TWENTY-SIX CENTURIES
OF AGRARIAN REFORM

TWENTY-SIX CENTURIES

OF

AGRARIAN

REFORM

A Comparative Analysis

by

ELIAS H. TUMA

UNIVERSITY OF CALIFORNIA PRESS

BERKELEY AND LOS ANGELES

1965

University of California Press
Berkeley and Los Angeles

Cambridge University Press
London, England

Library of Congress Catalog Card No. 65-24515

PRINTED IN THE UNITED STATES OF AMERICA

*To the peasants who are sustained
by hope and the expectation that
their life will one day be better*

PREFACE

Until about five years ago I held an attitude that is still fairly common among proponents of agrarian reform. In retrospect that attitude seems to have been based on no sound foundation. In fact, almost a full about-turn seemed forthcoming as soon as I began a critical evaluation of the effects of one of the most advertised and popularly acclaimed reforms in the postwar period. The figures defied the propaganda, and the sustained poverty and backwardness proved the reform to be a disappointment. The reformers in this and other cases subjected to scrutiny did not say what they did, nor did they do what they said. The problems that prevailed before the reform were not less serious after it. Obviously, these contradictions were not always the result of bad intentions; yet there was no reason to believe that these results and contradictions were unavoidable. Were there no alternatives? Was a similar trend apparent in other reforms in other countries and other historical periods? How did these results conform to modern trends of social change and economic development? And how were these "disappointing" results justified by the reformers?

These and many more questions impelled me to seek for possible answers. The initial fruits of my efforts were contained in my Ph.D. dissertation presented to the Department of Economics, University of California, Berkeley, in September, 1962.

Many people have helped me in this work. Foremost among them were Paul S. Taylor, Gregory Grossman, and Michael F. Brewer; they graciously gave me all the time and attention I asked for. The revision was guided by the detailed, insightful, and kind criticisms of Thomas P. Jenkin and Davis McEntire. Mortimer Chambers, a specialist in Greco-Roman history, read and criticized chapters iii and iv. Gustave E. von Grunebaum was kind enough to read and comment on the manuscript as a whole, but his major contribution was his constant encouragement to bring this effort to fruition. To each and all these scholars goes my deepest and most sincere gratitude. I also wish to thank R. Y. Zachary, Editor of the University of California Press, Los Angeles, for his helpful suggestions regarding the revision. I am grateful to the University of Saskatchewan for financing the typing of the manuscript and to Mrs. Anne Stanbury and Mrs. Patricia Abrahamson for taking full charge of the typing. Throughout, however, the responsibility for any errors of omission or commission are mine alone.

E. H. T.

University of Saskatchewan
Saskatoon, Canada
November 19, 1963

CONTENTS

CHARTS

TABLES

CONTENTS

CONTENTS

PART I

THE PROBLEM

I

INTRODUCTION

The purpose of this study is threefold: (1) to clarify the meaning of reform and suggest a general definition; (2) to construct a theory that may be applicable to various types of reform; and (3) to provide a critical evaluation of the function of reform and offer some views on current or prospective reform movements.

The history of land reform is as long as the history of the world, extending back into the medieval, ancient, and biblical times. Like many other socioeconomic and political movements, land reform movements have been sporadic and discontinuous, although the last two centuries have witnessed almost continuous struggles for reform, beginning with the French Revolution. It is certainly beyond the scope of this study to deal with the full history of reform; yet it is necessary to tap as much of it as possible.

Many attempts have been made in the present century, and particularly in the last two decades, to reform the land systems of underdeveloped countries. Land reform has become part and parcel of the United Nations' program, and is closely associated with attempts to industrialize, develop, and improve conditions in agrarian societies. It has also assumed primary importance in political platforms as a means of maintaining political stability and preventing revolutions; ironically, it has also been used to encourage or sustain revolutions.

Although there is a vast amount of literature on land reform, both theoretical and empirical, there is as yet no adequate theory or set of generalizations by which to guide and evaluate reform. The only theories available are those of socialist or radical doctrines, such as Henry George's single-tax theory of land tenure, and the more general back-to-nature theory of the physiocrats who advocate land to the tiller. The greater number of reform attempts, however, are not guided by these theories and are therefore lacking in theoretical basis.

Lack of an adequate theory may be due to insufficient knowledge or it may stem from one or more of the following four reasons.

1. Land reform usually has been carried out as an emergency measure to deal with specific circumstances, or in the course of a revolution with minimum planning or theoretical understanding. The motivation for re-

3

form was temporary and did not generate sufficient interest among scholars to study the movement and develop a theory.

2. Land reform has taken place within such different environmental contexts and has aimed at such a variety of objectives that theorizing is extremely difficult. As the development of a theory requires a comparison of reform movements separated by time, space, and cultural and other environmental conditions, the complexity of such an undertaking might have cast doubt on its feasibility and thus inhibited any effort to make such a study.

3. There has been no urgent need for theory, since up to the present century land reform was primarily a matter of land redistribution to reduce land concentration, appease the peasants, and control political restiveness. Only recently has it become essential to think of reform in relation to economic development and planning which require theoretical bases for implementation.

4. Attention has been directed to monographic case studies or to theoretical discussions as an extension of economic and social theory.[1] However, no attempt has been made to synthesize the knowledge contained in these monographs, and no one has tried to assess critically the applicability of the theoretical arguments or the degree to which they are borne out by historical experience.[2]

Now the need for theory has become evident. To construct a theory it is necessary to take historical experience into account, apply a comparative method of analysis, and utilize the knowledge that can be derived from individual case studies — the complications and pitfalls of such a comparison notwithstanding.[3]

This study is a modest attempt to fill the vacuum. Our procedure is to observe the general tendencies of past reforms, distinguish their common and their unique features, and note the relationships between these features and the environments in which these reforms have taken place From these relationships we shall derive generalizations which may serve as a basis for the construction of a theory. Thus, our problem is not merely to classify, but to explain and critically analyze these relationships and the processes of implementing reform.

For example, land reform has usually been enacted to reduce the concentration of land, wealth, and income. How effective has it been in reducing concentration or equalizing the distribution, and how far can one depend on it for that purpose? Again, land reform has been used to break the rigidity of social institutions that tend to hinder economic development and social mobility, but do historical experiences justify investment in land reform to enhance social and economic change and mobility? How useful has land reform been in promoting economic development, reallocating resources, or improving the standard of living?

Another basic objective of land reform has usually been to promote political stability and prevent a revolution. Has it usually done so? A cursory look would tend to cast doubt on the adequacy of land reform in
promoting stability or averting a revolution. Most of the reforms have
actually come during or after revolutions. Furthermore, to reform the
land tenure system by peaceful means it is necessary to win the coöperation of most of the landlords or the classes with vested interests. How coöperative have these groups been and is there any sound basis for the
optimism implied in contemplating reform by peaceful means as a preventive against revolution? What type of reform may and may not be
peacefully implemented? How well do historical facts bear out the optimistic attitude toward preventive and peaceful reform?

Land reform has often been recommended as a step toward political
democracy and reduction of conflict between classes — these being en-
visaged as natural results of distributing the land and enlarging the class
of small owners. Has reform been an effective tool to safeguard or create
political democracy? How far has it reduced conflict?

Cheyney's study [2] notes that reform has tended to be followed by a
period of reaction reflecting the trend of political change in society and
that political reaction often resulted in reversing the reform effects. Can
we generalize this observation to other reforms? If so, how significant is
it to contemporary reforms? Are the results usually permanent or do
they tend to be temporary, serving immediate purposes and subject to
reversal upon attainment of immediate objectives? Finally, can we historically associate specific reform processes with reform objectives and
thus predict the degree of success that a reform may achieve, or suggest
the best method of implementation?

Our study is based on a sample consisting of the following reform
movements:

1. The Greek reforms of Solon and Pisistratus in the sixth century B.C.
2. The Roman reform of the Gracchi in the second century B.C.
3. The English tenure changes, used here for contrast, covering the
commutations of the Middle Ages, and the enclosures of the sixteenth
and eighteenth centuries.
4. The French reforms that accompanied the French Revolution.
5. The Russian reforms, treated as three separate cases:
    a. The emancipation of 1861.
    b. The Stolypin reforms of 1906–1911.
    c. The Soviet reform commencing in 1917.
6. The Mexican reform following the 1910 revolution.
7. The Japanese reform following the Second World War.
8. The Egyptian reform that started in 1952 and has not been concluded.

These reforms have been selected according to two criteria: to satisfy the comparative method and to represent as much of the history of reform as possible. The comparative method requires fulfillment of two conditions:

A certain similarity or analogy between observed phenomena — that is obvious — and a certain dissimilarity between the environments in which they occur.[4]

These reforms have all involved a change of land tenure, to be defined below, and have been carried out by a conscious effort of the government. (The English case is an exception; its inclusion will be justified below.) However, they differ in the cultural, geographical, and chronological environments to which each of them belongs, and represent different historical periods and social and political systems.

The second criterion is fulfilled by the comprehensive representativeness of the sample. The Greek and Roman reforms represent the ancient period. The French reform represents the reforms that followed the French Revolution in Europe during the nineteenth century. The emancipation and the Stolypin reforms have unique features which warrant their selection, but they have been selected also for the sake of continuity with the Soviet reform which represents the socialist reforms. The Mexican, Japanese, and Egyptian reforms represent the modern era, and each of them goes a step further in the same direction. (Some might maintain that these reforms are not fully representative of the modern era, and undoubtedly it would be fruitful if it were possible to deal with such more recent reforms as the Chinese, the Iranian, and certainly the Cuban. Unfortunately, however, the lack of adequate data on some and the immediate recentness of others make it difficult to analyze them to any advantage within the framework of this study.)

The number of case studies is limited and statistical data are lacking for many of them. Even qualitative data are not fully comparable. Therefore, case presentation will not follow a perfectly uniform pattern, and the conclusions will be only tentative.

The plan of the study is as follows: In the next chapter we shall discuss the conceptual problem of land tenure and land reform and define the basic terms as we shall use them; we shall propose to substitute the term *land tenure reform* for the traditional concept of *land reform*, which has historically implied land redistribution, and suggest using *agrarian reform* where reform is general and comprehensive and goes beyond land distribution.

Part II includes the basic data or the case studies. Each case study will be divided into three main parts: (1) background material on land tenure and land distribution, and on the social and political conditions prevailing prior to the reform; (2) the process of reform covering the reform legislation and the methods of implementation; and (3) the effects and evaluation of each reform from the economic, social, and political aspects. The evaluation will be made against the objectives set by the reformers, and the problems characterizing the society as reflected in the literature.[5]

Part III comprises the analysis of the case studies and includes comparisons and contrasts of the background, processes, and effects featured in Part II. Also in Part III a theoretical construction will be presented showing the relationships between the background, process, and effects of reform as depicted in the historical perspective of the investigation.

Part IV is a summary presentation of the tentative generalizations and the implications of the findings to reform movements in underdeveloped countries.

II

LAND TENURE AND LAND REFORM

THE CONCEPTUAL PROBLEM

Land reform means different things to different people, but

. . . all these meanings and definitions appear to have two things in common. It seems, that whatever form land reform takes: 1. It is invariably a more or less direct, publicly controlled change in the existing ways of land ownership (i.e., a changing of the agrarian status quo). 2. It invariably involves a "diffusion" or "spreading" of wealth, income or productive capacity.[1]

This generalization is plausible, although many reforms do not share the common features it suggests, such as voluntary nongovernmental reforms, or even those like Stolypin's reform in Russia early this century. However, the differences between types of reform are as significant as the common grounds, since only by comparison and contrast can one get a clear conception of what land reform really means.

The differences between types of reform may be of substance or of emphasis. Differences of substance are those between reforms that relate to changes of land tenure or the system of ownership, as, for example, from private to public or from individual to collective ownership. Variation in substance may be exemplified by contrasting the western democratic and the socialist approaches to reform; the former tries to reform the land system within the framework of private property, and the latter by abolishing it and nationalizing the land.

Differences of emphasis relate to reforms that do not, or hardly, affect the system of tenure.[2] Such differences are reflected in the number of definitions applied by western reformers who advocate modifications of the tenure system without changing the form of tenure. They all agree on promoting private ownership, but they differ on details of the reform program. Ghonemy, for example, enumerates seven such definitions and adds one of his own. Between them, these definitions cover a wide area: "change for the better," change in "rental terms" or "resource ownership," greater equality and resource allocation, economic development, change in agricultural institutions, change in economic organization, redistribution of land in order to promote political stability — all these are definitions of land reform. Ghonemy's own definition emphasizes decision-making and ownership.[3]

For a better understanding of the reasons why there is this flexibility in the conception of reform and to present the definition used in this study, let us briefly trace the historical evolution of the concept.

Ordinarily land reform has meant redistribution of land to benefit the small farmer or landless agricultural worker.[4] The objective or purpose of the reformers has been to appease the small farmers, create small or peasant family farms, and reduce the inequality of income distribution. The indirect goals of this social policy have been to stabilize the political system and/or create a western-type democracy which has historically been associated with family farms. The attitude toward the family farm underlying this concept of reform has been summarized by Griswold:

The ancient tradition; the personal love of the soil; the theory of natural rights bequeathed by Locke to all liberal politicians of the age; the cause of American independence which became the cause of popular government versus the government of kings; the existing circumstances of the American frontier; the horror of the industrial revolution, fed by imagination as much as by a fleeting impression of England; the conception of the earth as a common stock; the belief in individual freedom and in private property as its means; the fact that farm land was the most typical and useful form of private property — the philosophical insight and the political sagacity — what does it matter which came first? All were present in the conclusion that small landholders, i.e., family farmers, were the "most precious part of a state," the classic American statement of the political theory of the family farm. [5]

However, this statement does not indicate the "appropriate" size of the family farm. It is possible to idealize the family farm where such is economically efficient and where land is free or easily accessible, as in the frontier days. Also, the statement says nothing regarding economic efficiency. Thus, guided by this attitude, land reform creates small family farms primarily for social and political objectives rather than for economic efficiency or higher production. Furthermore, it does not indicate the form of state or political system that would be consistent with the family farm institution, although Jefferson and those in the American tradition after him have had democracy in mind and have made this clear in their writings.[6]

But idealization of the small family farm is not peculiar to the American tradition or to the democratic political system. Griswold makes this clear when he says that

There is . . . no universal law that equates agrarianism and democracy or family farm and democracy. On the contrary, historical evidence to date seems to indicate that democracy has flourished most in the few countries, with the notable exception of Germany, that have attained a high degree of industrialization. It is true, nevertheless, that all the democratic countries except Great Britain have put a premium on family farming and the agrarian way of life, and none so great a premium as France . . . [which] has made a fetish of the small peasant farm.[7]

9

The French have kept that tradition both in theory and in practice. In spite of the theories of the physiocrats advocating large-scale farming and scientific and efficient technology in the tradition of Arthur Young, France has developed its rural area into small peasant farms. Not so in America; not only has the rural population been on the decline, but the family farm has also found itself in great trouble. Large-scale farming and tenancy have characterized the trend in America for a long time, contrary to the dictates of the ideals. This conflict between the ideal and the fact has been expressed by Hammer:

The thing most to regret in the matter is the schism that is opening between the ideal held by the proponents of owner-operation and facts: a counterpart of this schism has developed in the business world. That is, with stiffer and stiffer anti-monopoly laws, the drift . . . is toward greater and greater concentration of control in American business and industry. Competition is the ideal. The drift is toward monopoly. Tenure discussion almost universally extols owner-operatorship. The drift is, in fact, in the other direction and as the gap between the goal and fact widens, a cultural lag is created that will prove troublesome in time unless ideals are changed or developments brought more closely into harmony with the ideal. . . . Efficiency, too, is a social ideal and one may infer from the drift in tenure affairs that it may be a much more powerful ideal than that of operator-ownership of farms.[8]

Though the Jeffersonian tradition toward family farms has persisted as an ideal, the facts of the situation have caused a twofold change of attitude. First, the meanings of land reform, its objectives, and processes have become more comprehensive to accommodate agricultural policy and efficiency of production. Second, the term "land reform" has often been replaced by "agrarian reform" to express the new meaning of reform. Simultaneously, there has been a shift of emphasis from land distribution to production and development. In trying to explain this development, Doreen Warriner first acknowledges the importance of tradition in determining the American attitude toward reform and then introduces another element as follows:

Now a new conception of reform comes from America, which advocates reform as a comprehensive policy, including not only "opportunity or ownership," but also a variety of other measures to assist farmers by means of greater agricultural advisory services and education, and so on. This conception flowered in the course of the cold war, as an answer to Communism. The United States first made advocacy of land reform part of its official foreign policy in 1950, when it supported a Polish resolution in favour of land reform in the General Assembly of the United Nations, and thereby challenged the Communist claim to leadership in the use of land reform as a political warfare weapon.[9]

The new conception of reform has not, as suggested above, evolved out of tradition and the cold war alone. It also reflects the growing recognition of capitalistic tendencies in agriculture, which require an efficient production scale, credit facilities, contractual tenancies, and education. To develop capitalistic and commercial agriculture rapidly, economic planning has become more and more acceptable. Thus, the new conception has partly been an outgrowth of the increasing awareness of the need for economic development and planning, especially in underdeveloped countries where reform is most needed. The wider acceptance of planning has made it imperative to study the *total agrarian structure*, to be defined below, as it relates to development. As a result, *agrarian reform* has been recommended to overcome the obstacles to development arising from the agrarian structure. However, acceptance of planning implies moving away from the traditional conception of laissez-faire democracy in the direction of socialist methods of development. Simultaneously, a change has occurred in the substance of land reform, bringing it closer to the socialist conception which Mao Tse-tung has described as basically a method "to develop agricultural production and to clear the path for the industrialization of China." [10] Thus, the American tradition has sustained and augmented the drive for reform, but the cold war on one hand, and the growing importance of economic planning on the other, have been significant in pointing out the inadequacy of the old concept and the need for a new and more comprehensive one; hence, agrarian reform, which has, however, been vague and loosely used to mean any and all types of reform. [11]

To overcome vagueness and confusion we shall adopt a working definitional scheme as a basis of this analysis. This definitional scheme may also be applicable in analyzing any type of reform, regardless of its substance or emphasis or the extent of change it introduces.

The definitional scheme is based primarily on the United Nations approach, which suggests that certain defects in the agrarian structure hinder development and that it is the purpose of agrarian reform to overcome these obstacles. According to the United Nations, agrarian reform means any improvement in the agrarian structure, or

. . . the institutional framework of agricultural production. It includes, in the first place, land tenure, the legal or customary system under which land is owned; the distribution of ownership of farm property between large estates and peasant farms or among peasant farms of various sizes; land tenancy, the system under which land is operated and its product divided between operator and owner; the organization of credit, production and marketing; the mechanism through which agriculture is financed; the burdens imposed on rural populations by governments in the form of taxation; and the services supplied by governments to rural populations, such as

11

technical advice and educational facilities, health services, water supply and communication.[12]

We have reproduced the agrarian structure as Chart I, after some reorganization. As shown on the chart, the agrarian structure consists of three main sectors: tenure or title to the land, pattern of cultivation, and terms of holding and scale of operation. Each of these sectors may be subject to reform or change — reform implying an improvement, while change has no value implications. For example, a change in the form of tenure from individual to collective, or vice versa, may or may not be considered an improvement, depending upon the premium members of society put on each of these forms. These sectors are fairly independent of each other and reform of one may or may not entail reform in the others. Extension services may, for instance, transform production into supervised and diversified production without changing the title to the land, and without consolidating the holdings or the scale of operation. In other words, each of these sectors may be seen as an independent entity that may be the object of reform.

Yet these three sectors are also interdependent, and a change in one of them may have an impact on the others as well as be influenced by what goes on in them. For instance, a change of title may lead to a change in the terms of holding, such as status of the operator, the amount and type of rent he pays, and the scale of operation. Security of tenure may also lead to intensive diversified market production, although such results may not have been anticipated. Therefore, in studying reform according to this scheme, it is important to consider not only the direct results of the reform but also the indirect results that may ensue from this interdependence.

In constructing the chart, we have disregarded those aspects of the economy which are not peculiar to the agrarian sector, such as taxation, health services, education, and population, even though these are included in the United Nations definition. The reason for this modification is that these services may or may not be extended or improved with or without land reform, but not so with the main sectors of the agrarian structure mentioned above. In exceptional cases where, for example, education affects the pattern of cultivation directly, its impact will be represented by classifying that pattern as supervised vis-à-vis unsupervised. Credit has been included in the chart because of its important role in the activities of agricultural coöperatives, which have been almost totally independent of the nonagrarian sectors of the economy.

In reading the chart, horizontal lines represent continua. Thus security of tenure may vary in degree, while tenure can be either collective or individual but not in between. Similarly, agriculture may be extensive or intensive in different degrees, but the holding can be either consolidated or fragmented. In this scheme we differentiate between ownership and

12

CHART I
AGRARIAN STRUCTURE *

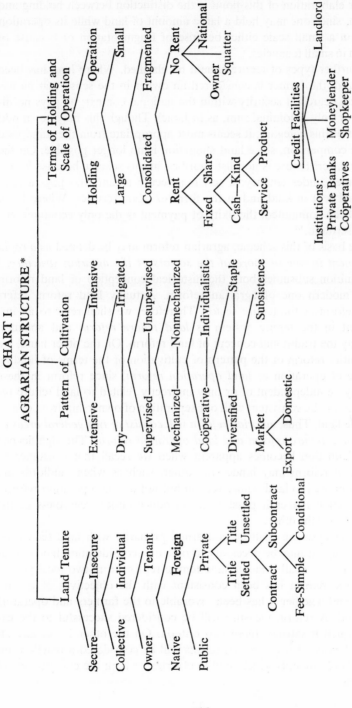

* An earlier version of this chart appeared in my "The Agrarian-Based Development Policy in Land Reform," *Land Economics*, XXXIX, 3 (Aug., 1963), 267.

operation of the land, since the owner may not himself be the operator. A further elaboration of this point is the distinction between holding and operation, since one may hold a large amount of land while its operation may be on a small scale either because of fragmentation or because of operation in small tenancies.

Two further types of tenure should be clarified. Where land has been nationalized, the farmer is considered an owner in the sense that he has the highest degree of security within the national context; he pays no direct rent or only a nominal sum, as in Israel. Though this may be an odd treatment of this category, it seems most appropriate from the standpoint of tenure comparison, since land alienation is no longer possible. On the other hand, serf tenure is not distinguished in this scheme because it may be subsumed under tenancy: a serf is a secure tenant who pays a relatively fixed rent in kind and in the form of labor services. Where labor rent has been commuted, the fixity of payment is the only economic criterion of serfdom.[13]

On the basis of this scheme, agrarian reform may be defined as *a rapid improvement in one or more of the sectors of the agrarian structure*.[14] This definition subsumes both the historical conception of land reform and the modern one of agrarian reform. Actually land reform refers only to reform of the tenure sector. Therefore, we shall refer to an improvement in the tenure system as *land tenure reform* and abandon completely the traditional concept of land reform. On the other hand, we shall identify reform of the pattern of cultivation or the terms of holding and scale of operation as *land operation reform*, since reform in these areas may be independent of or only indirectly related to land tenure reform. This will be consistent with our separation of ownership from operation of the land. Thus, *agrarian reform will consist of two general areas of reform: land tenure reform and land operation reform*. The significance of this distinction becomes apparent when we recall that resistance to one type of reform may hinder the other, such as when landlords are strongly opposed to land tenure reform but not to land operation reform. The distinction makes it possible to introduce either, regardless of the attitude toward the other.

In the analysis we shall be concerned primarily with land tenure reform, although it may be necessary to take into consideration land operation reform. We shall evaluate land tenure reform from two focal points: whether the reform has been consistent with the objectives of the reformers, and whether it has been favorable to the farmers and operators of the land. A reform measure will be considered successful to the extent to which it satisfies these two criteria. On the other hand, any attempt to hinder or reverse such results will be considered a reaction, including those attempts which tend to obstruct or limit the effectiveness of the reform.

PART II

LAND TENURE REFORM: CASE STUDIES

INTRODUCTION TO PART II

This part covers the case studies or basic data on which the analysis will depend. We have pointed out in Part I the complications of comparing these diverse experiences. One more complication arises from the different approaches of the numerous authors from whom we derive the data. Many of them give only qualitative or impressionistic information, but more significant is the unique way in which concepts are used by different writers. Equality or land concentration in one place or period may not have the same meaning in another place or period. Even the concept of ownership has one meaning in France, another in England, a third in Soviet Russia, and a fourth in Mexico. Therefore, to facilitate comparison and analysis of the data, we shall define some of the concepts used frequently in the study.

Land ownership means the right to dispose of the land. Though this right may be one of degree, we shall use as a standard the highest degree of disposal allowed by the constitution or the laws of the country under study.

Land and income concentration implies deviation from the line of equality, or inequality according to a Lorenz curve. However, since the data do not allow construction of such curves or computation of concentration coefficients, evaluation will depend on the sources of the data. We shall consider land to be concentrated, and the same applies to income, if these sources consider it to be so. However, as an objective criterion we shall use the ratio between the upper and lower limits of the size of individual ownership tolerated in the specific case under study.

Class differentiation implies unequal economic opportunities and wealth distribution if inequality seems to be of a permanent nature and tends to perpetuate class differences. As such, we deal with classes as economic groups in conflict with each other, on the assumption that material power produces social and political power. That is, economic class differentiation implies social and political class differentiation.

Crisis, which appears in practically every case study, implies the development of tension between tenure groups such that the stability or equilibrium of the social system is disturbed. Crises may be expressed in different ways, the most common of which is rising antagonism between tenure groups; in an extreme case the crisis leads to revolution and breakdown of the system.

17

Social or economic system implies a complex structure whose social and economic components are interdependent; disturbing any of these components would reflect on the other components and on the system as a whole. The economy in the aggregate is a system; the political order represents a system, and so does the society which lies within boundaries.

Large-scale versus small-scale operation is relative and depends on the availability of land, economic efficiency, and the techniques in use, and also on the assessment contained in the literature. A large farm in Japan or Egypt may be considered tiny in England, the United States, or Russia. Thus, the scale of operation is relative. In general it relates to the size of the farm. However, we shall use also the ratio between the high and the low limits on the size of holdings as an objective criterion of scale, as applied to concentration.

Land/Labor ratio refers to the relationship between the arable land and the rural labor dependent on it for a living. Effective land/labor ratio refers to the currently accessible land area, given the population, while the potential ratio describes the relationship that may arise from a change in the magnitude of either or both in the future.

Underemployment in agriculture refers to the situation in which the accessible arable land is inadequate to keep the rural population dependent on it for a living fully occupied, given the techniques and the institutional arrangements regarding the number of hours and the length of the work season. Underemployment may be disguised or revealed. The rural workers are disguisedly unemployed when they are *apparently* occupied full time but in fact less intensively than what is regarded optimal, such that some of them may be removed from the land without reducing total production, or they may be able to operate a larger farm with the same techniques during the same work time. Underemployment would be revealed if the rural workers are *partially* unemployed; that is, they are working less than the number of hours or weeks (i.e., a shorter season) customarily regarded as full employment. Again, the same number of workers will be able to operate a larger farm or some of them may be removed from the land without reducing the total product. The following two examples will clarify what we mean by underemployment.

1. A family of two operates a farm of a certain size, say 5 acres. Given the techniques, however, it is found that an average family of two can operate a 9-acre farm if fully occupied. In this case there is underemployment; it is disguised if the two workers are occupied the same number of hours, but less intensively, as the couple who operate the larger farm; their underemployment is revealed if they are occupied a smaller number of hours. In the case of disguised unemployment, they stretch their efforts over a longer time period than would normally be necessary.

2. Another example is that of the family that operates the 9-acre farm

this state of affairs and its threat of a revolution, and were therefore "eager that peace and calm should be restored. . . ."[14] This was the purpose that Solon adopted and to which he directed his efforts when elected. He was conscious of the impending danger, having publicized the grievances in his poems, and therefore immediately embarked on arresting it.[15]

SOLON'S REFORM: THE PROCESS

The exact measures are not fully known to us. He tells of four things he did "to bring immediate relief to the oppressed classes": he freed the land, he restored to their homes Athenians who had been sold into foreign slavery, he brought back those whom destitution had driven into exile, and he set at liberty those who were the slaves of Athenian masters.[16] All these were effects of his reforming the law of debt and applying it retroactively. By the *seisachtheia* or "shaking-off the burdens," as this law came to be known, he canceled all outstanding debts and freed the land that was enserfed or in danger of enserfment because of debt. He also demolished the *Horoi* or mortgage stones, freed the *Hektemors*, and restored the enserfed land to its former owners.[17] In the future no person could be held in mortgage and no personal freedom could be compromised because of debt. Thus Solon guaranteed the right of the peasant to personal freedom and deprived the landlord of the cheap labor he had found in the *Hektemor* status of the peasant; the landlord had now to search for new investment opportunities outside lending.[18]

There were other reforms attributed to Solon. He is said to have modified the law of inheritance. In the absence of male heirs, the owner was now entitled to bequeath his property to an adopted son or even by will as a form of "posthumous adoption."[19] Though the impact of this measure could not have been of significance to the peasant, it is considered a first step toward private ownership of the land by the individual and the beginning of the end of the family form of tenure.[20]

Solon is also credited with having introduced a monetary reform by appreciating the nominal value of the pound or mina from 70 to 100 drachmae. By this means he lightened the burden of the debtors upon repayment of the loan.[21]

Finally, Solon is said to have regulated exports, restricting them to oil and fine products and thus encouraging oil production and preserving grain for the domestic market. He also introduced regulations regarding distances between trees newly planted and made it easier for a person to acquire water in the absence of a well on his property. More relevant to the problem, however, was his encouragement of artisan training. Now each parent was expected to train his son to a trade; otherwise the son was not obligated to give relief to his parent in old age.[22]

Apart from reforming the law of debt and freeing the *Hektemors*, Solon's major relevant activity was concerned with social classes and the

23

distribution of power. He redefined social classes according to the product from the land, thus creating a timocracy and breaking the hereditary class barriers against those of non-noble birth. Merchants and newly landed people were thus admitted to social classes and enjoyed privileges formerly taboo to them. These classes were defined as follows: The first or upper class included the *pentacosiomedimnes*, those whose land-produce was 500 *medimnes* or more (1 *medimnos* = 1½ bushels, or the equivalent of a *metretes* which is more than 8½ gallons of liquid); the *chevaliers*, who produced about 300 *medimnes*; the *zeugities*, 200 *medimnes*; and all the rest were the *thetes*.[23] The upper three classes in the new timocracy were entitled to offices of the state in their respective ranking, while the *thetes* remained excluded. However, the *thetes* are said to have won two new privileges: to vote in the assembly (Ecclesia) as free men and to serve on the jury in the popular court (Dicasterion).[24]

EFFECTS AND EVALUATION

The Solonian reform was motivated by three major objectives, according to the point of view of the different social groups in the community — each group believing that Solon was the man to realize its objectives. The poor believed he would redress their grievances against the rich and redistribute the land; the rich thought he would restore calm without inflicting any losses on them; and the community in general trusted that he would create stability, prevent the impending revolution, and bring about long-overdue structural changes in the government.

It is safe to suggest that none of these groups was ignored or fully satisfied. The first two opponent groups were equally dissatisfied and angry with Solon. The *Hektemors* became free but they had little or no land to work on; their ambition to have the land redistributed was thwarted by Solon's resistance. The rich, on the other hand, though they lost little if anything, were angry because debts were canceled, even though they may have received more than they gave out in loan, and even though the debtors among them actually were compensated by the monetary reform.

In its time and place Solon's reform might have been considered radical, but in retrospect it seems clear that his measures were compromises and far short of what was needed to solve the problems plaguing the Attic society. The reform of the tenure had no significance to the distribution of land, size of holding, or level of techniques of cultivation. The family form of tenure remained virtually intact. Nor is there any evidence that the reform helped to solve the economic problems arising from the population increase or from the structural changes in the economy.[25] The impact was more pronounced on the social and political levels. The free peasants acquired a new civil status and the right to the product of their land. Their incomes were raised by the amount they formerly paid to their creditors. Nevertheless, the gap between rich and

24

poor remained wide, especially to the extent that the creditors were themselves debtors, and were actually compensated for the loss.

Solon did not hide his sentiments toward the different social classes or
his endeavor not to inflict any losses on the landlords. "He insists that
he had accomplished more for the lower orders than they would have
dared to hope for; but . . . he asserts with equal positiveness that he
was acting in the interests of the upper classes," [26] by saving them from a
greater disaster. In that sense, he insists that he fulfilled his promises to
all factions.

Finally, the community in general might have been satisfied with the
reform as a means of restoring stability and preventing a revolution. In
the immediate aftermath there was no revolution, but stability was not restored and most of the factors that constituted the original threat were
still there. The people who were freed had little or no land to work on or
to put up as security, and yet they were forbidden to borrow on the security of their person. They gained personal freedom but not economic
security; they even lost what security they had as *Hektemors*. At the
same time the landlords retained their estates. The economic gap and
social and political conflict between the two groups persisted. Herein lay
the seeds of instability which had threatened the whole society with a
revolution.

Political instability after Solon was quite evident. During the next fifteen years, there were two years of anarchy with no legally elected archon.
In 582–580 B.C. the archon Damasias was in office for one year and two
months unconstitutionally, and when ousted, he was replaced by ten
archons representing different social groups.[27] Solon may be said to have
postponed the revolution but not prevented it. The solution of the peasant problem had yet to come when Pisistratus seized power as a tyrant.

PISISTRATUS' REFORM: THE PROCESS

Little is known of the thirty-year period separating Solon's rule from that
of Pisistratus, except that political instability prevailed and unconstitu-
tional government was attempted. It is also agreed that the peasants were
dissatisfied and wanted redistribution of the land, and many landless people wanted better conditions. Solon's property qualification for public office proved ineffective and "nobles turned demagogues." [28] The same
three factions that had existed before Solon were involved in the strife:
the Shore (Coast) or the middle-road party led by Megacles; the Plain,
led by Lycurgus aimed at oligarchy; finally, the party of Pisistratus or the
Highlanders in which were affiliated the common people and "those who
lost money owed them, for they had now become poor, and those who
were not of pure descent, for they were apprehensive." [29]

In 561–560 B.C., after his military victory over Megara, Pisistratus was hailed in Athens as "the champion of the small holders." He then seized power as a tyrant but did not stay long, for the people of the Shore and the Plain united against him and twice forced him into exile. However, upon his second return he established himself as supreme ruler until his death in 528 B.C., during which period he carried out his reforms.

Politically, Pisistratus' triumph was a reversal of the trend set by Solon for a constitutional government based on compromise and harmony. However, his reforms may be considered a fulfillment of his own promises to the small and poor holders of land and a completion of Solon's reform or attempt to create an independent class of small farmers.[30] Pisistratus was able to retain the support of his followers, weaken his adversaries, and maintain his power, partly at least, by distributing the estates of those of his adversaries who had been killed or forced into exile.[31] He encouraged the small farmers also by extending loans to them, which he derived from a 10 per cent tax on agricultural produce. According to Aristotle, he succeeded by means of these loans to keep the poor people busy, prevented their dangerous concentration in towns, and stimulated cultivation and production in agriculture, thus raising the tax revenue.[32] He also encouraged olive growing and production of pottery by spreading security and justice into the rural areas.[33] Finally, he is said to have created employment by building temples and by expanding silver mining.[34]

EFFECTS AND EVALUATION

Pisistratus has been described as a very popular, benevolent, and capitalistic or economically-minded tyrant.[35] It is agreed that he distributed some land, but we do not know how much and to how many people, and we do not know the size of the newly created holdings. We are equally ignorant as to what amount or what percentage of the revenue was extended as loans to the farmers. However, since only land of dead or exiled adversaries was distributed, it may be safe to assume that the land area distributed was small and that land concentration was little affected. It is commonly suggested that he satisfied his followers and won acceptance of a large percentage of the population. The inference from all this is that he secured legitimacy for his rule.[36] Yet he and his sons after him ruled as tyrants, maintaining their positions by depending on a mercenary army and by suppressing their opponents. He actually shelved the constitution, even though he did not repeal any part of it. Therefore, it is hard to accept the claim that he won the approval of a majority or that he succeeded in legitimizing his rule, even though he might have tried to do that in every major activity he undertook.

Pisistratus' reforms did not involve any basic changes in the form of tenure, the social and political structure, or the constitutional foundation of the government. They were short-term measures dealing with immediate problems and were devoid of any perpetuating characteristics. As

26

soon as opportunity arose, his opponents violently overthrew his succes-
sors. We do not know how much of his reform effects survived, but
there is much speculation that some of them were reversed or modified.[37]
Finally, it should be mentioned that while Pisistratus' reform was more
far-reaching than Solon's in treating immediate problems of the peasants,
it took a revolution to introduce the reform and force and suppression to
execute it.

IV

THE ROMAN REFORM

This is another reform of the ancient period. Like the Greek reforms, it was a response to tension and disequilibrium in policy, effected from above, and carried out after a period of territorial expansion and colonization. It was also implemented within a traditional and intimate social environment. However, unlike the Greek experience, the Roman reform aimed at rehabilitating free people, rather than serfs or slaves, by redistributing usurped public domains; it was introduced in a state of civil war, and treated of short-term problems rather than basic constitutional questions.

The Roman reform, introduced by the Gracchi brothers in the second century B.C., dealt with agrarian and peasant problems that are still common in many contemporary societies. It used methods and responded to situations of disequilibrium and tension similar to those found in modern times, and similarly it was intended to prevent a revolution or political upheaval. The reform was executed with a rapidity and comprehensiveness reminiscent of the modern Japanese and Egyptian reforms. However, a unique feature of the Gracchan reform was its successful distribution of land without a revolution, in contrast to what happened in most other distributive reforms.

BACKGROUND: LAND TENURE AND SOCIAL CLASSES

Land in Rome was held in private or in public tenure. The private land was cultivated by small farmers, tenants, or slaves under direct supervision of the proprietor. The public domain or *ager publicus* was allotted to colonists, to veterans, or to creditors in payment of public debts. For all practical purposes, these allotments became private property and were not affected by the reform. The remaining part of undistributed public domain, approximately two million acres, formed the object of reform. This land was utilized in two ways: the better quality land was leased by the censors to individuals, presumably for cash rent, subject to efficient cultivation. The lower quality land was left for squatting as a means of relieving unemployment and to avoid its lying idle. The squatter paid as rent a variable share of the product according to the nature of the crop — between 10 per cent and 20 per cent — or a cash fee on grazers according to the nature of the beast.[1] Both types of leased land gradually passed into the hands of private holders who considered them their own and had no reason to fear eviction. However, to encourage small farming and to prevent abuse of the public domain, a limit was set on the area an individual could hold, but the restriction was easily evaded by counting relatives and friends among the family. Consequently many people held more land than the legal maximum.[2]

The Republic of Rome was formerly based on small farmers who produced the food and supplied the army with men. As long as these people performed their recognized functions, internal peace and harmonious class relations prevailed. However, this equilibrium was upset around the middle of the second century when fundamental changes occurred in the economy. The small farmers were being displaced and their farms appropriated by larger ones in response to the shift from cereal cultivation to grazing and pasturage; farms were becoming larger, the population was increasing, and unemployment spreading.[3]

Transformation of the arable land into pastures has been explained in different ways: (1) competition of imported grain grown by slave labor obliged landowners to seek alternative uses for their land; (2) farms were devastated by the long wars and absence of the farmers who had been conscripted and they could therefore be used only as pastures; (3) cattle and sheep-raising were more profitable than cultivation and the shift was economically more expedient; and (4) grazing was preferable to cultivation because the holder of public domain had no permanent title and would not invest in vine and olives, the most profitable crops at that time.[4]

Whatever the reasons, it is agreed that there was a shift to grazing. Since grazing needs large farms and big capital, the tendency was to acquire more land and apply extensive farming methods. However, there was no more unoccupied land. Therefore, the land of the small farmer was the easiest target, and the stronger farmers seized it with or without formal agreement of the peasant. Sometimes he was induced to sell by the offer of high prices,[5] or he sold the land because its relative productive value was low since he had no capital to shift to more profitable uses.[6] In both cases the farmer lost his land through the market, at least formally. But there were occasions when he was evacuated against his will. According to Mommsen:

The capitalists continued to bring out the small landholders, or indeed, if they remained obstinate, to seize their fields without title of purchase; in which case, as may be supposed, matters were not always amicably settled. A peculiarly favourite method was to eject the wife and children from the homestead, while he was in the field, and to bring him to compliance by means of the theory of "accomplished fact."[7]

Thus land was becoming more and more concentrated in the hands of a few people, but we have no data on the extent of this concentration. We can only infer its magnitude from the census estimates of the number of Roman citizens or propertied individuals. It is estimated that in 159 B.C. there were 328,000 citizens; 324,000 in 154 B.C., 322,000 in 147 B.C.; and in 131 B.C. only 319,000 citizens.[8] Other estimates differ a little but all seem to agree that the number of owners declined and that the class of small farmers was disappearing, both in absolute and in relative terms.

The growing gap between rich and poor and the decline in the number of owners reduced the number of citizens and of those eligible to serve in the army. Those who were deprived of their land were depressed further by competition of slave labor in the labor market as well as in employment on estates of the rich. As a result large groups of unemployed sought refuge in the city and became a source of political and social unrest.[9]

Who were the people who accumulated wealth and concentrated land? Following the Hannibalic wars, many acquired large sums of money in the conquered territories. The first to benefit were officials of the state: "Officials did not come home empty-handed, and the rising class of commercial adventurers had already embarked on those widespread and remunerative operations which by the end of the century were to become a powerful influence on the foreign policy of Rome." [10] But these officials did not hesitate to do so at the expense of the peasant:

After having, as praetors or consuls, pillaged the world in time of war, the nobles in time of peace pillaged as governors their subjects, and returning to Rome with vast wealth employed it in changing the modest heritage of their fathers into domains vast as provinces. The *lex Claudia* forbidding mercantile pursuits to senatorial families, a great amount of capital was thrown into landed property, and the formation of the *latifundia* was stimulated. These "landlords" were eager to enclose within their grounds, lakes, forests, and mountains. Where a hundred families had once lived in comfort, one now found itself cramped.[11]

According to a more recent author:

The soldiers were paid off with handsome war bonuses and often received a land allotment into the bargain. The senatorial class derived wealth from the proceeds of their war booty, from the administration of provinces, and from the scientific development of their *latifundia*. The fortune of P. Licinius Crassus [consul in 131] . . . was estimated at . . . a hundred million sesterces [c. £1,000,000] . . . Aemilius Paullus, the victor of Pydna, was reckoned a man of modest means, although he possessed one and a half million sesterces. . . .[12]

A group that benefited equally from these opportunities was the Equestrian Order who had originally formed the Roman cavalry. They were propertied people, capable of providing their horses and equipment. When business opportunities flourished in the new territories, they made good use of them and accumulated considerable wealth. In the second century

B.C. this Order included members "who possessed not less than 400,000 sesterces [c. £4,000]." [13]

Thus land concentration was not accompanied by the rise of a new middle class. It simply increased the wealth of those who had vested interests in the economic *status quo*. This concentration was significant because of the close association it had with political power and control of the government. The government itself was in the hands of two oligarchic factions, the Optimates and the Populares. The former "wished to give effect to the will of the best," and the latter "to that of the community." But

. . . There was in the Rome of that day neither a true aristocracy nor a truly self-determining community. Both parties contended alike for shadows, and numbered in their ranks none but enthusiasts or hypocrites. Both were equally affected by political corruption, and both were in fact equally worthless. Both were necessarily tied down to the *status quo*, for neither on the one side nor on the other was there found any political idea — to say nothing of any political plan — reaching beyond the existing state of things; and accordingly the two parties were so entirely in agreement that they met at every step as respected both means and ends, and a change of party was a change of political tactics more than of political sentiments. [14]

Even the Equites were excluded from political power — a reason why conflict arose between them and the prevailing aristocracy. [15]

Thus, when Tiberius Gracchus introduced his plan for reform, a stalemate had already developed: the government was in the hands of a corrupt oligarchy; wealth was concentrated by those in positions of power; the middle- and lower-class owners and also the army were on the decline; grazing was displacing cultivation and causing unemployment; and low-income rural people were migrating to and overcrowding the cities. These developments were sources of danger to the republic and to political stability, and these were the problems that Tiberius set himself to solve.

TIBERIUS' REFORM: THE PROCESS

Early in his political career, Tiberius Gracchus, the elder of the two reformer brothers, observed the fields of Etruria being worked by slaves and noted the absence of free peasants. He became aware of the danger to the Republic, inherent in the decline of the free peasantry, after the revolt of the slaves under their self-appointed King Eunus. It is then that he saw the need for reform, [16] although the need had been recognized before him, and attempts, though of a different nature, to introduce reform had been made. [17]

The direct motives of Tiberius are hard to determine. He may have pursued ideas ingrained in him in his early stoic education; or he may have introduced the reform out of loyalty to the Republic and to prevent a revolution which seemed highly probable. Some say that his mother, herself highly cultured, had a hand in his decision. Or he may have been the only one of a group who supported him among the nobility with enough courage and ability to bring about reforms contemplated by the group as a whole.[18] Finally, it is quite possible that he was socially-minded and had great sympathy for the poor and the oppressed.

It has also been suggested that he had personal reasons, such as proving his oratorical ability against a powerful rival, Spurius Postumius.[19] Another personal reason suggested is that his faction of the aristocracy was excluded from the seats of power, and that he hated the senate because of past experience; since he was the composer of the treaty of peace concluded by Mancinus with the Numantines in 137 B.C., the

recollection that the senate had cancelled it, that the general had been on its account surrendered to the enemy, and that Gracchus with the other superior officers had only escaped a like fate through the greater favour which he enjoyed among the burgesses could not put the young, upright, and proud man in better humour with the ruling aristocracy.[20]

It is significant to notice the absence in this manifold set of motives of any economic objectives other than distribution, which is more a social than an economic goal.

Tiberius was greatly concerned about political stability and the army, as he shows in his address to the Assembly:

Is it your judgement that the lands which belong to the people should be given to the people? That what was conquered by all should be divided amongst all? Do you believe that a citizen is more useful than a slave, a brave legionary than a man who cannot fight, a faithful Roman than a foreigner and an enemy? If so [he added, addressing the rich] . . . relinquish a portion of your wealth lest the whole be taken from you someday.[21]

Therefore, immediately upon his election as tribune in 134 B.C., he embarked on legislation for reform. With the support of the small farmers, tenants, landless people, and some of the ruling oligarchy, he had his *lex agraria* passed by popular vote, despite the veto of his opponents, without going through the senate, the formal channel of legislation. The main provisions of the new reform were as follows.

1. No holder of public land should hold more than 500 *iugera* (about 311 acres), as was decided in the law of 367 B.C.
2. According to a provision of the new law, a person may hold an additional 250 *iugera* for each of his sons, up to a total of 1,000 *iugera*.
3. Compensation should be rendered for improvements in the form of plantation or building made by the former holder.
4. Land surrendered should be divided into lots of 30 *iugera* and given to burgesses and Italian citizens outside of Rome.[22]

32

5. Rent should be exacted from all holders of public land.

6. All land thus held after adjudication should become private property on condition that it be inalienable by sale or any other form of transfer, including the land retained by former holders.

7. To ensure thorough application of the law, a *collegium* of three people should be elected yearly and kept as a standing body to enforce the law and determine what was public domain and what was private property.

Finally, the law set a limit on the number of stock that any individual might keep on public pastures and requested the landlords to maintain a certain percentage of free men among their workers.[23]

The first commission entrusted with enforcing the reform law consisted of Tiberius himself, his brother Gaius, and his father-in-law Appius Claudius. However, Tiberius was murdered the next year and did not live to see much work done by the commission, which nevertheless resumed its duties with great zeal. But the law was not passed and executed without a struggle. The reaction of the senate was anything but encouraging. At first they tried to obstruct passage of the bill by inducing another tribune, Octavius, to veto it, and the bill became law only after Octavius was deposed by popular vote. The senators and landlords then tried to arouse sentiment against Tiberius by charging him with robbing them of land in which they had invested their wives' dowries and in which were the graves of their ancestors.[24] Resistance continued after Tiberius' death, and the commission was suspended to appease the Latin and Italian allies of Rome. Even people formerly sympathetic to the reform, such as Scipio Aemilianus, now opposed it on political grounds. A decree was passed in 129 B.C. which "withdrew from the commission its jurisdiction, and remitted the decision respecting what were dominial, and what private possessions to the censors and, as proxies for them, the consuls, to whom according to the general principles of the law it pertained," [25] with the knowledge that they would not enforce the law. The commission was revived when Gaius was elected to the tribunate in the year 123 B.C. [26]

GAIUS GRACCHUS AND HIS REFORMS

Much of the credit for executing the reform law goes to Gaius, the younger brother of Tiberius and a fellow member on the commission since its inception. Gaius' efforts, however, went beyond the commission. Shortly after his election as tribune, he discovered that the work of the commission was coming to an end because there was no more land to be distributed, although many individuals still held more than the maximum 500 *iugera* and many more were landless and unemployed. He therefore resorted to other methods; he started a new program for colonization, selecting sites and colonists that would facilitate commercial and trade expansion. Among the colonists were many capitalists and among the sites were strategic points, such as Neptunia and Scolacium on the southern coast of Italy. But neither the colonies nor the laws upon which they were founded lived long enough to be of consequence or to realize the objectives of Gaius.[27]

Another of his measures was abolition of the quit rent on the small allotments of public domain, thus putting them on equal terms with the large holdings whose rents had been suspended as a way of compensation.[28] And to relieve poverty in the city, he regulated the supply of corn by rationing it and also by storing grains bought abroad and releasing them to the market when prices soared, thus attempting to stabilize prices and prevent speculation. Finally, he introduced political reforms to undermine the power of the senate, the most significant of these being abolition of the senatorial juries and vesting their authority in the Equestrian Order, thus managing to give a share of the political power to the class that had so far been excluded.[29] The end of reform came when in 121 B.C. Gaius and many of his supporters were brutally killed in the continuing civil war.

EFFECTS AND EVALUATION

Immediately upon Gaius' death a series of legislative acts was passed to undo what the Gracchi had done. In 121 B.C. alienation of public domain was made legal and thus the precaution against reconcentration removed. The land commission was formally dissolved in 119 B.C., and in 111 B.C. rent payments on public domain were abolished and the holdings were declared private property in perpetual tenure. Finally, the system of squatting was abolished altogether and in the future public land could only be leased piecemeal or kept as commons.[30] Before this wave of reactionary counter-legislation came to an end, colonization was stopped and some colonies were "broken up." [31]

The effects of land distribution are hard to evaluate precisely. The census lists suggest a rise in the number of citizens who owned property from 317,000 in 136–135 B.C. to 318,823 in 131–130 B.C., and 394,933 in 125–124 B.C. However, we do not know how much of this increase may be attributed to land distribution, since the law of citizenship was liberalized in 125 B.C. and many Italians were enrolled as citizens regardless of the impact of the reform.[32] It is agreed, nevertheless, that most of the *ager publicus* subject to reform was redistributed to about half a million people.[33] The overall effect of the distribution is expressed by Rostovtzeff as follows:

The great crisis of the Roman state was not surmounted by the Gracchi. Their activity did not even produce a redistribution of land on a large scale, much less a complete change in the political structure of the Roman state or a regeneration of the Roman peasantry. The Roman peasant state could not be restored; it was dead for ever. Some new peasant plots were of course created, some landless proletarians were provided with holdings, some large estates were confiscated. But soon the process was first arrested and then finally stopped by the stubborn resistance of the ruling oligarchy. The only result of the Gracchan revolution was that it stirred up large masses of the Italian population and, for the first time in the history of Rome, drew a sharp line of cleavage between rich and poor, "oppressors" and "oppressed." The struggle between these two classes once begun could not be ended.[34]

The effects of the reform were limited also by the exemptions and privileges enjoyed by the influential groups:

Some of the large estates which were confiscated by the military leaders in the civil wars may have been parcelled out among small holders. As a rule, however, either such estates were kept by the temporary rulers of the state and formed the basis of their personal influence . . . or the land was sold for cash to fill their continually depleted treasuries.[35]

In another overview of the achievements of the Gracchi, Plutarch holds that the "greatest detractors and their worst enemies could not but allow that they had a genius to virtue beyond all Romans. . . ."[36] This, however, does not prevent some from suggesting that

of all persons who initiated a revolution, Tiberius Gracchus was perhaps the most conservative. His land law was almost a model of compromise . . . [and] totally inadequate. As a means of checking the decline of the free cultivators it could have no more than a transient effect . . . . Far from infringing on any legal vested right, it treated the existing occupants of the public land with exemplary considerateness and safeguarded them against any further loss of territory. . . ."[37]

Tiberius has been accused of compromising also on account of his suspension of rent payments on land held by landlords and thus in effect compensating them.[38]

In any event, considering the circumstances under which the reforms were carried out and the obstructive reactions,[39] the achievement of the Gracchi was impressive. This does not mean that the problems were solved; in fact, it is hard to imagine that they could be solved by these reforms. For one reason, the reform law was a mild one, based on compromise and characterized by political expediency and concession to vested interests. The allowance for an individual to hold up to 1,000 *iugera* when the simple peasant received only 30 meant that the landlords retained most of their privileges and the gap between rich and poor remained wide. Suspension of the rent obligation, even though it later benefited the small owner as well, was certainly a concession to the large holders. They were not only relieved of the rent but their holdings were perpetuated under the new rules. Furthermore, the decision to compensate landlords for improvements on expropriated land, whatever the justification, undermined the impact of distribution on social differentiation. Finally, considering the exemptions to veterans, to those who received land as payment of the public debt, and what was retained as common pasture, it is hard to imagine that the land redistributed could have been extensive, particularly since the land of the allies was exempted.

The reforms were equally limited in their impact on political stability. As events have shown, civil war accompanied the reforms and did not come to an end until all the reform laws had either been modified or repealed and the old situation restored. The struggle among members of the oligarchy was a common feature of the reform era, which led Mommsen to ask "whether the legislators dealt altogether honourably, whether they did not on the contrary designedly evade a solution" — their major interest being to overpower their oligarchic opponents.[40] It is evident that the reform was used as a means to stabilize the political situation, but also to secure legitimacy of the group in power. These same objectives were also used by the counterrevolutionaries, and in the end we notice that neither stability nor legitimacy was in fact achieved and the reforms were of no lasting consequence on the political structure of the Republic.

V

EVOLUTION OF LAND TENURE IN ENGLAND: A CASE OF CONTRAST

Formally, the case of England is not an example of land tenure reform as used in the literature, even though it involved a great deal of change in the form of tenure and in the relations between rural groups. In contrast to usual reform movements, these changes were not government-directed or characterized by the rapidity implied in reform. They occurred within the span of centuries, the rate of change varying from one period to another. Furthermore, they were more economically and less politically motivated than most other cases in this study.

Three major changes took place in the English land system: the commutations of the second half of the middle ages; the sixteenth-century enclosures; and the eighteenth- and early nineteenth-century enclosures. These developments were not distinct from each other, nor was any one of them confined to a single century or to a definite period of time. However, knowledge of the exact time of change is not essential for this investigation, which will focus only on the factors leading to, and on the processes and effects of, that change.[1]

The tenure changes in England were a crystalization of the power of the capitalist, in both agriculture and industry, and as such they were directly related to the rate of economic and capitalist development. The specific forms of tenure which evolved and their consequences were colored by the social and political structure of the country and by the role of the government in socioeconomic changes.[2]

The primary justification for including the English experience in this study is to use it for purposes of contrast and to answer questions such as these: What form of tenure change can we expect in the absence of reform or when the changes are dictated by socioeconomic relations with a minimum of government intervention? What major factors influence the direction of nonplanned tenure change, and what alterations might occur in the agrarian structure when change is evolutionary rather than revolutionary?

The case of England also provides a unique opportunity to see, in a continuous manner, what adjustments have to be made in agriculture and tenure relations in response to economic and social change; it shows how one adjustment leads into another, what happens when a new form of tenure has evolved, and how to anticipate or prevent undesirable consequences. When, for example, small peasant farms are created, can one be sure that they will survive without special protective measures and, if not, what measures will suffice? What forces will be likely to interfere with the success of reform and how can they be controlled? The English experience shows with great clarity the problems that land tenure reform can create and which must be dealt with. It also points out the fact that tenure relations involve a certain amount of dynamism which makes further change inevitable and, therefore, should be taken into consideration to prevent the reversal of the reform effects. These questions will be treated more directly in Part III.

We shall treat the tenure changes in England as two rather than three major changes according to the processes of reform: (1) commutation of labor services and disorganization of manorial institutions and their replacement with free hold and tenancy by contract; and (2) enclosure of common land and consolidation of holdings of both the sixteenth and eighteenth centuries.

1. COMMUTATION

Commutation represented the substitution of money rent for labor services and marked the transition from the manorial or semimanorial system of landholding to a system of contractural tenancy subject to positive law, in contrast to the law of custom which had previously governed the villein-landlord relations. Vinogradoff suggests that commutation

. . . treats of nothing less than of the passage from medieval agrarian organization on the basis of natural husbandry to the modern management of land on the money-rent system and from the medieval arrangement of society according to customary relations to its modern arrangement under uniform legal protection.[3]

As such, commutation was the first step toward commercialization of agriculture as part of the general capitalistic development of the economy.

BACKGROUND OF COMMUTATION: LAND TENURE

As Cheyney stated: "At the end of the thirteenth century the majority of Englishmen were still unfree. . . . In the year 1300 about two-thirds of the people were serfs, one-third free. By the middle of the sixteenth century, or before, the mass of the English rural population were free men." [4] The transition from unfreedom to freedom was the outcome of commutation. What was the nature of this unfreedom and how did it exist?

Our starting point is the year 1300, about which time manorialism in England was in its prime. The manor, lay or ecclesiastical, was the unit of organization of the rural economy. A typical manor was characterized by

. . . a large demesne, cultivated by the hands and tools of the servile peasants; villein land covering the greater part of the tenants' land on the manor, and assuring the demesne of a supply of obligatory labour; an insignificant freehold: — a mere 'fringe', consisting of small knightly holdings and the tenements of the few free peasants, who paid money rents.[5]

However, Kosminsky shows that there were various manorial types:

Type (a) comprises all 'typical' manors with a demesne, villein land and free holdings. To Type (b) we refer manors with a demesne and villein land but no free holdings. . . .Type (c), a widely recurring type, is the manor with a demesne and free holdings but without villein land. Type (d) is the manor with villein land and free holdings but no demesne. Type (e) comprises free holdings alone, without demesne or villein land. . . . Type (f) is villein land alone, without demesne or free holdings. . . . Type (g) is demesne alone, without villein land or free holdings.[6]

Variation in manorial types is significant because it seems to be related to the size of the manor and the rate at which commutation took place. It has been suggested that large estates with demesnes cultivated by free or unfree peasants were the rule in this period.[7] But according to another view, large manors with an average of 1,600 acres comprised only about 41 per cent of all manors; medium-size manors, averaging 675 acres, accounted for 30 per cent; while the small ones with an average of 224 acres amounted to 29 per cent.[8]

Estates varied also according to the proportion of demesne land and the ratio of villeins to free tenants. Table 1 shows the relationship between the distribution of free and unfree land and size of the manor. It will be

TABLE 1

FREE AND UNFREE LAND BY SIZE OF MANOR IN ENGLAND *

	Size of Manor		
	Large	Medium	Small
Villein land as percentage of total	51	39	32
Free land as percentage of total	23	26	27
Demesne as percentage of total	25	35	41
Ratio of Demesne/Villein	33:67	49:51	56:44
Ratio of Free/Villein	31:69	40:60	48:52

* Figures arranged in tabular form by author from Kosminsky, *op. cit.*, pp. 99–101.

noted that an inverse relationship between size of the demesne and labor rents prevails. Labor rents were least common on small manors, in which the demesne occupied the highest percentage of land among the three sizes of manors. Conversely, rent in labor services was found mostly on large manors, where the demesne occupied the smallest percentage of total land.[9] Though the evidence is scant, we suggest that the form of rent was associated with the economic power and political status of the manor lord. Where the estate was large, the lord was powerful and the rent was more often in the form of labor services; on the small estates the lord was not so powerful and therefore agreed to rent in money form.

The form of rent was also associated with the status of the villein farmer himself as represented by the size of his holdings: "As a general rule it seems that money rent is more important for small villein holdings than for large. Most small (cottar) holdings are either free from labor dues, or owe very few by comparison with their money rent." [10] Unfortunately, it is not shown whether holders of relatively large villein holdings predominated on small or on large manors. If on large manors, which we suspect to be the case, it would be consistent with our hypothesis that large manorial lords were powerful enough to exact labor rent from their tenants, and that they would do so in view of the importance of villeinage in the economy of the manor.

Arable land was held in strips spread all over the village land area. The strips of different tenants were intermingled and distributed in accordance with the two- and three-field systems of cultivation. The land of the manor did not always coincide with that of the village: some manors included more than one village, or more than one manorial lord had land in the same village. Cultivation was carried out simultaneously by all the villagers in each sector of the land according to season and the nature of the work required. This has led Pirenne to conclude that collective cultivation was the natural consequence of the manorial tenure and that this system of holding and organization was based on equality among the villagers. He concludes further that this system of cultivation precluded any idea of profit or production for the market. Rather, the system was patriarchal, guided by the interest of the villagers and their need for protection. [11]

Class relations on the manor

The manorial organization presents three intimately connected aspects — the proprietary, the social and the political one. The manor is an estate surrounded by tenures; it is a combination of ruling and dependent, working and military classes; it is a unit of local government. . . . It is directed towards the two distinct aims: it represents and formulates the interests of the villagers, and it acts as the machinery for the collection of duties and enforcement of services on behalf of the lord. [12]

This does not mean that the manor catered to the welfare of the lord and the villagers on equal levels or that the villagers were all treated equally. On top of the social scale was the landlord, who, for all practical purposes, was the absolute proprietor of the manorial estate. Legally he held the land by a grant from the king, but this relationship was only a formality and had no significance in the affairs of the manor. The lord held sole authority in the manor and his power was augmented both by the rule of custom and by his juridical powers over the inhabitants. Below the lord stood the minority of freeholders, who, though protected by law and the king's court, were actually tenants of the lord. They had the power of alienation of their rights to the land, but the approval of the lord was requisite.[13] The unfree tenants, the villeins, came next. They were not protected by any law except the rule of custom which actually gave the lord absolute authority over them.[14] The villein was characterized by three main features: he was bound to the soil; he rendered service as dictated by the lord; and he was bound "to surrender to his lord any or all of his personalty, if his lord saw fit to seize it." [15] The lord was a perpetual proprietor of the villein land. Once the land had been in villeinage, it remained so unless the lord conceded to the contrary, even if it happened to fall in the hands of a free man. This rule, however, was not reversible: free land became subject to villeinage if held by a villein, since the lord had authority over the possessions of his villein, and he usually got the best of all situations.[16]

The lord's proprietary rights extended over the wastes and common pastures and meadows, contrary to the notion of communal property.[17] Furthermore, he had the right to "claim escheated tenements, to take into his hands the wardship of his tenants under age, to draw profits in cases of the marriage of heiresses, and to exact relief as a consequence of investiture of heirs, all . . . derived from the idea that the *dominium eminens* of the freeholders' tenements belonged to the lord." [18] These privileges of the lords were accentuated with regard to the villein, as compared with the rest of the community.[19]

THE PROCESS OF COMMUTATION

During the fourteenth and fifteenth centuries, many factors affected and were affected by the structure of the economy and might, thus, have led to the breakdown of manorialism and liberation of the serf. Some of these factors were internal to the manor and some external; some were social, political, or technological. However, the social and political factors have been usually regarded as contributing factors rather than primary ones. The primary factors have invariably been economic. Growth of money economy, revival of trade, and expansion of the market have been given primary importance by Pirenne. Thorold Rogers has suggested the Black Death and other plagues and famines as the most important causes. Vinogradoff thought that the Black Death only accelerated the process of commutation but did not initiate it. According to him, the manorial economy was unstable from the beginning. The same viewpoint has been held by Thompson. Thomas W. Page suggested that the manorial economy was unstable and as soon as the demesne's need for labor could be satisfied by free labor, it disintegrated. The Black Death, according to Page, contributed to the availability of free labor. Cheyney held the same position as Page, especially on the role of free labor as a substitute for villein services.[20] These factors usually functioned through rent, prices, wages of labor, and reactions of the lord and the peasant to the new developments and pressures ensuing from them.

While accepting most of these explanations, but utilizing a Marxist analysis, Kosminsky concludes that disintegration of the manor was due to the internal class struggle between the lord and peasant classes. Development of trade since the middle of the eleventh century, and growth of commodity production, increased the lord's pressure on his peasant. He tried to increase the amount of rent both in money and in services and to restrict the peasants' rights in the commons. The lord was supported in this action by the court and the state, as shown by the Statute of Merton and the second Statute of Westminster. The peasants reacted by appealing to court, to ancient custom, and by desertion and even violence. This class struggle was the direct cause for commutation as the last resort for the lord.[21]

Though Kosminsky's analysis is based on the same factors mentioned by other authors, it introduces as new elements the political relations within the manor and the role of the state in this transformation. Kosminsky finds the manor lords to be in alliance with the court and the state. The lord struggled to maintain his position by maintaining the *status quo* and thus contributed to the stability of the political order.[22]

Finally, an explanation that deserves treatment has been presented by Harriett Bradley. The changes in land tenure, according to her, were a result of soil exhaustion and decline of fertility of the land which necessitated rent reduction. Commutation of labor services was incidental and did not change the social conditions of the peasant or his status from unfree to free. The subsequent reduction of rent because of tenant shortage raised peasant real income and made it easier for him to accumulate capital and buy his freedom. The effects of the Black Death on population and the ease of desertion to vacant land made it necessary for the lord to accept the change as *fait accompli*.[23]

All these explanations share certain features leading to the same conclusion: the breakdown of villeinage in England was caused by internal evolutionary economic developments which also determined the direction of change.

In spite of its evolutionary character, the process of change was neither peaceful nor smooth. There was action and reaction by both the peasants and the authorities. The conflict became intense after the Black Death, when prices and wages started to rise, and the lord began to lose ground. As a result, the government introduced the Statute of Labourers in 1349 to stabilize wages and prices, regulate labor mobility, and make sure that the land was cultivated.[24] However, peasant discontent continued to rise.

42

They rose in open revolt in 1381 against oppression from the landlords and against the Statute of Labourers itself.[25] The immediate consequence was that the revolt was crushed violently. Government reaction was well expressed by Richard III when he addressed the rebels: "Villeins you were, and villeins you are. In bondage you shall abide, and that not your old bondage but worse."[26] He made his threats good, but economic forces were stronger than government reaction; the effects of the revolt were finally recognized by the manor lords and the government. They realized that the past could not be revived and new relations had to be devised; hence the speeding-up of land lease and commutation of the services and freeing of the villein.

EFFECTS AND EVALUATION OF COMMUTATION

Two distinct changes comprised the transition from the manorial organization of the rural economy: freeing the land from villeinage, and permitting the unfree peasant to buy his freedom. Commutation of labor services into money rent freed the land and reduced the lord's relationship with his tenant to the annual payment of rent. However, the landlord was able to retain his property intact and even to enlarge it by affirming his hold on the commons and waste land. Thus the English lord escaped the fate of his French counterpart who lost all his seigneurial rights and the land itself in the French Revolution. The second form of freedom — freedom of person of the peasant — evolved in the process until by the end of the fifteenth century it was virtually complete.

The new freedom had great effects on tenure, the distribution of power, the conditions of agriculture, and on social relations between the different classes. However, as with most other changes, the effects were differentially distributed among classes. Substitution of money rent benefited some sections of the peasantry more than others.

The rich peasant with his surplus, producing for the market, certainly found it an advantage. The poor man who paid a small rent and part of whose income was in money wages did not find it inconvenient. But the largely self-subsistent peasants who had few links with the market experienced great hardship in the transition to money rents.

They had to pay fixed rent and yet were at the mercy of natural and market fluctuation.[27] Similarly, the rich peasant could buy his freedom easily, but not so the other groups. This differential impact strengthened class differentiation among the peasantry.

Also as a result of commutation, law courts replaced manorial courts and the title to the land could now be formalized. The new title was issued in a document, based on the manorial court rolls, a copy of which was held by the peasant; hence the name copyholder.[28] But unless the copyholder had bought his freedom, he continued to hold the land in hereditary tenure as villein even though he paid money rent. However,

43

since the lord retained his holdings and the unfree peasant had to buy his freedom, and since no land redistribution took place, the land remained concentrated in the hands of a few. There was also no appreciable change in the distribution of income as a direct result of commutation, although there might have been indirect income advantage through payment of a fixed rent.

An indirect but important result of commutation was an increase in the power of the state. Decline of the manorial structure and the power of the manorial lord, and conflict between classes, augmented the power of the state and aided unification of the community as one nation.

Finally, though the effects were more personal and social than economic, they were economically important in the long run. The change from servile to free holding set the stage for more individualistic and commercial production in agriculture. As the land became free, the farmer was able to select the method of cultivation and the kind of crop he wished to grow, and when economic conditions warranted further change, he was free to introduce it.

2. ENCLOSURES

Enclosures refer to the process by which common rights on land were replaced by individual private ownership.[29] However, the form of enclosure differed according to the initiator and the kind of land he enclosed.

The most simple form was the enclosure of waste lands — moors, sandy stretches and swamps — over which villagers might have common rights, but from which the landlord drew little benefit. . . . Secondly, common pastures might be partially enclosed by the commoners or under certain conditions by the landlord. In a third form of enclosure the demesne arable strips were withdrawn from the village fields, consolidated and enclosed in a compact farm. . . . As a fourth method all the village lands might be enclosed at one step instead of piecemeal.[30]

In the last of these forms, each peasant would receive a piece of land to use according to his own wishes.

The enclosure movement has usually been divided into two separate periods, one of the sixteenth and the other of the eighteenth centuries. The two periods were distinctive in both causes and effects of enclosure. However, there was one feature common to both, namely rejection by a large part of the small and medium peasant farmers, indicating that the benefits were differentially distributed in favor of the big landowners. In this respect, the enclosures ran counter to one of the primary motives of land tenure reform: a more equitable distribution of land and income. The enclosures seem to represent what Schickele has termed the "Farm Business Theory of Tenure," in contrast to "Family Farm

Theory of Tenure," on which most land tenure reform is now based.[31] The former emphasizes production; the latter distribution.

MOTIVES OF ENCLOSURE

There are two main theories of enclosures: the first, which is the more accepted, is that the prevalent tenure system was not congenial to the commercial production necessitated by the economic development of the times. The inefficiency of common rights and the fragmentation of holding prevented individual adaptation to the predominant economic forces because they inhibited individual incentive and capital investment in agriculture. This theory has been generalized to both the sixteenth- and the eighteenth-century enclosures and may be called the *profitability theory*. The second theory, which has been applied primarily to the sixteenth-century enclosures, suggests that enclosure was a way of getting around the problem of soil exhaustion and decline of fertility of the land; this may be called the *soil exhaustion theory*.

The profitability theory has many protagonists. Johnson suggests that growth of the commercial spirit and the commercial class, and the rising demand for luxuries, made it logical for the landlord to pursue sheep farming, which gave higher income than cultivation, even if he had to evict some of his tenants. But sheep farming could not be undertaken on open fields in which holdings of different people intermingled; hence the inevitability of enclosure.[32] The pressure to derive a high income from the soil was generated by the landlord's need for capital to commercialize his agriculture, which was consistent with the economic philosophy of mercantilism prevalent at the time.[33]

Another reason is that sheep farming dispensed with labor, which was scarce after the Black Death, at a time of rising demand for wool because of the development of Flemish manufacturing, for which England was a good source for material.[34] And after the middle of the sixteenth century, pressure for conversion to pasture increased because of depreciation in the value of money, a change that "threatened with ruin those who did not" change to sheep farming.[35]

The theory of profitability applies to enclosures of the eighteenth century in a different manner. By this time industry had developed and towns had grown. Demand for agricultural products and for industrial labor rose but agriculture could not keep pace with the demand, nor could it provide labor for industry. At the same time a new philosophy of cultivation and agricultural organization was emerging. The teachings of Arthur Young and Jethro Tull about large-scale operation, intensive agriculture, and big capital coincided with the rise in demand for agricultural products. These forces, combined with growth of the capitalistic spirit and pressure of the Napoleonic war, stimulated the search for methods to improve cultivation and increase production. But the common field system, which had survived earlier enclosures, was an obstacle; therefore, new enclosures were indispensable. However, this time the purpose was to promote the use of arable land, rather than converting it to pasture, to meet the rising demand for food.[36]

Thus, according to the profitability theory of enclosure, both the sixteenth- and the eighteenth-century enclosures were motivated by economic forces and business "rationality," but land use was different in the two periods.

The soil exhaustion theory of enclosure is that decline in the fertility of the land was the driving force. This theory, used earlier in explaining the commutations, has been applied to the sixteenth-century enclosures by Harriett Bradley. Owing to the backward methods of agriculture and the pressure of increasing population, land was exhausted and crop cultivation ceased to be profitable, relative to sheep farming.[37] Bradley shows that even when the price of wool was declining in the seventeenth century, conversion to pasture did not cease.[38]

We shall not try to evaluate the validity of these two theories. Actually, they may be shown to be compatible. Both are based on economic development and rational economic and business motives. Except for Miss Warriner's objections,[36] no one has suggested political developments as a primary cause of enclosure. It is interesting to note that, except for detail, the above explanations of enclosure are compatible with those presented by Marxist and Soviet authorities. Commodity production and profit motives guided tenure change, according to the usual relationship between rent and tenure. Peasant ownership, which the enclosures destroyed, is inversely related to capitalistic and "improved" rent and to capitalistic utilization of the land and differentiation among rural classes.[39] Though the Marxist analysis is comprehensive and takes into account the economic, political, and social forces in explaining the evolution of English tenure, its emphasis is on the economic factors. As such, it simply strengthens the contention that the enclosures were economically motivated.

THE PROCESS OF ENCLOSURE

Enclosure implied three changes at least: extinction of common rights, establishment of individual title, and consolidation of holdings. The first two are technically complementary and attainment of the one implies that of the other. Even the third may be technically related to the first two, since enclosure involved loss of right-of-way through the holdings of others.

Enclosure was applied to wasteland, marshes, and other uncultivated land, as well as to arable common fields for communal purposes as a temporary measure. We shall not deal with these two types of enclosure in any detail. The most important and relevant type of enclosure was that of common fields and meadows for permanently replacing common rights with individual rights to the land. The common fields were enclosed:

1. By common agreement of all the collective owners, though many of the enclosures by agreement can hardly be described as of a voluntary nature for some were brought about by great pressure on the part of the lords, and others by the menace of a suit in chancery, and so were more compulsory than voluntary. . . .
2. By purchase by one owner of all conflicting rights.
3. By force and fraud.
4. By special licence of the monarch, in Tudor times.
5. By Act of Parliament, either by private act — the method most in use from 1760 to 1845, the most active period of enclosing — or under the General Act of 1845 and its amending acts.
The enclosure of the commons or wastes could be effected by any of the above methods, and also under the Statutes of Merton (1236) and Westminster the Second (1289).[40]

Except for the Private Acts and special licenses for enclosure, or control of commissioners appointed by a General Act of Parliament, enclosure was not supervised by legal bodies. There were provisions to correct injustices, but the process was tedious, expensive, and, therefore, of little use to the peasant.[41]

Enclosure by private act usually required the consent of a certain proportion of the community, but often this proportion was based on the value of land or the assessment in the poor law rates. If a two-thirds majority was necessary and the lord owned land at the value of two-thirds of the community land, then alone he constituted a majority. Even if the landlord did not constitute a majority, it was easy for him to secure it by using his influence with those who might have vested interests, or be bearing the heavy expense of enclosure, should the attempt fail.

Of course, the peasants were not passive. They opposed enclosure by various means, including open violence. They appealed to Parliament and sought the aid of the government and other public agencies and religious groups. Around the middle of the fifteenth century a rebellion broke out under Jack Cade, who presented a bill telling of the suffering of the commoners who had perfect title to the land and yet "dare not have hould claim nor pursue their right." [42] Another violent uprising was that of 1549 under Robert Kett in which many fences and enclosures were destroyed. The rebels were, as before, harshly subdued and their leaders executed. This rebellion, however, was the last of a national character by the peasants (although local riots took place as late as 1607).[43] Laws were passed to redress the peasant grievances, but no effective aid was forthcoming from a parliament controlled by the landlords and baronial interests.[44]

In contrast to its formal stand on the sixteenth-century enclosures, the government openly encouraged those of the eighteenth century in order to stimulate agriculture and increase production. And yet no violent rural uprisings took place during the latter period, even though unrest characterized the towns and the industrial sector. One reason for the absence of violent rural reaction might have been the existence of outlets for labor in the city and the growing industry. Another might have been that enclosure was carried out piecemeal and by private acts in isolated localities; there was no organized movement against which the peasantry could rise as a class. Finally, since the enclosures took place over a relatively long period, the impact might have seemed insignificant, having affected individuals rather than groups. Therefore, no group resistance could be organized.

EFFECTS AND EVALUATION OF ENCLOSURES: TENURE GROUPS AND RURAL POPULATION

The effects varied with the type of enclosure and the land enclosed. Enclosure of waste land and land newly reclaimed was approved by all groups; that of arable and common fields was opposed by most tenants and small holders. On the other hand, enclosure for sheep walks had no positive effect, if not a negative one, on the per capita real income, while enclosure for cultivation and improvement increased production and raised the standard of living.

By enclosing the commons, the landlords established private title to the land and consolidated their holdings, in which case they had to either exchange strips with others whose strips mingled with their own or buy them out. They also had to settle with copyhold-tenants by compensating them or by disproving their right; in either case they evicted them and established freehold title to their land. Finally, in the process of enclosure many small and medium peasant farmers and yeomen were unable to prove their title, share the expense, or withstand pressure of the landlord, and had therefore to sell and get out. The result was a system of land concentration on one side, and tenant farming and a landless proletariat on the other.

Unfortunately the data on the distribution of ownership before enclosure are inadequate. But it is an accepted fact that under manorialism the land was concentrated in the hands of the lords and most of the peasants were tenants. A rough estimate of the distribution of landholding for different periods between 1450 and 1650 in certain counties shows the following: freeholders were 19.5 per cent of all the landholding population; 61.1 per cent were customary tenants, including copyholders who were the majority in this group; 12.6 per cent were leaseholders; and 6.7 per cent were uncertain.[45] After the enclosures, land ownership continued to be concentrated but so also was the right of usufruct. The impact has been described by Slater as follows:

48

After enclosure the comparatively few surviving farmers, enriched, elevated intellectually as well as socially by the successful struggle with a new environment, faced, across a deep social gulf, the labourers who had now only their labour to depend upon. In the early part of the nineteenth century, at any rate, it was almost impossible for a labourer to cross that gulf; on his side the farmer henceforward, instead of easily becoming a farm labourer if bankrupt, would rather try his fortune in the growing industrial towns.[46]

The significance of this change may be seen from the pace of enclosure and the resulting distribution of landownership. From the fifteenth to the seventeenth century, the area enclosed by enclosure acts has been estimated at 744,000 acres, or 2.1 per cent of the total area of England. In the eighteenth and nineteenth centuries the area was at least 4,464,189 acres, plus an area of 2,100,617 acres of waste, together amounting to about 20 per cent of the total area.[47] The rate of enclosure is shown in table 2. These data show that enclosures of the sixteenth and seventeenth

TABLE 2

AREA ENCLOSED BY ACT IN ENGLAND *

Period	Common field and some waste		Waste only	
	Acts	Acreage	Acts	Acreage
1700–1760	152	237,845	56	74,518
1761–1801	1,479	2,428,721	521	752,150
1802–1844	1,075	1,610,302	808	939,043
1845 & after	164 awards	187,321	508 awards	334,906
Total	2,870	4,464,189	1,893	2,100,617

* Johnson, *op. cit.*, p. 90.

TABLE 3

LAND DISTRIBUTION IN ENGLAND AND WALES, 1883 *

Class of owner	Number of owners	Percentage of total†	Number of acres	Percentage of area†	Average acreage†
Peers and peeresses	400	0.04	5,729,979	18.16	14,324.9
Great landowners	1,288	0.13	8,497,699	26.93	6,597.6
Squires	2,529	0.26	4,319,271	13.69	1,707.9
Greater yeomen	9,585	1.00	4,782,627	15.16	499.0
Lesser yeomen	24,412	2.55	4,144,272	13.13	169.8
Small proprietors	217,049	22.64	3,931,806	12.46	18.1
Cottagers	703,289	73.37	151,148	0.48	0.2
Public bodies	14,459		1,433,548		
Waste			1,524,624		

* G. Garbury, Jr., and T. Bryan, *The Land and the Landless*, Social Service Handbooks, No. 3 (London: Headley Bros., 1908), p. 13.
† Computed by author.

centuries did not greatly affect the number of landowners, though they reduced employment. But enclosures of the eighteenth and nineteenth centuries had a great impact on the distribution of landownership, as shown in table 3. The private owners, who numbered 958,552 individuals, owned 31,556,802 acres; however, only 1.43 per cent of them owned 73.94 per cent of all the land, and 3.98 per cent owned 87.07 per cent of all the land privately owned. There is no need to dwell on the distribution any longer. It is generally agreed that the enclosures resulted in concentration of ownership and predominance of contractual tenant farming.

What became of those who had hereditary rights and lost them? This brings up the much-debated question of enclosure effects on population.[48] First it should be mentioned that the rural population engaged in agriculture was gradually declining while town and industrial areas were growing, until by 1880 only 12 per cent of the population were engaged in agriculture,[49] even though about 750,000 acres were reclaimed and brought under cultivation. During the sixteenth-century enclosures, conversion of arable land into pastures caused depopulation, since sheep raising requires less labor than does cultivation under two- and three-field systems and backward and unmechanized agriculture. Actually depopulation might have happened with or without enclosure, depending on the amount of conversion to pasture.

Whether or not enclosure caused depopulation depended on two main factors: the methods of cultivation, and the demand for labor in the city. It is important to know whether or not the new techniques of rotation, fertilization, and intensive cultivation were laborsaving. Consolidation of the farm and competitive rational farming reduced underemployment and inefficient use of labor-time, both common failings of the strip open field system. The best evidence on this is the constant decline in the number of people engaged in farming without any reduction in total farm acreage. Although total population was increasing rapidly — almost doubling during the nineteenth century — farm population declined both absolutely and relatively.

Most of those remaining to work the land became tenants or landless workers. When industry needed them they responded, since their attachment to the village was weakened or severed and labor mobility became possible.

The impact of enclosure was not distributed equally among social classes. It is extremely difficult to evaluate the differential effects because of the many other influences in the environment, such as industrialization and trade, which prevent isolation of the problem and assessment of its results. For example, a small holder who had been evicted might have been lucky and improved his situation upon coming to town. Did this man gain or lose because of the enclosures? If one looks at the problem from the standpoint of the conditions prior to enclosure, as a rule those who retained their own land prospered even when they had to rent land to supplement their own. Their prosperity was enhanced also by the consolidation of holdings and more efficient utilization of resources.

However, not many people could retain their holdings. To do so it was necessary to have capital to cover the expense of enclosure, to prove a legal right to the land, and, finally, to withstand pressure of the landlord in the case of a conflict. That many people were hurt by enclosure has been admitted even by such an advocate of enclosure as Arthur Young, who declared that "by nineteen Enclosure Acts out of twenty, the poor are injured, in some grossly injured. . . .The poor in these parishes may say, and with truth, *Parliament may be tender of property, all I know is, I had a cow, and an Act of Parliament has taken it from me.*" [50] The cottagers who had occupied but not owned the land were evicted. Those who had used it for a long time — thirty or forty years — were given too small an allotment to retain. So they ended by selling it and moving.[51]

Evacuation of copyholders had started long before the eighteenth-century enclosures. One method of evicting them was to increase revenue over the short term, and to obtain the right to terminate the lease in the long run, "by proving that the copyholds were for life or lives, and not of inheritance; or by substituting leases for lives, or leases for years at rack rent, for copyholds." [52] If, however, the tenant was a copyholder by inheritance, he could not be legally evicted, but illegal evictions were not uncommon. A more difficult problem was to determine the extent to which the laws protected the rights of copyholders.[53] Even if he was protected, court action was of little help because his allotment in the common would often be so small that he would have to sell. The conclusion one arrives at from this analysis is the classical one: only a small minority survived the enclosures as landowners; all the rest became agricultural proletarians or emigrated to towns. Those interested in farming continued to live in the village by renting land in large plots as business enterprisers.

EFFECTS ON AGRICULTURAL PRODUCTION

The impact on production differed according to the use to which the land was put after enclosure and the use it had been subject to before. When land was converted to pasture, gross production sometimes went down, but net production went up as did the rent. According to "Thoughts on Inclosures, by a Country Farmer," in one parish in which conversion to pasture took place the gross product went down from £4,101 5s. 0d. to £2,660 0s. 0d. after enclosure. In contrast, the gross rent rose from £1,137 17s. 0d. to £1,801 12s. 2d.[54] There is no doubt, however, that production increased when enclosure converted common pasture into arable. According to calculations made by the "Country Gentleman," the benefits were impressive, as shown in table 4. We see that the total product rose only when land was either kept in grass or converted to tillage. Where land remained in tillage, enclosure seems

TABLE 4

ENCLOSURE EFFECTS ON PRODUCTION IN ENGLAND *

(In £ sterling)

Type of land ten years before and after enclosure	Rent to landlord	Farmer's profit	Total cost†	Total product	Total product per:†	
					Acre	Unit cost
1. Before	300	364	1,733	2,400	2.4	1.38
After	750	500	250	1,500	1.5	6.00
2. Before	200	300	1,500	2,000	2.00	1.33
After	400	750	1,030	1,800	1.80	1.75
3. Before	100	240	130	470	0.47	3.62
After	750	500	250	1,500	1.50	6.00
4. Before	50	60	80	190	0.19	2.28
After	400	370	1,030	1,800	1.80	1.75
Total Before			3,443	5,060	1.26	1.47
Total After			2,560	6,600	1.65	2.58

* Curtler, *op. cit.*, pp. 234–235, from Tables I, II, and III. The results might be exaggerated because of inflationary prices at the time (end of nineteenth century).
† Computed by author.
Definitions: Type of land: 1. 1,000 acres of rich open field.
2. 1,000 acres of open field; poor land, kept in tillage after enclosure.
3. 1,000 acres of rich common pastures, apparently kept in grass.
4. 1,000 acres commons, heaths, and moors, apparently converted to tillage.
Total cost includes wages to self-employed

to have decreased total production, although rent went up as did net profits to the farmer — the reason being a reduction of costs. In other words, productivity per acre went down but productivity per man rose, as implied in the last column of the table.[55]

The rise in production and productivity would still be higher if we consider the innovations in methods of cultivation, such as rotation and manure application. But as Doreen Warriner has shown, there is no reason to make these innovations dependent on enclosure. The same cannot, however, be said regarding the impact of enclosure on the scale of operation, and whatever the impact of scale of operation on production, this was true after enclosure.

In summary, it seems that the *evolution* of tenure in England involved the following: (1) Servile land became free prior to or concurrently with transformation of the villein to free tenant. This was the process generally known as commutation. (2) Enclosure of the land reduced most small holders to landlessness or tenancy; it concentrated land use and was neutral in its effects on the concentration of ownership which had characterized the system before enclosure. (3) There was no effect on individual private ownership of the land. The main changes concerned the terms of holding and the scale of operation on one side, and the pattern of cultivation on the other. Holding continued to be individual and private, but there was an inclination toward contractual cash tenancy. The scale of operation was enlarged. Finally, the pattern of cultivation tended heavily toward intensive, commercial agriculture. (4) The change was evolutionary and extended over a number of centuries. Though it involved some violence, on the whole it was peaceful and neutral to the stability of the political system. (5) Profit was the major motivation for change, and to that purpose all economic, social, and legal tools available were put into operation. (6) As a result of commutation and enclosure, landholding was consolidated; production increased and could cope with the rising demand from the city and the town; and land transaction and alienation of rights became possible. (7) The social effects of the change included further differentiation between classes, and much hardship, though temporarily, to the poorer groups.

VI

THE FRENCH REFORMS

The reforms that accompanied the French Revolution have since been reënacted in almost every reform in other countries of the world. The French Revolution precipitated social movements in Europe and elsewhere in which the peasantry played a role similar to that of the French peasantry, and in which the middle class began to crystallize in modern history. Certainly there are differences between experiences of the different countries, and some, like Britain, approached the same historical objectives in unique ways. Yet, even today, writers about land tenure reform often associate current experiences with those of the French Revolution, and reformers are inspired by its events and achievements. Why is this so? Were the French reforms of 1789 and the years after really characteristic of the needs of Europe of the nineteenth century and most underdeveloped countries of today?

The French reforms abolished feudal relations and liberated the peasant, and secularized clerical property and sold it to the public. But the impact of the French reforms has been disproportionate to their actual results both at home and abroad. They have left an everlasting impress on all other reform movements, not only because they freed the peasant, but primarily because they have in effect institutionalized the idealized small family farm.

BACKGROUND: LAND TENURE

France of the eighteenth century was primarily an agrarian society, even though manufacturing and industry had progressed impressively and were second only to Britain's.[1] About the time of the Revolution some 20 million peasants lived on the land and cultivated the soil.[2] Land belonged to private owners, clergymen, and the state, while some was open common. The private owners were primarily the small owner-farmers, the noblemen, and a small group of bourgeoisie or capitalists who owned a considerable amount of land. Sometimes these capitalist-owners cultivated their land on a large scale and were known as *laboureurs*, but few of the noblemen, clergy, and the state agencies cultivated the land or supervised its operation directly. The vast majority of them had peasants work the land in small lots on terms determined by tradition.

The peasants constituted separate groups according to their relations with the lord. The *censiers* were those who paid a money quit-rent, or *cens*, fixed by custom from ancient times. The *cens* was "the most general obligation" of the free peasant and

marked the land as peasant land and subjected its peasant proprietor to the payment of various sales and mutation fees. The cens was almost always a money rent, and consequently it was neither high nor burdensome, since it had been fixed years earlier when the purchasing power of money was much greater than in the eighteenth century. In addition to the cens the peasant owner generally paid another land rent in the form of a specified share of the crop which was known as the *champart,* sometimes called *terrage,* and amounted on the average to one-eighth of the crop. This heavy burden the peasant endeavored to convert, whenever it was possible, into a money payment. The manorial rights most profitable for the lord, when they could be applied, were the various sales and mutation fees that he exacted whenever the land changed hands. The *lods et ventes* were a sales tax amounting theoretically to about one-eighth of the selling price. By the right known as *retrait* the lord could refuse, at any time within thirty years after the date of a given sale, to give his assent to it; a legal right that made for extortionate practices.[3]

Thus, the burden of the *cens* was mainly the additional obligations to which the *censier* was subjected, and its function was to identify those from whom these obligations could be extracted. Some *censiers*, however, had to pay a variable rent which the lord or his agent could adjust according to circumstances.[4] Although the *censiers* numbered about 4 million peasants.[5]

The second peasant group were the *metayers* or sharecroppers. Originally, the *metayers* were those who paid half the crop as the share of the landlord, but the term has come to be applied to all share tenancies.[6] The *metayers* usually paid their rent in money or in kind or both, the rent ranging from one to two thirds of the product, but usually it was half.[7] Also among the tenant groups were the *fermiers* who rented land from the privileged classes and operated it on a large scale as a capitalist enterprise. These were contractual tenants and the closest to the form of tenancy then evolving in England. The *fermiers* rented the land for periods ranging from three to nine years and paid rent in money or in kind.[8]

Two other groups in the countryside were the serfs and the landless workers. Though serfdom had gradually been abandoned, some serfs operated the royal domain until they were liberated by Louis XVI.[9] The serfs, *mainmortables*, numbered about one million people in 1789. They owed the lord three days labor every week on his estate,[10] but theoretically they were bound to the soil.[11] The landless laborers or proletarians of the countryside, if one may distinguish them that way, were approximately one-fourth of the rural population and earned their living as farm laborers, or in domestic service and rural industry.[12] An interesting observation has been made that these workers were in a better economic position than the sharecroppers. Their condition

. . . seems to have been as good as in many parts of England, better than in most countries of Europe. The districts where large farms held at a money rent abounded were among the best tilled, and the farmers were substantial men. The labourer earned tolerable wages, and sometimes saved enough to buy a patch of land. It was not these districts which broke out into anarchy in the first months of the meeting of the States General. It was the districts full of *metayers* and small proprietors that rose up against the *seigneurs*.[13]

The pattern of land distribution on the eve of the revolution depends greatly on whether the *censiers* are considered owners or tenants. Gershoy suggests that

between them the nobility and the clergy owned probably not more than one-third of the land. . . . The wealthy bourgeoisie also owned considerable property, particularly in the vicinity of the towns, their holdings ranging from twelve to forty-five per cent in different regions. . . .The most numerous proprietors were the free, non-servile peasants [*censiers*] . . . [holding] clearly not less than one-third and probably not more than one-half of all the land.[14]

But this estimate has not generally been accepted.

A recent writer of authority has accepted the opinion that before the Revolution one-fifth belonged to the crown or was communal property, one-fifth belonged to the clergy, one-fifth to the nobles, and two-fifths to the Third Estate. As few of the middle class were landowners, the share of the Third Estate belonged mostly to the peasants; and the peasants, who made up most of the rural communes, must be regarded as holding nearly all the communal lands.[15]

A more generally accepted, and probably more precise and accurate estimate, is that given by Loutchisky and Lefebvre and supported by H. Sée. Lefebvre estimates the holdings of the nobility to range from 9 to 44 per cent, that of the clergy from 1 to 20 per cent, the bourgeoisie from 12 to 45 per cent, and those of the peasants from 22 to 70 per cent, depending upon the region or district under consideration.[16] According to Henri Sée, the share of the peasants ranged from 20 to 50 per cent, that of the nobility from 11 to 35 per cent except in the west where it was larger; the share of the clergy, however, was much smaller than previous estimates and was about 6 per cent of all the land of France.[17]

Whichever set of estimates one accepts, it is agreed that the distribution was disproportionate to the size of the tenure groups. The nobility and the clergy held more and the peasants less than their proportionate share. But, if the *censiers* were considered tenants, in the words of H. Sée: "theoretically, the nobility and the clergy possessed almost all the land, but over peasant land they exercised only seigneurial authority." [18] This means that except for the "handful" of freeholders and the small number of bourgeois owners, all the land was concentrated in the hands of the nobility and the clergy. To simplify the analysis, we shall refer to the property of the lords as cens-land and freehold-land. The cens-land would be what otherwise is considered peasant property. This simplication permits evaluation of the effects of the Revolution on land tenure, as well as being consistent with our definition of ownership.

BACKGROUND: CLASS DIFFERENTIATION

Social classes in pre-Revolution agrarian France corresponded more or less to the forms of tenure. The clergy formed the first estate, followed by the nobility, and finally by the third estate, which was a conglomeration of the peasantry, bourgeoisie, and workers. One might actually think of the bourgeoisie as being in between the second and third estates, but traditionally it was part of the third. At the bottom of the scale were the serfs and proletarians. These classes were heterogeneous and the internal relations were not always harmonious.

The clergy, estimated at 100,000–130,000,[19] were privileged with economic and political autonomy beyond all proportion to their number. They were said to form "a state within a state." Their annual income was estimated at 200,000,000 *livres* or "about one-half of the revenue of the Crown at the accession of Louis XVI. Fully two-fifths of the whole was derived from tithes, the residue from landed estate." [20] But they were divided into high and low clergy. Like the nobility, the high clergy were distinguished by birth and closeness to the court, and had privileges and vested interests in the prevailing conditions. In contrast, the low clergy — monks, vicars, and parish priests — were poor, exploited, and despised by the high clergy. In fact, during the Revolution the low clergy sympathized with the peasants and common people: "In the first stage of the Revolution the sympathy of the parish priests ensured the victory of the Third Estate over the nobles and prelates";[21] ". . . at the end of the *ancien regime* the vicars began to revolt against this attitude of their bishops and to compare their miserable lot with opulence of their superiors." [22]

The clergy managed to get exemption from the *taille* (head tax), the *vingtièmes* (property tax), and the *capitation* (war tax). However, as if to maintain their position, they gave the Crown a subsidy every five years, *don gratuit*, which "by no means balanced their exemptions," [23] and was often offset by the annual grants they received from the king.[24]

As landlords, the clergy usually let their land to sharecroppers and directly supervised it or even cultivated it themselves. Thus clerical absentee-landlordism was less widespread than among large lay owner-groups. Church lands were said to be "the best cultivated in the kingdom," and the clergy treated their tenants better than other landlords did.[25] Nevertheless, the peasants were opposed to the burdensome tithe they paid and to their subjugation to landlordism.

It is more difficult to estimate the size of the nobility. Roughly, they numbered about 100,000 people or 25,000–30,000 families, and though less numerous than the clergy, they were wealthier.[26] Besides their manorial rights as lords of fiefs, their privileges included "the right of having a coat of arms, a lord's bench in the parish church, and special vaults or enfeux." They were exempt from the *taille*, forced labor on roads, and from billeting of troops, and when "accused of a crime their cases [were] judged by the parliaments."[27]

Like the clergy, the nobles were not a homogeneous class: some were prosperous and others poverty-stricken. The latter segment were hostile toward the nobility of the court. Both groups, however, were under pressure for higher income — the former because of the growing need in a world of new products and the limited income from the fixed *cens*, and the latter because of sheer poverty. Therefore, to the disadvantage of the peasants, they became more exacting of the dues and more literal in executing the laws of custom to squeeze more out of their custom-defined privileges. It is true that some nobles were influenced by new ideas of liberalism and were friendly to their peasants, but on the whole the nobility failed to meet their custom-defined obligations to their peasants. They plagued them with manorial rights, destroyed their corn in search of game, and the game itself was equally destructive of their crops. Yet the peasants were helpless against the lord and his game. The landlords' unkindness was aggravated by their absenteeism and ignorance of the peasants' conditions.

The bourgeoisie were mainly urban with a few large farmers cultivating their own land. Their grievances were primarily social and political rather than economic. The growth of industry and commerce on the eve of the Revolution had given rise to a well-educated capitalistic group who filled many "lucrative employments" and civil services, but they had no share in political power. The social system had no institutionalized place for them as an emerging class. In spite of their privileges, such as exemption from the *taille*, they felt deprived and discriminated against, especially since they could hold only positions unwanted by the nobles. This feeling of deprivation and discontent was a major link between them and the peasantry who neither occupied an enviable position nor threatened the emerging middle class. It was logical, therefore, that they should form an alliance with the peasants against the nobility and the clergy. Thus

it was the entire third estate that rose to demand the abolition of the privileges enjoyed by the aristocracy, the admission of all men to all positions, and, in the rural sections, the destruction of the manorial system. The latter demand was added to the program of the bourgeoisie at the insistence of the peasants, or at least in order to win them over to the cause of the urban third estate.[28]

As already implied, the peasants were poverty-stricken. They paid a big portion of the produce of their labor as *cens*, share-crop, tithe, or tax. They were burdened by traditional obligations which had survived the old manorial system long after that system had lost its social functions. Furthermore, their income was depressed because their farms were small and fragmented, and their techniques backward. Lefebvre found that in Limousin 58 per cent of the peasants held less than 2 hectares each; 76 per cent held a similar size in Leonais; three-quarters of the peasants in Nord at the south of Lys did not possess one hectare each.[29] Because of the backward techniques and the terms of holding, productivity was low and so was peasant real income. The increase of population and the lack of a corresponding increase of labor productivity depressed real income still further.[30]

On the eve of the Revolution, the relations between tenure and social groups had reached a critical point. The peasants were restive against their anachronistic manorial obligations. Though the government had taken over the responsibilities of the feudal lords, they continued to enjoy feudal privileges and even revived long-forgotten feudal rights: "The manorial dues were made heavier at the end of the *ancien regime*, and there came what is known as the 'feudal reaction.' This reaction is not manifested in the creation of new obligations, but in the arbitrary increase of the old ones, or in the revival of those that had fallen into disuse." [31] This was true even though the peasants had been increasing their land holdings.[32]

The crisis was accentuated by the financial difficulties of the state. Increasing demands of the administration were met by higher taxes, most of which fell on the peasantry. The *taille*, which was paid only by the peasantry, was gradually raised "until on the eve of the Revolution it produced 91 million *livres*." The people had also to pay *capitation* or war tax, which was maintained until 1791. The *vingtième* or property tax, both personal and real, was gradually concentrated on real property and shifted onto the peasants. The tax burden was especially heavy owing to the corruption and arbitrariness with which taxes were collected. "The wealthiest classes, by the purchase of official posts or otherwise, joined the ranks of the privileged, and secured complete or partial exemption," putting the burden of taxation primarily on the peasants.[33]

The peasantry, however, was not passive toward these developments. The tide continued to rise until by July 14, 1789, tension had reached a breaking-point and peasant revolts and war against feudalism broke out and spread quickly. According to Duchemin, "more than three hundred riots occurred in the four months preceding the taking of the Bastille." [34]

It is against this background of extremes of poverty and wealth, deprivation and privilege, ancient institutions and the crystallization of capitalism and a middle class, with rising tension and class conflict, that we shall discuss the tenure reforms of the French Revolution.

LAND TENURE REFORM: THE PROCESS

Among the first accomplishments of the Revolution "was the destruction of French feudalism and creation of an independent propertied peasantry. What the benevolent despots had been vainly attempting to achieve for fifty years was accomplished by liberal parliamentarians in the course of the single night of August 4, 1789." [35] Though this may sound rhetorical, there is no doubt that as an agent of the Revolution, the National Assembly dealt the *ancien régime* a fatal blow in the week of August 4 to 11, 1789. The reform laws passed in the first week of the Revolution may be summarized as follows:

(1) The National Assembly entirely destroys the feudal system, and decrees that, of the feudal rights, those which are derived from real or personal *mainmorte* and personal servitude, and those which represent them, are abolished without indemnity; all others are declared to be redeemable, and the price and method of their redemption shall be fixed by the National Assembly. Those of the said rights which are not suppressed by this decree shall, nevertheless, continue to be levied till their reimbursement.
(2) The exclusive right to pigeon-houses is abolished; pigeons shall be shut up at the periods fixed by the communities; during these times they shall be regarded as game, and any person has the right to kill them on his land.
(3) The monopoly of hunting-rights and open warrens is similarly abolished; every proprietor has the right to destroy and cause to be destroyed, on his own possessions, all species of game. . . .
(4) All feudal jurisdictions are suppressed without indemnity; nevertheless, their officers shall continue to fulfill their functions till the National Assembly shall have provided for a new juridical system.
(5) Tithes of all kinds and dues which take the place of them, under whatever name they may be known and levied . . . are abolished. However, until such provision shall have been made [for their replacement] . . . the National Assembly orders that the said tithes shall continue to be levied according to the laws and in the customary manner. As to other tithes, of whatever kind they may be, they are redeemable in the manner which

60

shall be decided by the Assembly, and until such decision the Assembly orders that their collection shall be continued also.

(6) All perpetual rents, whether in money or in kind, whatever their character and origin, and to whatever persons they may be due. . . shall be redeemable; the *champarts* of all kinds, and under all names, are equally redeemable at the rate to be fixed by the Assembly. It is forbidden to create irredeemable rent in the future.[36]

The peasants understood these laws to mean complete destruction of feudalism, but the facts were not so. The ambiguity inherent in the distinction between feudal rights that were personal and thus redeemable and those which were real and based on land concessions and thus unredeemable, permitted the landlords to obstruct liberation of the peasant and his land. The serfs were freed of all servitude and some feudal rights were abolished, but obligations based on land concession remained, including "all land rents (cens and champart), all real corvees, lods et ventes, and all dues which had been commuted into money payments. These which were the most lucrative of the noble's rights were to be repurchased from the proprietor."[37]

Putting the burden of proof of title on the peasants was a concession to the nobility, who nevertheless opposed the new legislation for depriving them of social privileges and honors without offering any material advantages. The peasants were equally disappointed because the burden of redemption was unbearable and because their hopes of complete freedom were not realized. They reacted violently and the "disturbances of the fall and winter of 1789 and the spring of 1790 were more extensive and more profound than the peasant insurrection prior to August, 1789."[38] They believed that "the old days were no more" and therefore refused to pay rents. On June 18, 1790, the Assembly renewed its orders to resume the customary collection of dues and dispatched members of the National Guard to enforce these orders. The peasants' answer was further rioting and violence.

In June, 1792, a decree was passed abolishing all casual rights such as *quint, requint, treizieme, lods et ventes*, milods, *rachets*, reliefs . . . *acapte*, and *arriere-acapte*, unless they were proved to have been based on land concessions. Another decree was passed on August 20, 1792, allowing redemption of annual rights and casual rights separately; casual rights were also made redeemable individually. It was decreed also that each individual landholder could redeem himself separately from the other tenants of the same landlord. Finally, on August 25, 1792, the earlier laws were reaffirmed, but a new tone was set when the burden of proof of title was shifted from the peasant to the landlord, who usually lacked such proof in writing. "The wheel had swung full circle; the policy of the first revolutionary legislature was completely reversed."[39]

On August 28, 1792, a measure was introduced declaring all previous legislation on common land void, and that

if the properties of which the communes had been dispossessed were still in the hands of the *seigneurs*, they could be reclaimed within five years without indemnity. In the same way the communes could recover any property in rights of usage of which they had been despoiled unless the lord were able to show that he had acquired them by legal purchase. Further, even if the communes could not prove that they had formerly owned any commons, wastes, or *landes* which might exist within their borders, they could now claim ownership of them unless the former *seigneur* were able to show an adequate title, or prove that he had been in peaceable and uncontested possession of them for forty years.[40]

Nevertheless, the destruction of feudalism was not fully accomplished nor were the peasants gratified until political circumstances made further reform necessary. When national safety required peasant support against the impending war, the Convention completed the agrarian revolution to the satisfaction of the peasants. On June 10, 1790, common lands were ordered distributed among the inhabitants of the communes; on June 17 another decree ordered that "all dues formerly seigneurial, feudal rights whether fixed or casual, even those maintained by the decree of the 25 August last, are suppressed without indemnity." [41]

In the meantime, the government confiscated land of the clergy, the emigrants, and political opponents of the Revolution. These acquisitions together with the land originally held by the state became public land. Initially it was decided to sell public land in small lots and on easy terms to encourage peasant purchase.[42] The peasants, however, afraid of speculation, "demanded that this land continue to be used as it had been since times immemorial." Others held that "selling public land would be dangerous to the peasants since only partition could prevent speculation by the rich." [43] Talleyrand initially supported the attitude of the peasants to the public land. He suggested its distribution in small lots among state creditors and other citizens. That, he thought, would transform the old order into a new one and prevent restoration of the old regime.

By May 14, 1790, the Assembly had made arrangements facilitating purchase of public land by the poor, the payment being in twelve installments with an interest rate of 5 per cent on the debt.[44] But the attitude toward public land changed rapidly:

By a series of decrees of June 25, 26, and 29, the Assembly confirmed its resolution of May 14. But the attitude of the deputies was already changed by August and September, now being convinced of a need to modify the May 14 decree. The same Talleyrand whose eloquence had been expended to convince the Assembly of the usefulness of increasing the number of small proprietors now considers only the state's obligation to satisfy its creditors, and Pinteville-Cernon contends that the sale of public land and that the great vice of its operation comes from considering this indulgence as a consequence or as a simple effect, instead of considering it as a principle and as a means.[45]

The grave financial difficulties of the state and the change of attitude regarding public land were reflected in the decree of November 3, 1790, which suspended division of the land, recommended sale *en-bloc*, and modified payment terms. Now the buyer had to pay at least three-tenths of the total at the time of purchase and the rest in four installments instead of twelve. As a concession to the advocates of partition, the new decree was not to go into effect until May 14, 1791. In evaluating the measures to promote small proprietorship, Loutchisky points out that "these were only beautiful phrases. In all the districts, those responsible for the sale were recommended to give preference to buyers *en-bloc* over small buyers, given the prices offered were the same."[46] The obstacles created by the new policy were sometimes circumvented by the small buyers who bought land collectively and divided it later. But this did not prevent speculation. The speculators also formed associations to buy collectively and take advantage of the new opportunities.[47]

Another decree was passed on June 10, 1793, when the Montagnards triumphed over the Girondins and wanted to retain the support of the peasants, suppressing sale on cash and readmitting installment payments. It also provided for distribution of land to the poor without reverting to auction, either against payment of a certain rent or against capitalization of the rent, the option being left to the buyer.[48]

Finally, a decree was passed on November 6, 1796, to ease the terms of purchase of public land. According to the new policy, one-tenth of the cost would be paid immediately upon purchase; five-tenths were to be paid in two installments, one after ten days and the other after six months; the remaining four-tenths were to be paid over a period of four years.[49]

Effects and Evaluation

The reforms have so far been discussed as formal measures and laws enacted and handed over to committees and officials for implementation. The effects were sometimes positive, but not always. It is, says Dovring,

. . . a big mistake to state that the French Revolution abolished feudalism. . . . The Revolution abolished the land rent derived from Medieval feudal tenures. It did not change very profoundly the agrarian structure of the countries it touched at first hand, and scarcely needed to do so either, since the farm structure was already essentially the family farm structure we know. The 'inferior' ownership of French and neighboring peasants was converted into full ownership. . . . The abolition of feudalism had gone on silently during the Late Middle Ages.[50]

Comparing this statement with that of Hamerow on the achievements of the French Revolution shows the complexity of evaluating the French reform. It is certain that the Revolution abolished the *main-morte* and the *cens* and transformed the cens-land into freehold or private property of the peasants who had cultivated it. But the results were not so clear-cut with regard to the commons. The attitude of the policy makers was indecisive, and often unfavorable to small proprietorship. At the beginning, the Revolution recognized the right of the peasant in the commons; in 1792 division was made obligatory except for woodlands, but within a year it was made optional. In 1803 a law forbade further division of commons. The results obtained until then varied according to regions. In the town areas, common land almost vanished, while in the north the commons were either cut up or sold extensively. In 1815 one-tenth of France was still owned in common tenure, although this was mostly woodlands. We have no way of determining how much of the commons reverted to small owners.[51]

The policy on public land was equally flexible and unfavorable to the peasants. The results have been evaluated differently by different writers. Some have suggested that peasant property did not increase nor was there any change in the number of small owners. These people, like Tocqueville and Lavergne, suggest that small owners had been acquiring land before the Revolution, and that the bourgeoisie only speeded up that movement, regardless of the sale of public lands. Others, like Molinari, attribute to the sales a change in medium-sized holdings but not in small or large ones. Sybel suggests that land exchanged hands without changing the number of proprietors and that small owners did not benefit much from the sale. In contrast, L. von Stein claims that both small and large owners benefited from the sales, but not the medium-size owners. Bourdaux holds that the bourgeoisie intentionally allowed other groups to have the public land "comme dot à la Constitution." [52]

In his extensive study of the subject, Loutchisky finds that the sale of public land had the following tendencies: (1) Inequality of land distribution was not diminished; those who had more were able to buy more. (2) Big farmers, *laboureurs*, and merchants were great beneficiaries of the sale. (3) Ecclesiastic property, by nature of its structure, was sold in small and medium lots, contrary to the previously held opinion. (4) Contrary to M. Marion's findings, most of the sales passed to rural rather than to urban people; some variation existed among regions and according to locality. And (5) the sales strengthened two already prevalent tendencies: differentiation between and among rural

64

groups, and enhancement of the small bourgeoisie and people with economic power.[53]

These observations have been subjected to criticism by Lefebvre, who says: "As far as possible, all the heads of families have become proprietors, thanks to the division of the public and common land, without becoming of equal wealth, for some had inherited land. When the minimum was assured for each family, the rest of the land was put up for sale, by general agreement." [54] The process of sale and the changes of policy on public land do not support Lefebvre's conclusion, unless we were to give much weight to the qualifying phrase "as far as possible." Later views have held that land was bought by bourgeoisie or by agents of the former owners. Some wealthy peasants, however, did acquire land, but few of the landless people or the small proprietors could buy any. The share of the peasants was proportionately smaller than that of the other social classes.[55]

Finally, since the sale was open to everybody, sale *en-bloc* was preferred, and since the bourgeoisie were in command it seems plausible that economic endowment was decisive as to who bought how much. The only other channel by which small peasants could have acquired land was purchase from speculators, but this could not have been any easier for them than direct purchase of public land.

To summarize our evaluation of the reform:

1. The benefits were neither generally nor equally distributed, as is evident from contrasting the advantages of the serfs and the *censiers* with those of the landless workers and *metayers*. The first two groups were liberated from their manorial obligations. The landless and tenant groups, unless they acquired land by purchase, which is doubtful, remained as they were before the Revolution. Similarly, the policy on public land and commons was biased in favor of the wealthier peasants and capitalists. The small landowners, the *metayers*, and the landless workers hardly benefited from the sale of public land. Also unaffected, to their advantage, were the former nobility who had title to the land. Their estates remained intact, unless they were political enemies of the Revolution.[56] Sometimes they even took advantage of sale opportunities and increased their landholdings. These observations suggest that the bourgeois government did not intend to break the large estates to create small owners but to weaken the nobility as a class. The reforms seem to have been an expression of class conflict in which the new middle class fortified its position against the old order by alliance with the small peasantry and proletariat. Yet, the declared objective always was to create and strengthen the class of small proprietors.

2. There was a close association between political events and the policy on tenure. Triumph of the bourgeoisie freed the land from its

seigneurial ties, encouraged its transferability, and enhanced private property regardless of the farm size. It also ended domination of the clergy as a tenure group. Victory of the Montagnards changed the policy on public land in favor of the poorer groups whose support they wanted; when national safety was endangered, all indemnity requirements were canceled to appease the peasants, but the triumph of Napoleon encouraged the emergence of a new landed bourgeoisie.[57] The land policy of the government was often determined by financial crisis, as a result of which land sale replaced land distribution, and large size rather than small size lots became the unit of transaction. Also, the terms of payment were shortened. Finally, political restoration caused a setback to the reform, since it rehabilitated the defeated nobility and restored most of their wealth to them.

3. The reform policy was replete with reaction. By differentiating personal from real rights, abolition of manorial relations was obstructed for a relatively long period, and triumph of the republic did not automatically represent a triumph of the peasants. Though feudalism was considered an institution of the past, the "bourgeoisie none the less could not approve of its abolition except by legal methods and with compensation, lest a dangerous precedent for other forms of property be set." [58] Reaction was expressed also by putting the burden of proving title to the land on the peasants, which obstructed thorough and rapid implementation of the law. In all cases, reaction was overcome only by peasant action and by favorable political circumstances. Also, the policy on public land was reactionary and unfavorable to the peasants, even though it might have been justified by national conditions.[59] These reactionary policies were finally made the rule rather than the exception when the Restoration managed to undo many of the reform effects. Material rehabilitation of the nobility, recovery of their estates, and the payment to them of a large indemnity in 1823 reversed many of the reform effects. The loss of the peasantry after the Restoration was aggravated by the emergence of a new class of landowners among the supporters of Napoleon. These people acquired land that was potentially accessible to the peasantry.

4. The reforms were not guided by economic objectives, nor were they especially conducive to higher production or productivity. They might have encouraged production by releasing the common land for enclosure and by entitling the peasant to make his own farming decisions.[60] They might have been useful also in increasing peasant incentive, but all these would be indirect effects of the tenure change. They were not direct results or planned objectives. The effects on the distribution of income and wealth are vague, but they cannot have been too extensive, especially if one regards the *censiers* as owners. In that case the changes would necessarily be minor. Even if they were considered tenants, the distribu-

66

tive effects would still be limited, since the holdings of the *censiers* continued to be very small and also because some peasants had redeemed their rights before redemption was abolished.[61] Finally, as Loutchisky has concluded, sale of public land and of the commons did not reduce inequality. There might have been some narrowing of the gap between the extremes of poverty and wealth, but the emergence of wealthy capitalists and the partial recovery of the nobility were almost sufficient to offset that equalization.[62] These forms of reaction suggest that the impact of the reform on economic equality was limited.

5. In terms of the classificatory scheme of this study, there was no change in land tenure relations: tenure remained individual and private. The cens-land which became peasant freehold simply changed hands from one private owner to another.[63]

But a more pronounced change was the transformation of state and common land into private property. This change respectively from public and collective to private and individual ownership reflected the tendency of tenure change toward private tenure, and represented the triumph of capitalism and *laissez-faire*. In fact, this tendency was well expressed in and institutionalized by Articles 544–546 of the Code of Napoleon,[64] which formalized the victory of the middle class over the old order. The agrarian structure underwent change with respect to the terms of holding: cens-land became freehold; serf holdings were abolished and the tenure relation between serf and *seigneur* ceased to exist. But there was no direct effect on the scale of operation of the farm nor on the pattern of cultivation. Whatever change took place in this respect might or might not have been related to tenure reform. It is probably safe to attribute most of the subsequent improvements in the pattern of cultivation to the change of political and economic leadership rather than to the reform of tenure.

VII

THE RUSSIAN REFORMS

INTRODUCTION

The three tenure reforms treated in this chapter are interconnected and form links in one chain of events. Each reform, directly or indirectly, provided the means and objectives of the next, or the background within which the new reform seemed imperative. Emancipation of the serf (1861) freed him from the rule of the landlord, but made him subject to the commune as a whole. The various measures enacted between Emancipation and the Stolypin reforms (1906–1911) had important effects on the agrarian system as a whole, but these were not always favorable to the peasant. The peasant expressed his disappointment in many ways, including open violence and uprisings up to the eve of the Soviet reform. Whether or not the Soviet reforms satisfied the peasants depends on which phase of the reform is under consideration, and also on which peasant group one has in mind. The peasant class was not a homogeneous group and therefore was differentially affected.

Looking at the problem from the point of view of the landlord, we also observe a direct connection between the measures taken in each of the three periods. Each reform period seems to have put new restrictions on the power of the lord, ultimately leaving him without title, land, or power. In the meantime, he continuously and vigorously attempted to maintain his position in a rapidly changing social system by both action and reaction. The lord was against social change; therefore, he worked hand-in-hand with the state to preserve stability of the political order in which he had vested interests. And to that end the earlier tenure reforms were utilized. In a similar manner, after the Soviet authorities overthrew the old regime, they sought to stabilize the new system and legitimize the new political order at least partly by means of land tenure change. In each case, so it seems, land tenure has been used for the same purpose: stabilizing or legitimizing the political order. However, this might be an oversimplification, but we shall come back to this point.

In view of this interconnection between the three Russian reforms, the presentation will be more or less continuous — the results of each stage of reform comprising the background of the following one.

A. EMANCIPATION OF THE SERF, 1861

BACKGROUND: LAND TENURE

In the middle of the nineteenth century Russia was an agricultural society in which land was owned privately or by the state. The private owners were noblemen whose rights and privileges had evolved through centuries past and who had lived on the income from land cultivated by the peasants. The land was held in one of two forms: absolute ownership or in allotment tenure. The former may be called private ownership in absolute tenure according to which land could be transferred or leased by contract. Allotment land was held by cultivators of the land, the peasants, who owed the individual landlord, or the state, rents or dues for usufruct of that land. It was on these lands that serfdom prevailed. Distribution of the land among these categories cannot be determined with precision. Though many sources offer bits of information on this, the data are incomplete and some manipulation is necessary.

TABLE 5

PRIVATELY OWNED LAND, RUSSIA, 1877–1878

	Million desiatines		Per cent of total [a]
Allotment land		131	55
Privately owned		109	45
Imperial family	7		2.9
Clergy	6		2.5
Commercial institutions	2		0.8
Towns and cities	2[b]		0.8
Nobles	73[c]		30.4
Other private families	19		7.9
Total		240	100

[a] Computed by author.

[b] V. I. Lenin, *Alliance of the Working Class and the Peasantry* (Moscow: Foreign Languages Publishing House, 1959), pp. 33–35.

[c] Litoshenko estimates this share to be 77 million des. in 1877; L. Litoshenko, "Landed Property in Russia," *Russian Review*, II (1913), no. 4. Florinsky estimates the holdings of 102,870 members of the nobility to be 30.6 per cent of the total land area of Russia in 1859; M. T. Florinsky, *Russia, A History and an Interpretation*, II (New York: Macmillan, 1953), p. 784.

The total land area in European Russia was estimated in 1877–1878 at 390 million *desiatines* (1 des. = 2.7 acres), of which 150 millions were owned by the state and 240 millions divided as in table 5. Owing to the lack of the data I have estimated the distribution for 1861.[1] The results, based on Lenin's figures, are as follows:

69

$73 + 9.5 = 82.5$ million des., land of nobility including acquisition from settlement up to 1877.

$82.5 - 16.5 = 66$ million des., land of nobility before acquisition: 1862.

$131 - 5.7 = 125.3$ million des., land of peasantry before acquisition by purchase.

$125.3 + 16.5 = 141.8$ million des., land of peasantry before Emancipation: 1862; or before application of the law.

Lenin, however, regards the figures on state land as misleading in the sense that only 4 million desiatines of the 150 millions were cultivable, the rest being forests and waste land. This theory does not seem plausible, considering the size of the serf population on state land compared with that on private estates. In 1859 there were 10.7 million and 12.8 million male serfs on private and state land respectively. Twenty-four years earlier the estimates were 10.9 million and 10.6 million respectively.[2] Accordingly, it is difficult to imagine that the area of state land could be much less, if at all, than that of private estates, and yet support this comparatively large number of serfs. It is true that some state serfs were in industrial enterprises and factories, but their number could not have been large enough to validate Lenin's assumptions.

The lord, usually an absentee owner, controlled whole villages, both land and people. He received dues from the inhabitants, either in the form of services on his own domain, or in money, or both. Though these dues were fixed by custom, the lord had the power to vary them according to his wishes. The village community had some internal autonomy, especially regarding the use of land, which was periodically redistributed among the families according to the labor force available, to maintain equality and to cope with the changes in the size and composition of the peasant family. The system of redistribution varied according to regions and fertility of the soil, both in timing and in size of allotment.[3] The peasants were free to grow what they wanted and to pursue the methods they thought best. As long as they paid the dues, they were left in peace unless dues were paid in service, in which case the lord interfered according to the needs of his domain. If the peasants were unable to meet their obligations, or when better earning opportunities prevailed outside the village, the lord did not hesitate to send them to work and remit their earnings to the village to meet their obligations. Or the lord might himself establish a factory and employ his serfs in it on similar terms as on the land, since they were his property. In fact, he considered the serfs, rather than the land, to be his main capital.[4]

Though the lord originally derived his rights over the land as compensation for services rendered to the state, he retained his privileges long after he was freed of his obligations to the state, in 1762. In practice, his power over the land and the serf was absolute. He could sell either or both, together or separately, although there was no auction market for serfs as in slavery. He could "liberate" the serf by relieving him of his obligation to work on the land, which meant depriving him of his only source of income. The serf could not leave the estate without permission of his master, nor transfer his rights to others except by inheritance and through the village commune to which he belonged.[5]

In his domain the lord had juridical powers and could hold court and inflict punishment, except in cases of crime where the power of jurisdiction was vested in a public court. He could subject his peasants to physical punishment or exile by enlisting them for military services away from home and family for years — a punishment the peasant dreaded.[6] It is true that the law prohibited cruelty on the part of the lord, but the law was hardly ever invoked; on the contrary, the peasant was forbidden to complain against his master. In return, the lord was obligated to provide his peasants with food and seeds in time of famine. Otherwise, "he ruled a little monarchy within the great one, and the central government utilized him as its viceroy, or (in the phrase of the Emperor Paul) its 'gratuitous chief-of-police.' "[7]

Finally, the conditions of the peasant were bad because of extreme poverty. About 40 million serfs lived on approximately 135 million desiatines of allotment land. Yet they had to surrender part of the product to the lord. In contrast, a minority of nobles owned privately about 80 million desiatines in addition to their share in the product from allotment land.[8]

This is a brief summary of the relations between the peasants and private landlords. The same, only in a milder form, applies to the serfs on state domain. State serfs paid dues in money form at a lower rate than those paid to private landlords. These dues were assessed in proportion to income so as to take into consideration work done in state factories or in crafts. Finally, the state serfs were less closely supervised and therefore enjoyed more freedom than private serfs.[9]

BACKGROUND: CLASS DIFFERENTIATION

Social differentiation within classes was as significant as between classes and was closely related to economic status of the individual. The economic power of the landlords was quite unequally distributed. Among the private family-owners in 1877–1878 about half owned less than 10 desiatines each; 16,000 families owned more than 1,000 desiatines each, and of these 924 families owned more than 10,000 desiatines each, totaling about 65 million desiatines.[10] The power of these owners varied according to their wealth and the quality of their land. Those who owned smaller amounts of land were new bourgeoisie coming into title, since capital had started to play a role in land ownership.

The peasants also were differentiated according to wealth and size and quality of landholding. Some were freeholders and aspired to more wealth and higher income. Others could rent land and thus increase their economic resources, while thousands had to find outside work to supplement their income. Even among the serfs there was differentiation, and burdens were not of equal weight. This inequality reflected on the relations among the peasants, and the richer oppressed the poorer even "worse than the landlords." [11]

In the last few decades before Emancipation great changes were taking place. Economic development in Russia and abroad and the growth of towns and urban areas had caused a sort of transition from a barter to a money economy. Concurrently, there was increasing pressure on the landlords to acquire more income, especially in money form, to enjoy new products appearing on the market. One way of raising money was to borrow on the security of their lands and serfs. It is estimated that on the eve of Emancipation they had mortgaged about two-thirds of the serfs to state institutions for an amount totaling about 400 million rubles, besides what they had borrowed from private sources.[12] Or they pressured the peasants for higher and prompter payment of dues. Some landlords took up cultivation and sometimes enlarged their holdings at the expense of the peasant.[13] But the landlord was unable to save himself; a decline in the price of grain attributed to surplus production, lack of transportation to carry the grain to the market, and insufficiency of storage facilities aggravated his dilemma.[14]

The condition of the peasant was not any more pleasant. The economic forces that had burdened the landlord did not spare him; he sold his product at low prices in order to pay his lord in money form; he lost some of the allotment land when the landlord took up cultivation and yet he had to feed a larger number of people since the population was increasing.[15] His only hope, unless great changes took place, was supplementary employment elsewhere.

In the face of this tension the lord was willing to commute the services of his peasants into money payments, and the peasant was willing to have them commuted and free himself of subjugation to the lord. Therefore, commutation was underway even before Emancipation.[16] Nevertheless, at the time of Emancipation more than two-thirds of the private serfs still paid rent in kind in forty-one *guberniias* (provinces). However, money rent predominated in the guberniias from Moscow northward.[17]

A more important result of this crisis was the growing peasant disobedience, refusal to pay dues, and even violent uprisings. (Table 6 shows the growing insubordination.)

The peasants wanted freedom and the land they cultivated. In their craving for reform they were aided by several factors. The uneconomical character of serfdom and its obstructive influence on development were

72

strong arguments for change. Another was the weakness of the Russian society which became apparent in the Crimean War. Finally, there was the personality of Tsar Alexander II, without whom, some suggest, Emancipation would not have been possible.[18] The Tsar and even some members of the nobility were aware of the crisis and were willing to emancipate the peasants as a liberal gesture or to overcome the uneconomical influence of serfdom.[19] Or it might have been in appreciation of the Tsar's realism when he said that "it is better to abolish serfdom from above than to await the day when it will begin to abolish itself from below."[20] Undoubtedly interest in political stability was a major reason why Emancipation was accepted by many of the nobility. Even Rostovtzev, the right-hand man of the Tsar in the struggle for reform, though "well disposed towards drastic improvement of the conditions of the peasants, he was, nevertheless, concerned chiefly with the maintenance of order and with the security of the Government."[21]

TABLE 6

INSTANCES OF INSUBORDINATION ON THE
PRIVATE ESTATES *

Period	Total number	Average per year
1826–1829	88	22
1830–1834	60	12
1835–1839	78	16
1840–1844	138	28
1845–1849	207	41
1850–1854	141	28
1855–1861	474	68
Total	1,186	34

* Robinson, *op. cit.*, p. 49.

But this was not the general attitude of the nobility; indeed, reaction and hesitation were more common. The Tsar himself, at the same time that he expressed his apprehensions in 1856, made it clear that he did not "at the present intend to abolish serfdom." In fact, the reactionary attitude of the government was formalized in the Code of 1857 which

declared that the proprietor might lay upon his serf every kind of labor, and demand of him any sort of payment in goods and in money, with only these two restrictions of importance: that the serf should not be required to work for his master on Sunday, or on certain holidays, or for more than three days per week, and that he should not be ruined by the master's exactions.[22]

The interest in tenure change and improvement of peasant conditions was not a new phenomenon. As early as 1803 a law was passed allowing the landlord to free the serfs by villages or by families, on conditions mutually agreed upon, with the stipulation that the peasant be given land upon emancipation. Another law was passed in 1842 which

73

empowered the pomestchiki (landlords) to conclude agreements with their peasants under which the former retained the ownership of the land while the latter received an allotment for their own use under certain stipulated obligations. Under this law the bonded serf could become an "obligated peasant" whose forced labour on the pomestchik's land was thereby transformed into an agrarian obligation representing an indemnification to the pomestchik for the "peasant's" use of his land.[23]

The effects were negligible, and in retrospect it appears that the reaction of the late 1850's represented the necessary climax of the crisis. It heralded the end of one era and the beginning of another, the era of Emancipation.

THE REFORM PROCESS

There is no need to relate here the story of how abolition of serfdom was brought to consummation in the Emancipation Act.[24] On January 14, 1861, the Emancipation Act was passed by the Main Committee and, after passing the Council of State, was signed by the Tsar on the 19th, but was to take effect two years later. The relevant contents of this eagerly awaited Act may be summarized as follows:

1. "Serfdom is abolished forever."

2. Emancipated serfs shall be given the land they have been cultivating: this includes the homestead and the field land.

3. Only the house and surrounding garden or plot of land will become hereditary property of the individual peasant. The field land will be hereditary property of the village as a whole and will be subject to repartition as seen fit by the village assembly.

4. All rights to the land and claims for dues from the peasant to the landlord shall be transferred to the community or abolished by redemption as compensation of the lord for his losses.

The law also provided detailed rules concerning implementation of the law, recommending flexibility according to regions, to status of the peasant, and to the wishes of the parties concerned whenever agreement was possible.

Although the Act abolished serfdom, the serf had to pay ransom to the lord to be relieved of rendering the services.[25] Formally the government forbade any discussion of ransoming the person of the serf, but in practice ransoms were collected indirectly by manipulating the value of the land, as suggested by the inverse relationship between the size of allotment to be redeemed and the value put on it. For example, a higher value was put on a given acreage in "some of the clay-soiled central-industrial guberniias, than in the rich black-soil guberniias farther south . . . not because the land was here more valuable (actually it was less so), but because the person of the peasant had here a greater value, by reason of the greater development of side-earnings in the household crafts and in wage work in the towns." [26]

74

One may get an idea of the value put on the person of the serf from the arrangement with regard to the "beggarly allotments" or "poverty lots" as Dobb calls them. According to the Act, the landlord might free the peasant without redemption by appropriating three-quarters of the allotment land, leaving him with one quarter.[27] It is reasonable to assume that if the peasant were to redeem only his one quarter of the land, it would be sufficient to give up his right of usufruct to an equal amount of land or the equivalent of working-time which he previously rendered in services. Why, then, did he give up his rights of usufruct to an additional half of the total allotment land if not for his person? In other words, it seems that the peasant redeemed one quarter of his allotment land by surrendering an equivalent amount to the landlord, and redeemed his person by giving up his rights to the rest. Thus he became free, but with rights of ownership to only one quarter of the holdings he worked originally.[28]

Emancipation of the serf became final only upon completion of redemption payment, and until then he remained in "temporary obligation" to pay redemption instalment in kind if requested by his former lord. However, temporary obligation was abolished in 1881.[29]

There were other ways in which implementation of the Act was biased against the peasants. Formally the peasants were entitled to all their land, homes, and the surrounding lots,[30] but in application this was not so. The law provided only for a minimum and a maximum limit to the size of the allotment land to be redeemed, leaving the final decision for agreement between the parties. If no agreement was possible, the landlord made the decision, except in the case of forced redemption, a practice permissible until 1870. But the lord would seldom enforce redemption unless he found it to his advantage. However, since the peasants were opposed to the lord's power over them and were anxious to be rid of it, they usually sought redemption, thus giving the lord the right to determine the size of their allotment. The lord used that right against the peasant in at least two ways. First, he reduced the area of redeemable land and seized the rest as his own private property. Secondly, he cut off from the peasants resources essential for their life, such as forests for fuel or timber and "such essential elements of village economy as water resources and meadow land."[31] Consequently, the emancipated peasant had to render services to secure access to the pastures.[32]

The process of redemption was facilitated by the government. Upon agreement to redeem, the lord received 80 or 75 per cent of the total value, according to whether he surrendered his rights to all or a part of the allotment land. He received interest-bearing government bonds, which the peasant repaid with an additional 6 per cent interest over a period of forty-nine years. The redemption payments were determined by mutual agreement or, in case of disagreement, by settlement under governmental supervision, with little regard to the rental value of the land.

Therefore, the charges were frequently prohibitive and, as a result, 6 per cent of the peasants preferred to receive "beggarly allotments" rather than pay the redemption charges.[33]

The above discussion applies only to serfs on private estates. The state and imperial serfs who had been paying money rent[34] were emancipated later by separate laws. In 1863 a special statute gave imperial serfs the maximum amount of land fixed by law as allotment with redemption payments starting two years later for forty-nine years. Actually, they fared better than the private serfs in terms of the size of allotment and of the redemption payments, which were based on the rental value of the land.[35]

The state serfs were emancipated by a statute in 1866 which gave them in perpetuity all the land they had occupied, except the forests, against money rent. The rent was based on the total peasant income, from whatever source it was derived, not on the value of the allotment. In 1886 the status of the former state serfs was changed and the money rent replaced by a somewhat larger redemption payment spread over a period of forty-nine years. But as far as village organization was concerned, the same rules applied to private, state, and imperial serfs: they all held the land in communal tenure, subject to periodic repartition. The state serfs were not entitled, however, to the same rights of separation from the commune as the private serfs, but were subject to indefinite local restrictions.[36]

Another law was passed in 1869 dealing with the Cossacks. It gave them about two-thirds of their land, the rest to be put at the disposal of the army. They were to hold the land in common subject to repartition, but instead of redemption, they were required to serve for twenty years in the army, active or reserve, and provide their own horses and arms.

Finally, the serfs in the mines and factories, and those in household service were made free, but in contrast to the others, the former group received very small allotments while the household serfs received no land at all. They became proletarians dependent on wage work in agriculture and industry.[37]

EFFECTS AND EVALUATION

This was the "Great Reform" for which the Tsar struggled for years, and which the peasantry awaited eagerly. Even the nobility who opposed emancipation had hopes that it would circumvent future troubles with the peasantry. How successful was this reform and what were its economic and sociopolitical effects?

1. *Effects on Land Tenure.* The tenure status of the different groups remained unaltered during the rest of the nineteenth century, except in the case of hereditary communes in which redemption payment was completed,[38] or when the landlords sold their property. The collective owners were not, as individuals or in groups, full owners yet and the individual peasant was no more an owner or freeholder then he was before. He was restricted in his rights of disposal and freedom to leave the commune.[39]

Furthermore, the peasants were left with less land than they had before. The individual allotments became smaller and the total amount of allotment land was reduced. The loss varied from one province to another, ranging from zero to 45 per cent, according to the fertility of the soil, the value put on the person of the serf, and on the power of the landlord vis-à-vis the communes. Only in exceptional cases was there a gain. The results are shown in table 7.

TABLE 7

AVERAGE SIZE OF ALLOTMENT LAND BEFORE
AND AFTER EMANCIPATION *
(In desiatines per person)

	Black soil			Non-Black soil	
Province	Pre-Reform allotment	Post-Reform allotment	Province	Pre-Reform allotment	Post-Reform allotment
Kursk	2.3	2.2	Yaroslavl	5.2	3.8
Oryol	2.6	2.6	Kostroma	6.8	4.9
Ryazan	2.6	2.3	Vladimir	3.1	3.9
Tula	2.6	2.8	Moscow	2.6	2.9
Tambov	3.1	2.4	Kaluga	2.5	3.8
Voronezh	2.6	2.7	Petersburg	3.3	4.8
Penza	2.8	2.2	Novgorod	2.7	5.7
Kharkov	2.5	2.6	Smolensk	3.6	4.8
Yekaterinoslav	2.8	2.0			
Kiev	6.6	2.1			
Podol	5.5	2.2			
Saratov	3.8	2.4			
Simbirsk	2.9	2.4			
Kazan	3.0	2.3			
Vyatka	3.2	3.0			
Perm	5.5	4.0			

* P. I. Lyashchenko, *History of the National Economy of Russia to the 1917 Revolution*, tr. by L. M. Herman (New York: Macmillan, 1949), pp. 382–283.

Comparing the pre-reform and post-reform area cultivated by the peasants in 36 provinces, Lyaschenko finds that pre-reform peasant landholdings in 15 non-black soil provinces amounted to 14,550,000 desiatines; the reform reduced them by 9.9 per cent, or by 1,437,000 desiatines. Those in 21 black-soil provinces were reduced from 14,619,000 desiatines by 3,825,000 desiatines or by 26.2 per cent. The total loss amounted to 18.1 per cent,[40] although its impact was more significant because of its differential effects on individual peasants. Some peasants became freeholders of their house and garden lot, but had no claim on allotment land; others accepted beggarly lots amounting to only 25 per cent of what they had before. Still others lost everything for having been in household service or almost everything for having been assigned to mines and factories. A few lost nothing or even gained. Finally, the imperial state peasants kept all the land they had before. Thus, one result of the Emancipation was to increase differentiation among the peasants — between those who received allotment land and those who did not, and between those who were private serfs and the imperial and state serfs — and also among private serfs who continued to belong to repartitional communes, and between members in different communes and provinces.

2. *Effects on Social Classes.* Obviously, the loss to the peasant was a gain to the landlord and a new source of inequality between the two groups. Inequality was aggravated by the redemption-valuation system. The overvalued redemption payments sometimes exceeded the peasant's total income from the land. Overvaluation ranged between 25 and 33 per cent of the land value at market prices, as shown in table 8. Diminution of the peasant landholding and overvaluation put the peasant in a peculiar economic and social position. Investigating these conditions in 1877, Professor Yanson found that the "total of peasant payments exceeded the return from their lands." [41] Even the Procurator of the Harkov Appeal Court, though questioning the accuracy of Yanson's findings, did not deny that the peasants in some provinces were unable to meet their living needs and pay taxes and redemption out of income from the land. [42]

TABLE 8

COMPARISON OF REDEMPTION PAYMENTS WITH
VALUE AT MARKET PRICES OF LAND *
(In rubles)

Guberniias	Value at market prices, 1863–1872	Original redemption loans of government to landlords (to be recovered from peasants)	Excess (+) or shortage (−) of redemption loans as compared with market value of land
Non-black soil	179,900,000	342,000,000	+162,100,000
Black-soil	283,900,000	341,500,000	+57,600,000
Nine western	184,000,000	183,100,000	−900,000

* Robinson, *op. cit.*, p. 88.

The peasants' inability to meet their obligations resulted in accumulation of arrears in redemption payments, the nonagricultural sources of revenue notwithstanding. At the end of the period 1871–1875, arrears of payments to the state were 22 per cent of the average annual assessment for that period, and they rose to 27 per cent in 1880. The government acknowledged the problem and in 1881, 1884, and 1896 tried to alleviate it by reducing the debt, deferring payment, or even canceling it altogether. [43]

The peasant was hurt in another way. Prior to emancipation, he used his time fully on his allotment land and on the lord's domain, or he sometimes found outside employment. After emancipation, since he no longer worked for the lord and did not have enough land to occupy his time, he became more underemployed than before. Unless he had means to buy land, he had to rent it from the lord or work for wages. In other words, the Emancipation created holdings so small that it necessarily made the holder a tenant and a potential proletarian.

The nobility, as a class, did not fare better. The Emancipation might have postponed their troubles, but it did not solve them. The nobility were not equipped to defray the rising living expenses or to invest in business and commercial agricultural production. A large part of the redemption money was absorbed in payment of debts which they had incurred. To make matters worse, the redemption bonds gradually depreciated owing to inflation; by 1880 they had lost about 23 per cent of the bond value.[44] Since the landlord lost his previous source of permanent income, in the form of land and the person of the serf, he had to find new sources. Some landlords took up cultivation, using redemption payments to develop agriculture. Others leased the land to peasants for rent in money or kind. Some went as far as reviving the old institution of leasing land against service on their own estates.[45]

But the most significant source of income for distressed landlords was land sale. Throughout the rest of the century the land of the gentry was declining, as table 9 shows. In an attempt to save the nobility, the Government established the Nobles' Land Bank in 1885. The Bank extended large loans to the nobles, "with combined interest-and-amortization pay-

TABLE 9

LAND OWNED BY GENTRY IN FORTY-FIVE
PROVINCES OF EUROPEAN RUSSIA,
1861–1906 *
(In thousands of desiatines)

Year	Total	Per cent (of whole land area)
1862	87,088	100
1867	83,900	96
1872	80,641	93
1877	76,959	88
1882	71,231	82
1887	66,829	77
1892	62,922	71
1897	58,440	67
1902	53,137	61
1903	52,438	60
1904	51,813	59
1905	51,248	59
1906	49,906	57

* Litoshenko, *op. cit.*, p. 191.

ments always lower than those charged upon the loans made to the peasantry by the official Peasants' Land Bank." [46] Nevertheless, between 1862 and 1906, the nobility sold about 37 million desiatines or about 43 per cent of their landed property. An indirect effect of this sale was further class differentiation, since, while some of the nobility were selling land, others were buying, especially in the first thirty years after Emancipation, as shown in table 10.

TABLE 10

LAND BOUGHT AND SOLD IN RUSSIA BY
ECONOMIC GROUPS, 1863–1906 *

(As percentages of total land areas changing hands per year)

Years	Gentry		Merchants		Peasants		Corporations		Other Classes	
	Bought	Sold	Bought	Sold	Bought	Sold	Bought	Sold	Bought	Sold
1863–1872	51.6	80.4	22.6	4.3	12.7	4.6	4.1	3.2	9.0	8.5
1872–1882	42.9	71.4	24.2	9.5	17.7	7.1	4.8	4.3	10.4	7.7
1883–1892	34.6	65.2	20.8	12.7	29.2	10.2	4.6	2.3	10.8	9.6
1893–1897	33.2	60.9	18.2	14.7	27.0	11.2	8.8	2.5	12.8	10.7
1898–1902	27.0	54.2	17.8	13.9	36.7	13.3	6.4	6.6	12.1	11.0
1903	25.0	47.0	14.8	16.8	41.4	17.4	7.4	7.0	11.4	11.8
1904	28.3	54.4	12.8	14.9	42.4	17.8	3.9	4.5	12.6	8.4
1905	25.7	50.7	13.2	15.7	36.7	17.4	11.5	5.2	12.9	11.0
1906	15.8	61.9	7.5	16.3	33.0	11.7	37.0	1.0	6.7	8.2

* Litoshenko, *op. cit.*, p. 199.

If the gentry lost almost half of its landholdings in less than fifty years, who were the buyers of land? One group was the rising bourgeoisie, others were members of the nobility and the peasantry. The merchants and the Peasants' Bank were substantial buyers until 1906. However, the merchants did not buy to hold, but as middlemen and speculators. Between the years 1863 and 1906, the merchants bought 24,268,500 desiatines and sold 13,130,000 desiatines, the amount sold being 54.1 per cent of that bought, thus retaining only 46 per cent of the land that came into their hands.[47]

With the help of the Peasants' Bank the peasants were gradually becoming important elements in the land market. Between 1863 and 1906 they bought 30,223,800 desiatines, but they sold 11,481,700 desiatines or 37.9 per cent of what they had bought, probably because the small peasants could not hold their own or because of capitalistic elements among the peasantry.[48] A summary of all buying and selling of land for the same period is reproduced in table 10.

One significant effect of the land transaction was the concentration of new holdings, as in England and Prussia. As Lenin put it, the tenure changes and capitalistic development of agriculture after 1861 followed the Prussian rather than the American type. It did not break up and destroy the owners' *latifundia* and replace it by a free capitalistic peasant economy, but, as in Prussia, the "landowners' feudal economy [which] is slowly transformed into the bourgeois *Junker* variety of farming, condemned the peasantry to decades of agonizing expropriation and indebtedness, while a small minority of *grossbauers* [wealthy peasants] make their appearance." [49] Rich peasants were emerging, the landlord class survived, but the peasantry remained distressed and dependent.[50]

Some light may be shed on this problem by looking at the size distribution of private estates. In 1877–1878, 481,358 families owned 92 million desiatines; half these families owned less than 10 desiatines each, while 16,000 families owned more than 1,000 desiatines each, with a total of 65 million desiatines; of these, 924 families owned more than 10,000 desiatines each.[51]

Since a commune is a legal person, one might regard it as a single large owner. However, this would be incompatible with the fact that differentiation was developing among commune members and causing class conflict between the rich and the poor peasants. In a detailed analysis of the *Zemstvo Statistics*, covering European Russia, Lenin shows that differentiation was occurring inside as well as outside the commune. From this survey of "The Disintegration of the Peasantry" Lenin concludes that

the system of social-economic relations existing among the peasantry (agricultural and village-community) shows us that all those contradictions are present which are inherent in every commodity economy and every order of capitalism: competition, the struggle for economic independence, the snatching up of land (purchasable and rentable), the concentration of production in the hands of a minority, the forcing of the majority into the ranks of the proletariat, their exploitation by a minority through the medium of merchant capital and hiring of farmworkers. There is not a single economic phenomenon among the peasantry that does not bear this contradictory form, one specifically peculiar to the capitalist system, i.e., that does not express a struggle and antagonism of interests, that does not express advantage for some and disadvantage for others. It is the case with the renting of land, the purchase of land, and with "industries" in their diametrically opposite types; it is also the case with the technical progress of farming.[52]

3. *Effects on Production and Productivity.* There is no indication that Emancipation improved methods of cultivation or productivity. On the contrary, improvement "was rendered almost impossible because the method of possession and cultivation of the land remained as it had been under the *regime* of serfdom: the community system known as the 'mir.' . . . A class of small individual peasant proprietors had not been created." [53] Emancipation did not increase investment in agriculture either. Little of the redemption payments found its way back to agriculture; the peasants did not have the knowledge or the capital to invest; and the

merchants were largely speculators, little interested in farming. Yet, it is estimated, without explanation, that grain yield per acre sown in European Russia rose from 29 *puds* per desiatine in 1861–1870 to 39 puds in 1891–1900[54] (1 pud = [or pood] 16.38 kilograms).

Lenin suggests that productivity increased throughout the period 1864 to 1905 except in 1885–1894, when productivity declined owing to the crisis of 1891–1892 "which tremendously intensified the expropriation of the peasantry." [55] Foreign trade also increased and grain export was eight times more in 1901 than it was in 1861.

The rise in grain export may have been due to better transportation and railroad building or the development of a money economy and the commercial spirit.[56] But there seems to be no direct connection between Emancipation and the rise in production or growth of the commercial spirit. Emancipation may have contributed indirectly by transferring land into the hands of the more efficient farmers, or by encouraging money circulation and increasing demand for money income to pay redemption.[57]

4. *Effects on Political Stability.* Owing to the ignorance or hopeful expectation of the restive groups, the Emancipation had immediate but temporary effects on political stability. However, it did not prevent a *jacquerie* or a "1789" as the Tsar had hoped. Both were repeated in Russian form in 1905 and 1917 respectively. The 1905 revolution climaxed a wave of peasant dissatisfaction extending over the previous two decades. Rising tension and class conflict, growth of revolutionary elements, peasant violence and destruction of property, and the reactionary behavior of the government in the 'eighties and 'nineties of the nineteenth century suggest failure of the reform to create political stability.

In fact, there were new sources of tension and instability. Some peasants were becoming rich and rural bourgeoisie, while others suffered "depeasantizing," as Lenin put it, and became partly or wholly dependent on others for work. A class of capitalists also was evolving but, as in the French society before 1789, it had no institutionalized place in the system. It had to carve such a place at the expense of the old nobility. Finally, the influence of capital tended to split up both the peasantry and the gentry.[58] However, class conflict was a result not merely of economic differentiation but of group awareness and the conflict of interest — a conflict whose fire was fanned by revolutionary elements and the closer contact with Western societies. Revolutionary elements recruited from universities and professional institutions and colleges penetrated the rural areas and aroused peasant discontent regarding results of the Emancipation.[59] Revolutionary and terrorist actions were widespread in the 'seventies and up to 1881, the end of the Reformer Emperor's rule, despite government repression. The final blow in the lifetime of Alexander II was his own death by explosives at the hands of terrorists, while the attitude of the people was one "of indifference and curiosity." [60]

Alexander III did not bring any more stability into the country. His early years as Tsar were characterized by a period of reaction and instability. In the 'eighties,

Disorders in the villages were frequent, and in the towns riots occurred through conflicts of people of different races. There were outbreaks of brigandage in the Caucasus, and pillage was committed in many places. Murders became more numerous. Industrial strikes in factories produced many disturbances and much loss of life. In the industrial cities of Poland there was much unemployment and much unrest. In Russia proper there were strikes of weavers at Ivanovo-Voznesensk, of railwaymen at Sevastopol, and of dock labourers at Fibinsk. Jewish pogroms occurred in Rovno. . . . Property was damaged everywhere. In 1885, 192,000 complaints were made of damage to forests, a number about a fourth more than that of the previous year.[61]

Though the government made some compromises regarding redemption payment, the policy was generally one of reaction and oppression. Besides the suppression and restriction of freedom inflicted on revolutionaries and academic institutions, tenure changes were made reversing some provisions of the Emancipation Act. Under the influence of the old nobility, a law was passed in 1889 providing for the appointment of *zemskii* chiefs, chosen as a rule from the local nobility, to "exercise a general guardianship over the economic and moral condition of the peasantry, to review the acts of the peasant assemblies, and to recommend the repeal by higher authority of any of these acts." They were also given limited juridical powers to levy fines and inflict punishment on individual peasants and to discipline their officials. In 1893 their power extended to redistribution of communal land, "and in fact their powers showed more than a little resemblance to those of the serf-owners of other days." [62]

Three years earlier, in 1890, peasant representation in the *zemstvo* assemblies was reduced in number and that of the nobility increased. The peasants were stopped from electing their own representatives. They could only nominate candidates from among whom the governor appointed the representatives. The purpose was to maintain the influence of the nobility and leave them in complete control.[63] This policy was not an isolated act of bureaucracy; behind it was a reversal of attitude toward the individual peasant and his rights of tenure. A law of December 27, 1893, restricted the right of the individual to hereditary tenure upon completing redemption payments so as to perpetuate the commune.[64]

The government went further in its reactionary policies against the peasant. It placated the nobility by vacating many official positions of their common occupiers to fill them with nobility. It tried to win the bourgeoisie by subsidizing industry and by protective tariffs.[65]

All these developments lead to one conclusion: the political order was not stabilized and the reform failed in its objective, as suggested by the violent upsurge in 1905, the herald of the second stage of tenure reform.

B. THE STOLYPIN REFORMS: 1906–1911

This era of reform is significant for several reasons. First, it reflects the consequences of Emancipation and, as such, it serves as an indicator of its success or failure. Second, it signifies the socioeconomic struggle between the old forces and the new. The role played by the former nobility in these reforms represents the desperate efforts they undertook to safeguard their wealth and privileges. Third, the reform decrees represent the gentry's compromise with the emerging forces of capitalism. The attempt to create simultaneously a class of individual well-to-do peasant-owners and a class of proletarians is a concession to capitalistic forces. Not that it could be avoided, but it is significant that the old nobility should use the emerging bourgeoisie for its own purposes. Finally, it is significant because it shows that by sponsoring this alliance and disregarding peasant interests the reforms fell short of achieving their objectives.

BACKGROUND: LAND TENURE AND CLASS DIFFERENTIATION

After the Emancipation two tenure types emerged besides individual ownership: the repartitional and the hereditary communes. All attempts to convert repartitional into hereditary tenure were precluded by the amendment of 1881. On the eve of the Stolypin reforms village land was divided into 124.9 million desiatines of allotment land and 24.6 million desiatines of nonallotment land, of which 11.4 millions were held by peasant collectives not subject to repartition.[66] Allotment land was unequally distributed among members of the commune with an apparent rise of differentiation as shown in table 11 and the following data. In 1905 about 23.8 per cent of all communal households belonged to communes in which the average allotment was 5 desiatines or less, with a total of nine million desiatines, while 0.02 per cent of the households had a total of 3.6 million desiatines, averaging more than 100 desiatines per household.[67]

While the large farmers were gaining as landowners or independent farmers, the small peasant lived on part-time farming and outside work as a supplement; or he gave up his allotment land in informal sale or in lease to free himself of the farm and become a proletarian. Yet by law the peasant had to maintain his ties with the village because of his redemption obligations. Therefore, any solution of his problem or settlement outside the village was only temporary and incomplete.[68]

The lot of the peasants and landless workers was worsened by the general economic conditions in the country; either prices of grain were low and they were unemployed, or the prices were high and they suffered as

84

buyers of food. Thus, the economic improvements resulted in higher exports and profits favorable to the seller or exporter and businessman, but were adverse to the local consumer. To make matters worse, production of food on allotment land in all fifty provinces of European Russia was about 11.5 per cent short of the food and seed needs of the peasants.[69]

The level of wages was also unsatisfactory; it was not only low but was further depressed by the system of advance payment in anticipation of the crop season. Advance wages were fixed at a much lower level than they would otherwise have been.[70] This is what Lenin called semibondage.[71]

TABLE 11

LAND DISTRIBUTION IN RUSSIA IN 1905 *
(In millions of desiatines)

State land	137.4
Communal "mir" land	136.3
Land of nobility	49.8
Merchants, bourgeoisie, and associations	22.7
Private property of peasants	13.2
Holdings of Imperial family	7.8
Cossack land	3.5
Towns and corporations	3.5
Churches and monasteries	2.5

* Kokovtzoff, op. cit., p. 365.

The farmer who rented land was equally dissatisfied because of the high rent he had to pay in view of the high demand for land and competition of the sharecroppers. In the 1880's more than one-third of the peasants rented land amounting to about 19.5 million desiatines.[72]

The peasantry were also socially and politically depressed. The period of reaction, initiated in the 1880's, had not subsided and the peasant was under the yoke of a revived nobility. He was tied to the commune and the land, and had lost some of his former rights in local administration and management of the commune and the district. He was obligated to pay redemption for land that, so he felt, belonged to him in the first place. Deferment of payment or even partial cancellation by the government was ineffective; his debts were accumulating and he saw no way out. On the other hand, there were active forces in the environment which made him impatient and unwilling to submit to these circumstances. On one side were the revolutionary parties which were penetrating the countryside; on the other, the nobility continued its oppressive action, aided by the government which they controlled.

In contrast, the nobility received aid from the Nobles' Land Bank to maintain their estates. Their privileges in the countryside were rehabilitated and even augmented by the legislation of the 1880's and 1890's.

85

Yet their condition was deteriorating, their debts were rising, and by 1904 they had mortgaged about a third of their land to the Bank alone against loans amounting to 707 million rubles.[73] The nobles suffered mainly from two weaknesses: the decline of their power through loss of land, and the rift in their lines due to economic differentiation and/or growth of liberalism. There were among them those who served in the central government and those who were associated with provincial affairs. Among the latter group there was a strong tendency toward liberal solutions to the problems of the peasantry, including better standards of education and health. Both groups, however, agreed that the influence of the peasants in decision-making and voting should not be extended.[74]

The peasantry responded to this state of affairs in several ways. First, they openly refrained from paying redemption. The arrears had accumulated until by 1904 they reached 130 million rubles. Similarly, deficits were mounting in loan payments to the Peasants' Bank.[75] In many places they refused to pay taxes. They also entertained revolutionary ideas and in some instances openly participated in revolutionary activities despite or because of oppression.[76] They even attacked the estates of the nobility. Though disturbances prevailed throughout the latter part of the nineteenth century, the tide rose rapidly after 1902 until the explosion in 1905. The peasants proclaimed a general strike, attacked estates, and cut wood from forests that were forbidden to them. From October through December, 1905, disturbances spread over 47 provinces. More than a thousand manorial houses were ravaged and burned. With awareness and determination, their aim was to "drive out the squires and transfer the land to the people," while the "intellectuals wanted more political freedom for the people." [77]

The threat of the peasants and their attacks caused animated discussions among the nobility and stimulated some reorganization. First, they questioned the usefulness of communal tenure and the "*mir*" as stabilizing elements in society. As early as 1898, Witte expressed his apprehensions concerning the *mir* in these words:

Woe to the country that has not nurtured in its population a sense of law and of property, but on the contrary has established different forms of collective possession which have not been precisely defined in the law, but are regulated by uncertain custom or simply by individual judgment. In such a country, there may take place, sooner or later, such grievous events as have nowhere been known before.[78]

Witte's views of a solution were similar to those later contained in the Stolypin reforms.[79] Skepticism toward the *mir* was encouraged by the waning enthusiasm of the government after the commune proved ineffective in collecting taxes and redemption payments.

Another strand of thinking on these problems, which supplements the former, was to expropriate the landlords and distribute the land among the peasants. This idea was advocated by, among others, people such as M. Chuprov, Professor Magulin, and N. Kutler, and by the Cadet Party; also, it was the view of the First Duma.[80] This sort of thinking touched upon the essence of reform; namely, how to justify expropriating some private owners in order to augment the holdings of other private owners, and how to deal with efficiently run estates which were a great asset to the economy. The former argument points out the contradictions in the logic of a law that orders breaking estates for redistribution. As far as efficient estates were concerned, it was proposed that they be maintained in some way, as was to happen under the Soviets.[81] But there was no theoretical solution to the arguments against expropriation.

A third approach was the one applied by Stolypin, and the reforms bearing his name aimed at strengthening private property not by expropriating large private owners but by encouraging the dissolution of the commune and substituting private for communal tenure. Thus, the commune was the target of the Stolypin reforms and private ownership the objective.

THE REFORM PROCESS

The Stolypin reforms were embodied in three main laws, enacted between 1906 and 1911. They were preceded by concessions from the Tsar in the form of edicts: on November 3, 1905, all redemption payments were cancelled; on March 4, 1906, Land Organization Commissions were established; and on October 5, 1906, some restrictions on personal rights were abolished, among which were: (1) Joint responsibility of the commune for public obligations, which had been gradually declining since 1903. (2) Communal assemblies were deprived of authority to subject any member of the commune to forced labor or to control his passport. Thenceforward, the individual was free to choose his residence, give up his membership in the commune and acquire membership-at-large in the district of his choice, and that district was obligated to grant him membership.[82]

The reforms proper, however, remained for Peter Stolypin to introduce. He wanted to stabilize the political system by creating an independent middle-class peasantry without encroaching upon the rights of the nobility. The edict of November 9, 1906, was the first step. It provided that:

1. Every individual had the right to claim appropriation of his allotment land as private ownership with or without the consent of the commune.

2. If no land redistribution had taken place in the *mir* during the last twenty-four years, the land in the peasant's possession automatically became his hereditary property; otherwise, the peasant was entitled to any extra land that happened to be in his possession, at the original redemption rate.

3. If a peasant requested separation from the commune, he was entitled to receive his holding in one bloc, as far as that was possible.

4. "Individual peasant holdings . . . are the private property of heads of households, in whose possession they are," rather than property of the family as was previously the case.

The edict, however, retained the rule that required a two-thirds majority in a village community to effect separation and consolidation of holdings.[83]

Finally, the edict entitled the individual member of the commune to extract his share from common holdings such as meadows and pastures. Land Commissions were established all over the country to implement the edict.

The law of June 14, 1910, was a legislative confirmation of the 1906 edict, since the latter was inconsistent with the 1905 Constitutional reform embodied in the October Manifesto. The 1906 edict was passed as an order after the dissolution of the First Duma without legislative action on it. Now it was submitted to the Assembly for confirmation as a law. However, this law was more extensive than the previous measure. While it retained the spirit of the 1906 edict, it also

made distinction between village-communities which had redistributed their holdings since the original Emancipation Allotment and those which had not done so. Land communes whose land had been allocated before January 1, 1887, and which had never effected a general distribution since that date (i.e., for the last twenty-three years) were considered to have tacitly adopted a system of heritable tenure. Therefore all such villages became automatically in the eyes of the law identical with those under podvornee vladenie (hereditary tenure). To achieve the physical enclosure of their land, individual holders in such cases were relieved of the necessity of obtaining titles to their land.[84]

Finally, the Stolypin reforms were completed by the law of May 29, 1911, which seriously attempted to promote consolidation of holdings.

The Act of 1911 allowed compulsion upon one party in certain cases, where enclosure was impeded. By Clause 35, any number of individuals could require enclosure at a general redistribution if their application had preceded the decision of the assembly to redistribute holdings. Clause 36 provided that apart from general redistributions, enclosures could be enforced if the applicants amounted to at least one-fifth of the families in a commune (of which the total membership did not exceed 250) or to at least 50 (if the membership of the commune did not exceed that number). Where injury to the rest of the village was unlikely even a single member could ask for it. . . . Clause 37 allowed enclosure at the request of a simple majority of peasants of a communal village, where portions of arable land had been permanently appropriated. No agreement at all was needed under Clauses 23-7, with regard to parts of arable land which were appropriated as private property. Again, under Clause 37 no single peasant was allowed to prevent the technical perfection of a neighbor's farm by refusing to exchange strips to allow consolidation.[85]

I have presented some details of this law because of its uniqueness in taking into consideration the problems of efficiency and production. It is also significant that the Land Commissions were given the responsibility of implementing the law chiefly at public expense.[86]

EFFECTS AND EVALUATION

There is no doubt that the reforms succeeded in creating a class of rich peasants. But they failed to create stability, for good reasons. One such reason was the weakness of the agencies directly or indirectly responsible for implementing the law, such as the Land Banks and the Land Commissions. Their composition was biased in favor of the nobility and the bureaucracy. Not only were these committees under the influence of the nobility and the bureaucrats, but they were constantly manipulated by the ministerial authorities. Similar bias and distortion were demonstrated in the activities of the Land Banks, which overvalued the land designed for transfer to the peasants. As a result, the Peasant Banks sank huge funds which could not be realized because they were beyond the value of the land. Another result was that the price of land rose enormously, from 71 to 140 rubles per desiatine between 1895 and 1910. Consequently, the peasant felt cheated and was unable to take full advantage of the reforms. Even when the peasants could buy land, it was in localities where land was least needed. For example, in 18 provinces where peasants were most in need of land, the Bank had at its disposal 588,000 desiatines to be sold to 1,447,000 small holders. In contrast, in 18 provinces least in need of land, with a total of 145,000 small holders, the Bank had 1,987,000 desiatines available, or an average of 13.7 desiatines per household. This misallocation was further aggravated by the freedom bestowed upon the peasant to leave the commune, alienate his holdings, and change his residence. Thus, where additional land was not available, the peasant was inclined to sell his small lot and leave, and where land was available, he could not afford the prices and therefore was willing to sell and move on. Between 1908 and 1915, about 1.2 million peasant households sold about 3.9 million desiatines, usually because of economic pressure.[87]

Who were the purchasers of these and the Peasant Bank's lands? Between 1907 and 1916, 54.6 per cent of the land was bought by peasants separating from the communes; 23.4 per cent by small homesteaders; 17 per cent by rural societies, and 5 per cent by others. Altogether the merchants and bourgeois elements acquired about a fourth of all the land sold.[88]

Another weakness of the reform was its bureaucratic character and failure to consult commune members. One contemporary of the reform observed that the "agrarian reform meets a serious need of the rural population of Russia. But it has approached this object from a purely bureaucratic point of view, which is to be found in every police-ruled state such as Russia is even to the present time, in spite of the transition to constitutionalism proclaimed by the Manifesto of October 30, 1905." [89] Consequently, about 70.8 per cent of those requesting separation were able to acquire land and separate, but these constituted only 21.8 per cent of the householders on communal land. The area finally separated amounted to 13,382,927 desiatines, or 16.4 per cent of the total area of allotment land.[90]

Manuilov questions the soundness of the decision to substitute private for communal tenure on economic grounds and the wisdom of applying Arthur Young's theory to Russia. Does not the experience of England itself, asks Manuilov, necessitate modification of Young's dictum that "give a man a rock as his own property and he will turn it into a garden; give him a garden on a year's lease, and he will make it a wilderness"? Communal tenure has not hindered improvement in agriculture, and when communal villages lagged behind farms of other tenure, as on farms of Bohemian and German colonists in the same provinces, the differences were due mainly to "comparatively larger proportions of the holdings of the colonists, but chiefly to their possession of the necessary capital for rational farming, and to the higher level of culture among the colonists themselves." If communal tenure is defective, adds Manuilov, let it be changed by natural evolution, not by bureaucratic action.[91]

The reforms gave rise to a Kulak or rich peasant class, but side by side with this the class of proletarians continued to grow. The differentiation that had been in progress since the Emancipation now received a push because the Bank's policy favored individual over collective buyers, and the price level favored the richer peasants over the poorer. The gap between the haves and have-nots was widened rather than narrowed.[92] This, of course, was consistent with the goals of the Stolypin policy, even though maximum limits were put on the amount of land any one individual could buy in a single region.[93]

Many problems complicate evaluation of the success or failure of the Stolypin reforms; they include the limited available land, the conflict of interests of the different classes, the unwillingness of these classes to give up some of their advantages, the atmosphere within which these reforms were undertaken, and the fundamental interest of the reformers in stabilizing the political order and maintaining the status quo with respect to the landed nobility. The short life of the reform before the whole system broke down adds to the difficulties of an evaluation. In view of the reactionary, arbitrary, and bureaucratic character of the reforms, and of the economic forces facing the reformer-class, it should not be surprising that their measures failed in their main objectives. The failure is indicated by the limited number of separations from the commune, and by hostility to the land surveyors and executors of the reform. The peasants continued to encourage and participate in revolutionary activities. They never ceased to struggle until the explosive events led to the fall of tsardom, seizure of the land, and overthrowing of the nobility and its new allies, the capitalists.[94]

C. THE SOVIET REFORMS

INTRODUCTION

This reform period is unique in its features, and as it relates to our study. Its uniqueness derives primarily from its own characteristics. First, it includes reform policies that were conceived as part of a national program. Second, the series of reform measures undertaken during the Soviet period were progressively complementary to each other, in the sense that each measure was another step toward realizing the original plan. Third, the reforms were always undertaken with a view to the needs of other sectors of the economy, especially as means toward the fulfillment of political and economic aspirations of the party in power. In the latter sense the reforms were not unique, but the openness with which the policymakers declared their intentions was a new phenomenon. Finally, the plan on which the reform policy was based concerned itself with agricultural production and development of the economy as a whole rather than with formal tenure.

The Soviet agrarian policy may be studied in a long-term perspective, or with regard to the immediate goals. The immediate goals were invariably to strengthen the Soviet state by enhancing its economic and political foundations and to forestall any counterrevolution. The economic objective was higher and more strategic production; the political one was alliance with various classes and subclasses against the prevalent enemy of the Revolution, the remaining elements of the old regime. The long-term goals were based on socialist theories and Marxist views of economics and class relations. Land nationalization was designed to eliminate private ownership and to prevent any land transfer or accumulation. It was deemed necessary to eliminate private *holding* of the land and replace it with collective holding and operation. Large-scale coöperative operation was therefore the goal. Nationalization and equal distribution of the land were declared insufficient, since these would only create *petite bourgeois* farmers and would neither guarantee equality nor prevent differentiation.[95]

The Soviet agrarian policies must be viewed against the sociopolitical background directly preceding the Revolution, or during the period of the Provisional Government headed by Kerensky. This government probably had the opportunity to win the confidence of the peasantry and prevent a Soviet victory. But the hesitation with which it handled the agrarian question was well reflected in the proclamation of July 8, 1917:

In the immediate future the Government intends: — (1) to abandon completely the old land policy which ruined and demoralized the peasantry; (2) to secure complete freedom for the Constituent Assembly in the matter of the disposal of the nation's land; (3) to regulate agrarian relations in the interests of national defence and welfare by extending and strengthening the network of land committees; these will be endowed with carefully defined rights of dealing with the current problems of agrarian policy, but the fundamental question of ownership of land, which is to be settled by the Constituent Assembly, will not be prejudged. (4) By thus introducing order into agrarian relations, to obviate the serious danger to the country and to the future land-reform, arising from seizures of land and other arbitrary methods of dealing with the matter locally, in contravention of the principle that the future land-reform is to include the whole of Russia in its scope. Announcing its aims, the Provisional Government believes it has a right to reckon in its hard and responsible task upon the whole-hearted support of all the living forces of the country.[96]

The Provisional Government did not do what the French Assembly did in the first week of the French Revolution, but was content with issuing a proclamation and calling on all parties concerned to coöperate and observe order in the service of the country. The government acknowledged that the peasants had been ruined and yet promised them nothing concrete even though they had begun to seize the land and distribute it. Soldiers were deserting and returning to their villages to share in the booty. Law and order were being undermined while the government was helpless. The peasants had waited too long and would wait no more. The former ruling class was equally disappointed and felt that the Social Revolutionaries and their associates in the Provisional Government were "little better than Bolsheviks. . . . [while to the cantonal assemblies] they were compromisers with the old order."[97] This chaos was aggravated by the devastating effects of the war and the apparent weakness of the social structure. These problems were fertile soil for the revolutionary agitation of the Social Democrats and for Soviet rule. Thus came the October Revolution.

THE REFORM PROCESS

When the Soviets took over, the peasants had already started to seize the land, distribute it, and liquidate the class of landlords. The Bolsheviks therefore seized the opportunity to win the alliance of the peasantry and passed a land decree on November 8, 1917, partly to that effect. Some of the more relevant articles of the decree are the following:

1. The Landowners' right of property in land is herewith abolished without compensation.
2. The Landowners' estates as well as all the lands of the Imperial family,

of the monasteries and of the Church, with all their live and inanimate stocks, manor buildings and all appurtenances are placed in the charge of the cantonal Land Committees and District Soviets of Peasants' Delegates pending the decision of the Constituent Assembly on the land question.

. . . .

5. The lands of the rank-and-file peasants and rank-and-file Cossacks are not subject to confiscation.

In "The Land Instructions of the Peasants" section of the Decree, it is continued:

1. The right of private property in land is to be abolished for all time. The land shall not be bought, sold, leased or otherwise alienated.

. . . .

6. The right to use the land shall be given to all citizens, regardless of sex, of the Russian State, who desire to work it by their own hands, that is, by the labour of their respective families or on co-operative principles, for such periods only as they are able to do so. Hired labour is not permissible. . . .

7. The lands shall be distributed among those who use them on the principle of equalization, that is, on the basis, as determined by local conditions, of the normal units of labour or food. No restrictions shall be placed on the mode of land-tenure, the individual villages determining whether it should be by households, individuals, village communities, or co-operative organizations.[98]

Thus, in its first agrarian measure, the Soviet government did away with private ownership, forbade alienation of land, prohibited tenancy, and decreed equalization of holding — making tilling of the land the basis of both the right and size of holding. But nothing was said in this decree about production, nor was there any provision defining the rank-and-file category of landowners exempted from confiscation.

The decree was complete as far as landownership or tenure was concerned. Ownership was made public and land alienation prohibited. Emphasis or the focus of attention was transferred from the legal title to the right of holding and operating the land. Hence, the later reforms were concerned with the terms of holding the land and the pattern of its cultivation.

The Decree of February 19, 1918, confirmed the provisions of the earlier decrees and made some additions, among which was Article 4 of the General Principles, which decreed that the "right to use the land shall not be restricted either by sex, religion, race or nationality (including foreign)," thus declaring religion, race, and nationality as irrelevant to landholding. Other relevant provisions of the decree included:

Article 11. Over and above the equitable distribution of agricultural land among the labouring population and the most productive exploitation of natural riches, the land administration of the Land Departments of the local and cantonal Soviet authority aims at the following objects:

(a) To bring about such conditions as would favour the growth of the productive forces of the country, such as an increase in the fertility of the soil, the improvement of the technical methods of agriculture, and the increase of agricultural knowledge among the labouring masses of the agricultural population.

(b) To form a reserve stock of lands having agricultural value.

(c) To develop such kindred industries as horticulture, agriculture, vegetable gardening, cattle-breeding, dairy farming, etc.

(d) To accelerate the passage from inadequate to more productive systems of land-tillage in the different zones by an even distribution of working farmers.

(e) To foster collective farming as the more advantageous system in point of labour-saving and productivity, at the expense of individual farming, with a view to transition to Socialist agriculture.

. . . .

Article 18. The trade in agricultural machinery and seeds constitutes a monopoly of the Soviet authorities.

Article 19. Both external and internal corn trade shall be a monopoly of the State.[99]

Finally, in Part III of the Decree, "The Mode of Granting Land for Use," a note was included to emphasize that "in determining the mode and order of granting the use of lands, preference is to be given to working agricultural cooperatives as against individuals." [100]

As far as the policy and substance of the Soviet agrarian reform are concerned, the law is complete and clear. Whatever remained to be done must be interpreted as a means toward the fulfillment of that policy, and in that light it should be evaluated. Three points should be kept in sight: the intention to promote collectives, and the improvement of agricultural production, while safety of the state and stabilization of Soviet power continued to enjoy top priority. Finally, the decree of February 14, 1919, described individual farming as transitional, pending the establishment of collective farming.[101]

Legislation and decreeing is one thing, but application of the law is another, and conflict between the two is not uncommon. Such discrepancy was demonstrated during the first few months of Soviet rule. The peasantry, eager to get hold of the land and property of the landlords, did not wait for the Land Committees to manage confiscation and distribution. They felt free to seize land and property while the government "was . . . only a spectator." Consequently, acquisition and distribution were neither uniform nor equal. The stronger and richer were better rewarded because they had means to transport seized property.[102] The government, however, soon took over and formalized landholding.

The agrarian policy of the Soviets, after land nationalization and declaration of their intentions, may be studied as three main stages: War Communism, the New Economic Policy (NEP), and the Drive for Collectivization.

THE PERIOD OF WAR COMMUNISM

This period extended from 1918 to 1921 and witnessed the first rupture in the alliance between the peasantry and the new government, although only a part of the peasantry was involved. When land was confiscated in 1917, the peasantry remained differentiated; there were poor, middle, and rich peasants (kulaks). Until the October Revolution, the policy was to be: "Together with the whole peasantry, against the tsar and the landlords, with the bourgeoisie neutralized, for the victory of the bourgeois-democratic revolution."[103] This had been the slogan of the Communists in the first stage of the revolution, 1905–1917. However, pressure of the civil war, the need for farm products to feed the towns and industrial workers, and reluctance of the peasantry to sell their products to the government for inflated paper money set the stage for the second slogan: "Together with the poor peasantry, against the capitalist bourgeoisie in town and country, with the middle peasantry neutralized, for the power of the proletariat."[104] Interpreted into action, this slogan meant that the Soviet authorities, failing to obtain sufficient food from the countryside, would resort to a policy of splitting the peasantry and imposing their will on the richer peasants. Thus, when they could not get the farm product by purchase, they resorted to requisition of all surplus product and gave the responsibility to seize these surpluses to the poor peasants. In the later part of this period the Soviet policy changed from one of neutralizing the middle peasants to that of forming an alliance with them against the kulaks. To consolidate this alliance, the Committees of the Village Poor, delegated to requisition farm surplus, were dissolved. The army units who replaced them were instructed to pay special attention to the middle peasants.[105]

The policies of War Communism were an attempt to deal with the immediate problems, and an experiment to abolish the market and create conditions for the highest ideal of equality: from everyone according to his abilities, to each according to his needs.[106] The results of War Communism were economically disastrous. The peasants reduced production by restricting the sown area, and by destroying farm livestock and implements to avoid requisition. The effects of this policy are reflected in table 12.

Reduction of the livestock and area sown was only partly due to Soviet policy. It was a joint result of the World War, the decline in the number of large and efficient farms, and crop failures in 1920 and 1921. Nevertheless, the Soviets bore the consequences. To deal with food shortages, they inaugurated the NEP on December 1, 1922.

THE NEW ECONOMIC POLICY (NEP)

In principle, the NEP upheld the earlier decrees, but it modified their implementation to cope with the immediate problems. The modifications, however, reached to the essence of the reforms decreed previously. For example, the new decree formally permitted land-leasing or tenancy,

TABLE 12

SOME INDICATORS OF THE RURAL ECONOMY OF
RUSSIA, 1909–1921*
(In millions)

Year	Sown area (desiatines)	Gross yield of crops (poods)†	No. of horses	No. of cattle	No. of sheep and goats
1909–1913	83.1	3,850	—	—	—
1916	79.0	3,482	31.5	49.9	80.9
1917	79.4	3,350	—	—	—
1920	62.9	2,082	25.4	39.1	49.8
1921	58.3	1,689	23.3	36.8	48.4

Baykov, *op. cit.*, p. 23. Unfortunately, it is not clear exactly to what instant of time the figures in the last three columns apply; we may assume that they were taken consistently at the same time of each year.

† One *pood* [*pud*] = 16.38 kg. = 36.113 lb.

on the conditions that the land be leased only to cultivators and in an amount just sufficient to employ the farmer's family. Hiring labor was also permitted, provided it was to enable the farmer to carry out farm work at the right time, and provided all able-bodied members of the employer family were working on the farm at the same rate as the paid worker.[107] A special feature of the NEP which both Lenin and Stalin regarded as a major change of policy was the substitution of tax in kind for requisition of farm surplus. After fulfilling the "fixed" tax obligations, the farmer was allowed to sell his products privately to the towns.[108] Taxes were assessed as a proportion of the net produce above the minimum needs of the family.[109]

The purpose of the NEP was both economic and political. Economically it was to restore production and to "pave the way for further socialization of the country's national economy." [110] It was political in that it sought to regain confidence of the peasants. As Lenin put it:

The important thing is that we changed our economic policy exclusively out of practical consideration dictated by the circumstances. Crop failure, shortage of fodder, lack of fuel — all this naturally exercises a decisive effect on economy as a whole, peasant economy included. . . . The peasantry had to be shown that we can and want to change our policy quickly, in order to alleviate their need immediately.[111]

In another place Lenin was more explicit on this point:

The question of substituting a tax in kind for requisitioning is primarily a political one. Its essence lies in the relations between the workers and the peasants. The interests of these classes do not coincide: the small farmer does not desire what the worker is striving for. Nevertheless, only by coming to agreement with the peasants can we save the socialist revolution. We must either satisfy the middle peasant economically and restore the free market, or else we shall be unable to maintain the power of the working class.[112]

Effects and Evaluation of the NEP. The economic effects of the NEP were immediate. The area ploughed increased from 158 million acres in 1922 to 205 millions in 1923, 217 millions in 1924, and in 1927 it reached 236 million acres. The number of horses increased from 24.1 millions in 1922 to 27.1 millions in 1925. Cattle increased from 45.8 millions to 62.1 millions; sheep and goats from 91.1 to 122.9 millions, and pigs from 12.1 to 21.8 millions during the same period.[113]

The NEP encouraged differentiation among the peasants and reëmergence or strengthening of the richer peasants or kulaks, as suggested by table 13.

TABLE 13

DIFFERENTIATION AMONG RUSSIAN PEASANTRY, 1927 *

By cropland holding		By value of principal means of production	
Hectares per household	Per cent of total	Household group range in rubles	Per cent of total
Under 0.10	6.3	None	3.0
0.10–1.19	13.1	Not over 100	10.6
1.20–2.29	17.3	100–200	12.1
2.30–3.38	17.1	200–400	26.2
3.39–4.47	13.5	400–800	30.9
4.48–6.66	16.2	800–1,600	13.8
6.67–8.84	7.7	Over 1,600	3.2
8.85–11.03	3.7		
11.04–17.59	3.7		
17.60 and over	1.4		

* Jasny, *The Socialized Agriculture of the U.S.S.R., op. cit.,* pp. 181–182.

These figures do not reveal the distribution of households by size or number of able-bodied workers, or the role of the NEP in this differentiation; however, there seems to be full agreement that the NEP favored the richer peasants who had surplus products for trading.[114]

The NEP represented reaction, since it reversed the existing policy and obstructed reform implementation. But it would not be reactionary if one looks at it from the point of view of the peasants or of the long-range objectives of the reformers. Lenin regarded the NEP as the only way to save the revolution and the reforms it had instituted, and as a transitional measure facilitating further socialization of the economy.[115] Similarly, while admitting it as a retreat, Stalin considered the NEP as unavoidable and a necessary preparation for a new offensive. In Stalin's view, the NEP was "a link that will ensure the victory of socialism"; and he confessed that "if we adhere to the NEP it is because it serves the cause of socialism. When it ceases to serve the cause of socialism we will cast it to the devil." [116]

More light is thrown on the nature of the NEP by studying the manner in which it was executed. Initially the tax in kind was not progressive, but as production increased it was made more so, thus increasing the pressure on the richer peasants. In contrast, the poor peasants benefited by tax rebates and by government assistance in case of crop failure. In other words, once production pressures were somewhat relieved, the slogan of the second stage was revived and war against the richer peasants resumed.

Whether a reaction or not, the NEP was a compromise that halted execution of the Soviet agrarian policy and reversed it. The NEP not only reverted to free trading, hiring of workers, and leasing of land, but it also tolerated small peasant farming in the greater sector of the rural economy. The handicaps created by small peasant farming were becoming increasingly more evident when the Soviets embarked on a program of rapid industrialization. Grain for the market had increased gradually in the mid-'twenties but was still below the prerevolution level. Grain export, which was necessary to pay for imported machinery, had also not been recovered because the small peasantry lacked the efficiency of large-scale farming, and because they increased their consumption over prerevolution levels.[117] Therefore, to facilitate industrialization, agricultural production had to be revolutionized and exportation of grain and other farm products increased. As Stalin saw it:

The way out is to turn the small and scattered peasant farms into larger united farms based on the common cultivation of the soil on the basis of new and higher techniques. The way out is to unite the small and dwarf peasant farms gradually and surely, not by pressure but by example and persuasion, into large farms based on common, cooperative cultivation of the soil, with the use of agricultural machines and tractors and scientific methods of intensive agriculture. There is no other way out.[118]

Hence the transition to the third stage of Soviet agrarian policy and "reform."

THE DRIVE FOR COLLECTIVIZATION

Collectivization of the farms in Russia involved major changes in the terms of land holding and in the scale of operation. Both changes were motivated by the same policy objectives, namely, increasing agricultural production and promoting socialism in agriculture, as in industry. This

98

was also seen as the only way to relieve the peasant of poverty, and Russia of its economic and political problems.[119]

The policy to encourage large-scale coöperative farming was, as mentioned above, expressed in the Land Decree of 1918. Some collectives had been established when the issue was almost completely abandoned and the trend reversed by the NEP. As late as 1927–1928 collective farms occupied only 1.1 million hectares and state farms 1.2 million hectares out of a total area of 115.6 million hectares of sown land, while the remaining 113.3 million hectares were cultivated by individual peasant farmers.[120] Even after the Soviet government had made its intentions known regarding organization and scale of farming, the extent of collectivization remained limited. In 1929 the area of grain crops amounting to 96.0 million hectares was divided as follows: 1.5 million hectares in state farms; 3.4 million in collectives; and the remaining 91.1 million hectares in individual farms.[121] Owing to the limited success of voluntary collectivization, Stalin and some of his associates thought it imperative to pursue a new policy if rapid industrialization was to be achieved; hence the drive for collectivization and the slogan for union between the workers and the poor peasants against the bourgeoisie — the kulaks in this case — and neutralization of the middle peasants.

In pursuing the new policy, the boundaries between poor, middle, and rich peasant were defined more precisely. It was made clear at the outset that the rich peasants were not fit for membership in the collectives and therefore had to be eliminated as a class. For this purpose the tax in kind was used very harshly against them: "If they paid the first time, they were reassessed at twice or three times the original sum. Sooner or later the rich peasant failed to pay his taxes; thereupon his property was nominally sold for the amount of the arrears and handed over to the nearest kolkhoz." [122] The middle peasants were treated less harshly, but severely enough to induce them to join collectives. The poor peasants who did not have much to lose by joining the collectives were induced to join voluntarily by tax exemption and subsidization.[123]

As a positive measure, the new drive planned to show convincing results of collective farming and efficient operation to induce voluntary acceptance of the collectives. The government therefore facilitated credit and provided tractor service for the collectives.[124]

The policy of squeezing the kulaks later became a direct offensive against them. Village Soviets were authorized to expropriate their machinery, working implements, and cattle above a certain minimum. Police authority was used in this offensive. But the results were disastrous. The reaction of the richer peasants was very drastic and politically and economically destructive. They reacted with passive resistance, boycott, slaughter of livestock, violence, and arson. But their most destructive weapon was their influence on the middle peasants, half of whom took sides with the kulaks.[125] The drastic economic and political effects could not be ignored. That is why Stalin wrote his article "Dizzy with Success," [126] in which he criticized compulsory collectivization and violation of the principle of persuasion toward the middle peasants. He reiterated the need for flexibility according to local conditions. As a result, the pace of collectivization slowed, and members of the collectives were allowed to leave if they wished to — and many did.

Suspension of the drive for collectivization was temporary, however, and before long it was resumed with full force until its virtual completion in the late 'thirties. In 1938 collective farms occupied 85.6 per cent of the sown area; collective farmers (personal homesteads) occupied 3.9 per cent; all state and coöperative farms occupied 9.1 per cent, of which individual peasants held only 0.6 per cent of the sown area.[127] The job was complete, but the cost was very high; as late as 1939 the loss of the livestock had not been made good.[128]

Effects and Evaluation of Collectivization. To evaluate the effects of collectivization in terms of costs and benefits is difficult and probably unrealistic, since collectivization was not an isolated policy with measurable costs and benefits. It must be seen within the framework of the whole agrarian and general plan for the economy. It should also be seen as part of a long-range policy concerned with the total economic and political structure of the Soviet society. Furthermore, the economic effects of collectivization are difficult to evaluate before the new structure has had enough time with stable conditions to show fairly representative results. The evaluation is still more complicated because of the Second World War, which necessarily distorted the normal course of events and interfered with allocation of resources. The effects of the war were heavy on the rural population, particularly by conscripting the able-bodied males and being partly responsible for replacing them on the farm with women and youth.[129] Finally, no reliable data are available. Most of the official data are exaggerated and contradictory, while data presented by other scholars are merely good estimates. However, although prohibiting rigorous evaluation, these complications do not prevent a survey of the available results.[130]

Speaking in 1943, before the flow of data in the 1950's, Sir John Maynard gave a concise evaluation of the "material results of collectivization" as follows:

(1) It has made mechanization possible on a very large scale.
(2) It has made possible the application of science to agriculture by its introduction of organization.
(3) It has greatly facilitated the collection of produce for the army and the towns, and has thus facilitated more rapid industrialization.

100

(4) Supplemented by a great and widespread system of storage and processing . . . it has made possible the saving of much waste.

(5) It has not at present increased production per acre, and the partial change-over from cereal to industrial crop is to be attributed rather to general industrialization than to collectivization.

(6) By making mechanization on a large scale possible it has given to the rural population a turn in the direction of machine-mindedness, a consequence which has been very apparent during the present war, and gives promise of still more industrialization later on.[131]

Roughly speaking, this description seems correct. Mechanization of agriculture has advanced rapidly since 1928, though it was partly to replace the animal draft power which was destroyed in the early years of collectivization. Taking total animal and mechanical draft power in 1928 to be 100, all mechanization up to the late 1930's was to replace the lost animal power. The index rose by 5 per cent by 1950 and by 50–55 per cent by 1956. If animal draft were excluded from this index, the index of mechanization would have increased from 100 in 1928 to 450 in 1956. Mechanization has increased further since then.[132]

The degree of mechanization does not indicate the efficiency of production brought about by this change of technique. Though labor productivity may have improved as a result of mechanization, the use of agricultural machinery has been highly inefficient. Much waste has accompanied mechanization, and a large part of the farm machinery lay idle for long periods because of poor maintenance.[133]

Mechanization has, however, saved labor to be utilized elsewhere. Despite the great human loss in the war, the rural areas have contributed a large number of people to towns and industry and to the opening of new territories for farming. Labor saving implies that the same number of workers could cultivate a larger area of land within the same period of time, or that less people operated the same land area either by increasing productivity per man day, or by increasing the working time. The latter could be in terms of days in the year or hours in the day. Labor saving involved both raising productivity and increasing the work days of able-bodied workers. On the other hand, it has been claimed that working hours have been cut.[134]

Table 14 testifies to increased productivity per labor day. These figures show that productivity began to rise in 1940, after the trauma of the drive for collectivization had passed. The war years are not shown, but it is generally agreed that productivity declined during that period. It took several years for productivity to return to the prewar level. Since 1952, however, the improvement has been almost continuous. In commenting on his own findings, Kahan concludes that productivity per unit of land has also increased.[135] On the other hand, workers have been employed more days during the year and thus idle capacity has been utilized. The average number of days worked in a year by agricultural able-bodied workers has risen from about 120 in 1927 to about 155 days in 1940, and to 175–180 in the 1950's. In collectives the number has risen from about 130 days in 1933 to about 160–170 days during the 1950's. If all productive

TABLE 14

INDEXES OF OUTPUT PER UNIT OF LABOR INPUT
IN SOVIET AGRICULTURE *

(1926–1929 = 100)

Year	Per unit of actual input
1933	87.8
1934	79.6
1935	86.3
1936	85.6
1937	107.1
1938	87.5
1940	102.1
1950	102.3
1951	101.7
1952	119.9
1953	124.7
1954	123.5
1955	131.1
1956	148.8†

* A. Kahan, "Changes in Labor Inputs in Soviet Agriculture," *Journal of Political Economy*, LXVII, no. 5 (Oct., 1959), 460.
† The year 1956 was exceptionally good and does not represent the trend accurately.

services rendered by collective farmers were added, the number of days worked would be about 200 for the middle 1950's.[136] In other words, surplus labor has been greatly reduced by transferring such labor to industry and to newly opened territory.

The effect on total agricultural production is shown in table 15. These figures show two things in addition to the overall increase of output: first, that livestock products lagged behind until 1956, taking a longer period than other products to recover the initial setbacks; and, second, they show the relatively large increase in industrial crops, thus contributing to rapid industrialization.

The impact on the standard of living of the peasant is hard to estimate. The per capita national income has certainly multiplied several fold, but not so the living standards of the peasant. Per capita income is not an accurate measure of the standard of living of the peasant. The rate of increase in production of capital goods has been higher than that of consumption goods. There has also been substantial differentiation between the real incomes of the industrial and agricultural workers and among the agricultural workers themselves; thus, the average per capita income conceals the condition of the low-paid groups.

The peasant standard of living was greatly depressed during the 1930's and 1940's. It was only in the 1950's that the per capita real income

TABLE 15

INDEXES OF GROSS AND NET OUTPUT OF LIVESTOCK PRODUCTS,
TECHNICAL CROPS, AND FOOD CROPS IN THE SOVIET UNION *

	Gross output			Net output		
Year	Livestock	Food crops	Industrial crops	Livestock	Food crops	Industrial crops
1928	100	100	100	100	100	100
1932	61	91	126	61	101	119
1937	71	131	218	71	161	213
1940	102	125	201	98	137	192
1950	107	124	240	100	140	240
1953	120	120	261	114	128	266
1954	127	125	267	120	131	266
1955	137	146	307	129	151	310
1956	149	176	342	142	183	343
1957	165	152	332	158	145	333

* Johnson and Kahan, *op. cit.*, p. 206.

started to rise. Goldman has estimated the improvement as reflected in retail trade in the countryside, which rose by about 31 per cent in 1953.[137] This approach points only the direction of change. A. Nove has tried to estimate the peasant income directly, but lack of data made it impossible. Yet he concludes that "it is certain that all major components of peasant income except revenue from free-market sales show a definite upward trend. It is also certain that the aggregate increase has been impressively large." [138] Jasny estimates that the peasant real income in 1958 was still less than it was in 1928. He agrees, however, that a big increase has occurred during the 1950's, and suggests that this period may prove to be the start.[139]

There is no denying that during the 1930's and 1940's the peasant lived at or near subsistence, but was this because of collective farming? Undoubtedly the process of collectivization was accompanied by a great decline of production and therefore of the per capita real income. At the same time, the Soviet authorities continued to collect the tax in kind, thus depressing the peasant income still further. The latter result was more a consequence of rapid industrialization than of the institution of collectivism in agriculture. Had there been no collectivization, peasant income might still have been greatly reduced because of the dependence of industrialization on internal capital. The bulk of this capital came from the peasants and rural population as forced saving. The collectives provided a convenient mechanism of procuring the product. These procurements could have been made by other means, as was done in Japan and in England during their periods of industrialization. The peasants in Japan and the workers in England lived at or near subsistence during rapid industrialization, even though there was no collectivization in either case. And in all three countries, when industrialization was underway, and probably when the peasants and workers became restive, incomes started to rise. This occurred in Russia for several years in the mid-'fifties, without abolishing collective tenure. Collectivization may have been partly responsible for the low standard of living, but only indirectly by generating specific social responses from the rural population.

To summarize, it appears that the Soviets have realized the objectives of their agrarian policies: they have industrialized rapidly, making use of agriculture for that purpose; they have increased labor productivity and, after delay, productivity per unit of land also. They have reduced surplus population in the rural areas and put it to use in industry and in new land, and thus increased both total production and per capita output. They have also created large-scale mechanized farming in conformity with their Land Decree of 1918. And, finally, they have recently embarked on raising the standard of living of the peasant and urban workers out of the rising agricultural productivity and national product.[140]

GENERAL REMARKS ON THE SOVIET AGRARIAN POLICIES

1. Viewed as a whole, the Soviet agrarian policy seems general and comprehensive. It touched all rural groups and all sectors of the agrarian structure. Nationalization covered all the land, whether held by rich or poor, and most of it was collectivized, the rest being state farms and private garden lots; that is, even though the reforms were carried out on behalf of the proletariat, they did not favor one group over another.[141] They leveled rural classes by eliminating class differentiation deriving from ownership of land or other means of production, but not of income within the rural community or between rural communities, nor between rural and urban people.[142]

The Soviet reforms were comprehensive also in terms of the agrarian structure. Unlike those of the pre-Soviet era, these reforms covered tenure, the pattern of cultivation, the terms of holding and scale of operation, and credit. Once and for all, tenure was made public and mostly collective; the pattern of cultivation was redirected toward intensive, supervised, coöperative and commercial production to promote industrialization and progressive agriculture. Similarly, the terms of holding were changed into collective, nonrent holding on the basis of tilling. The scale of operation was enlarged as decreed by the theoretical convictions of the "reformers" regarding efficient production.

2. The process of reform was neither smooth nor peaceful. Although a large portion of the peasantry was landless, there is no evidence that the landless rural population approved of the Soviet reforms. They may have refrained from open resistance, but there is no clear indication that they would not have preferred individualistic landholding and operation. However, open resistance was expressed mainly by those who had land and capital subject to confiscation. Only firmness of the authorities could overcome resistance, at a high cost to the community and to the peasants.[143]

3. A counterpart of peasant resistance to collectivization was the tendency for reaction or reversal of policy by the government. At least two such instances took place before collectivization was completed. The first was the inauguration of the NEP and the readmission of private trading. The second was suspension of the drive for collectivization, and permission to leave the collective if desired. It is true that both actions were tactics to cope with emergencies and serious problems. It is also true that these reversals were temporary measures, known to be so in advance and probably justified on those grounds. But it is equally true that the reform was halted temporarily. It was also subjected to modification and change in details such that the results were different from those anticipated, at least in the short run. However, reaction in this context differs from reaction by former regimes or privileged classes which tends to restore or perpetuate prereform conditions. The Soviet reaction was rather a postponement of action to gain time and reduce the overhead cost of the reform, and probably to save the reform and the revolution before it was too late.

4. The Soviet agrarian policy was closely associated with the internal and external political developments. To gain support of the peasantry, the government declared that land belongs to the peasants in general, overlooking class differentiation among them.[144] When civil war and foreign danger were apparent, War Communism was declared. When resistance of the peasants became strong, the NEP was inaugurated, giving them concessions. When the opponents of Stalin were ousted and his power entrenched, both of which coincided with a relative increase in the economic power of the state and collective farms, the NEP was abandoned and the drive for collectivization announced. And to reduce internal dissatisfaction and destructive opposition, the drive was halted. Nothing was held rigidly in the short run. Security of the state and achievement of the long-run objectives dictated the agrarian short-term policy.

5. Finally, in contrast to the pre-Soviet Russian reforms, the Soviets were constantly guided by national economic considerations. As mentioned earlier, the whole agrarian plan was developed along the Marxist economic doctrine which advocated nationalization of the means of production, the commercialization of agriculture, and large-scale operation.

Not only was the general plan influenced by these economic considerations but the details of its implementation were determined also by the immediate economic needs of the economy. The NEP was introduced to restore production. The drive for collectivization was pushed to give the state more power over composition and disposal of the product and facilitate rapid industrialization. The changes made in the terms of holding and scale of operation and also in the pattern of cultivation were similarly guided by economic objectives, namely, higher production for domestic and foreign markets. In this respect, the Soviet reforms were the first to pursue economic objectives to so large an extent. In fact, these reforms have set the stage for wider recognition of economic factors in planning reform.

VIII

THE MEXICAN REFORMS

Mexico is the only case in this study in which the population is racially differentiated; it is also the only case which has a background of colonization.[1] These two factors have helped to shape the processes and tendencies of tenure change. It is significant that the Mexican community has neither developed into a replica of the mother country nor been assimilated into a culturally homogeneous nation. On the contrary, it has been socially differentiated into classes according to purity of racial and ethnic origin and economic wealth; these criteria are closely related. The social class differentiation has in turn sustained the system of ranking and cultural exclusion, of which it was an outgrowth, making the integration of ideals and objectives hardly possible. This conflict has been well demonstrated in land tenure relations before and since the modern reforms.

One distinctive feature of the prereform Mexican land system was the high percentage of land ownership by foreign elements. Another was the multiplicity of tenure types, each being associated with a different social and ethnic group. For example, the *hacienda* (plantation) combined two racial groups: the Spanish and the Indian — the former on top and the latter at the bottom, while the *rancho* (small family farm) was usually owned by the *mestizos*, who are of mixed blood.

In still another way the Mexican case differs from the rest. Theoretically, the Mexican *peon* (plantation worker) was free and protected by law, but in practice he was bound to the soil, as in manorial England and pre-Emancipation Russia, by the system of advance payments used by the *hacendado* (lord or plantation owner). Therefore, there was no need to formally emancipate the peasant. It was necessary only to restore to him the land he had lost through illegal seizure.

The Mexican reforms comprised two main operations: the restoration of land and settlement of the title, and the creation of new owners by redistributing public land or land requisitioned from neighboring estates. In either case, private ownership and operation of the land were maintained. In the early years of reform the title was vested in the village as a whole, but after 1925 it became a joint title between the village and the individual member. However, throughout the reform the newly acquired land has remained inalienable.

The Mexican reforms were motivated primarily by social and political factors, and therefore were of relatively limited economic impact. Their primary objective was to promote political stability through the communal farm (*ejido*).

BACKGROUND: LAND TENURE

Two forms of land tenure existed in Mexico on the eve of the Revolution which precipitated the reform. The public land consisted primarily of uncultivated areas for which no concessions had as yet been granted. The private individual tenure, or freehold, applied to the hacienda and the rancho. The former was comparable with the English manor or the Russian commune, while the latter represented the small family farm.

A third form retained in violation of the law was collective ownership. This form of tenure was abolished in 1857, and accordingly most Indian village-holdings were broken up into ranchos or swallowed by the neighboring haciendas. But some such villages were still in existence in 1910, having evaded the law by being in isolated areas, or by formally transferring the titles to individuals.[2] Sometimes a whole clan or family shared the property, although the title remained vested in one individual; such arrangements did not in fact exclude sale or inheritance of the land. In a sense many held property as joint stock companies.[3]

The hacienda was usually owned by an hacendado, managed centrally, and operated by resident workers, the *peones*. Its size ranged from 1,000 to 400,000 acres — at least one of the upper limit existed in 1910. The population ranged from less than one hundred to a thousand. The hacienda was characterized by a variety of soil types which made village life tend toward economic self-sufficiency. Moreover, the village had its own church and priest, school — if such existed at all — post office, and so forth.[4]

Though the hacienda was similar to the English manor and to the Russian commune in some ways, it differed from both in organization. It was centrally managed and the peasants were theoretically wage workers; it was more like a Roman *latifundium* without slave labor. The hacendado had no legal title or authorization to most of the land, in contrast to the manor lord or the *pometschik* in Russia, who was formally granted a concession to the land and the serfs working on it. The Mexican hacendado might have a formal concession to some of the land, but most of his estate was usurped by exploiting the weakness of the Indian who was ignorant of the Spanish laws of tenure. This is why a primary objective of the reforms was to restore the land to its legal owners from whom it had been appropriated without compensation.

The hacendado, predominantly of European descent, was usually an absentee landlord. He enjoyed the luxury of city life and lived on the income from his estate or by borrowing on the security of the land. In contrast, the peones working the land were usually of Indian blood or mestizos in whom Indian blood predominated. These people had been reduced to bondage by their attachment to the land and by the system of advance payment practiced by the hacendados.[5] Now they worked these lands for very low wages in kind or money. The money wages, however, were spent in the village store owned by the hacendado and in which they could buy on credit in the form of advance payment. Since the peon was not allowed to leave the village before clearing himself of debt, and since he was never able to do so out of his poor wages, gradually he found himself tied to the land and the landlord.

Production concentrated on those commodities needed by the hacienda, given the soil and nature of the terrain, and the primitive methods of cultivation. However, the hacienda had a special significance to the hacendado because of the anticipated incremental value of the land — the country's cultivable area was limited while population was increasing and the means of transportation expanding.[6] The significance of the hacienda in the national land tenure structure may be seen from the figures in table 16.

TABLE 16

LARGE HOLDINGS IN TEN MEXICAN STATES, 1910 *
(In hectares)

Number	Size of holding
1,611	1,000 or more
589	5,000 or more
336	10,000 or more
116	25,000 or more
51	50,000 or more
11	100,000 or more
2	200,000 or more
1	400,000 or more

* McBride, op. cit., p. 79.

The second major group were the rancheros or peasant owners who usually owned enough to keep the family employed. Thus the rancho was a subsistence economy and catered to the market only on rare occasions. The rancheros were sometimes Europeans, but more often were of mixed blood. Except with respect to the scale of operation, which in this case was small, and the absence of wage labor, there was no difference in methods of cultivation between the rancho and the hacienda. In 1910 there were 47,939 ranchos in Mexico geographically distributed in an inverse ratio with haciendas, since in most cases they survived encroachments of the hacendado by occupying hilly terrain or where water was not abundant.[7]

The significance of these tenure groups may be seen more clearly by comparing the wealth in land of each of these groups, and by contrasting them with the landless rural population, as in table 17. Columns 3 and 4 of this table distinguish the owners from the nonowners, but concentration of ownership may be seen among the owners who constituted only 3 per cent of the population. Though detailed statistics are not available, it has been estimated that as late as 1923, several years after the Revolution,

TABLE 17

LANDOWNERSHIP IN MEXICO, 1910

State	Rural population as per cent of total population	Percentage of heads of families who own individual property	Percentage of heads of families who own no individual property
Aguascalientes	58.5	3.6	96.4
Baja California	89.4	11.8	88.2
Campeche	73.1	2.3	97.7
Chiapas	82.3	4.0	96.0
Chihuahua	77.7	4.5	95.5
Coahuila	66.2	2.3	97.7
Colima	67.6	3.1	96.9
Durango	84.4	3.2	96.8
Guanajuato	71.7	2.9	97.1
Guerrero	91.7	1.5	98.5
Hidalgo	91.4	1.3	98.7
Jalisco	77.1	3.8	96.2
México	84.0	0.5	99.5
Michoacán	83.6	2.7	97.3
Morelos	77.7	0.5	99.5
Nuevo Leon	72.2	5.4	94.6
Oaxaca	86.7	0.2	99.8
Pueblo	81.4	0.7	99.3
Querétaro	81.8	1.6	98.4
Quintana Roo	100.0	1.4	98.6
San Luis Potosí	77.9	1.8	98.2
Sinaloa	86.0	5.3	94.7
Sonora	82.7	4.2	95.8
Tabasco	93.4	4.8	92.3
Tamaulipas	79.6	7.7	92.3
Tepic (Nayarit)	81.4	6.0	94.0
Tlaxcala	85.3	0.7	99.3
Veracruz	78.3	1.1	98.9
Yucatán	73.3	3.6	96.4
Zacatecas	85.1	1.9	98.1

SOURCE: Extracted from McBride, *op. cit.*, Table 1, p. 154.

less than 2 per cent of the haciendas held 58.2 per cent of the area, and 110 of them owned 19.32 per cent of the land in private hands. In some states the haciendas occupied over 90 per cent of all the privately owned land. . . . In contrast to these great holdings, 59 per cent of all proprietors in Mexico had less than five hectares each. . . . Of three per cent of the population who did have land at this time . . . the vast majority had not enough to make a bare living.[8]

In 1910 in the state of Mexico, where only 856 people owned any land, excluding the surviving Indian villages, 64 hacendados owned more than half the land of all the haciendas and ranchos. In the state of Morelos in the same year 41 farms covered about 222,249 hectares, while the largest three occupied 99,254 hectares, in contrast to 68 small farms under 100 hectares with a total of 2,100 hectares only.[9] This pattern of distribution was the rule rather than the exception.

The problem of concentration was not only one of poverty and riches; it extended to the basic sociopolitical relations in the country because of the significant percentage of foreigners among the big owners. Tannenbaum has gone as far as saying that the "Mexican Revolution cannot be understood without an insight into the irritation produced by the foreign ownership of land in the country." In 1923 the foreigners owned about 20.1 per cent of all privately owned land, or 32,044,947 hectares, "an extent equal to the combined areas of all the New England states, New York, and New Jersey."[10]

Finally, a word should be said about the Indian village or *pueblo*. During the Diaz regime, 1876–1910, these villages were "raped" of their land by several legal and illegal means. The law against communal ownership, the law of "denunciation" by which unoccupied land (or land claimed to be "unoccupied") could be appropriated by the denunciator, pressure from the haciendas, and the tax laws — all were tools by which the Indian villages were reduced to about 10 per cent of their area in the middle of the last century.[11] Part of the Indian land — about one million hectares — was retained by individual members in private ownership, but most of it was sold to outsiders or allotted to the members of the villages in such small quantities that they had to sell out. Thus, "in proportion as communal property and small individual holdings declined during the Diaz regime, large estates grew," so that by the end of the regime the Indian villages had lost their autonomy and local government, and their communal structure became insignificant.[12]

SOCIAL CLASSES AND POLITICAL CONDITIONS

On the eve of the Revolution,

economic power, political power, and the power exercised by those who spoke in the name of supernatural beings was concentrated socially and geographically. Mexico City was the undisputed metropolis. The small "upper-upper" class came close to being a caste which was tied together by family, personal, political, and ideological bonds and fear of the wrath of the masses whom some of them abused.[13]

111

It is almost natural to find economic and political power and, until the time when church and state separated, power of the clergy going hand in hand. They might or might not be associated with the same persons, but would still be in the hands of the powerful class. The social structure in Mexico was, and still is, complicated by racial differentiation. Economic and political power were associated with racial and ethnic origin. On top of the social structure were the *creoles* who were presumably of pure European stock. Below them, the mestizos were "ethnically, people of Spanish and Indian blood; in practice, all who adopted mestizo mores." Below them still were the Indians and the Negroes.[14]

These groups were neither homogeneous nor united. The creoles, for instance, were composed of three subgroups: the old creoles who were of ancient Spanish lineage; the new creoles who were not always of Spanish origin and who came into power after the War of Reform (1858–1861) and the Maximilian period; and the clerical creoles who were the extreme clericals. The interests of these groups were not the same and sometimes were in conflict with each other. However, they united on at least two grounds: attachment to their continent of origin, and attitude to the land and mass of the population. They were kept in harmony with each other and with the government of Diaz by the latter's ability to satisfy each of them separately. The old creoles — usually hacendados — were contented by being left alone to pursue their own interests. The new creoles were given political positions and power in the service of the government. The clergy and their supporters were appeased by nonenforcement of the anticlerical Laws of Reform which, if applied, would have deprived them of property and power.[15] Thus, the contribution of these groups to political stability was not substantive or dependable when seen from the standpoint of the rest of the population or the letter of the law.

The mestizos, on the other hand, though of mixed blood, would not admit any connection with the Indian and would even look down upon him.[16] They were not homogeneous either in race or in interests, and many of them occupied high government positions. It has been suggested that by 1910 the government bureaucracy had expanded so much that it had employed about 70 per cent of the mestizos and that "with rare exceptions, the chief ministers, the state governors, and the superior officers of the army were mestizos." [17] Among the mestizos were also the rancheros, who were more or less self-sufficient and conservative, and thus a source of stability in the political system.[18]

The Indians were quite important numerically, but were of little significance in the social and political structure. Diaz did not even attempt to appease them; on the contrary, he saw them lose their land and did not try to help them.[19]

The numerical significance of these social groups is hard to determine precisely. According to Cumberland, in 1876 the mestizos constituted about half the population and the Indians 35 per cent.[20] A similar distribution seems to have existed in 1910, in which year the whites were 7.5 per cent, the mestizos 53.5 per cent, and the Indians 39.0 per cent.[21] On the basis of the 1895 census, Senior estimates what he calls the upper class to be 1.4 per cent of the population, the middle class 7.8 per cent, and 90.8 per cent to be in the lower class.[22] This is more consistent with economic class differentiation and the distribution of land.

A more significant aspect of this class differentiation was the degree of rigidity characterizing it. Being sustained by monopoly of economic and political power, and roughly parallel to racial or overt features, the immobility has approximated a caste system.[23] Senior has gone as far as trying to explain the Mexican Revolution in terms of what he called a "closed system" of classes. Out of this social rigidity arose the frustration and tension which have been considered basic causes of the Revolution.[24]

The last decade of the rule of Diaz witnessed a crisis manifested by the steady deterioration of the living standards of ten million out of the twelve million people of Mexico.[25] Land monopoly and peonage had reached "unprecedented proportions under the Diaz administration." [26] The crisis has, however, been explained differently by different people. One view contends that

it is the upper and middle class "misfit" who is at once both conscious of his thwarted ambitions and able to clothe his dissatisfaction with significant meaning. And so it was in Mexico. The intellectual leaders of the revolution sprang from the upper and middle classes, from those who could not (or would not) find a place either in the closed circle of the Diaz bureaucracy or in the foreign-dominated new industries. For it was this group which was caught between the upper and nether millstones. There was an ever increasing pressure to emulate the high standards of conspicuous expenditure introduced by the inner circles of the Diaz bureaucracy, fattening on the new industrialism, while, at the same time, the wherewithal to keep up with the procession was made more and more difficult to come by.[27]

In contrast, according to McBride,

the situation would have been different if Mexico had had a great number of small proprietors, with a proprietor's devotion to law and order, and if the Diaz administration had not countenanced the despoiling of many small holders, who, notwithstanding the irregularity of their legal claims to the land, were justified in expecting the full protection to which, as the rightful owners, they were entitled. Furthermore, the revolution would have been impossible but for the vast army of Indians and mestizos who had neither soil, crops, houses, nor cattle that would suffer in the turmoil and who welcomed the chance to gain plunder or perhaps a confiscated hacienda by rousing the other landless hordes against the government that made such conditions possible.[28]

These two statements are not contradictory. Both point out a crisis, but they differ on its source. They show not only that land concentration, increased poverty, and discontent of both the landless people and misfits were taking place, but also that those in power positions were experiencing pressure of rising needs.[29]

The crisis, though latent for a long time, was not unnoticed. Sporadic revolts were not uncommon. There were thousands of cases of individual acts of rebellion, such as banditry and murder of local chiefs.[30] Labor rebelled in 1906. There were strikes in mining and textile enterprises. The strikes took a violent turn at Cananea, Sonora, and even the mediation of President Diaz was rejected by the workers, and riots erupted. Order was restored only when federal troops were used against the workers.[31] The tide continued to rise until in 1910 the President announced his intention to seek reëlection after a rule of thirty-four years. His announcement was the excuse for political change and an occasion for reform.

THE PROCESS OF REFORM

The year 1911 saw the end of the Diaz regime and the dawn of a new era, the era of tenure reform. Yet there seems to have been no direct connection between the Revolution and the program for reform. The Revolution had no plan for reforming the tenure. Madero, hero of the Revolution, had no idea of reform or intention to inaugurate any radical changes in that respect. The only mention of reform was a paragraph in the Plan de San Luis Potosi concerning small proprietors, as follows:

In abuse of the law on public lands numerous proprietors of small holdings, in their greater part Indians, have been dispossessed of their lands by ruling of the Department of Public Improvement (Fomento) or by the decisions of the tribunals of the Republic. As it is just to restore to their former owners the lands of which they were dispossessed in such an arbitrary manner, such rulings and decisions are declared subject to revision, and those who have acquired them in such an immoral manner, or their heirs, will be required to restore them to their former owners, to whom they shall also pay an indemnity for the damages suffered. Solely in case those lands have passed to third persons before the promulgation of this plan shall the former owners receive an indemnity from those in whose favor the dispossession was made.[32]

The extent of the plan, then, was the restitution of land to small holders. Nothing was implied about the *ejidos* (common property of the Indian villages) or about breaking up large estates for redistribution. Under pressure from Zapata, the Indian leader who assisted Madero in the Revolution, a commission was established to study the land problem. The commission was a conservative one consisting of three engineers, two lawyers, and four landowners and public administrators under the presidency of Minister of Fomento Hernandez. It reported in 1911, but made

114

no suggestions concerning the Indian village land.[33] Nothing further was done until the Decree of 1915 was passed; it was later embodied as Article 27 in the 1917 Constitution.

However, when the Revolution took place, the Indians and mestizos thought it opportune to recover the land of their ancestors and would not wait for the government and the law to gratify them.[34] In small armed groups they took over large amounts of land from haciendas and began operating them under armed guard. This was especially noticeable in the states of Chihuahua, Durango, Jalisco and Hidalgo. "Villagers moved back upon the land they had so recently lost. In other instances it [the movement] was more indirect — it was an extension of the right to plant and till, harvest and use the land that the village needed but to which it had no access." [35] Vain attempts were made by Madero, Huerta, and Carranza to stop that movement, but the villagers would not give up what they considered to be their right. Peasant uprisings were in fact part of a country-wide movement. Zapata, in the south, continued to occupy land until his death in 1919, and military commanders supported peasant occupation of the land to win their support.[36] In his Plan de Ayala, Zapata advocated "immediate seizure of those lands which had been taken from the villages, the expropriation of one-third of the lands held by hacendados who did not obstruct the revolution course, and complete expropriation of lands held by men who 'directly or indirectly' opposed the plan." [37] Zapata's Plan was quite significant in arousing sentiments for and bringing about the reform. According to Tannenbaum, "there would probably have been no agrarian law at all if the agrarian revolution and expropriation had not already occurred." [38]

Reform legislation was passed at intervals starting in 1915, during the rule of Carranza, after Madero had been killed and several presidents had followed him in succession. The 1915 Decree, after acknowledging the sad condition to which the villagers had been reduced, ordered that

(1) All alienation of village lands, forests, and waters affected by the mis-application of the law of June 26, 1856, through illegal acts of surveying companies, through enclosures, or other illegal means are null and void.

This was the principle of distributing land by restitution.

(2) Villages which, needing them, do not have ejidos or which cannot secure their restoration because of lack of titles, difficulty of identification, or because they have been legally alienated shall have the right to obtain a sufficient portion of land to reconstruct them in accordance of the necessities of the community, the National government expropriating the necessary lands to that effect from those immediately adjoining the communities in question.

Articles 3 to 6 provided that legal machinery should be set up consisting of a National Agrarian Commission, State Agrarian Commissions for each state, and Executive Committees in the villages. Initiative for restoration or dotation should come from the villages themselves. Expropriated owners should have the right to apply to court for legal adjudication within a year after expropriation. Only villages that had *calegoria politica* (political status) could petition for land.[39]

The provisions of the 1915 Decree were reaffirmed two years later as Article 27 of the 1917 Constitution, with some additions and elaborations. These provisions included:

The ownership of lands and waters comprised within the limits of the national territory is vested originally in the Nation, which has had and has the right to transmit title thereof to private persons, thereby constituting private property.

. . . .

Private property shall not be *expropriated* except for reasons of public utility and by means of indemnification.

The rest of this section was an elaboration of these two principles. The law then defined the legal capacity to own lands and waters as follows: Only Mexicans by birth or naturalization and Mexican companies have the right to acquire ownership in lands, waters. . . . The Nation may grant the same rights to foreigners, provided they agree before the Ministry of Foreign Relations to be considered Mexicans in respect to such property, and accordingly not to invoke the protection of their Governments in respect to the same, under penalty, in case of breach, of forfeiture to the Nation of property so acquired. Within a zone of one hundred kilometers from the frontiers, and of fifty kilometers from the sea coast, no foreigner shall under any conditions acquire direct ownership of lands and waters.

Sections II to VII declared that religious, public, or commercial corporations and institutions should not own land, with a few exceptions, including state, federal and municipal authorities. A special mention was made of communal villages in Section VI as follows:

Properties held in common by co-owners, hamlets situated on private property, peublos, tribal congregations and other settlements which, as a matter of fact or law, conserve their communal character, shall have legal capacity to enjoy in common the waters, woods and lands belonging to them.[40]

Except for the communal or corporate bodies excepted above, civil corporations could own property only for their own use. The rest of Article 27 was an elaboration of these principles and a summary of procedures regarding their application, plus a definition of public utility which would justify expropriation of private property, and of methods of compensation. However, to deal with the land problem, Article 27 reiterated the provision of previous laws regarding restitution and dotation, adding that

116

all contracts and concessions made by former governments from and after 1876 which shall have resulted in the monopoly of lands, waters and natural resources of the Nation by a single individual or corporation, are declared subject to revision, and the Executive is authorized to declare those null and void which seriously prejudice the public interest.[41]

Generally speaking, Article 27 contained "the ideas, the principles, and in some respects the detailed items of all the laws about landholding that have been placed on the statute books since 1917." [42] It also provided the "legal basis for the solution of the agrarian problem." [43]

A few observations may be made regarding these two laws:

1. They did not provide for breaking up haciendas; they allowed only restoration or acquisition of parts of haciendas in conformity with the principles of restitution and dotation.

2. They limited the right of petitioning for land to villages with a political status. This excluded half of the population — those living on haciendas who were most in need of land.

3. They left the initiative to the villagers regardless of the red tape which might discourage illiterate and destitute people from fighting for their rights.

4. The new land laws made holding of land contingent upon use and emphasized communal against individual interest. But the restriction of ownership according to use did not apply to owners of haciendas, although they imposed limitations on the right of foreigners to own or to dispose of property.

5. Though these laws legalized communal holdings, they did not unconditionally provide for restoration of the communal or ejidal Indian village land. Land received in restitution continued to be communal "until such time as the law finally determines the distribution of the lands to the villagers." [44] The ultimate purpose was to create private holdings.[45]

Further legislation followed during the 'twenties and early 'thirties. However, most of this legislation was concerned with detail. Three important laws, those of 1922, 1923, and 1927, will be reviewed briefly. The law of April 10, 1922, concerned three main questions: who is entitled to petition for land; what land is subject for requisition; and how is the land to be distributed. The law sustained the restriction on the identity of the petitioner, but it redefined more broadly the political status of the village and thus excluded those living in the suburbs of villages and towns and who are thus politically dependent, and those living on haciendas. In this sense, this law was consistent with Article 27.

The land subject to distribution was expanded to cover more categories of holdings, but exemptions were still made for "(a) lands legally distributed under the law of June 25, 1856; and (b) properties not larger than fifty hectares to which the owner can prove a clear title for a period of ten years or more." [46] The law of 1922 also restricted the size of holding a person could receive from 3 to 5 hectares of irrigated or humid land, from 4 to 6 hectares of temporal land which receives regular but abundant rainfall, and from 6 to 8 hectares of other seasonal land. The amount of land a village could receive would be determined according to a census.[47] Finally, the law established formal procedures for receiving land by villages.

The law of August 2, 1923, concerned itself with colonization of public land, providing that

any Mexican over eighteen years of age could obtain title to national lands in an amount varying from 25 hectares of irrigable land up to 200 hectares of nonirrigable, pasture or mountain land, by occupying and tilling it for a period of two years. Title was granted to the individual settler upon the payment of fifty pesos and the presentation of proof of occupancy.[48]

The new owner, however, was not allowed to sell this land to anyone owning an amount equal to or more than the limit set by this law.

The law of 1927 dealt with details and procedures, which we will not discuss, but it also generalized the right to petition for land and abolished the arbitrariness that characterized previous legislation. Subsequently, it covered all villages having more than 25 families.[49] Thus the only groups that remained excluded were those of less than 25 families and the peon settlements on haciendas. However, because of these limitations more than half the rural communities were automatically excluded, or 46,000 out of a possible 60,000 rural communities.[50]

On the other hand, this law made concessions to the landlords. It gave them representation on the boards that conducted the census and fixed the amount of land to be allotted. It also exempted from expropriation estates not exceeding 150 hectares, regardless of the needs of the neighboring villages. Finally, it restricted the right of villages to petition for extra land to enlarge their holdings. Such petitions could be presented only ten years after the first dotation.[51]

One other law in this period should be mentioned, though it was not concerned with distribution — namely, the Regulatory Law Concerning the Division of Ejido Lands and the Constitution of the Ejido Patrimony of December 19, 1925. This law reflected the personal attitude of President Calles toward small private property. Among other things, it ordered that ejido crop lands be divided into parcels and the titles be vested in individuals jointly with the village. That is, land was to be subject to joint ownership so as "(a) to curtail the power of the village agrarian authorities; and (b) to take the first step in converting the ejidatarios from members of a commune into proprietors of individually-owned and independent private properties." [52]

This attitude toward private ownership in small holdings was augmented by the laws of 1930 and 1931 which reversed the reform trend. The tendency had been to restore land to villages without paying attention to agricultural efficiency or to the creation of private tenure. Under the direct influence of Calles, then ex-President, a decree was passed on December 26, 1930, redefining the peon communities, and making the communities attached to haciendas by a wage-labor contract ineligible to petition for land. And a redefinition of property subject to expropriation exempted lands of industrial importance, such as those involved in the production of milk, sisal fiber, and sugar. Finally, it made the right of villages to apply for land to enlarge their holdings dependent on the budgetary conditions of the treasury and on the efficiency standards, as follows:

(a) No petition for the enlargement of an ejido should be valid unless it could be demonstrated that efficient use has been made of the land previously granted to the village; and (b) expropriation for the purpose of making additional grants of land to villages with ejidos should be made only "after payment . . . and for this purpose provision shall be made each year in the budget of the Ministry of Agriculture and Development for the corresponding amounts." [53]

The decree of December 23, 1931, was another policy reversal; this time it was against the landlords. Following a ruling of the Supreme Court, "landowners affected by orders granting or restoring lands or waters in ejidos, which have been, or which in the future may be, dictated in favor of villages, shall have no right of legal recourse to *amparos*." [54]

Legislation in the following period aimed at completing the reform laws and synthesizing them. In 1933, Article 27 of the Constitution was expanded. The new version upheld the previous text and added a few provisions allowing division of ejidos and abolishing land distribution that had taken place by mistake or fraud. It also restricted the right for *amparo* or court injunction and thus upheld the amendment of 1931.

But the important legislative act of the period was the Agrarian Code of 1934, which not only synthesized the previous laws but also made significant new contributions. The relevant additions or amendments were roughly as follows: the Code limited the autonomy of the commissions by appointing representatives of the federal government to them and by shortening the period during which action on petitions could be completed. It abolished the political-status criterion of eligibility to petition for land. The only remaining requirement was that the group be a center of population, which also included the peones living on haciendas. The peones were not made unconditionally eligible, nor did the new law provide for breaking up haciendas. The peones, as "permanent resident laborers . . . on agricultural properties who occupy a house without paying rent and who depend for their living on the wages they receive for their services" could receive land under the following conditions:

119

I. Should there be vacant parcels in existing ejidos within a radius of ten kilometers from any point of the boundary lines of the property on which the particular "permanent laborers" are employed, and provided the needs of the centers of population have been fulfilled, such "permanent resident farm laborers" who so request shall be granted parcels of ground;

II. Should the agrarian cases referring to lands allocated within a radius of ten kilometers calculated in the manner set forth in the preceding Fraction be in course of proceedings, the "permanent laborers" who expressly petition the Agrarian Mixed Commission or the Census Board to be included in the census, may be included therein and become entitled to a parcel;

III. Should petitions for extensions of ejidos be in course of proceedings covering lands within a radius of ten kilometers, or should such cases be eligible for procedure in the terms of this Code, the "permanent laborers" who expressly so petition shall be entitled to consideration in the respective agrarian census.[55]

The only group that was excluded from the benefits of land redistribution was the tenants. Finally, the Code expanded the provisions for colonization of vacant land and increased the size of holding that could be acquired by the colonists.

Though the 1934 Agrarian Code was a great step forward in the history of reform in Mexico, it had limitations. It restricted the rights of the peones and it exempted haciendas from division. These limitations remained for President Cardenas to abolish in 1937 when he abolished Article 45 and made the peones automatically eligible for land distribution.[56]

Two more points should be mentioned: (1) The Agrarian Code was revised in 1942, guaranteeing the "inalienability of stock-breeding estates, with the purpose of protecting the country's stock-breeding industry, which was declining because the large ranch owners would not expand their undertakings for fear of losing the capital invested in livestock if their lands were affected by redistribution." [57] And (2), the movement for agrarian reform included legislation on labor relations. Article 123 of the Constitution regulated the relations between the worker and the employer, including agricultural workers, and set minimum wage limits. Thus, unlike previous reform movements, the Mexican reform took the agricultural worker into consideration, even though it created no revolutionary improvement in his conditions.

EFFECTS OF THE REFORM ON LAND TENURE

Half a century has passed since the Mexican Revolution and a little less than that since the first law on land tenure. During this period there has been a great change in the agrarian structure. The state has reasserted its right to absolute authority over the land, but private property has been maintained while, as well, the ejido system of tenure has been revived in a new form. Originally ejido meant common land. In the new structure this title has applied to two forms of villages: collective ejidos and individual ejidos. In the former, crop land as well as pastures and all other supplements are held and operated in common. Crop land in the latter is parceled out to the members and is operated individually by them, but the pastures and woodlands are held in common. However, in spite of these changes, a large number of people have remained landless.

In 1950 there were 1,365,633 private holdings and 1,378,326 *ejidatarios*.[58] The private holders held 11,137,395 hectares of the total crop land while the ejidos held 8,790,866 hectares or 44.1 per cent of all crop land. The distribution of ejido and private holdings according to farm size is shown in tables 18 and 19.

TABLE 18

DISTRIBUTION OF EJIDO CROP LAND HOLDINGS
ACCORDING TO SIZE; MEXICO, 1950

Size of holding (hectares)	Number of *ejidatarios*	Per cent of total
None	11,071	0.8
0–1	101,848	7.4
1–4	467,873	33.9
4–10	580,891	42.1
More than 10	216,643	15.7
Total	1,378,326	

SOURCE: Bradsher, *op. cit.*, from Table 18, pp. 214–215.

TABLE 19

DISTRIBUTION OF PRIVATE HOLDINGS OF CROP LAND
ACCORDING TO SIZE; MEXICO, 1950

Size in hectares	Number of holdings	Per cent	Total area (hectares)	Per cent
0–5	1,149,659	84.2	1,504,397	13.5
5.1–25	160,158	11.7	1,894,757	17.0
25.1–200	52,413	3.8	3,188,222	28.6
200.1–800	2,695	0.2	1,001,189	9.0
800 and over	708	0.05	3,548,830	31.9
Total	1,365,633	99.95	11,137,395	100

SOURCE: Bradsher, *op. cit.*, p. 187.

The distribution pattern apparent in these tables applies also to noncrop land, except that in the latter land has been more concentrated in larger units. This is shown in tables 20 and 21. Several conclusions may be drawn from these statistics:

1. The number of landowners in both the private and *ejidal* sectors has greatly increased. From less than 3 per cent of the agricultural popu-

TABLE 20

DISTRIBUTION OF TOTAL PRIVATE HOLDINGS
ACCORDING TO SIZE; MEXICO, 1950

Size of holding (hectares)	Number of holdings	Per cent of total
Under 1	498,399	36.5
1–5	506,436	37.1
5–10	90,213	6.6
10–25	101,112	7.4
25–50	59,523	4.4
50–100	43,290	3.2
100–200	27,795	2.0
200–500	20,932	1.5
500–1,000	7,414	0.5
1,000–5,000	4,335	0.5
5,000–10,000	1,523	0.1
Over 10,000	1,661	0.1

SOURCE: Bradsher, *op. cit.*, p. 185.

TABLE 21

DISTRIBUTION OF LANDHOLDINGS IN MEXICO, 1940, ACCORDING TO SIZE, EXCLUDING EJIDOS

Size (hectares)	Total holdings Number	Per cent of all Holdings	Per cent of all Private holdings	Area held (000 omitted)	Per cent of All private holdings	Per cent of Total land area
Under 1	497,372	17.6	76.2			0.1
1–5	431,221	15.3		1,157.3	1.1	0.7
5.1–10	74,187	2.6	12.8	1,969.5	1.9	0.4
10.1–25	82,013	2.9				1.0
25.1–50	46,466	1.7	3.8	1,742.5	1.7	1.3
50.1–100	31,763	1.1	2.6	2,374.9	2.4	1.8
100.1–200	22,695	0.8	3.3	9,041.8	9.0	2.6
200.1–500	17,428	0.6				4.4
500.1–1,000	6,087	0.2	0.5	4,455.4	4.4	3.4
1,000.1–5,000	6,883	0.2				12.0
5,000.1–10,000	1,342	0.1				7.5
10,000.1–20,000	751	0.02	0.8	79,747.0	79.5	8.2
20,000.1–40,000	420	0.01				9.2
Over 40,000	301	0.01				25.0
Total	1,218,929	43.2	100.0	100,488.4	100.0	77.6
Ejidatarios	1,601,392	56.8		28,921.7		22.4

SOURCE: Columns 2 and 3, from Whetten, *op. cit.*, Table 17, p. 592; column 5 from Whetten, Table 23, p. 177; columns 4, 6, and 7 from U.N., *Progress in Land Reform* . . . (1954), *op. cit.*, p. 39.

122

lation in 1910, the owners have increased to more than 50 per cent. The meaning of ownership has been modified, however, and many of the "new" owners may not be considered owners after all. This point will be discussed further below.

2. The increase in the number of owners has been accompanied by an expansion in the number of small holdings, many of which may be considered uneconomical and certainly below the size that permits mechanization. For example, 73.6 per cent of all owners own 5 hectares of land or less. The situation is even more striking with respect to crop land, of which 84.2 per cent of the owners have 5 hectares or less each, totaling only 13.5 per cent of the crop land or 1,504,397 hectares, and averaging not much more than one hectare per holding.

3. Land concentration may have been diminished, but it has nevertheless remained a common feature. In 1950 0.25 per cent of the owners of crop land owned about 40.9 per cent of all the crop land in farms greater than 200 hectares each. In 1940 less than 1 per cent of the holdings occupied about 79.5 per cent of all privately owned land. In contrast, 76.2 per cent of all private holders had 1.1 per cent of the land in the same year, as shown in table 21. This distribution pattern has not changed substantially since 1940. Since part of the ejido land came from public and uncultivated land, acquisition and distribution did not significantly reduce concentration of private ownership.

4. The fragmentation that had characterized private holdings remained a pronounced feature of the ejido crop land, since most of this land was parceled out and handed to individual members in small lots.

5. Total production declined and productivity per unit of land has been lower on ejido land than on private holdings.[59] These observations have been based on averages and do not give a complete picture. The differences in yield per acre have been attributed to, among other things, differences in size, degree of mechanization, credit facilities, type of land and fertility of the soil, and educational level of the population. Since mechanization, credit facilities, and education are usually associated with large farms, it is plausible to assume that partition of the land was at least partly responsible for the lower yield on ejidos. It has been observed more recently that a threefold rise has taken place in the last two decades, after the slump of the early years of reform, although productivity on ejido farms has remained lower than on private farms.[60]

EFFECTS ON SOCIAL CLASSES

The motto of the agrarians was land and liberty. The reform gave them a little of both without greatly altering social class differentiation. A small group of large owners, or a class of landlords, has survived side by side with a large class of agricultural laborers. The landless agricultural workers have diminished in numbers and the small owners have increased. If the small owners are classified as middle class, then it can be said that the reforms have created a middle class, even though members of ejidos did not become free owners. They depended on the village community for common pasture, woodland, and similar resources, and were restricted in choosing the crop they grew. The *ejidatario* was liberated from the yoke of landlordism only to submit to the authority of the ejido and the agrarian commission. His rights to the land were of usufruct only and both this and his title to the land were inalienable. In contrast, these restrictions did not apply to the private owners, who enjoyed the right of disposal over the land.

Finally, the reforms did nothing, nor alone could they have done anything, to alleviate racial differentiation of classes. The class structure remained virtually as it had been for a long time prior to the Revolution, in violation of the Constitution.

The effects of the reform on the class structure are suggested in table 22, which defines classes according to occupation. The lower class de-

TABLE 22

MEXICO: CHANGES IN CLASS STRUCTURE, 1895–1940

Social class	1895		1940		Proportional change
	Number	Per cent	Number	Per cent	
Total population	12,698,330	100.0	19,653,552	100.0	
Upper	183,006	1.44	205,572	1.05	−27.1
Urban	49,542	0.39	110,868	0.57	+46.2
Rural	133,464	1.05	94,704	0.48	−54.3
Middle	989,783	7.78	3,118,958	15.87	+104.0
Urban	776,439	6.12	2,382,464	12.12	+98.0
Rural	213,344	1.66	736,494	3.75	+125.9
Lower	11,525,541	90.78	16,329,022	83.08	−8.5
Urban	1,799,898	14.17	4,403,337	22.40	+58.1
Rural	9,725,643	76.61	11,925,685	60.68	−20.8

SOURCE: Senior, *op. cit.*, p. 41, from Jose E. Iturriaga, *La Estrutura Social y Cultural de Mexico*, pp. 28–30.

creased from 90.78 per cent of the population in 1895 to 83.08 per cent in 1940, or during almost half a century. The upper class declined from 1.44 to 1.05 per cent while the middle class doubled, rising from 7.78 to 15.87 per cent. However, the effect of this change in the class structure on the political structure has been limited, since the new middle class has remained small and the concentration of richness and poverty have persisted. And, inasmuch as democracy relates to the economic class structure, there seems to have been little change.

EVALUATION

(1) The Mexican reform has caused many changes in society. The social and economic status of many people, though still low, has improved considerably. Tenure has become a mixture of private and public, individual and collective ownership. The public authority over land and other natural resources has been formalized, but ownership has now become restricted to citizens: foreigners are allowed to hold property only conditionally.

Yet, these tenure changes have not been extensive and the major part of the land has remained in private hands. The ejido tenure has not been a creation of the revolution, and much of the land accruing to the ejidos has simply been restored to them. Nor has collective tenure been an innovation; some form of collectivism had existed among the Indians long ago. At the same time, the number and extent of collectives have remained relatively limited.

Some writers consider the change to be a social and agrarian revolution. Tannenbaum, for example, suggests that a whole new concept of property has emerged. The new concept is "flexible" and "can be made to mean many sorts of different things, and may be defined differently for different purposes," as these are conceived by public authority for public interest.[61] Even this conception of property is not new in Mexico, and certainly not outside it.[62] In summing up his evaluation, Tannenbaum says:

What Mexicans have established cannot be described as socialism or nationalization or communism, nor is it private property in the accepted use of that phrase. It is more inclusive than any one of these descriptions. The limitations already developed could perhaps be duplicated in American property law that has arisen in one or another form of the exercise of the police powers. But here all these forms co-exist on one equal basis and require no special justification or legal defense. They are all constitutional, and any other form that may be established by the legislature in the name of public interest will be equally constitutional within the concept contained in Article 27. This attitude toward property may perhaps be described as conditional ownership — ownership in a variety of forms existing side by side, limited in different ways, but meeting the general requirements of "public interest."[63]

Actually the Mexican conception of property is not so revolutionary as Tannenbaum implies. It is almost universal that private property may be alienated in the service of public interest. Furthermore, conditional ownership in Mexico is discriminatory in that it applies only to the ejidos, but not to private property. As conditional owners, the *ejidatarios* may be classified as perpetual holders or secure tenants paying no rent,[64] in contrast to the other tenure groups who enjoy the rights of operation and disposal of their property. Finally, the functional basis of ownership ap-

125

plied to the ejidos has not been generalized to all the agrarian population; many have remained absentee landlords, while about half the rural population is landless.

(2) A significant, though seemingly backward, change was the transformation of many large-scale, latifundia farms into tiny farms or minifundia; rather than consolidation of farms, there was fragmentation. This change theoretically has negative effects on production efficiency. The small size of the farm and the low level of techniques and standard of education of the peasant tended to keep his living standard at subsistence.

(3) The effect on agricultural production and efficiency was minor and little attention was paid to these problems by the reformers. Legal protection for efficient farms was introduced only two decades later and even then there was no hesitation in sidestepping the law and breaking up and redistributing these farms, especially during the term of Cardenas.[65] Therefore, productive efficiency suffered because of the reform. There was an apparent inverse relationship between extensive distribution of land and considerations of production: when production was taken into account, land distribution was limited and slow; when distribution was rapid, production became irrelevant. This phenomenon is apparent in comparing the periods before and after 1934. The methods of cultivation have not been modernized. There was no push for mechanization or supervision of agriculture. The smallness of the newly created farms might have obstructed such innovations. Even though total production has increased in the last two decades, the increase seems to stem from opening-up of new lands rather than from redistribution. In fact, the indications suggest that redistribution reduced both production and productivity on the reformed estates.

(4) The impact of the reform on political stability and the class structure or democracy has not been any more extensive than it was on agricultural production and efficiency.

Although it is true that there has been no major political upheaval or revolt in the agrarian sector since 1920, local uprisings and attempts to seize land have been recurrent until the present time. Actually some such attempts were almost mass movements and involved clashes with the troops on account of land.[66] It is difficult, therefore, to see how the reform has created political stability or augmented democracy — effects often attributed to it.[67] The apparent stability has probably been due to the fact that land tenure reform has come in strides over the whole period, thus appeasing the restive people in time to prevent their consolidation and uprising. The slow but continuing distribution may also have kept up the hope of many that they will yet be gratified. If so, then stability has prevailed as a temporary condition sustained primarily by hopeful expectations rather than by genuine accomplishments.

(5) Finally, the reform was slow in application and devoid of any

126

positive shock-effect on the economy or the polity. Unlike the French or the Soviet revolutions, the Mexican Revolution has spread the distribution over a long period and distribution has been interrupted several times.[68] Setbacks had to be overcome before reform could be resumed.[69] The peak year of distribution was 1937, more than twenty years after the first land tenure reform law was passed. In fact, up to 1934, except for the year 1929 when 1,850,532 hectares were distributed, all other years were of modest results.[70] In no other year during this period (1915–1934) did distribution amount to one per cent of the land of Mexico. The rate of distribution would seem more impressive, however, if measured in terms of crop land alone. Yet, the total crop land distributed was less than 25 per cent of all the land affected by reform.

The slow pace of reform stemmed from the ambiguity of the law toward the ejido, the red tape and complexity of executing the law, and from the attitude of the incumbent president. After many revisions, the law was still unclear regarding the status of the ejido in the economy, thus permitting hesitancy of implementation. Until the days of Cardenas, the ejido was considered a stepping-stone to private ownership, without a well-defined attitude toward it as an institution. This indefiniteness has been described as the "perhaps most serious of all weaknesses" of the Code.[71]

Another obstacle inherent in the Constitution, until 1933, was to allow the landlord to seek an injunction against expropriation. The differential influence of the landlord and his ability to delay action were well demonstrated in the case of San Juan and Ejido. The case extended over five years and the results were unsatisfactory to the peasants.[72] Up to December, 1928, the landlords had applied for injunction 5,500 times. In 1,800 of the 2,000 cases concluded the decision was favorable to them. Their right to seek injunction was

a most effective weapon for protecting themselves against the ejido. Indeed, the charge was freely made that the courts were sabotaging the land reform; that the president of the Republic would hand down a decision granting land to a village and a week later the courts would turn around and restore the land to the *hacendados* from whom it had been taken.[73]

The attitude of the incumbent president was at least a partial determinant of the rate of land distribution. Carranza obstructed execution of the law, but when the radical Cardenas became president, land distribution hit a record high. Cardenas also revised the law and reduced the restrictions on eligibility to petition for land. Lopez Mateos has also pushed redistribution since his election in 1958.[74]

Finally, the effects of the reform were limited by the fear of foreign intervention and by the landlords' right to choose the land they wanted to retain: "Fear of American intervention has prevented any attempts on general confiscation of the large estates." [75] The landlords' right to choose the land they retained meant that land for distribution was

secured only by nibbling at the edges of the large estates . . . [consequently] most of the land distributed by the revolutionary governments from 1915 to 1934 was poor land, badly located from the standpoint of either selling products or procuring supplies. . . . After fifteen years of land distribution, the 1930 census showed the agrarians in possession of only 9.9 per cent of the actual or potential farming land of the country.[76]

These limitations and obstructive measures were offset to some extent by peasant pressure for distribution. Without peasant pressure as a catalyst, it is doubtful that land tenure reform in Mexico would have been as extensive or more than just enough to pacify the peasants and recruit their political support.

IX

THE JAPANESE REFORM

The 1946 Japanese reform differs from the reforms studied so far in the following ways:

1. The Japanese reform was carried out under the pressure of an occupation army after the national forces had surrendered. Some have actually suggested that without this external pressure the reform probably would not have taken place. Of course, the reforming army did not act arbitrarily; it relied on experts representing an important school of thought on land tenure reform, predominant in the United States and most western nations. As long as the results were consistent with these western social and political ideals, the native reformers were free from all restriction.

2. It was the only reform carried out in a context of high literacy and industrialization and, except for the Egyptian reform, intensive cultivation. Even agriculture, though mechanized and characterized by extreme fragmentation of farm land and widely spread tenancy, was efficient in comparison with other agricultural societies in Asia and the Far East.

However, in common with other reforms, the Japanese experience took place in an environment of land concentration, aimed at wider ownership and paid compensation, and was limited by instances of reaction. It also tended to perpetuate private property and peasant family ownership. Finally, although primarily politically motivated, it paid at least formal attention to production and efficiency of cultivation which traditional reforms disregarded.

BACKGROUND: LAND TENURE

Since the beginning of the Meiji period in 1868, the Japanese land tenure system has consisted of private and public ownership, although the latter only on a small scale. In their attempt to abolish the feudal relations of the Tokugawa period, the Meiji government declared that "agricultural land was the property of the peasants."[1] Accordingly, the land was surveyed and title deeds issued to those recognized by custom to be in possession of land. All restrictions on land alienation were abolished and the institution of private property became firmly established.

However, the rule of custom created many disputes and deprived some farmers of the land they had been cultivating. Land held in common by the village was either seized by the rich peasants or confiscated by the state. Mortgagees were given title deeds, while hereditary tenants were often evicted or reduced to contractual tenancy. Consequently, a class of full-time tenants emerged, ranging from 20 to 30 per cent of all farmers, while another 35 per cent were part-time tenants.[2]

When the Meiji government instituted the new tenure relations, it replaced the feudal tax in kind with a money tax based on land value. The tax, 3 per cent at the beginning, was fixed independently of conditions and therefore was unfavorable to the small peasant owner who was susceptible to ruin in the event of crop failure. Many peasants fell into debt, mortgaged their land, and eventually lost it.

The new tenancy was characterized by a high rate of rent paid mostly in kind. It is estimated that in 1943 66 per cent of the cultivated area was held against rent in kind, averaging 48 per cent of the yield in rice paddies.[3] This high rental was another stimulus for tenancy, as the landowners found it more profitable to lease the land than to operate it. The tenant, on the other hand, could not escape the high rent because of population pressure on the land and high demand for it. Even government efforts to halt the growth of tenancy during the first quarter of this century were of no avail. By 1941 only 30 per cent of the cultivators owned their land in full, while 70 per cent were full or part-tenants, holding 46 per cent of the farm area.[4]

However, the trend was arrested when other factors prevailed. First, the increase in productivity during the last quarter of the nineteenth century, plus the increase in cultivated area, helped to raise the standard of living of both the owner and the tenant and thus reduced the danger of indebtedness. Second, the government extended credit facilities and encouraged coöperatives to help the small peasant. Finally, the depressing impact of rice imports, after the Rice Riots of 1918, on the profitability of the land reduced the incentive to acquire more land and lease it to tenants.[5]

Thus we find three major agrarian groups in Japan on the eve of the reform: "(1) those who owned and cultivated land, (2) those who cultivated but did not own land, and (3) those who owned but did not cultivate." [6] The relative strength of these groups may be seen from the figures in table 23.

Who were the landlords who leased their land to tenants? Accurate figures are not available, but one estimate suggests that in 1947 18 per cent of the tenanted land was owned by absentee landlords, another 24 per cent by resident noncultivating landlords, while the remaining 58 per cent was owned by owner-farmers.[7] The absentee landlords were sons of families who had moved to the city or elsewhere for jobs but had retained their land. Many of them were "officials and professors of agricultural economics who helped in the drafting of the Land Reform Bill." [8] Or they were merchants or moneylenders from towns and neighboring villages who bought the land from needy farmers. Finally, there was a small group of absentee landlords temporarily in that status, such as schoolteachers engaged in another village, or someone who had bought a piece of land to come back to on retirement.

The resident landlords comprised the "large-scale" owner, who earned

TABLE 23

TENURE GROUPS IN JAPAN BY HOUSEHOLD AND AREA OCCUPIED AS
PER CENT OF TOTAL[a]

Tenure status[b]	Per cent of households	Per cent of area occupied
Owners	32.0	54.2
Part-owners–Part-tenants	39.8	—
Tenants	28.2	45.8[c]
Total	100.0	100.0

[a] Hewes, "On the Current Readjustment . . .," *op. cit.*, p. 251.
[b] According to official classification, "owners are those who own at least 90 per cent of the land they cultivate; part-owners own between 50 and 90 per cent of the land they operate; part-tenants own less than 50 per cent and more than 10 per cent; and tenants own less than 10 per cent of the land they operate."
[c] Includes all land under tenant operation whether cultivated by tenant or part-owner.

enough rent to be free to devote himself to politics and financial activities, and the owner-cultivator. The latter let part of his land because he had more than could be worked by his family, or because his children were still too young to work.

In 1947, prior to the reform implementation, about 6 million families worked on an area of less than 6 million *cho* (1 *cho* = 10 *tan* = 2.45072 acres), or an average of about 2 acres per family,[9] often characterized by extreme fragmentation. As shown in table 24, 47.7 per cent of the owners owned less than one-half *cho* each, while 74.1 per cent owned less than 1 *cho* each. On the other hand, 33.6 per cent of the cultivators operated less than one-half *cho* each, while 63.6 per cent operated less than 1 *cho* each. In fact, these figures underestimate the degree of fragmentation, since there is no reason to believe that each of these farmers operated all his land in one plot.

Another important fact arises from table 24: land ownership as well as operation were concentrated in different degrees at the upper end of the distribution curve. Those owning three or more *cho* comprised 7.4 per cent of all owners and owned 43.4 per cent of all agricultural land. Operators of three or more *cho* comprised 9.6 per cent of the cultivators but controlled 33.6 per cent of the agricultural land. The concentration of ownership and operation reflected the differential distribution of power, which in turn had an important impact on the nature of the subsequent reform, its time, and its effects.

Finally, a significant feature of the prereform period was the high demand for land and the high rent which often caused antagonism between landlord and tenant. The conflict of interest between them led to the con-

TABLE 24

ESTIMATES OF LAND DISTRIBUTION IN JAPAN BY SCALE
OF OWNERSHIP AND OPERATION *
(In percentages, 1941–1945)

Size	Ownership		Operation	
(cho)	Owners	Area	Households	Area
0.0–0.5	47.7	14.7	33.6	9.5
0.5–1.0	26.4	17.1	30.0	21.2
1.0–3.0	18.6	24.9	26.8	35.7
3.0–5.0	4.4	14.4	6.1	13.9
5.0–10.0	2.1	12.6	2.2	7.7
10.0–50.0	0.8	12.1	0.9	6.2
Over 50.0	0.1	4.2	0.4	5.8

* Hewes, "On the Current Readjustment . . . ," op. cit., p. 250.

solidation of each of the two groups as social classes opposed to each other. Their conflicting interests were represented by landlord and tenant unions, which reached a peak in 1933, numbering 4,810 tenant and 686 landlord unions.[10]

BACKGROUND: SOCIAL CLASSES

Before the Meiji restoration of 1868, Japan had a fairly rigid class structure. At the top was the Imperial Family, followed by the Samurai or warrior class, the farmers, the artisans, and the merchants, and at the bottom were the pariahs and immigrants.[11] Formally the restoration destroyed this structure, leaving two classes only: the nobility (kazoku) and the commoners (heimin). However, the previous stratification left a great impression on social relations long after its formal abolition. At the same time, the transition to an industrial and commercial economic system changed the criteria of class status and made social mobility possible. Birth origin no longer determined class status except for the nobility.

In general, length of residence in an area, economic conditions, and social status were correlated. Taking into consideration these factors, plus the ethnic and birth origins, Embree divided the pre-reform Japanese society roughly into the following social classes: [12] an upper class comprising (a) the Imperial Family whose members were not allowed to participate actively in any economic or political activity; (b) the hereditary nobility who exerted great influence in the affairs of government; and (c) the big business families who as a class included older financial and commercial families and the new big industrialists. "Behind the scenes these families have influenced not only the political parties but also certain army cliques." Yet, in view of the traditional distrust of financiers and money-makers, this group found it necessary to contribute generously to social services and research projects, as well as to the army to allay criticism and maintain their position.

The middle class included: (a) the upper middle class, or the businessmen and industrialists who engaged mostly in foreign trade and manufacturing for export, and some civil servants or new rich; (b) the white-collar workers and professions; and (c) a new group of technicians who had acquired importance in recent years. The peasantry was looked upon with an attitude of patronage as the class of virtue and dedication. Their status in society was below the urban classes mentioned above, but above the urban workers and the submerged minorities or *eta* class of outcasts.

These same classes featured on the local scene; each town and village had its own class structure which ran roughly in the same order. The landowning group, for example, was on top of the hierarchy in every village and controlled the political and social affairs of the community. However, except for the nobility and the *eta* or outcast group, mobility was possible, especially through the medium of business and wealth.

As usual, these classes were not homogeneous. The landowners did not act as a united group. The bigger owners were either of the older hierarchy or big business and financial people, both deriving influence from sources other than land. It was this group, rather than the landowners in general, that was in conflict with the tenants. The conflict was usually intensified in periods of bad harvest and when the tenants requested reduction of rent, as happened after the First World War. Antagonism also reflected tenant attitude to idleness of many of the rentier landlords, who showed no sympathy toward their tenants. The conflict of interest between landlord and tenant was well expressed by the mushrooming of their respective unions, as table 25 shows.

The tenants requested a general reduction of rents by 30 per cent — a demand greatly intensified in 1923. In response, the landlords evicted some of them from the land, which induced the tenant unions to seek greater security of tenancy.[18] The degree of tenant restiveness and the number of disputes were closely associated with the rise and decline of political organization, and with encouragement by intellectual leaders and left-wing groups, including the communists who demanded nationalization of all the land. Interestingly enough, when in 1928 the communists were suppressed, the number of disputes declined (to 1,866 from the previous year's 2,053). The government tried to reform the tenant-landlord relationship, but its efforts were thwarted by the landlords' influence, especially in the House of Peers. It passed the Tenancy Conciliation Law

133

in 1924 to control disputes and in 1926 it enacted the Regulations for the Establishment of Owner-Farmers as an expansion of a previous Post Office Insurance Fund giving long-term loans to encourage land purchase.[14]

The government, however, also resorted to repression of the radical groups. On the local level, "police frequently intervened in disputes, sometimes with an objective fair-mindedness which operated to the tenant's

TABLE 25

NUMBERS OF DISPUTES AND TENANT, LANDLORD, AND
CONCILIATION UNIONS, JAPAN, 1917–1941 *

Year	Tenant unions	Landlord unions	Conciliation unions	Disputes
1917				85
1918				256
1919				326
1920				408
1921	681	192	85	1,680
1922	1,114	247	176	1,578
1923	1,530	290	347	1,917
1924	2,337	414	542	1,532
1925	3,496	532	1,371	2,206
1926	3,926	605	1,491	2,751
1927	4,582	734	1,703	2,053
1928	4,353	695	1,909	1,866
1929	4,156	655	1,986	2,434
1930	4,208	640	1,980	2,478
1931	4,414	645	2,047	3,419
1932	4,650	662	2,098	3,414
1933	4,810	686	2,309	4,000
1934	4,390	633	2,219	4,828
1935	4,011	531	1,748	6,824
1936	3,915	513	2,878	6,804
1937	3,879	497	2,849	6,170
1938	3,643	473	3,158	4,615
1939	3,509	474	3,152	3,578
1940	1,029	304	4,025	3,165
1941	293	144	764	3,308

* Extracted from Dore, *Land Reform in Japan, op. cit.*, Table 2, p.72.

advantage, but generally there is no doubt that their powers were mobilized in the landlord's interest." [15] In retrospect, it seems that peasant violence was prevented only by police action.

The conflict over tenure was aggravated by the depression of the early 'thirties. The tenants, the small owners, and the small owner-farmers were hit so severely that the broader rural problem overshadowed that of tenancy. Now the conflict was between the "peasants as a whole on the one hand, and 'the towns,' 'the capitalists,' and 'the Government' on the other." [16] Again the government tried to alleviate grievances by construction work, creation of agricultural coöperatives, stabilization of agricultural prices, and direct relief to the debtors. The most successful measure was the creation of owner-farmers, but even this was of limited effect; it helped to transfer 86,000 *cho* or one-thirtieth of the tenanted land to owners between 1926 and 1936. Up to the end of the war the landlords were able to obstruct the passage of laws of reform.

The 1930's were important for the peasants because in this period they found an ally in the army. This army–peasant alliance had a scissors' effect: on one hand it silenced the peasants by recruiting their nationalistic sentiments; on the other, it emboldened the rebellious elements in the army against governments, political parties, and the House of Peers.[17] Thus when national mobilization started in 1939, the farm problem receded into the background and all symptoms of instability were suppressed. Rents were frozen by the Rent Control Order of that year. The Land Control Order of 1941 regulated prices and land use to guarantee maximum food production. In 1943 an administrative order amended the Agricultural Land Adjustment Law to promote owner-farmers, but the voluntary character of this scheme rendered it ineffective and left the land system as it had been for a long time.[18]

In retrospect, it seems that the instability and crises of the 1930's and even the war might have been partly due to tenure relations. The Japanese expansion overseas has been attributed to: (1) population pressure on the land; (2) lack of an adequate domestic market; (3) the desire to divert attention from domestic problems; (4) the fact that the army found support for its expansionist policy in the distress of the peasants; (5) the social structure of the village and the authority of the landlord which were congenial for the development of totalitarianism; and (6) poverty which breeds aggression.[19] More explicitly, it has been suggested that "fascism in Japan is related to the struggle which arose between the landlords and the tenants of that country as the latter began to dissolve their feudal duties following World War I, and to the vigorous opposition of the landlords to proposed programs of reconstruction."[20] Although it is impossible to test their validity, these hypotheses seemed logical enough for the Allied Powers to justify land tenure reform directly after Japan surrendered.

THE PROCESS OF REFORM

The farm problem, which lay dormant for a while, erupted again around the end of the war. Food shortages and breakdown of the city economy brought some of the absentee landlords back to the villages, where they hoped to secure food and alleviate their business hardships. Their only outlet was to evict their tenants and settle on the land, which they attempted by ruthless methods while the authorities were too busy to maintain order.[21] This conflict, triggered by the war, brought the broader land issue back into prominence and emphasized the need for reform. Yet there is no assurance that the Japanese would have carried out a reform without outside pressure [22] or for the sake of the peasants. Reform was assured only when the Occupation Army conceived a relationship between the Japanese political and expansionist policies and the land tenure systems. The reform was ordered as a preventive against new expansionist policies, as shown by the Army directives discussed below.

The philosophy of the postwar reform, then, was not indigenous. It was imported and foreign to the country. The theory was that small peasant farming in place of the prevalent tenant-landlord system would help democratize the community and stabilize its political system. Some Japanese groups believed in that philosophy, but such was not the attitude of the majority or of the government.

Soon after Japan's surrender the government hinted at the need for reform, a gesture that received wide support from the press, both at home and abroad. It is not known whether the Japanese authorities had really wanted reform or whether they took the initiative to forestall reform by the Occupation Army. The latter possibility has been suggested on the assumption that an imposed program would be more far-reaching than a self-imposed one and more damaging to Japanese national pride. Even the landlords preferred an internally sponsored reform to one imposed from the outside.[23]

Whatever the reason, the Japanese government drafted a reform bill providing for (1) the commutation of rent in kind to a lower rate of money rent, (2) the compulsory transfer of absentee landlord holdings to the cultivators and the establishment of a limit on the size of individual holding at 3 *cho*, and finally (3) the reorganization of land committees to administer the transfer with equal representation of landlords and tenants. This bill, however, was not accepted by the cabinet until the maximum limit was raised from 3 to 5 *cho*.[24]

The bill passed the Diet on December 9, 1945, but on the same day it was rejected by the Supreme Commander of the Allied Powers (SCAP). The SCAP message embodied both the philosophy and the concrete objectives of what the land reform should be. Among other things the memorandum said:

In order that the Imperial Japanese Government shall remove economic obstacles to the revival and strengthening of democratic tendencies, establish respect for the dignity of man, and destroy the economic bondage which has enslaved the Japanese farmer to centuries of feudal oppression, the Japanese Imperial Government is directed to take measures to insure that those who till the soil of Japan shall have more equal opportunity to enjoy the fruits of their labor.

. . . .

The purpose of this order is to exterminate those pernicious ills which

136

have long blighted the agrarian structure of a land where almost half the total population is engaged in husbandry.[25]

The memorandum enumerated the "ills" as intense overcrowding of the land; widespread tenancy under conditions highly unfavorable to tenants; a heavy burden of indebtedness combined with high rates of interest on farm loans; government fiscal policies which discriminate against agriculture in favor of industry and trade; and authoritative government control over farmers and farm organizations without regard for farmer interests. The government was ordered to submit on or before March 15, 1946, a program which

. . . shall contain plans for:

a. Transfer of land ownership from absentee land owners to land operators.

b. Provisions for purchase of farm lands from non-operating owners at equitable rates.

c. Provisions for tenant purchase of land at annual installments commensurate with tenant income.

d. Provisions for reasonable protection of former tenants against reversion to tenancy status. Such necessary safeguards should include:

    (1) Access to long and short term farm credit at reasonable rates.

    (2) Measures to protect the farmer against exploitation by processors and distributors.

    (3) Measures to stabilize prices of agricultural produce.

    (4) Plans for the diffusion of technical and other information of assistance to the agrarian population.

    (5) A program to foster and encourage an agricultural cooperative movement free of domination by non-agrarian interests and dedicated to the economic and cultural advancement of the Japanese farmer.[26]

The Japanese authorities had no choice but to comply. The directive of SCAP required a comprehensive "agrarian reform" rather than the conservative and narrow program of the government. The original bill had intended to maintain the social structure of the village community with a few modifications; in contrast, the SCAP order had one central purpose: "destruction of feudal social relations in Japanese villages and removal of agricultural production as an element of economic support of the political power of autocratic government." [27]

After deliberation the Diet passed a second reform law on October 21, 1946, partly as an amendment to the Agricultural Land Adjustment Law of 1938, and partly in a separate Owner-Farmer Establishment Special Measures Law. The new reform law provided that:

1. The government should buy the land defined by this law and resell it to the tenants and those who would devote all their energies to cultivation.

2. The government should compensate the landlords for the land sur-

rendered at a price calculated according to prewar levels, to be paid in cash and bonds within thirty years at a rate of interest of 3.6 per cent.

3. Recipients of land should fully reimburse the government.

4. The remaining tenancy should be protected by a written contract and the restriction of rent to cash payments not exceeding 25 per cent of the product.

5. Land transfer should be administered by Land Committees, the most important of which were the town and village committees. Each committee should consist of five tenants, three landlords, and two owner-farmers. The Prefectural Land Committee should be elected by the town and village committees, in the same proportion as the other committees. Finally, a Central Land Committee as the general policy-making body should be formed consisting of eight tenants, eight landlords, two representatives of peasant unions, and five university professors.

The land subject to purchase was defined as:

All the land of absentee landowners, the latter being defined as landlords who did not have their place of normal residence within the same town or village as the land in question or within such areas of neighboring towns or villages as may be designated by the Village (or Town) Land Committee.

. . . .

All tenanted land owned by resident landlords in excess of 4 *cho* in Hokkaido and an average of 1 *cho* in the rest of Japan . . . plus such additional land as to bring the total holding of leased and cultivated land to a total of not more than 12 *cho* in Hokkaido and an average of 3 *cho* . . . in the rest of Japan.

. . . .

All land cultivated by the owner in excess of 12 *cho* in Hokkaido and an average of 3 *cho* . . . . for the rest of Japan, where it was considered by the Land Committee that the holding was "not of appropriate (size) for cultivation."

. . . .

Any uncultivated land suitable for cultivation that was needed, in the view of the Prefectural Land Committees, for the expansion of existing holdings or the settlement of new farmers.

. . . .

Other residential land, building, or grass land, rented by a tenant and necessary to his livelihood as an owner-farmer, at the discretion of Village and Prefectural Land Committees and on the specific request of the tenant himself.[28]

The land thus redistributed should be inalienable, but this was modified by Cabinet Order No. 288 of September 11, 1950, to permit land transaction subject to size restriction. Land prices also were decontrolled.[29]

The restriction on land transaction was intended as a preventive against resurgence of the tenant-land system. For further prevention and to protect the farmer's income, the government promoted extension programs and credit facilities. It also encouraged formation of credit and marketing coöperatives.[30]

EFFECTS OF THE REFORM

By August, 1950, a total of 1,337,000 *cho* of rice land and 796,000 *cho* of upland had been bought from 2,341,000 landlords and sold to 4,748,000 tenants. Owner-cultivated land was expanded from 46.9 per cent of the total in 1941 to 55.9 per cent in 1947, and to 88.9 per cent in 1950. Similarly, the upland cultivated by the owners increased from 62.7 per cent of the total in 1941 to 66.5 per cent in 1947, and to 91.2 per cent in 1950. In contrast, tenant-cultivated land decreased from 53.1 per cent of the total rice land to 10.9 per cent; and the upland tenant-cultivated land decreased from 37.2 per cent in 1941 to 8.5 per cent of the total in 1950.[31] These effects are shown in table 26.

However, the reform reduced the average farm size and thus increased fragmentation and the number of tiny holdings. Though the statistics on this are not adequate, the trend is beyond doubt, as indicated in table 27. Operating units under 1 *cho* increased from 63.3 per cent to 72.3 per cent between 1941 and 1954. Those above 3 *cho* — the maximum size allowed by law outside Hokkaido — decreased from 3.5 per cent to 2.3 per cent of all operating units.[32]

There are no data on equalization of ownership by the reform, but it is presumed that equality of ownership was increased by spreading the distribution and reducing the average size of the unit of ownership.[33] According to Dore, the reform has leveled incomes in the village enough to change the power structure. The owner group became strong enough to "set the pace" for the whole community. This group, which now ranges from 10 per cent to more than half the village households, dominates the Parent-Teacher Association and sets the standard for the rest.[34]

The reform also raised the farmers' income. The total family real income rose from an index of 100 in 1934–1936 to 144 in 1955, owing partly to the reform and partly to a rise in the real income from nonagricultural employment. While nonagricultural income rose from an index 100 to 260 between 1934–1936 and 1955, agricultural income rose only to 118.[35] This differential change reflects the growing importance of the nonagricultural sector of the economy and the decline of the agricultural sector. In the postreform period, agricultural income has progressively formed a smaller percentage of the national income, declining from 31.1 per cent in 1946 to 16.0 per cent in 1953, but rising again to 16.4 per cent in 1954 and 17.1 in 1955.[36]

An increase in productivity per acre has been particularly evident in the production of rice. The yield of rice was 80 *koku* in 1955 compared

TABLE 26

COMPARATIVE DISTRIBUTION OF FARMERS BY TITLE STATUS, JAPAN, 1941–1955
(In 1,000's of households)

Status	Aug. 1, 1941		Aug. 1, 1947		Feb. 1, 1950		Feb. 1, 1955	
Owner-operator	1,711	(31.2%)	2,157	(36.5%)	3,822	(61.8%)	4,199	(69.5%)
Owner-tenant	1,139	(20.7%)	1,183	(20.0%)	1,591	(25.7%)	1,308	(21.6%)
Tenant-owner	1,100	(20.0%)	997	(16.0%)	411	(6.7%)	285	(4.7%)
Tenant farmer	1,527	(27.7%)	1,574	(26.6%)	312	(5.1%)	239	(4.0%)
Other	24	(0.4%)	1	(0.0%)	41	(0.7%)	11	(0.2%)
Total	5,499	(100.0%)	5,909	(100.0%)	6,176	(100.0%)	6,043	(100.0%)

SOURCE: "Orientation of Farmland," *Oriental Economist*, 25 (1957), 462.
NOTE: "Other" means, up to 1947, nonoperating farm households (owners); and after 1950, those whose acreage worked is neither rented nor owned in excess of 50 per cent.

with 71 *koku* in 1933, climatic conditions being comparable. Yet this increase in per-acre productivity has been accompanied by a decline in productivity per man on the farm because of "increased intensity of labor input due to the post-war inflation of the agricultural population." [37] The rise in productivity has resulted from better utilization of land, use of

TABLE 27

DISTRIBUTION OF FARM LAND ACCORDING TO SIZE OF HOLDING,
JAPAN, 1941–1954
(Percentages)

Size bracket	1941	1946	1949	1950	1954
Under 5 *tan*	33.3	39.2	43.0	36.1	39.8
5 *tan*–1 *cho*	30.0	31.3	31.1	30.9	32.5
1 *cho*–2 *cho*	26.7	23.5	20.8	24.5	22.1
2 *cho*–3 *cho*	6.1	3.7	3.2		3.4
3 *cho*–5 *cho*	2.2	1.4	1.2	8.5	1.5
More than 5 *cho*	1.3	0.8	0.7		0.8

SOURCE: Dore, *Land Reform in Japan, op. cit.*, p. 181, except the 1950 column which is taken from "Farmland Status," *Oriental Economist*, 23 (1955), 400. Figures from Dore do not total 100 because owners not cultivating the land are excluded (e.g., apiarists and livestock breeders).

fertilizer and other extension services. It is hard to say how much credit for these improvements should be given to a change of land tenure. Some have concluded that the reform had no effect on efficiency of production, nor was any intended.[38]

SOCIOPOLITICAL EFFECTS OF THE REFORM

A major objective of the reform was to "democratize" the village and the community. The success or failure of the reform in that respect is extremely difficult to measure. Japan had just come out of a war in which it was defeated. Life was disorganized and the social structure had proved a failure, and there is no way of telling what form reconstruction would have taken had there been no reform. Finally, the policy towards democratization consisted of other measures in addition to the land tenure program. Agrarian reform was not even the major effort in that direction. By introducing the Local Autonomy Law in 1947, SCAP hoped to decentralize the power structure, increase autonomy, and thus change the political structure of the locality, but this was not agrarian reform.

Nevertheless, the land tenure reform was sociopolitically effective in several ways: (1) It elevated the social status of most of the tenants to that of owners, thus eliminating the gap between the two tenure groups, owners and tenants. (2) The reform made the village the source of its own power, since absentee landlords no longer existed and only those in the village could interfere in village affairs. The total amount of power in which the new owners could share became larger. (3) The reform under-

mined the influence of the former landlord group and weakened the rigidity of the social structure which obstructed social mobility.

These were the formal results of the land distribution program, but the
actual leveling of social classes brought about by the reform may easily
be exaggerated. The gain to the former tenants was not all loss to the landlords in terms of prestige and influence. Only the absentee landlords lost
all their land. Resident landlords outside of Hokkaido could keep up to
3 *cho*, one of which might be tenanted. But not many had that much to
begin with and even those left with only 3 *cho* were still wealthier and
higher on the economic scale than the new owners. Thus, though social
differentiation between owner and tenant has been destroyed, a new type
of differentiation has taken its place: that between the owners of the tiny
holdings of less than 1 *cho* and those of more. That the tenants have become owners does not mean that conflict between owners has been controlled, since there is still a high degree of differentiation among them.
Emergence of the new owners did not submerge the former influential
groups, most of whom remained owners of more than the average new
owner-holding. If this analysis is correct, the land tenure reform seems
to have been of limited effect on the class structure and, if that structure
has indeed been changed, the primary causes must be sought outside the
reform.

Empirical observations may shed some light on this problem. As Dore
has observed, the former landlord group has not been destroyed. Since
the road to local power was now open to all inhabitants, the former landlords had advantages over the new owners. Their background in administration, their traditional influence, better education, and higher economic power gave them more than their proportional share of power and
allowed them to retain much of their traditional influence. Dore's view is
that the "ex-landlords, then, still have the cards stacked in their favor,
but this is not to say that they can exercise anything like their prewar
dominance." [39] This implies that inasmuch as economic differentiation remains the basis of class differentiation, the land tenure reform's effect
was insufficient to change the class structure considerably.

EVALUATION

Three questions may be asked in evaluating the reforms: (1) What are
the formal tenure changes caused by the reform? (2) How smooth was
the process of reform? And (3) what are the prospects for these changes
to be permanent and lasting?

(1) In terms of our classificatory scheme, land tenure has continued
to be private and individual. Even where coöperation has evolved, it has
been only in marketing, processing, and credit, and not in ownership or
operation of the land. These reforms affected the tenure of individual

owners by changing their status from tenants to owners within the institutional tenure arrangements that had prevailed prior to the reform.

By restricting land transaction, the Japanese reform restricted the right of ownership. However, the restrictions on who buys the land and how much may be bought guarantee only that the buyer does not come out with a holding larger than the legal maximum. In a sense, this limitation affects the buyer rather than the owner or seller of the land. Land ownership in fee simple has remained the effective tenure arrangement in Japan.

(2) Superficially, the land tenure reform program has been implemented rapidly and smoothly. No sooner had the land committees been formed than land purchase and resale got underway. There was no violence either in the application or in the attempts to obstruct the reform. This does not mean that the landlords were happy with the program or willing to adopt it without resistance. Though they knew that there was nothing they could do in face of the determination of the occupation forces, they were not passive in their submission. They reacted in several ways.

First, they tried to intercept the reform effects before the reform laws were enacted, by drafting and passing a bill much less extensive than the one finally passed. Second, they challenged the legality of land redistribution through the courts, where their success was considerable. In 1949, for example, they were able to recover 53,000 acres from their tenants and prevent their redistribution. In other cases they kept the land by intimidating their tenants and in that same year they were able to retain 196,000 acres and thus prevent their redistribution.[40]

Third, the landlords could enforce their will against the tenants by making use of their economic power. They could confer favors by allowing them to use their forest and pasture lands which were excluded from reform. Finally, they were able to influence the land commissions by promoting the election of conservative members. As a result the landlords kept the best land and have managed to sell much of the rest to tenants they approved of. Sometimes they kept the land by avoiding its registration, or by subdividing it formally among relatives.[41] However, their most effective weapon was to evict the tenants from at least part of the land, take up farming, and thus escape expropriation. When this was done by agreement, it was legal. However, the tenant often found it difficult to oppose the landlord, in which case also there was no dispute, and eviction was concluded peacefully. According to estimates of the Ministry of Agriculture, during a period of ten months after the end of the war there were 250,000 cases of landlords trying to reclaim land from their tenants, of which only 23,000 cases were disputed.[42] Even disputed cases often ended favorably for the landlord, especially when the case remained in the hands of the local land committees and did not reach the Prefectural Governor. Between November, 1946, and December, 1949, the local committees dealt with 305,601 petitions by landlords to repossess their land from tenants, and in 261,999 cases, or 86 per cent of the total, the petitions were approved and only 14 per cent were rejected. When reviewed by the Prefectural Governor, only 162,380 approvals or 53 per cent were sustained, 92,735 or 30 per cent reversed, and 50,486 cases or 17 per cent left pending.

These figures show that local committees were biased in favor of the landlords. The SCAP found it necessary to deal with this problem in a memorandum on February 4, 1948. After reiterating the objectives of the reform laws passed until then, the memorandum reminded the Japanese Government that "since the enactment of these land reform laws . . . efforts have been made by certain adversely affected interests to obstruct the accomplishment of the rural land reform program." Therefore, the Government was directed that

a. The Ministry of Agriculture and Forestry will instruct prefectural and local agricultural land commissions to purchase without delay all land subject to Land Reform Law in accordance with existing procedures and without regard to unauthorized action by pressure organizations seeking to impede the objective of the Land Reform Program.
b. The Japanese Government will take prompt and vigorous action against any and all persons who, by bribery, intimidation or other unlawful means, obstruct the implementation of land reform measures. Reports of such actions will be submitted to this headquarters.[44]

The attempts to evade the law helped to reduce the amount of land available for redistribution and to maintain a larger number of owners of maximum size than otherwise would have been the case.

There has also been reaction in the form of reversal. After land sale was made permissible in 1950, the smaller owners tended to sell their land to the larger owners. This trend has been disturbing to some elements in the community, since it suggests reëmergence of a powerful landed class. First observed in the early 'fifties, this tendency has continued on a larger scale through the late 'fifties.

Between February 1, 1950, and February 1, 1954, the group of small holders of less than 3 *tan* [10 *tan* = 1*cho*] decreased from 20.3 per cent of total households to 17.1 per cent of total owner households. In contrast, those owning from 5 *tan* to 1 *cho* increased from 30.9 per cent to 32.4 per cent, those of 1–1.5 *cho* from 16.9 per cent to 18.1 per cent, and the owners of 1.5–2 *cho* from 7.6 per cent to 8.0 per cent. But those owning more than 2 *cho* remained constant.[45] Finally, while the area operated by tenant farmers has been diminishing, "bigger acquisition of farm land by the upper-class owner-operators" has been increasing. In fact, recent government efforts have been directed to save the achievements of the reform and combat those contrary tendencies, although they seem to reflect production and efficiency requirements.[46]

An equally disturbing tendency has been the widespread incidence of "black market" rates of rent in view of the rent control. "A nationwide survey of rice paddies conducted in 1953 by the Hypothec Bank revealed that of the 2,599 cases investigated 1,049 (40 per cent) involved black-market rentals for tenant holdings." [47]

(3) As for the permanence of the reform,[48] we should remember that the reform was imposed by outside forces and therefore might be susceptible to rejection and its results to reversal as soon as those outside forces withdrew. Its permanence is also threatened by four other factors. (a) Its discriminatory character, in that it favored certain former owners over others, according to the size of their holdings and the use to which they had put the land. Regardless of its justification, the rationale behind this action has yet to be accepted by the people concerned. (b) The contradiction inherent in restricting the size of holding contrary to the rule of economic forces in the economy. Although tenure is individual and private, the farmer is prevented from complying with efficiency implications. He is frustrated by the inability to increase his holdings for mechanization, investment, or more income. Why should the landlord accept this system and lend support to its legitimacy? As a corollary, the law controlling rent runs counter to the traditions of a *laissez-faire* economy, which the reform tried to promote. Rent is not permitted to reflect the conditions of the land market. (c) The fact that the land tenure reform law does not have a counterpart in the industrial and commercial sectors. This discriminatory feature might be of importance should the landowners attempt to reverse the reform effects. This, however, has not been openly attempted yet. (d) The relatively low per capita income of the rural population which is necessarily a destabilizing factor in an industrialized economy. While more than 33 per cent of the total population — 33,600,000 in Japan proper — were in 1955 occupied in agriculture,[49] agricultural income comprised only 17.1 per cent of the national income in that year. The per capita farm income is depressed by underemployment and insufficient mechanization and hence low labor productivity. It is hard to estimate how long a literate community will tolerate these conditions, but there is no theoretical basis why they should accept them permanently. Yet, this is what the reform has demanded of them.

Finally, it may be difficult to tell whether political democracy and stability have fundamentally been promoted by the reform. The tendency of tenure changes in the postreform period has been in the opposite direction, but this tendency is part of a slow process which needs more time before meaningful conclusions may be drawn. The reform effects on class relations and differentiation have not been extensive; the former landlord group is still privileged and yet they continue to strive for further rehabilitation. In the current session of the Diet a bill was introduced to recompensate former landlords for losses suffered in the reform.[50]

As far as tenure change is concerned, the new structure is inherently unstable because it generates conflict between the economic forces of a capitalistic economy without providing the necessary checks and balances to contain that conflict. Whether attitudes have changed enough to eliminate the need for these checks and whether the new structure has acquired legitimacy can only be seen by allowing the system more time to unveil itself.

X

THE EGYPTIAN REFORM

The Egyptian reform was initiated after the revolution of 1952, but the law has since been modified and the area subject to reform expanded. Since the reform is still in the process of implementation, its evaluation can only be tentative, particularly in that some observers think it will be modified again before consummation. This reform has been the most comprehensive in scope outside the socialist countries, touching on all aspects of the agrarian structure. In fact, among the nonsocialist reforms it was the first to pay attention to the impact of the scale of operation on the efficiency of production. To cope with these problems, an integral part of the reform has been the creation of agricultural producer coöperatives. Being applied to a land system characterized by intensive cultivation and high land productivity, the reform was concerned not nearly so much with increasing production as it was with preventing the possible negative effects of land distribution on the efficiency of cultivation.

Another unique feature of the Egyptian reform was the role it played as part of a comprehensive effort to secure political independence from foreign occupation. The reform policy derived much support from the unifying sentiment of nationalism and opposition to the foreign armies. This observation may partially account for the rapid and highly efficient execution of the reform.

Otherwise, the reform followed a standard pattern: redistribution into small holdings of a limited land area which had little effect on the pattern of land distribution; compensation for requisitioned land; differential treatment of tenure groups and restriction of the rights of the new owners; and extension services within the framework of coöperatives in which membership was made mandatory upon all land recipients. It regulated tenancy and rents to protect the tenant and raise his living standard. And, like many other reforms, it had limited effects because of reaction in different forms. Finally, though the reform had long-term objectives, its results seemed to be primarily of a short-term social and political nature.

BACKGROUND: LAND TENURE

Immediately preceding the 1952 revolution,[1] Egypt had two main types of tenure: private and *wakf* (mortmain), while some unreclaimed land

147

was held by the state. The *wakf* land was either charitable or *ahli* (private), and both were under the supervision of trustees and the Ministry of *Wakf*. *Wakf* land was inalienable and the beneficiaries had control over the product only.[2] The restriction on alienation and the limited control over *wakf* land have often been considered handicaps in the way of improving the land or revolutionizing its cultivation. This applies especially to the *ahli wakf* whose product usually reverted to many beneficiaries, reducing the share of each to very small amounts.[3]

The private land was owned individually without any restrictions on the right of disposal and was operated by owners, tenants, or by subtenants. However, the land concentration and the high population density rendered landless 16.5 million of the approximately 19 million people in 1948.[4] About one million landless laborers lived in the rural areas, and half the landowners did not earn from their land enough for subsistence and had to supplement their income with other occupations. The pattern of land distribution is represented in table 28.

TABLE 28

LAND DISTRIBUTION BY SIZE OF HOLDING, EGYPT, 1950 *

Size of holding (*feddan*)	Number of owners	Percentage of total †	Area held (*feddan*)	Percentage of total †	Average size (*feddan*) †
1 or less	1,981,343	71.77	780,046	13.08	0.30
1–5	618,860	22.41	1,324,030	22.20	2.14
5–10	80,019	2.89	531,024	8.90	6.46
10–20	46,123	1.67	626,700	10.51	13.59
20–30	13,073	0.47	313,078	5.25	23.95
30–50	9,356	0.338	351,577	5.89	37.58
50–100	6,575	0.238	445,111	7.46	67.70
100–200	3,194	0.115	436,403	7.31	136.69
200–400	1,350	0.049	362,317	6.07	268.31
400–600	344	0.012	164,445	2.75	478.04
600–800	141	0.005	98,430	1.65	698.08
800–1,000	92	.0.003	82,673	1.38	898.62
1,000–1,500	99	0.004	122,216	2.04	1,234.51
1,500–2,000	28	0.001	47,454	0.79	1,694.79
More than 2,000	61	0.002	277,258	4.64	4,545.21
Total†	2,760,658	99.98	5,962,762	99.92	2.16

* Hasan Abu al-Su'ud, "A study on Land Reform in Egypt," *Islamic Review*, XLV (April, 1957), 14; unfortunately Abu al-Su'ud does not explain the composition of the table and we suspect that there is double counting in the number of owners; however, after checking with other sources, the discrepancy, if any, seems minor.

† Computed by author.

The upper one per cent of the owners held about 20 per cent, but the upper 7 per cent held about two-thirds of the cultivable land. In contrast, 94.18 per cent of all the holdings occupied only 35.28 per cent of the land. The number of farms of less than one *feddan* (1 *feddan* = 1.038 acres) amounted to 71.77 per cent of all the holdings, averaging about 0.3 *feddan*.[5]

The high dependence of the Egyptian people on agriculture for their living and the unequal land distribution resulted in a high rate of tenancy and exorbitant rates of rent. It has been estimated that about 60–75 per cent of the cultivated land was operated by tenants who rented the land from middlemen on short-term leases at a rent that sometimes exceeded the net income of the land.[6] The rate of rent, whether in cash or kind, depended on the degree to which the landlord defrayed the cost of production and on the locality and kind of crop.[7]

Because of the high rent and the small size of his holding, the tenant was hardly in a better position than the laborer. The same applies to the small owner, particularly because of his primitive techniques, low productivity, and underemployment, although productivity per acre was 5 or 6 times that in Britain.[8] Labor productivity suffered also from inefficiency and the high waste of capital, in seed and fertilizer.[9] Thus the peasant, whether small owner or tenant, lived on subsistence, in idleness and despair.

BACKGROUND: SOCIOPOLITICAL CONDITIONS

Formally there was no nobility in Egypt, but in practice the class of large landowners have been described as feudal lords similar to the lords of Roman *latifundia* and of the English manor, and to the *seigneurs* of pre-revolutionary France. The product from the land — the main form of wealth — supported a small wealthy group at the top and a broad base of poverty-stricken and ignorant *fellahin* (peasants) at the bottom. The landlord employed the peasant, represented him in the government, and made his decisions for him in the village. Interaction between them was designed to maintain this master-servant relationship, making social mobility extremely difficult. Thus, the economic monopoly by the landlord depended on and sustained his political monopoly.[10]

Between these two classes, or rather beside them, was a middle class consisting of minority groups, businessmen, and some intellectuals and army officers, many of whom came from the peasantry. In the middle class were the Christian Copts, the Greeks, and the Jews, but its "backbone" were foreigners whose interests were "bound with those of the landowners." Nevertheless, the members of this class engaged in the national struggle for independence although their impact on local issues was minor.[11] Gradually, however, the upper and middle classes grew more and more interdependent as the landlords increasingly participated in business and commercial enterprise.

The rigidity of the class structure reflected the land tenure relations. Therefore no serious attempts at reform were made prior to the 1952 revolution. It is true that the land problem was sometimes discussed in Parliament, which was dominated by the landlords, but when they talked of reform they meant prevention of further land concentration rather than equalization of the distribution or change of tenure. Usually it was suggested that *wakf* and public land be redistributed to increase the number of small holdings.[12] These programs, however, had no backing. The influential political parties preferred the *status quo* in which they had vested interests. According to one observer:

The most striking feature in the parties' approach to the agrarian question was their common opposition to any reform in the existing distribution of land in Egypt, a position which they maintained even after the 1952 Revolution. All the parties believed that it was possible to evade drastic reform through the sale of state domain to small farmers, although none of them ever in fact carried out that programme.[13]

On the contrary, in the name of reform the government patronized the landowners and supported their monopoly power. It used public money to help them pay debts; it reduced the land tax from 28.6 per cent of the rental value to 16 per cent in 1937 and to 14 per cent in 1948; and when public land was reclaimed, it was more often sold to big than to small owners, contrary to official proclamations and party platforms.[14]

The conflict between the rural social classes culminated in crises that became quite apparent on the eve of the reform. The price of land soared to £E800–1,000 while the real value of one *feddan* was estimated at £E150; and the rental value per feddan ranged between £E40 and £E60 although the real value was not more than £E20.[15] High prices and rents were disastrous to the peasants, who reacted by riots and local violence. They even revolted sporadically between 1944 and the revolution, and attacked estates of the rich and sometimes were killed in those clashes.[16]

The crises that preceded the revolution were not caused by the land distribution or the landlord-peasant conflict alone. Other factors contributed to the disequilibrium of the society. The middle class had reached a stage of development that called for recognition, and the urban workers had started to organize and demand rights and privileges. Corruption in the government and meddling by the King in the affairs of the country intensified the conflict. Failure of the government to end foreign occupation, defeat in the Palestine war, and inflation and unemployment following the withdrawal of foreign armies after the war increased the misery and restiveness of the people.

In its struggle for social recognition, the rebelling middle class found common grounds with the peasantry. Together they rose against the ruling class and its ally, the King, while the unstable government was unable to correct the situation in time. Between 1942 and 1952, the year of revolution, the government changed hands 17 times, its lifetime averaging 7 months. It resorted to martial law while the workers struck and rioted and spread terror and murder; Prime Minister Ahmed Maher was killed in 1945; in 1946 Finance Minister Osman was murdered, and Nokrashi Pasha in 1948; in the same year an attempt was made on the life of the *Wafd* leader and Prime Minister Nahas by blowing up his car.

Thus, when the reform was introduced, the ruling class was fighting desperately for its life as a class while the middle class was carving a place for itself in the social structure. The peasantry anxiously took advantage of this conflict to improve its own conditions.[17]

THE PROCESS AND OBJECTIVES OF REFORM

Political revolution by the army officers brought a new regime into power, changing the basic institutional structure of the country, and passing the agrarian reform law in the same year.

The revolutionary government had several motives for reform. It did not hope to increase land productivity, since cultivation was already intensive and use of fertilizer widespread; but it was possible to improve techniques, encourage land reclamation, and redirect capital away from the sterile financial investment in land speculation into productive investment. It also could consolidate holdings and promote mechanization. However, only some of these objectives were taken into consideration, namely, those of redirecting investment into land improvement, commerce, and industry.[18]

The revolution sought to raise the peasant living standard by redistributing wealth and income both as a humanitarian act and with an eye on the effects of this action on incentives and investment.[19] But the basic objectives were political, namely, to break the power of the old regime by checking its control over the land and by strengthening the peasantry. As described by President Nasser, abolition of feudalism was the primary aim of the reform.[20] In other words, the reform was a preventive measure against attempts to restore the old order and a means of gaining the support of the peasants to strengthen the revolution. The reformers took advantage of the fact that some landowners were of foreign origin, including the royal family, to recruit nationalistic sentiments and legitimize the revolution.[21]

While acknowledging the importance of these domestic motives for reform, Doreen Warriner suggests that American influence played a significant role in the reform: "America's advocacy of land reform was said to be a green light, and State Department influence certainly played a part in the preparation of the decree, probably strengthening the revolutionary element in the Group." [22] In other words, the revolutionary government sought acceptance in the international community by introducing a widely supported reform.

Finally, the reformers wanted to stabilize the political system, pacify the *fellahin*, and "forestall Communist revolution." In the words of Sayed Marei, the Egyptian Minister of Agriculture who played a major role in the reform movement:

We all remember the days preceding the revolution of July, 1952; we remember how the Egyptian village became restless as a result of dangerous agitation; we remember the events which led to bloodshed and destruction of property — for the first time in the history of the Egyptian village. Would the large owners have preferred to be left exposed to the wind blowing through this unrest, exploiting want and poverty, until it became a tempest uprooting everything . . . and endangering, perhaps, the peace of our fatherland? Do they not fare better under stable conditions, the income from the land being given to its tillers and its price to its former owners to be invested by them in the development of Egyptian industry and commerce? [23]

The political objectives, then, were to legitimize the new regime, stabilize the political order, and avert a Communist revolution or a grave disaster. Although no direct mention was made of democracy as an objective, this was clearly implied.

The Egyptian Agrarian Reform Law was the first extensive measure of land tenure change in the Arab countries and probably in the Middle East. Its most relevant provisions may be *paraphrased* as follows:

1. No person may possess more than 200 feddans of agricultural land. Exempted from this provision are: (a) companies and societies holding land under reclamation for purposes of sale; (b) private individuals holding fallow or desert land for improvement unless acquired 25 years or more earlier; (c) industrial companies holding the land for industrial exploitation; (d) agricultural and scientific societies holding land for research purposes; (e) benevolent societies; (f) creditors owning the land as a result of expropriation, for one year after the government has the right to requisition that land; (g) private individuals who own the land as a result of a bequest in a will of inheritance or other than a contractual process, for a period of a year after which the government has the right to requisition it. Wakf land is also exempted.

2. During the five years following the coming into force of this Law, the Government shall requisition the area in excess of 200 feddans retained by the proprietor for himself provided that the land requisitioned each year is not less than one fifth of the total area of the land to be requisitioned.

3. The proprietor may, however, in the course of five years after the enactment of this law, transfer the ownership of such agricultural land in excess of 200 feddans as may not so far have been requisitioned, as follows:

(a) To small farmers provided that they must satisfy the following conditions:

(1) They must be working in agriculture.

(2) They must be tenants of farmers (fellahin) cultivating the land disposed of or inhabiting the village wherein the land exists.

(3) Their total ownership thereafter must not exceed 10 feddans.

(4) No more than 5 feddans shall be disposed of to any one individual.

(5) Land so disposed of must not be less than two feddans unless the total amount of land disposed of is actually less than that or unless the land transferred is specified for building houses. . . . Such land must be built on within one year of disposal. . . .

. . . .

(c) To graduates of Agricultural Institutes according to the following conditions:

(1) The land so disposed of must be orchards.

(2) The individual ownership of any one graduate must not exceed 20 feddans.

(3) No individual shall get more than 20 or less than 10 feddans, unless the actual area of the parcel disposed of is less than that amount.

The law provided for compensation equal to ten times the rent of such land, the rent to be assessed as seven times the basic land tax. This indemnity was to be paid in the form of state bonds redeemable within 30 years and carrying a 3 per cent rate of interest. These bonds would be negotiable for purchasing fallow land for improvement, and for payment of tax or inheritance duties.

4. The areas requisitioned in each village shall be distributed among small farmers, so that each one of them shall have a small holding of not less than two feddans and not more than five feddans, according to the quality of the land.

Persons to whom the land shall thus be distributed must satisfy the following conditions:

(a) They must be Egyptians of age, who have not been convicted of any dishonorable crime.

(b) They must be working in agriculture.

(c) They must own less than five feddans of agricultural land. . . . Land so distributed may not be acquired by pre-emption.

. . . .

Other provisions include the following:

6. Land recipients shall repay the indemnity plus an annual interest of 3 per cent, and an additional overall sum equal to 15 per cent of the price for administrative expenses. The total amount shall be paid by installments within 30 years (later changed to 40).

7. Recipients of land shall belong to coöperative societies whose membership is restricted to owners of 5 feddans or less; these cooperatives

shall aid in production, marketing, and credit, under government super-vision and guidance.

8. A supplementary tax is imposed "on land holdings in excess of 200 feddans, at the rate of five times the amount of the basic tax."

9. The law regulates the conditions of tenancy:

Agricultural land may be let only to a person undertaking to farm it per-sonally. . . .

The rent of agricultural land may not exceed seven times the amount of the basic tax assessed upon such land. In the case of a rent based on crop-sharing the owner's share shall not exceed one half after deduction of all expenses. . . .

Leases of agricultural land may not be concluded for less than three years. . . . The contract shall be concluded in writing irrespective of its value.

Finally, the law takes into consideration the wages and rights of agricul-tural workers and protects them by specific legislation,[24] but this pro-vision has not been executed.

The law has recently been revised. As of July 25, 1961, it has been ordered that no person shall own more than 100 feddans, in place of the previous limit of 200 feddans. The new legislation restricts the total area that may be held in tenancy to 50 feddans per family. The new size restriction is expected to redistribute 500,000 feddans to 150,000 families.[25]

In order to implement the reform, the government had yet to over-come many obstacles. The military regime first entrusted the government to a veteran statesman of the former ruling class, but soon found that the reform was in danger of being shelved. Ali Maher, the Prime Minis-ter, tried to prevent passage of the law "under the pretext of 'studying the experience of other countries.' " The army group had to dismiss him and assume the government, which they had formerly planned to leave in civilian hands.[26]

The landlords then tried to obstruct the law by questioning its justifi-cation and usefulness. In a petition to the Cabinet they invoked the Mos-lem faith as protector of private property, raised the question of econ-omies of scale, and suggested progressive taxation as an alternative to land redistribution. And should these arguments fail, they requested fair compensation in cash and help from the government to pay off their debts.[27] The reformers countered with opposite arguments and went ahead with the program.

EFFECTS OF THE REFORM

To pass a law is one thing, but to apply it may be another. In Egypt the two were actually the same in the sense that implementation was quick and complete.

154

ECONOMIC EFFECTS

There has been a lot of theoretical analysis of the possible effects of the reform on production and development, both regarding Egypt and in general. Reform has been described as useless for increasing productivity in Egypt, since it decreases the scale of operation and because of the high pressure of population on the land.[28] Even the Egyptian Agrarian Reform Board anticipated adverse effects on pdocution on sugar cane plantations, but later the Board found the results to be positive.[29] However, production was expected to rise because of the incentive effects of becoming an owner.[30]

Generally speaking, productivity has not suffered because of the reduced scale of operation since the possible adverse effects were offset by cooperative operation of the land on a large scale. The average annual return of sugar cane per feddan rose from 679 *cantars* (1 *cantar* = 99.5 lb.) in 1951–52 to 837 in 1952–53 and to 908 *cantars* in 1953–54;[31] in 1957 it was 941, in 1958 1,061, 981 in 1959 and 1,016 in 1960.[32]

However, hardly any improvement in productivity has been observed in any other commodity, especially if the 1945–1949 period is taken into consideration, as table 29 shows. Even if the rise were significant, according to Doreen Warriner:

The overall production results cannot, however, be attributed to the redistribution which up to the present [1956] has affected only a small proportion of the land. But the reduction of rents, which affects a very large proportion of the land, has been accompanied by heavier use of fertilizers, so that the reform has certainly contributed to the increase in production.[33]

There are no data on the impact of reform on investment. One of the major purposes of the reform was to redirect capital from land specula-

TABLE 29

LAND PRODUCTIVITY BEFORE AND AFTER REFORM IN EGYPT *
(*Egyptian* quintals per hectare)

Harvest year	Cotton	Wheat	Rice	Maize
1945–1949	5.7	17.3	37.3	20.9
1950	4.6	17.7	42.2	21.4
1951	4.4	19.2	30.3	20.4
1952	5.4	18.5	32.9	21.0
1953	5.7	20.6	36.7	21.9
1954		22.9		

* Thweatt, "The Egyptian Agrarian Reform," *op. cit.*; 1 *Egyptian* quintal = 99.05 lb.; cotton production has been estimated at 4.3 quintals per hectare in 1957, 5.7 in 1958, 5.7 in 1959, and 5.9 in 1960; converted from Public Relations Dept., Agrarian Reform General Organization, *Replies to United Nations Questionnaire*, p. 37.

tion to productive investment.[34] Since the bonds were not generally negotiable, investment could not have been stimulated. Even if the bonds were negotiable, as in the case of land reclamation, the uncertainty created by the reform regarding future property rights must have discouraged the landlords from investing their compensation bonds in agriculture. The reform may have had an indirect impact by forcing land transactions whose proceeds may have been invested.[35]

Finally, the reform did not create any employment, nor did it induce the surplus population to migrate. On the contrary, by allotting a small piece of land to the family, it strengthened the tie between the peasant and his land, and discouraged him from migrating. Underemployment in agriculture has persisted and waste of resources has not been eliminated by the reform.

SOCIOPOLITICAL EFFECTS

To the extent that land concentration has been reduced, wealth redistribution must have taken place and class relations reconstructed. Change in the pattern of income distribution must have also contributed to the reconstruction of class relations. However, the land redistribution was too limited to have extensive effects on the class structure. The effects were limited also by discriminating against the new owners, and by compensating the expropriated landlords at a reasonable rate. Compensation helped to maintain the landlords' relative class ranking as it was before the reform.[36]

According to official figures, the reform applied to 566,000 feddans, of which 425,000 had been redistributed by 1960 to 161,413 individual families.[37] To this should be added 300,000 feddans made available by the 1961 modification. The average new family allotment is 2.63 feddans. Assuming that all the land subject to reform has been redistributed, the major impact would be a large increase in the number of holders of less than 5 feddans and a modest increase of the area they hold. After the reform, which has not been concluded, about 95 per cent of the owners would have a little more than half the private agricultural land, while the remaining half would be in the hands of only 5 per cent of the owners.

Thus, the results seem to be limited and conservative, as has been suggested by other writers.[38] The ratio between the maximum limit of 200 feddans per family with two children and the *maximum* received by a beneficiary family, 5 feddans, is 40:1.[39] This means that the reform has hardly reduced the equality of distribution or the concentration of ownership.

The distributive effects on the landlords were positive or negative according to whether the market value or the real value of the land was the basis of compensation. If the former, then the landlords suffered a great loss; otherwise, the effect would be limited to a change in the composi-

156

tion of their wealth rather than in its level or relative importance. The social and political power of the landlords has been diminished and in that sense the distributive effects of the reform unfavorable to them. It should be noticed, however, that the loss of the landlord cannot be measured simply by the number of feddans he surrendered. In general, he retained the best land and sold other good parts freely before the law was put into effect.[40]

But the main social effect of the reform was the redistribution of income by land transfer and regulation of rent. The benefits were common to the former tenant peasants, whether they remained tenants or became owners. The latter group benefited because the installments they paid for the land were remarkably lower than the original rent. The magnitude of this change is shown in table 30.

TABLE 30

INSTALLMENT PAYMENTS COMPARED WITH PRE-REFORM RENTS
IN SELECTED ESTATES IN EGYPT, 1955 *
(In £E)

Estate	Rent per feddan before reform	Annual installment per feddan	Installment as per cent of rent †
Mataay (El Menya Prov.)	44.750	18.650	41.6%
Drine (Gharbiah Prov.)	35.100	14.500	41.4%
Nagah Hamady (Upper Egypt, Kena Prov.)	43.890	15.430	35.6%
Arment (Upper Egypt, Kena Prov.)	32.250	15.120	47.0%
El Nakas (Sharkiah Prov.)	35.00	9.305	26.6%
Menshat Rahmy (El-Fayoum Prov.)	28.000	9.305	33.2%

* Marei, *op. cit.*, p. 245.

† Computed by author; this comparison may be an exaggeration of the benefits, since it overlooks the cost of production, part of which may have been borne by the landlord but after reform is paid by the new owner. According to Darling and also Warriner, the average net gain of the new owner was £E7 per *feddan* or £E20 per holding, which boosted the peasant's income by about 50 per cent. Warriner, *Land Reform and Development in the Middle East, op. cit.*, p. 36.

The total gain of the tenants has been estimated at £E35 million out of a total agricultural income of £E300 million, or an average of £E10 per feddan.[41] As Doreen Warriner describes it, "this improvement in income and legal status for a very large section of the farm population is by far the most valuable achievement of the reform, greatly exceeding in importance the benefits of redistribution."[42] Recently it has been observed that rent regulations are being violated. A black-

157

market rental is being charged the tenants, who submit to it because of the high demand for land.[43] If so, the social benefits may be less than estimated above.

The political effects of the reform have been the most impressive. The change represented a political revolution in which the middle class played the major role in trying to replace the former ruling oligarchy and abolish feudalism. If feudalism meant breaking up large estates, originally identified as those above 200 feddans, the reform certainly achieved its objectives.[44] But if the aim was to narrow the gap between rural classes or to create a small peasant class of owners as a foundation of democracy, it did not succeed. The gap in rural wealth has remained vast between owners and tenants, and between small and large owners. Though the income of the peasants has been increased (relative to the income of the large owners), it has remained very low and not much higher than subsistence. Furthermore, the new owners are only partial owners, since they are restricted by the coöperative organization.

Apparently the new regime did not consider owners of 200 feddans, and 100 feddans after amendment of the law, as part of the feudal regime, but as part of the middle class and therefore tried to win their support by sparing their property from redistribution.[45] Except for the uncertainty concerning the future of their land, they had no reason to oppose the new regime. Thus, the regime won the support of those who identified themselves with the middle class, and neutralized those who sympathized with the displaced oligarchy by exempting their land from expropriation. Finally, by conferring benefits on the peasants, and by vigorous propaganda, it won the support of practically all the peasantry.

The regime was thus able to gain short-term acceptance, but we are not so certain that it has achieved legitimacy or created a long-term stability. It is too early to judge the degree of realization of the long-term objectives. The political atmosphere has not been free enough for opposing views to be expressed, nor do we know if the middle class has become strong enough to maintain a stable democracy.[46] The government has, however, introduced radical laws since 1961. In addition to the land tenure reform, it has regulated industry by controlling or nationalizing about 82 per cent of the financial and industrial enterprises of the country. It has put a ceiling on salaries at £E5,000 a year, except on that of the President.[47] These daring policies may suggest that the regime still feels unstable and needs to weaken the wealthy class still further to prevent a restoration or that state control seems the only way to development and the regime feels secure enough to impose the change. It is possible that both factors have been important.[48]

Therefore it is not possible to conclude that the new political structure is stable until all the forces in the community have been allowed to act freely. The recent movement to recruit popular support by participation in open forum preparatory to rewriting the constitution may be the beginning.[49]

Political stability may also be discussed from the point of view of the peasants. Though benefiting from the reform, the peasants are still living on low incomes while the revolution has sustained their hopes for better conditions. The changes have not been radical, nor have alternative occupations been provided. Furthermore, many of them must feel discriminated against — those who remained tenants, the landless workers who received no benefits, and those who received much less land than others.[50] How long will the peasants tolerate these conditions and how long will they live on hope? With the land/labor ratio low as it is, unless industry and commerce flourish it is not expected that conditions will improve substantially. Hope alone may prove inadequate for political stability.

EVALUATION

1. The economic effects of the reform have been positive but limited, and have accrued mainly from regulation of rent and coöperative organization. Underemployment and land fragmentation have persisted, the latter being overcome only on redistributed land, although attempts to consolidate other lands have been made. Techniques have remained generally the same. The impact on productivity has been modest, and on investment and employment almost nil.

2. The social effects of the reform have been limited, since redistribution of wealth has been negligible. Redistribution of rural income has resulted from rent control, but inequality has remained and the peasants, though benefiting from the reform, still live on very low incomes.[51]

3. The primary objectives and results have been political. The distribution program seems to have been oriented toward weakening the old regime and preventing restoration. Through reform and the highly effective propaganda machinery, the revolution has been able to win acceptance and legitimacy over the short term, and probably in the long run also.

4. The reform has been characterized by reaction. By allowing a large-size holding limit, the reform has permitted a *rentier* group to exist. And by compensating the expropriated landlords, the government has limited the distributive effects of the reform. Furthermore, the government compromised by permitting the landlord to retain the best part of his land, within the legal limits, and to sell other parts to persons he approved of.

Nevertheless, the landlords have tried to obstruct reform through the procrastination of Ali Maher to prevent passage of the law and by arguing and spreading slanders against the new order. They also tried to subvert it by smuggling out the livestock, grain, and other capital before surrendering their land, in violation of the law.[52] Finally, the new tendency toward charging black-market or illegal rent may be a sign of the surviving power of the landlord and a form of reversal of the socioeconomic effects of the reform.

5. The reform law was discriminatory in its effects. There was discrimination between those who became owners and those who remained tenants; also between tenants who had less than 5 feddans and have now increased their holdings and those who operated more and now have lost part of the land. Also, privileges were accorded the graduates of agricultural institutes. The impact of this discriminatory policy is hard to assess, but there is no reason to believe that it has been approvingly accepted by all concerned.

6. Finally, the reform has left unaffected the private individual tenure that had existed prior to the revolution. There has been a transfer of land from one owner to another, while the new coöperative organization regulated the operation of land only. However, a dual tenure arrangement has resulted, since newly acquired land has been subjected to special restrictions, though temporary, which are inconsistent with the private ownership rights enjoyed by other owners. But the amount of land affected by these restrictions is so small that it could not impress its character on the tenure arrangements in general.

PART III

COMPARATIVE ANALYSIS

CHART II

Summary of Reform Features and Findings*

Criteria of comparison	Greek Solon	Greek Pisis.	Roman	English Comm.	English Enclos.	French	Russian Emanc.	Russian Stolypin	Russian Soviet	Mexican	Japanese	Egyptian
I. Background Features												
a. Tenure of cultiv. area:												
Private	x	x	x	x	x	x	x	x	x	x	x	x
Public			x			x	x	x				
Individual	x	x	x	x	x	x	x	x	x	x	x	x
Collective						x	x	x	x	x	x	
Feudal tenancy	x			x		x	x					
Contractual tenancy				x	x	x						
b. Land concentration	x	x	x	x	x	x	x	x	x	x	x	x
c. Scale of operation:												
Small	?	?		x	x	x	x	x?	x	x	x	x
Large	?	?	x	x?	x?		-?			x		x
d. Sociopolitical:												
Polemic class division	x	x	x	x	x	x	x	x?	x?	x	x	x
Concentration of power	x	x	x	x	x	x	x	x	x	x	x	x
e. Dynamic features:												
Change in econ. organ.	x	x	x	x	x	x	x	x	x	x?	x	x
Change in class struc.	x	x	x	x	x	x	x	x	x	x	x	x
Econ. & pol. crises	x	x	x	?	?	x	x	x	x	x	x	x
II. Objectives & Processes												
a. Objectives:												
Economic	–	?	–	x	–	–	–	x?	x?	–?	x?	x?
Social	x	x	x	–	–	x	x	–	x	x	x	x
Political	x	x	x	–	–	x	x	x	x	x	x	x
b. Processes:												
Non-Revolution	x		x	x	x	x	x	–	x	x	x	x
Revolution		x	x	x	x	x	x	x?	x	x	x	x

Compensation	–	–?	x		x	x?	x	–?		x	x
Discrimination	x	x	x	x	x	x	x	x		x	x
Reaction:											
Compromise	x		x	x	x	x	x	x		x	x
Obstruction		x	x	x	x	x	x	x?	Nega-tive	x	x
Reversal		x?	x	x	x	x?	x?	x?	x?	x	x?
III. Effects											
a. Tenure:											
Private	x	x	x	x	x	x	x		x	x	x
Public	x	x	x	x		x		x	x		x
Individual		x	x	x	x	x	x	x	x	x	x
Collective				x			x	x	x		x
Feudal tenancy											
Contractual tenancy	x	x	x	x	x?	x	x		x	x	x
Land concentration			x	x	x?	x?	x?	x?	x?		x?
Scale of operation:											
Small		x	x	x	x	x	x	x			
Large	x		x	x			x?		x	x	x?
b. Economic conditions (production, allocation, investment)			x		x		x	Nega-tive	x?	x?	x?
c. Social conditions:											
Personal	x		x		x	x	x		x		
Material —				Nega-tive	x?	Nega-tive	Nega-tive	x†	x?	x?	x?
Distribution & standard of living	x?	x?	x?		x?	tive	tive				
d. Political:											
Short-term	x?	x	x	–	x	x	x	x	x	x	x
Long-term		x	–	–	x	x	–	x	x	?	?

* x = yes or positive effect.

blank space = no information, or irrelevant.

x? = considered but not realized, or partially positive results.

– = was not warranted or considered.

–? = considered but not realized, even though not warranted.

? = uncertain.

Negative = the effects were in the opposite direction from the peasant welfare.

† Improved partially after a delay of two decades.

INTRODUCTION TO PART III

Some of the basic elements of the agrarian structure are the effective and potential land/labor ratios. The growth of population, given a limited amount of land or an amount that increases at a slower rate than the population, by necessity leads to the problems that have usually been the concern of land tenure reform.[1] The relative scarcity of arable land as a source of wealth and income usually renders land a tool of power and a symbol of high social status. Acquisition of land becomes the objective of everybody, but what one gains another loses. Consequently, a common feature of agrarian societies has been land concentration, inequality of wealth and income distribution, and abject poverty for a large number of people.

Even a cursory analysis of tenure relations suggests that under private tenure, land concentration and inequality of rural wealth and income are almost inevitable. In contrast, concentration may be avoided by nationalizing the land and tying its control to tillage in the sense that only those who work on the land may hold it, as has occurred in the socialist countries. Yet, unless nonagricultural employment is made available, or productivity increases greatly, the per capita income would remain low and the standard of living very modest. However, even if land is nationalized, productivity increases, and nonagricultural employment abounds, inequality of income may only be reduced but not eliminated unless distribution of the product is divorced from factor contribution and some radical criteria of equality are adopted. Such criteria are often regarded as utopian — such as distribution according to need in the final stage of Communism.

Historically, two courses of action, or inaction, have been followed under these rural circumstances. The people have been resigned to their fate, in which case the economy remained agrarian, underemployment increased, per capita incomes declined, and pressure on the land and the peasants mounted. This has been the fortune of most densely populated agrarian societies of today in which land tenure reform has been in vogue. The alternative to the above situation has been industrialization and growth at a rate sufficient to cope with population increase, migration to the city, and operation of the land by a number of people that

165

may earn an acceptable income, as has occurred in England and Scandinavia.

It is in the light of these alternatives that we shall analyze the land tenure reforms in this study. First we shall explore the common features and problems that have formed the background of the cases studied. Next we shall compare and contrast the processes and objectives of reform. Finally, we shall compare and contrast the effects, taking into consideration their impact on the problems pointed out in the background material. A summary of the findings is presented in Chart II.

XI

COMPARISON AND CONTRAST I:
REFORM BACKGROUND

Several features, as shown on Chart II, seem to have been common prior to reform in almost all the societies studied. All the reforms were introduced when land tenure was primarily private and individual, when land ownership was concentrated and often when its operation was on a relatively small scale. The class structure was highly polemic and the power concentrated. These are static features, which may last for a long time without causing change, but the reforms were almost invariably preceded by disequilibrating developments which may be called dynamic features, such as changes in economic organization and class structure, and crises in the economic and political relations.

The static features may seem inconsequential when treated in isolation, but when their effects and implications are investigated it appears that reform, or at least change, was inevitable. The distinction between static and dynamic features is not easy — the two being overlapping and interdependent — but for analytical purposes we shall treat them separately.

STATIC FEATURES

1. FORM OF TENURE

When reform was introduced, in all cases the form of tenure was primarily private and individualistic. Collective holding existed only in Mexico, in violation of the law, and in the Russian commune (*mir*) between emancipation and the Stolypin reform. However, though ownership in Russia was collective, operation of the land was individual and the majority of the communes repartitioned the land periodically.[1] Public tenure also existed in most cases, mainly on uncultivated land. The cultivable area was held in public tenure only in three instances: the Roman, French, and pre-emancipation Russia, while in the pre-Stolypin era state land was in a transitory stage headed for private individual tenure. The differentiation between private and public land has a direct relationship with the distribution of land among owners and farmers and with the concentration of wealth and income. Insofar as public land is not subject to market transaction, it has little impact on the concentration of ownership. Public land, when available, may also be an important outlet for population pressure and colonization, as happened in Rome and in

Mexico after the revolution. In other words, given the objectives, the preëxisting land tenure may determine the reform policy to the extent to which it permits land alienation and concentration of holdings.[2]

2. LAND CONCENTRATION

The predominance of private tenure was invariably accompanied by a high degree of land concentration. Table 31 gives an idea of the degree of concentration and shows that land distribution was far from the line of equality in all cases, though in varying degrees. But the causes of concentration were varied. In the Greek society where ownership was a family or clan affair and land was inalienable, concentration resulted from indebtedness of the peasant and his having to mortgage his land and person into perpetual servitude to the creditor as *Hektemor*. In the Roman and Mexican cases, concentration resulted from land purchase on one hand, and from usurpation of public land and land concessions from the government on the other.

In the French, English, Russian, Japanese, and Egyptian cases, land concentration was a survival of serfdom, or its variant as in Egypt, in which the ruler granted land concessions, including the service of the peasants on it in lieu of specific services by the grantee. Though the functions performed by the latter had been taken over by the national government, the land grants remained in the hands of the landlords. In some cases, however, land was accumulated through the market, the wealthier owners absorbing the poorer, in which case the buyer either evicted the peasant and incorporated the land in his estate, or leased it, possibly to the original owner.

3. SMALL-SCALE OPERATION

In addition to private tenure and land concentration, and probably as a result, a fairly common feature was the fragmentation of landholdings into small units of operation. Uneconomic small-scale operation characterized all except the Roman and Mexican cases, and possibly the Greek on which we have no information. The Roman and Mexican large estates were operated as *latifundia* and hence as big enterprises. In contrast, the English manor, except for the demesne land, was operated in small strips. The French farm was a small enterprise whose scale was declining because of the increased population depending on the limited land area. The same was true of pre-Soviet Russia. The serf peasant, and later the member of the *mir*, operated land repartitioned periodically in amounts just enough to keep him busy. In fact, the average size of operation unit declined after emancipation because part of the allotment land fell to the landlord and also because of the increase in population. The extreme cases of fragmentation, however, were in Japan and Egypt.

The data in Part II of this volume show that about 66 per cent of the French peasants operated less than 4.9 acres each; the average holding

TABLE 31

High and Low Brackets of Land Ownership as Indicators of Land Concentration Before Reform *

	Proportion of owners or of total population	Proportion of land area held
Greek[a]	low	high
Roman[a]	low	high
French[b]		
Nobility	0.9% of adult pop.	23–26%
Peasants	70–80% of adult pop.	35–36%
Russian[c]		
Pre-emanc.		
Nobility	±250,000 or 2% of pop.	40%
State & other		
owners	——	±35%
Peasants	53% of pop. (74 million, 1859)	25% in allotment land
Pre-Stolypin		
Nobility	low	23%
Peasants	——	62%
Soviet[d]	——	——
Mexican		
Total owners	3% of population	100% of private land
Hacienda owners	2% of haciendas	58% of private land
Japanese		
Big owners		
(above 10 *cho*)	1.8% of owners	16.7%
Small owners		
(up to 1 *cho*)	74.1% of owners	31.8%
Egyptian		
Big holders	7% of owners	66%
Small holders	93% of owners	34%

* Lack of data allows presenting only selected and ununiform examples of land distribution.

[a] No quantitative data are available; this qualitative estimate is based on the opinion of students of the problem.

[b] Formally, the nobility, the clergy, and the state owned all the land; however, I have presented the separate holdings of the nobility and the peasantry on the assumption that *cens* land was owned by the peasants.

[c] Accurate figures on the size of the nobility have not been available. The amount of land owned by the two groups takes into consideration the share of the nobility in the product of the allotment land, and assumes the nobility to have an average of four children to a family.

[d] The results of the Stolypin reforms were minor, and therefore the distribution in pre-Stolypin time applies to the pre-Soviet period.

in Russia was 9.45 acres before emancipation and 8.18 acres after it, and 23.8 per cent of all the peasants operated less than 13.5 acres each; and 59 per cent of the Mexican peasants operated less than 12.355 acres each. In the English manors the small scale is suggested by the fact that demesne land occupied an average of one-third of the manor land while the rest was repartitioned among the population and held in strips. In Japan 63.6 per cent operated less than 2.45 acres each, and another 26.8 per cent operated between 2.45 and 7.35 acres each; in Egypt 71.77 per cent of all holders held no more than 1.038 acres each, and 94.18 per cent held less than 5.19 acres each.

Given the backward techniques and the high population pressure on the land, fragmentation and small-scale operation imply poverty in the sense that output per man cannot be high and the worker is underemployed unless supplementary nonfarm employment is accessible. They also imply misutilization of nonhuman resources and a low total product, which again results in low rural per capita income, especially when the small scale operation and the fragmented holdings preclude indivisible capital investment. Even investment in the form of fertilizer and pesticide may require larger-scale operation than that represented above.

Looking at these common features in combination, and considering the scarcity of arable land relative to population growth, it is easy to understand why there was a high degree of tenancy and absentee landlordism and what impact these conditions might have on the distribution of income, wealth, and power, and on class structure. We shall deal with each of these points separately.

(a) Tenancy and Absenteeism. Tenancy and absenteeism do not always occur together. Concentration of ownership may lead to either or both of them. When owners operate their land directly, neither tenancy nor absenteeism exists. If they supervise their estates through agents, there will be absenteeism but no tenancy. If the landlord leases his land to one or more tenants and goes to live in the city, however, there will be both absentee landlordism and tenancy.[3]

The cases under study illustrate all these variants. Absenteeism with or without tenancy characterized all of them. In the English (manorial), Roman and Mexican land systems the big estates were operated under supervision of an agent of the lord who had little contact with the land. The French, Russian, Japanese, and Egyptian pre-reform systems represented tenancy and absenteeism with regard to almost 75 per cent of the farmers.[4] The pre-Stolypin and pre-Soviet periods in Russia are more complicated because peasants in the process of acquiring individual ownership were neither tenants nor yet owners. In both cases absenteeism was common.

Of course, absenteeism as such need not carry any value or efficiency implications. Where the agent of the landlord is trustworthy and efficient, or where absenteeism is combined with contractual and protected tenancy, the effects may be neutral and little different from what they would be under owner-operators, as in modern England. But this was not the common form of tenancy or absenteeism. Except in England, the landlord looked upon the land as a source of income, charged relatively high rents, and paid little attention to the conditions of the peasant or the land and its cultivation. He did not provide capital for reinvestment or for improving the methods of cultivation. The result was stagnation of the French, Russian — up to the late nineteenth century — Mexican, Egyptian, and partly Japanese agriculture, even though better methods of cultivation had already become common in other countries.[5]

Thus, the high rent exacted from the farmer, the lack of other economic outlets for surplus population, the carelessness of the lord, and the ignorance and economic backwardness of the peasant all tended to sustain backward agriculture, low average productivity, and low per capita income.

(b) Income and Wealth Distribution. By definition, land concentration implies inequality of wealth and consequently of income from the land. Given the land/labor ratio, the higher the degree of ownership concentration, the more unequal the distribution and the greater the gap between the income and wealth of the different groups of landowners. Similarly, the higher the degree of concentration, the smaller the number of owners and the larger the number of landless people; and, assuming no significant increase in the nonagricultural demand for rural labor, the wider will be the gap between the wealth and income of the owners and nonowners. Furthermore, if we take into consideration the possible decline of the land/labor ratio because of the natural increase of the rural population, the gap should become wider and wider, both between different owner-groups and between owners and nonowners.

Low per capita income and concentration, or unequal distribution of wealth and income, were common in every single case from the ancient Greeks to the Egyptians. This was so even in Japan and Egypt where agriculture was intensive and land productivity high. In all these cases, land concentration caused unequal distribution, but the low average income was due to the relatively low and declining land/labor ratio, the widespread underemployment, and the absence of nonagricultural economic activities to absorb the surplus labor. In contrast, land concentration continued in England, but the rise in the land/labor ratio after the industrial revolution increased per capita income greatly while higher productivity and rationalized agriculture reflected positively on the rural standard of living. However, inequality of wealth and income distribution was not affected, or only aggravated, according to whether or not the degree of concentration was changed.

4. SOCIOPOLITICAL FEATURES

To separate the economic from the sociopolitical characteristics is difficult and probably unrealistic, especially in agrarian societies where land is the main source of both wealth and power; we do it here to simplify the analysis. In the societies under study, as a rule class differentiation

171

was associated with or even based on land ownership. In the Greek and Roman societies, this association went even farther by identifying ownership and property tax liability with citizenship and eligibility to serve in the army. Identification of landownership with class status is, of course, not peculiar to the ancient and medieval or medieval-type societies; in modern societies wealth has remained an important criterion of class status.

As shown in Chart II, almost all the cases were characterized by a bimodal class division and power concentration—a small upper class on one side and a large lower class on the other. The one was the nobility who were the big landowners, and the other the peasants and workers who owned little or no land. The power structure corresponded to the class structure so that on top were the rulers and on the levels below them the ruled. The dichotomy was sharp in terms of both accessible resources and functions. Even though these two classes were not internally homogeneous, each class was fairly distinguished from the other and mobility between them was hardly possible. Their interests were diametrically opposed and each class acquired power only at the expense of the other.

It is true that there were other classes and status groups, but these were small in membership and usually ineffective or uninvolved in the tenure problems and conflicts between the landlords and the peasantry. In each case, for example, there was a small middle class, though of a different composition. Besides the merchants who occupied such a position in all cases, there were the medium size landowners, as in Rome, England, and Mexico; the army and professionals in Japan; and the professionals and intellectuals in Egypt—all were considered middle class. It is true that their interests were not the same as those of the peasantry, but they often united with them for political purposes and calculated objectives. The revolt of the middle classes, when it happened, was to unseat the ruling class politically, but the revolt of the peasants was to unseat them economically by requisitioning the land. The middle classes tried to alter the class structure by modifying the criteria of status and the sources of power, but the peasantry wanted to retain the same criteria. They only wanted a larger share of power by redistributing the land— the symbol of power and class status. In other words, the middle class struggled to break the concentration of power by substituting capital for land as criterion, and by abolishing the hereditary status privileges in order to carve a place for themselves in the social structure. The peasantry wanted only to break the concentration of landownership in order to improve its standard of living. This dissimilarity, and sometimes conflict, of interests has had a great influence on the process and effects of reform, as we shall see in the next chapter.[6]

To summarize, it seems that certain static features were common to all the environments in which reform was introduced. Among them were private tenure, a high degree of land concentration, widespread tenancy and absenteeism, small-scale operation and backward techniques, low per capita productivity and income, and a high degree of maldistribution of both wealth and income. Equally common were a bimodal class structure and a wide gap between the upper and lower classes, while in each case the influence of a middle class had become apparent. Finally, it seems common for the middle and lower or peasant classes to unite against the upper class, although each with different objectives in mind.

DYNAMIC FEATURES

While the above "static" characteristics might have seemed to be sources of conflict, actually they became disturbingly so only when other disequilibrating developments took place, which we have called dynamic features. The community had remained fairly passive toward the *status quo* for a multiplicity of reasons until the social equilibrium had been shaken. It is then that reform seemed imperative to restore equilibrium in the society. These dynamic features include changes in economic organization and class structure, and the development of economic and political crises.

1. CHANGE IN ECONOMIC ORGANIZATION

By economic organization we mean the internal structure of the economy, such as the system of exchange, international trade, technology, and methods of production. In its broadest sense, economic organization implies the "mode of production" as used by Marx, which signifies the transition from one stage to another in the Marxist system of analysis.

In almost all cases, as Chart II shows, a fundamental change in economic organization took place during the few decades preceding the land tenure reforms. Each of these changes was a cause of disequilibrium in the economy and led to inconsistencies which made reform necessary. The Greek economy, for example, had been undergoing transformation from a barter to a money ecnonomy, and international trade had been assuming greater importance. To take advantage of the luxuries appearing on the market, the landlords geared production toward export goods to finance their imports, increased their pressure on the peasants, and enslaved many of them. In Rome cultivation was giving way to grazing or livestock breeding in response to the competition of cheap imported grain, and the competition of commerce and manufacturing for capital. The competition for capital has also been suggested as a cause for the decline of farming and the expansion of livestock, and the rise of unemployment.

In France, in Russia in the Stolypin period, and later in Japan, there was an expansion of industry, manufacturing, and trade, and yet agriculture maintained its old tenure relations. French industry and manufacturing and international trade were entering the capitalistic stage while agriculture was still based on the *seigneurial* relations that had prevailed since the middle ages. This anachronism was recognized and attacked by champions of the Enlightenment and the Physiocrats who stressed that land belonged to the tillers. Tenure relations were subjected to pressure in response to the new tendency toward freer trade and abolition of tariffs which culminated in the 1786 Anglo-French treaty.

The Russian emancipation was preceded by a transition from a barter to a money economy in which economic development and international trade were also becoming more significant. Yet the position of the peasant, the methods of cultivation, and the relations between the landlord and tenant had not changed. These relations were inconsistent with the economic trends, especially late in the nineteenth and early twentieth centuries. Actually, a capitalistic development had started in agriculture but the tenure system, the scale of production, and the methods of cultivation were not congenial to expansion. Production of food was short even of the needs of the peasants themselves.

The change in Japan was still more apparent and the discrepancy between development in industry and agriculture greater. Japanese industry and manufacturing had expanded and were in need of markets, yet agriculture was relatively backward and the income of the rural population was too depressed to provide a market. Furthermore, the lag of agriculture was a source of tension in the relations between the absentee landlords and their tenants and between town and country, particularly during the 'thirties, at which time the preparations for war started.

The Mexican experience offers a peculiar example. The most important changes in economic organization were the rapid drift of the economy into foreign hands, and the reduction of the Indians—almost 40 per cent of the population—to virtual bondage. Also, the economic structure was drifting into what is known as a colonial economy, that is, export of raw material and import of manufactured consumer and luxury goods, which hindered productive investment and development. The creation of a colonial economy was aided in the decades preceding reform by Diaz' policies of concessions and subsidies to foreigners, and of expanding railroad construction and the market for the *hacendado* producer-exporter. In other words, the change tended toward greater dependence on foreign capital and entrepreneurship and deterioration of the political and economic status of the nationals.

In Egypt the change represented a transition into a capitalistic economy sustained by foreign capital which had become entrenched long ago. In fact, Egypt had become a dual economy: a well-developed urban sector and a contrasting backward rural sector which failed to cope with the needs of development and to produce sufficient food for the increasing population.

The fact that reform has usually been preceded by a drastic change in the organizational structure suggests certain relationships between the two. It seems that the land tenure system must roughly be consistent with the prevailing economic organization. Whenever a change of organization takes place or is contemplated, land tenure reform becomes imperative. A new tenure system becomes essential to promote or sustain the new form of economic organization. This hypothesis has important implications to contemporary societies seeking change, namely, one of the preconditions of change is a new tenure system. What that system should be depends on the type of economic organization aspired for. However, the more radical the change in economic organization, the more fundamental and comprehensive the land tenure reform must be in order to create or sustain social stability. Finally, if a modest land tenure reform follows a radical change in economic organization, one should expect friction and instability to continue; and if such a reform is intended to facilitate a radical change, it may actually prove to be an obstacle rather than a facility. We have in fact already encountered examples of these relationships in the case studies and they will be elaborated further below.

2. CHANGES IN THE CLASS STRUCTURE

At the same time as economic organization was changing, and probably as a result of it, the class structure was being altered. The number of landless people or proletarians was growing at the expense of the small owners, thus altering the relative positions of both the big and the small owners, as well as that of the middle class. On one hand, the group of small and middle owners or the rural middle class was declining, leaving behind a vacuum in the social system; on the other, a counterpart urban middle class was evolving in the commercial and industrial areas.

The change, of course, varied in detail and extent from one case to the other and in its relation to reform. In general, the internal strength of the reformers or their ability to introduce reform depended on the position of the urban middle class, unless they were externally supported.[7] In Athens, the class of small peasants was being replaced by the "bonded" *Hektemors* and this was disturbing to Solon, who initiated the reform. When the "shore" of Attica opposed distribution of land, Solon avoided it. Pisistratus, in contrast, ignored this opposition, having established himself as tyrant with external support. In Rome also the middle class was disappearing; the small owners were losing the land and joining the rural and urban proletariat, while unemployment in the cities was becoming serious.

175

In all the other cases, a new bourgeoisie was growing at a rapid pace by accumulating commercial and industrial wealth. Yet, because the social structure had no institutionalized place for them thus far, they were a source of instability and a threat to the established ruling group. This was true in France and in Russia of the second half of the nineteenth century and the early part of the twentieth, but more significantly after emancipation. In fact, after the Stolypin reform the middle class was purposely augmented by the creation of a rich peasantry.

A similar situation prevailed in England beginning with the enclosures and even earlier. In Mexico, though to a smaller extent, a new middle class had evolved among the *mestizos* and occupied an important position in the administration of Diaz. Similarly, the army officers and some of the intellectuals in Japan were the backbone of the middle class and were an important element in the class conflict that preceded the reform. Industrialization in Japan also created an urban bourgeoisie while the small and middle owners were being reduced to tenants. Finally, a class of intellectuals, financiers, and businessmen had been evolving in Egypt for a number of decades previous to reform and yet they had no significant place in the power structure. The same was true of the army officers, many of whom came from rural areas.

The significance of the changing position of the middle class lies in the relationship between the strength of that class and political stability. A strong middle class has traditionally been associated with democracy and political stability. It has been regarded as a source of checks and balances which maintain stability and contain conflict. Therefore, decline of the landed middle class or small and medium owners has been interpreted as a threat to democracy and a source of instability. On the other hand, the growth of an urban bourgeoisie has been conceived as a source of instability and a threat to the *status quo* in which it had no legitimate social position. Hence, to create stability it has been thought necessary to rehabilitate the class of small owners and to legitimize the existence of the urban bourgeoisie. These ideas were common in all cases prior to reform. Put more formally, it appears that a change in the class structure may result from or lead to land tenure reform. The more instability the changing class structure tends to generate, the more imperative would land tenure reform seem to be, and the more radical it has to be to maintain or restore stability or to create a western democracy. Of primary importance, however, is the position of the middle class within the social structure: the more dissatisfied this class is, the more imperative and likely the reform tends to be.

3. ECONOMIC AND POLITICAL CRISIS

The third common dynamic feature, which is connected with the class structure, is the economic and political discontent or class conflict. The conflict seems to have taken the form of a struggle by the ruling elite to maintain the *status quo* and by one of the other classes to change it. The remaining class has usually allied itself with one or the other of the two conflicting classes. Thus each of the reforms was preceded by a crisis. Reform seemed indispensable because political stability was endangered and the threat of revolution was in the air.

The transition from a barter to a money economy and expansion of international trade led the landlords in Athens to regulate production and increase export by depriving the peasants of the product of the land. As a result the gap between the landlords and the peasants was widening. The peasants expressed their indignation by requesting distribution of the land. This economic crisis led to a political crisis, since by losing the land the peasants were disenfranchised and made *Hektemors* without political status. When the conflict became serioues enough to endanger political stability and threatened a revolution, Solon tried to contain it and avert the revolution by introducing land tenure reform.

The crisis in Rome was reflected in corruption in government, widespread unemployment, and restiveness of the slaves. The peasants were burdened with huge debts at exorbitant rates of interest. Furthermore, decline of the small owners had a demoralizing effect on the army and the democracy of the republic. As in Athens, the Roman reformers anticipated a revolution and wished to avert it by introducing reform. The crisis in France was more openly expressed by both the nobility and the peasants. The nobility responded with what has been called "feudal reaction," or revival of old feudal rights and pressure on the peasants for more income. The state also increased taxation, which fell mainly on the peasants. In response, the peasants rose in open revolt against feudalism at an increasing rate. Even in England, where the social structure was less rigid and the landlords were more willing to compromise, a crisis developed and conflict was sometimes expressed in violence.

Open conflict in Russia was common in all three periods of reform. Prior to emancipation the lords were greatly in need of a larger revenue, which they obtained by borrowing and by squeezing higher payments from the peasants, and sometimes evicting them. The peasants reacted by disobeying, by refusing to pay dues, and by destroying the property of the nobility. Instability and conflict were even more apparent prior to the Stolypin reform. Pressure of the nobility had not subsided; on the contrary, they increased their pressure by using the Nobles' Bank to further their interests. Again the peasants reacted by refusing to pay dues, by violence, by destruction of the nobles' property, and by supporting the intellectuals and the revolutionaries. Peasant violence reached its climax in the explosion of 1905. By the time the Soviet revolution had occurred, tsarism had been overthrown and the peasants had started to seize the land and cultivate it for themselves.

177

The experience of Mexico is less clear because the role of the peasants was submerged in the background prior to the 1911 revolution. It is true that peasant leaders supported the revolutionary movement, but the general crisis was more an expression of the dissatisfaction of the urban and industrial workers. There was an uprising in 1906, and strikes and violence were widespread in urban areas, but there is no evidence of such uprisings in the rural areas. However, if we consider the period preceding 1915, the year the reform commenced, as the background, Mexico then offers an example similar to all the others. Soon after 1911, the peasants rose against the landlords and the government and started to seize the land violently and to cultivate it under protection of armed guard.

In analyzing Japan's experience one must concentrate on the years preceding the Second World War, because the war years witnessed a policy of repression, mobilization, and control which helped to obscure the real situation. Looking a little farther back shows that tension and conflict between the landlords and the tenants began around the end of the First World War. Encouraged by increasing demand for land owing to increasing population, the landlords raised the rents at the same time as they acquired more land. The peasants reacted by requesting rent reduction and formed unions to protect themselves. They also allied themselves with the army, which they hoped would champion their cause. The landlords counteracted by establishing their own unions, and resorted to oppression, utilizing the local and state forces for that purpose, and thus they succeeded in averting violence.

Once the war was over, disputes were revived with greater zeal. This time, the landlords were not seeking higher rents but eviction of the peasants by whatever means were necessary. Though there is no evidence of violence prior to the reform, it is clear that a crisis had developed and conflict between the landlords and the peasant tenants had become grave.

The crisis in Egypt was evident in both rural and urban areas. Besides the strikes and violence in urban areas, throughout the 1940's and up to 1952 the peasants attacked the property of the landlords and there was some bloodshed. The pressure from below was so great that it threatened the stability of the whole social structure and the position of the nobility.

It seems evident, in conclusion, that land tenure reform has been commonly associated with a crisis in the economy which may be instrumental in bringing about the reform. It is possible that land tenure reform serves as a means of tackling the crisis. Whether or not it was in each specific case will be seen in the next chapter. The crisis may also be the mechanism by which reform is rendered imperative and justifiable by making it easier to overcome opposition of the vested-interest groups who will not permit a reform unless they see in it a chance to augment their interests or to safeguard them. It may be suggested, therefore, that the more fundamental the crisis and the more widespread it is, the more imperative, radical, and likely the reform appears to be.

XII

COMPARISON AND CONTRAST II:
REFORM OBJECTIVES AND PROCESSES

I. OBJECTIVES

In the previous chapter we investigated the problems that prevailed prior to reform. The reform might or might not have been designed to solve these problems. It is necessary, therefore, to find out what were the objectives of reform and the processes of their realization.

First we must differentiate between the objectives of the pre-reform advocates of reform and those of the actual reformers. The advocates may not be in positions of power or be policy-makers. However, as outsiders they see the problems more clearly and prescribe the reform accordingly. Or they may be proponents of a certain political philosophy which prescribes reform. But there is no reason why their objectives and those of the actual reformers should always be the same. Of course, the difference between the two may be a difference in roles and policies only, though the persons may be the same.[1] In this chapter we shall deal with the objectives of the actual reformers only.

The objectives of reform may be distinguished as economic, social, and political. Economic objectives deal with production and allocation. Social objectives include distribution of income and wealth, and status of the peasant in society. Political objectives include promotion of political stability, legitimacy of the political system, and national security.[2]

(A) ECONOMIC OBJECTIVES

Prior to the Soviet reforms, economic objectives were not common features of the reforms under study. Problems of investment and allocation or productivity and growth were not even mentioned. The only economic action of the Greek reforms was Solon's regulation of exports to reallocate factors of production and to maintain the supply of food in the domestic market. Pisistratus extended credit to small farmers, encouraged production in mining, and promoted construction work to alleviate unemployment, but these policies were separate from and independent of his land tenure program, and had little or no effect on agricultural production or productivity.

Similarly, the Roman reforms had no direct interest in economic problems. Except for Gaius' colonization program, which was designed partially to relieve urban unemployment, no economic objectives appeared

180

in the program. Even the colonization program was more a political maneuver and a revival of an old policy of colonizing occupied territory. Failure to deal with economic problems was even more pronounced in the French reforms. They not only failed to include economic objectives but tended to have negative effects on production by encouraging fragmentation and small-scale operation. In Russia the emancipation was neutral to economic problems. However, economic objectives started to win recognition with the Stolypin reform, which had consolidation of holdings and commercial production among its objectives. It also was concerned with economies of scale in agriculture.

The Soviet reforms were the beginning of the contemporary era in which agrarian reform has been comprehensive, extending to all sectors of the agrarian structure. Thus, the Soviet reforms were concerned with the scale of operation, with techniques of cultivation, with capital investment, and with allocation of resources, although they fell short of their objectives in application. Soviet emphasis on economic objectives was comparable to that of the English tenure changes which were responses to economic developments and business rationality. The main difference between the English tenure changes and the Soviet reforms was that the former were motivated by and planned according to the business interests of the individual owners, while the latter were motivated and planned collectively by the Communist Party in the name of the national economy.[3]

The new era was only ushered in by the Soviet reform, but not all reforms since have been that comprehensive. Especially during its first two decades, the Mexican reform had no economic goals. Actually it had negative effects on production whenever it broke up efficiently run estates. Although this was formally prohibited in 1934 and later in 1942, the precaution to preserve efficient farms was often disregarded, especially in the 1930's during the presidency of Cardenas.

The Japanese and Egyptian reforms, comprehensive in objectives and effects, both took economic problems into consideration, but the results were limited. Though Japan provided extension services and encouraged coöperatives, the effects were more social than economic, and altered distribution and the standard of living rather than the conditions of production and allocation. The coöperatives were limited to credit and marketing activities. They had no direct impact on the scale of operation, physical productivity, or allocation of resources. Therefore, the impact on investment was not labor-saving and there was hardly any effect on labor productivity.

The Egyptian reform was more directly concerned with production than was the Japanese. By instituting mandatory membership in producer coöperatives, it guaranteed the use of machinery, fertilizer, insecticide, and pesticide, which were contingent upon large-scale operation. The coöperatives also assumed marketing, credit, and educational responsibilities. The reform also aimed at increasing mobility of capital to encourage productive investment in industry. Therefore the Egyptian reform, as an example of agrarian reform, is the one most comparable to the Soviet reform in proclaimed objectives. But unlike it, the Egyptian reform was not integrated within a national economic plan. However, this difference may be insignificant, since agriculture in Egypt is relatively efficient and has little room for flexibility of production planning.

Thus, even though economic problems characterized all the societies under study, the only reforms with economic objectives were the Soviet, Japanese, and Egyptian. The Stolypin reform was concerned only indirectly. The English tenure changes were concerned primarily with economic objectives and will be discussed later.

The above analysis may be objected to on the ground that all the reforms have served economic goals by promoting individual ownership, thus increasing security of tenure and raising incentives. If true, this is an indirect objective or only an effect rather than an objective. Furthermore, there is no conclusive evidence that individual ownership encourages incentives more than tenancy. It may do so if it promotes security of tenure, but security was not necessarily advanced by the reforms that created individual ownership. A serf in bondage is also secure, probably more so than the newly created owner, since he is reasonably assured of an amount of land proportional to the size of his family through periodic repartition. The new owner did not have this security, since his land was too small to guarantee an adequate income capable of creating security. It was also subject to fragmentation and diminution through inheritance, even though the new owner might feel secure.[4] The reformers who have tried to rehabilitate or promote privately owned family farms have justified their action as a means to strengthen or create political democracy and stability, rather than to stimulate incentives and increase production.

(B) SOCIAL OBJECTIVES

The social objectives of reform are difficult to isolate from the economic and political, since the social problems were causes of low productivity and of unrest and political instability. Low per capita income and unemployment, for example, are social problems, but whether the reformers dealt with them because of their social or their political implications is hard to say. These problems are therefore, separated in this section only for analytical purposes.

The social objectives have centered around freedom of the person of the peasant, freedom of the land, correction of injustices, lower unemployment, and higher living standards. The first two are problems of serfdom and bondage. The other three are results of corruption, inequality of distribution, and low per capita output.

182

Freedom of the peasant and his land were two separate questions and their treatment was not the same. Solon freed the *Hektemors* by freeing their land from debt, and by taking measures to prevent recurrence of land enserfment. The English commutations freed the land by commuting labor rent into money rent, but the person of the villein had to be ransomed in order to obtain his freedom from the lord. The French reform and the Russian emancipation were designed to free the person of the peasant, but not the land unless redeemed separately. In the French reform, all dues to the lords were abolished without compensation under pressure from the peasants. This was not the original objective of the reform; it was forced on the Assembly by circumstances. The Russian emancipation freed the person of the peasant but made ownership conditional upon redemption.

Poverty is a relative concept. It relates to low per capita income of the whole community, or to low per capita income of specific groups relative to the other groups. Low per capita income of the whole community is a problem of the size of total production given the total population, while that of specific groups is one of distribution, or of what share of the product goes to each specific sector of the population relative to its size. Inequality of distribution is a social problem which several reforms aimed at tackling. However, only the Soviet reform ideally aimed at eliminating inequality and at raising the total per capita income or standard of living.[5]

Only the Stolypin reform did not have social objectives, unless one considers separation from the *mir* to be a sort of freedom,[6] although the reformers themselves did not consider this freedom as one of their objectives. However, like the Stolypin reform, the English enclosures were not motivated by social objectives, but social effects may be observed when evaluating them in a long-run perspective.

Low living standards loomed large prior to the Greek reform, the French reform, and the Russian Emancipation. The reformers were aware of that, but no attempts were made to deal with this problem from the standpoint of distribution of land and wealth. In other words, there was no attempt to redistribute the land and raise the living standard of the peasant. Except for Pisistratus' distribution of the estates of his adversaries, nothing in the nature of the reforms was appropriate to deal with the problem.

Peasant low income and social distress were central to the Roman, Mexican, Japanese, and Egyptian reforms. In the Roman and Mexican, the problem was perceived as a result of injustices and corruption. Therefore, it was treated by restoration and distribution of usurped *ager publicus* in Rome and land of the Indians in Mexico. Mexico also distributed public and private land to improve conditions of the peasants, but this was conditional and ineffective, as we shall see below.

The Japanese and Egyptian reformers proclaimed their intention to

183

deal with low income and unequal distribution by redistributing privately owned land, regulating rent, and redistributing the agricultural product. The extent of redistribution will be discussed in the next chapter.

(C) POLITICAL OBJECTIVES

Having surveyed the background features and having seen that crisis and political instability were common, we are not surprised to find that the primary objectives of reform were political. Except for the tenure changes in England and the Soviet reforms, political objectives were primary in all the reforms, as shown in Chart II. Political objectives, however, differed according to whether reform was introduced before or after a political upheaval.[7] When reform preceded political upheaval, its main objectives have usually been to create stability, prevent a revolution, and maintain the existing political order with a minimum modification. If reform was introduced after a revolution, it has usually been to maintain and strengthen the new political order, or give it legitimacy. In either case, political stability has been the goal, but the object of stability was different — the old or the new order.

Another political objective of reform, which is related to the above, has been the establishment of a western type of democracy. This resulted from the conviction that a middle class is necessary for democracy and that creating a class of small owner-farmers strengthens the middle class and thus democracy.[8]

We have seen that Solon wanted to reduce the danger of revolution and stabilize the political system which was endangered by the heavy concentration of wealth and power and the loss of citizenship by the enserfed *Hektemors*. He therefore tried to narrow the gap between classes and lessen the danger of conflict. In contrast, Pisistratus wanted to strengthen his own position and legitimize the revolution and his dictatorship. For this purpose he distributed land to fulfill his promises to his supporters and to weaken the power of his adversaries.[9]

The Gracchi brothers wanted to stabilize the political system which had been endangered by concentration of wealth and power, unemployment, poverty, and restiveness among the slaves. It is probable that Tiberius had other political reasons, such as switching the pendulum of power in favor of the plebian aristocracy that he led, but his main purpose was to prevent a revolution from below and restore political stability. Tiberius wanted also to rehabilitate democracy and strengthen the army, both of which had been undermined by disappearance of the middle-class farmers.

The French reforms, as part of the total program of the middle class or bourgeois revolution, were geared to win the confidence of the peasants and weaken the power of the old nobility, that is, to establish and legitimize the new political structure. The reform was therefore modified gradually according to political circumstances, such as the external dan-

184

ger to national security and the need for peasant support. These objectives were held strongly as potential instruments to contain peasant discontent and restlessness which the revolutionaries exploited to strengthen their own position and legitimize the new political system.

Though the Russian emancipation aimed at improving conditions of the peasants, its primary purpose was to avoid political upheaval. This was the opinion of the Tsar and of Rostovtzev, who supported the reform as his right-hand man. Both were aware of the potentialities for political disorder and were anxious to introduce changes from above rather than have them enforced from below. This attitude became especially strong after the Crimean War demonstrated the weakness of the Russian social structure. Even the form of organization imposed on the liberated serfs was determined by the need for political stability; besides being an easy way of collecting taxes and dues, the *mir* was considered a stabilizing element in society. When this proved to be untrue the government changed its attitude and sought to dissolve the *mir* and strengthen private ownership. The change was based on the belief that a strong middle class composed of rich and secure peasants would be a stabilizing factor; this was the essence of the Stolypin reform. Stolypin wanted to dissolve the *mir* and encourage individual ownership to maintain the status of the nobility and counteract the influence of the leftists and revolutionaries. The nobility, represented by Stolypin, allied itself with the middle class and adopted their techniques to intercept any uprising and to salvage what they could. The reform was a means to that end.

The interdependence between Soviet political objectives and their reform policy is known, both in general and in detail. The Communist Party had planned to nationalize the land and create collectives, but the policy and application of reform were guided, partly at least, by political objectives. For example, once nationalization was decreed, the peasants were allowed to seize the land and hold it individually. The authorities permitted such acts, to win peasant support and strengthen the revolution while attending to other matters. When War Communism proved economically and politically disastrous, once again the Soviets modified their policy and introduced the NEP to regain the confidence of the peasants and guarantee the security of the new political system. When the rich peasants became powerful — at this time the economic objectives of the NEP had roughly been realized — the government changed its policy and initiated the drive for collectivization. Finally, when collectivization met with strong opposition, Stalin interfered and, at least formally, ordered re-adherence to voluntary collectivization. Though the drive did not become voluntary, the change of policy shows how closely the agrarian policy was influenced by politics to serve the regime and augment the security of the state.

The Soviet reform was in fact more politically oriented than any other reform. In its totality, the program was based on the intellectual and philosophical doctrines of socialism regarding class and power structure and position of the individual vis-à-vis the state. The Soviets intended to destroy the old political order and build a new one based on nationalization and collectivization of the land. This was what their reform was meant to achieve.

The Mexican reforms also were motivated by political objectives, and were implemented accordingly. The reform law of 1915 was passed under the pressure of Zapata, the Indian leader who, with others, was causing enough rural disturbance to endanger the Revolution. The peasants had already started to seize the land by force and settle on it, and the reform was politically expedient to quiet them and to help the revolutionaries entrench themselves in the country. Restriction of the rights of ownership by foreigners was another political objective of the reform intended to strengthen the political independence of the state. Since the foreigners had received extensive concessions from the old regime, the reform sought to destroy that regime by eliminating foreign influence as one of its main effects. These objectives clearly indicate that the reform was used by the reformers to ensure security of the new political structure, as occurred in the French reform.

Application and direction of the reform depended also on the political views and objectives of the incumbent president of the republic. When Carranza was president, even though he had supported the Reform Law of 1915, its application was obstructed by the administrative complications he introduced. His primary objective was to stabilize his own political position, and once that was done, he tried to slow the reform; he succeeded. Similarly, when Calles changed his views about the *ejido* in favor of private ownership, he ordered parcelization of the ejido land.

Finally, upon his election to the presidency, the radical Cardenas revitalized the reform and strengthened the ejido tenure. The next distribution revival had to wait until the presidency of Lopez Mateos in 1958. It appears that neither the orientation, direction, nor pace of the reform was determined primarily by the objective economic and social needs of the rural population. They were determined largely by the attitude of the president and his political and social philosophy.

The significance of political objectives in the Japanese reform needs no proof. Coming in the form of directives from the Occupation Army, the reforms were intended to create democracy and eliminate future dangers of war. All details of the program were chosen to fit these ideals. Democracy was associated with small owner-farmers and therefore a class of these was to be created. Control of rent and limitation of the size of holding were additional measures to ensure the creation and stability of a middle class as a basis for democracy.

Finally, the Egyptian reformers aimed at breaking up the "feudal" oli-

186

garchy to free the peasants from political dependence and strengthen the relative position of the emerging middle class. Even the reform policy on coöperation was politically determined, placing the decision-making responsibilities in the hands of state officials. Furthermore, the Egyptian reformers compromised with the fairly large landowners in order to neutralize them and thus safeguard the new political structure. When their neutrality was no longer essential to the security of the Revolution, the reform law was revised to expropriate some of their holdings. Even regulation of rent was not devoid of political orientation, for it helped to win peasant support in return for improving peasant conditions.

This survey of reform objectives leads to one of the most important hypotheses about reform. It clearly suggests that the main objectives of the reformers were political. The reformers use land distribution and other tenure changes, according to each situation, to win support of specific groups, to create or restore political stability, to legitimize their own positions, and to create what they consider to be democracy. The timing and scope of the reform are determined more by the political pressure for reform than by the economic and social needs of the people. To a large extent, the timing and objectives of reform are interdependent with the processes or ways and means of executing the reform, as will be seen in the next section. Therefore, planning reform for economic development and improvement of social conditions should not ignore the political implications and the feasibility of these reforms. To do so may render the reform plan futile.

II. PROCESSES

Two types of reform processes may be distinguishable: those which determine the objectives, and those which, at least partly, are determined by the objectives. The processes that determine the objectives involve timing of the reform and the extent to which it is meant to deal with the problems of the rural population. The processes determined by the objectives include those dealing mainly with implementation of the reform. To separate these two classes of processes is not easy, because a process may be both a function and a determinant of the objectives of reform.

(A) OBJECTIVE-DETERMINING PROCESSES

Most of the reforms under study came during, or directly following, a political revolution. Those which neither accompanied nor followed a revolution did not involve redistribution of private estates, at least when land was held by legal title. These reforms were usually timed to prevent a revolution. In contrast, the reforms involving redistribution of land accompanied a revolution, coming only after the power structure had been changed and a new elite had emerged. The pattern of implementation was determined by the degree to which the new elite aspired to the status and power position of the deposed elite. The specific objectives of reform

187

were defined according to whether or not the reform was intended to prevent a revolution or to support one. We shall call the former group nonrevolutionary reforms and the latter revolutionary reforms and shall deal with them separately.[10]

1. Nonrevolutionary Reforms. Among these were Solon's and the Gracchan reforms, the Russian emancipation, and possibly the Stolypin reforms. These also include the tenure changes in England. All the nonrevolution reforms came at a time of crisis and only when the reformers believed a revolution to be imminent. Solon's reform involved no land distribution. It centered around abolition of debt which freed the enserfed land and restored it to its legal owners. The Gracchan reform, on the other hand, was declared indispensable if a revolution were to be averted and democracy rehabilitated. Though the Gracchan reforms included land distribution, this land was not legally owned by the immediate holders. Formally, it was public land held in violation of the size limit on individual holding. The legally held private estates remained intact.

The Russian emancipation was also necessitated by the apparent crisis and the determination of the tsar to prevent the eruption of violence and the overthrow of the political system. Therefore, its timing was important in determining the objectives which excluded distribution of privately owned land. The land affected was held by concession from the state in lieu of specific obligations by the landlord. The landlord held his private land separately and this land was not affected by emancipation. It is therefore hard to classify the Emancipation among the reforms that distributed private land, increased the holdings of the peasants, or diminished land concentration.

Though the Stolypin reform followed a violent uprising, it did not follow a revolution but was designed to prevent one. While it did not involve land distribution, it did change the form of tenure of *mir* land from collective to individual. Now the peasants owned individually what they had owned collectively. Otherwise, there was no change except that resulting from private land transactions.

While the nonrevolutionary reforms are too few to permit generalization, it may be suggested that such reforms usually avoid land distribution, fundamental tenure changes, and basic changes in the political structures. They are usually intended to pacify rather than to change the social order or to solve fundamental rural problems.

2. Revolutionary Reforms. These include the reform of Pisistratus, the French, Soviet, Mexican, Japanese, and Egyptian reforms. In each of these, reform was carried out by a new regime during or directly after revolution had altered the political structure and installed a new class in power.[11]

Two things are common to the revolutionary reforms: privately held land was distributed to the peasants, and the distribution was carried out by

188

a new elite. Of course, the revolutionary reforms did not all follow the same pattern of land distribution. Pisistratus, as far as could be ascertained, distributed public land or the land of his adversaries which he confiscated and treated as public land. The French reform did not distribute land, but established title to land already in the hands of the peasant; also, it relieved the peasants from paying feudal rent. In other words, it changed the status of the peasants from tenants to owners. The Soviet reform did not distribute land, but redistributed the right of use of the land after abolishing the right of private ownership. Inasmuch as the right to use the land became the highest form of tenure in Soviet Russia, this right was redistributed in favor of the tillers of the land, that is, the peasants. The Mexican reform concentrated on usurped land and restored it to the peasants, and opened public land to colonization. Especially since 1934 the Mexicans have not hesitated to requisition and redistribute parts of the private estates when land was needed. The Japanese and Egyptian reforms were similar in that both transferred land from private owners to tenants or landless peasants.

In all these reforms the revolutionary process of reform and the time at which it was introduced determined the objective and scope of reform. Land distribution was necessary to gain support of the beneficiaries and to weaken the adversaries. The need for political acceptance made distribution necessary, but only to the extent that the revolution and the new elite needed legitimacy. Furthermore, it appears that land distribution is closely associated with revolution and a change of the ruling elite. In contrast, the entrenched elite try to maintain the old tenure structure as intact as possible. Whenever they permit basic changes, it is because they are convinced that change is imminent and larger losses are to be anticipated.

(B) OBJECTIVE-DETERMINED PROCESSES

Three such processes may be distinguished: compensation, discrimination, and reaction. They are interrelated, but for analytical purposes are treated separately.

1. Compensation. The act of compensation refers to the redemption or compensatory payment for any rights or property expropriated as a result of land tenure reform. Except for the reforms of Pisistratus and the French, all others that involved transfer of private estates to other private owners were based on payment of compensation or redemption fees.[12]

The reforms of Pisistratus and the French were noncompensatory because of unique circumstances. Distribution of land in the former applied only to public land or to private land made public for political reasons, but there was no distribution of private land and no reason for compensation. In the French reform, provision was made initially to compensate all rights based on land concession. Owing to political circumstances and the threat to national security discussed above, and the pressure of the peasants, redemption payments were cancelled and the feudal tenants became owners without paying compensation. Therefore, it may be unrealistic to classify the French reform as noncompensatory. The reformers, as long as they had a say in the matter, were insistent that compensation be paid.[13]

Formally, the Gracchan distribution was not compensatory. Since the expropriated land was held illegally, no compensation was owing. Yet, Tiberius had contemplated compensating the landlords but withheld compensation from them after their opposition became intolerable. He compensated them indirectly, however, by increasing the land allowance for their children and by exempting them from rent on their holdings of public land. In that sense the reform was compensatory.

The only other reform that renders classification difficult is the Mexican, in which distributed land was either restored or dotated. The restored land was simply returned to its legal owners and required no compensation, and the land for dotation was extracted from public land or from neighboring private estates. Public land warranted no compensation, but the policy on privately held land was unique. The law permitted compensation, whether the land was restored or dotated, subject to examination of each petition for compensation according to the economic needs of the petitioner. If approved, compensation was paid by the treasury rather than by the land recipient.

In contrast, compensation was paid automatically in the Russian emancipation, in the Japanese and Egyptian reforms, and in the English tenure changes. Since the English tenure changes were based on land transaction rather than on expropriation, and were carried out without direct government intervention on a national level, they are not discussed here. The Russian emancipation and the Japanese and the Egyptian reforms were compensatory by design and in fact. Compensation was paid in government bonds to be amortized by the land recipients.[14]

From the above it appears that in all cases of distribution of privately owned land, legal provision was made for compensation even when reform was carried out by a new elite representing a class generally opposed to the old regime. The principle of compensation reflects two kinds of attitudes: first, a sense of justice, and second, hesitation and insecurity of the reformers. We shall not discuss the former, since it relates to one's philosophy and value judgment concerning private ownership and wealth. The latter attitude, however, reflects the apprehensions of the reformers which arise from contradictions in the logic of such reforms. The contradictions are: (1) why redistribute landed property and not industrial and commercial property?, and (2) if landed property were redistributed without compensation, how is a different policy for urban wealth justified, should the question arise? These contradictions have actually been pointed out in relation to the French and the Stolypin reforms. In France the revolutionary middle class insisted on reform by legal means and with compensation "lest a dangerous precedent for other forms of property be set." In the Stolypin reform the question was raised differently: Is the expropriation of certain landowners justified in order to establish private ownership by others? This hesitation led to the Stolypin policy discussed above.

2. *Discrimination.* Two types of discrimination [15] were common: discrimination by exclusion or nonapplication of the reform law, and discrimination by inclusion. The former relates more to the differential effects of reform on social and economic classes; the latter to the nature of tenure or rights of ownership. An example of the former is the exclusion of the *metayers* and landless rural workers from the benefits of the French reform. This type of discrimination will be discussed in conjunction with the effects of reform in the next chapter; discrimination by inclusion will be discussed presently.

Several of the reforms have been discriminatory in handling tenure arrangements. These include the Roman and Russian emancipation, Mexican, Japanese, and Egyptian reforms. Because of their discriminatory character, they have resulted in what may be considered a dual tenure arrangement, one form of which applied to the veteran landowners, and the other to the new owners or beneficiaries of the reform. The duality, however, has not been uniform. For example, land distributed by the Roman reform became private property but was made inalienable, in contrast to the private owner's right of disposal. Thus, the new owners, like all other owners, had full use of the land, but unlike them their right of disposal was restricted. Even though the restriction was intended to protect them against losing the land by sale, their tenure status fell short of the right enjoyed by the veteran owners.

The problem of duality was more pronounced in the Russian emancipation where emancipated peasants were given perpetual rights to the land, but these were not rights of ownership as the term applied to other owners. The peasants held the land in communal tenure and neither the individual peasant nor the commune could alienate the land. The individual could forego his rights upon meeting certain conditions and winning the approval of the commune, but he could not transfer his rights freely. The commune, on the other hand, could alienate the land after completing redemption payments, but even then alienation was conditional. No such restrictions were placed on other owners.

The same form of duality resulted in Mexico.[16] The recipients of land were members of *ejidos* and held the land collectively. In contrast to the private owners, they could not alienate it either individually or collectively. This is why we have suggested that these new "owners" were secure tenants rather than owners. Whichever classification we apply, the resulting tenure implies tenure relations discriminatory against the beneficiaries of reform; hence the duality.

The Japanese experience was different. Land alienation was restricted in two ways, one specific and the other general. The specific restriction prevented the new owners from alienating their land except by returning it to the land committees for resale. This restriction was abolished in 1950. The general restriction required that land be sold only to people who owned less than the legal maximum size of holding. Since this regulation was general to all owners, it is irrelevant to the question of duality.

The Egyptian reform represents the most extensive discrimination among those under study. The recipient of land was subject to at least three restrictions: he had to join a coöperative, could not alienate the land, and was obliged to observe inheritance laws which applied only to small owners. For this reason, it appears that the Egyptian *fellah* was made a secure tenant only, like the Mexican *ejidatorio*. The Egyptian *fellah* was restricted also regarding production methods through membership in the coöperative. Although the motives of these restrictions were to raise his income and improve his conditions, they created a dual tenure system and in that way set him apart from other owners.

In contrast to these discriminatory reforms, the Greek, French, Stolypin, and Soviet reforms and the English tenure changes applied the law equally to all, and a uniform tenure system emerged. The variety of backgrounds within which these reforms or tenure changes have taken place does not encourage generalizations; yet, some hypotheses may be suggested.

One possible hypothesis is that the discriminatory tenure policy was a reflection of the government's interest in regulating tenure. The dual tenure system resulted from government indecision on policy. Some governments would not let tenure change occur spontaneously as in England, and they did not have the courage to go all the way in directing change as the Soviets did in Russia. This hesitation might be a reflection of the surviving influence of old regimes, or of the fact that the new elite aspired to the position of the old regime, or of both. Thus, the reformers were neither willing to preserve the old tenure nor ready to destroy it. The result was a compromise; they modified the old tenure system by creating small owners and protecting them through a dual tenure system.

This hypothesis is borne out by the Roman, Mexican, Japanese, and Egyptian reforms, as these are contrasted with the English and Soviet tenure policies which went to extremes of government control in that it was either nonexistent or complete. The only discriminatory case that deviates from this hypothesis is the Russian emancipation, which, besides maintaining the influence of the old regime, kept the peasants under supervision to facilitate collection of taxes and redemption payments. When both these objectives failed, government policy on the duality of tenure changed. The Stolypin reform reversed the policy and provided for uniform tenure arrangements.

Another possible hypothesis is that a close relationship exists between duality and reform planning. Reforms planned in advance tend to result in duality, while spontaneous reforms are beyond the control of the reformers and therefore lead to a uniform system. Thus, Pisistratus' distribution policy was part of the process of revolution and nothing indicates that land tenure reform was planned in advance. The same was true in France and, of course, in England. Two cases do not fit this hypothesis — the Stolypin and the Soviet reforms. The former involved a policy reversal: a change of tenure rather than distribution of land. In a sense, this policy reversal may be seen as government decision to let tenure change follow a spontaneous course free of government intervention. Even the Soviet reform, which was planned, resulted in duality at least with regard to the form of land holding. The Soviet policy provides an example of complete control which may be considered an extreme case of the duality system represented here as partial government control over tenure groups.

The duality problem has significance in evaluating the efficiency of reform and in predicting future developments and stability; for example how can the creation of a double-standard tenure system be justified when it allows the veteran owners full rights of disposal while it puts the newly created owners under government control? And how can the latter group be reassured they are not being discriminated against and thus be prevented from becoming a threat to the new political order? These questions will be dealt with in chapter xiv.

3. *Reaction.* Reaction, as used here, means an attempt to limit the effects of land tenure reform or prevent its consummation and/or permanence. Reaction may take any of three forms: compromise, obstruction, or reversal. Compromise implies purposeful limitation of the effects of reform by the reformers in an attempt to ensure acceptance of reform, to avoid failure, or simply for lack of intention to achieve more radical changes in the tenure system. Obstruction may be caused either by the reformers or by their opponents. The reformers may obstruct execution of the law when they have legislated more extensive changes than they had intended, or when they are satisfied that their primary objectives have been realized without a more thorough implementation of the reform law. In contrast, the opponents of reform may obstruct implementation at any stage of the process, to protect vested interests inherent in the old order. Compromise and obstruction occur only during the reform period, but reversal occurs only after the era of reform. Reversal reflects the policy of a group other than the original reformers. The most characteristic example of reversal occurred after the death of the Gracchi: the successor government reversed the policy of its predecessors and undid their work.

These forms of reaction are encountered to one degree or another in most of the reforms under study. One of the difficulties of analysis is to determine whether a particular reaction policy was compromise or obstruction. How can one determine, for instance, whether or not a compromise was indispensable to save the reform? Another problem is how to evaluate a policy which if taken by itself may appear to be a form of reaction, but when considered in context proves otherwise. An example is the reversal of Soviet policy on agriculture in 1921, and again in 1932–33. In order to avoid this problem we will consider both situations.

Finally, in determining whether or not the reform effects have been limited because of reaction by compromise, we shall base the evaluation on proclamations of the reformers and on the objective needs of the rural population, both socially and economically. Thus, a policy may or may not be a compromise according to whether or not it falls short of the originally proclaimed objectives of the reformers.

Both compromise and reversal were apparent in the Greek reform. Compromise during Solon's reform caused peasant dissatisfaction, while the landlords were not overly disappointed. First, Solon refrained from land distribution despite loud cries for it and despite the concentration of poverty and wealth. His policy might have been guided by an honest perception of the problems rather than by an intent to compromise, but his second measure tended to support the view that his was a policy of compromise. By debasing the currency, Solon indirectly compensated the landlords who themselves were debtors and reduced the impact of the reform on their standing in the social and economic class structure. The two policies together tended to undermine the effectiveness of the reform as a solution of the problems plaguing the society.

A second instance of reaction was the reversal following the rule of Pisistratus when his dynasty was overthrown and his sons killed. The fact of reversal is significant in the sense that the reform was not built on a solid foundation sufficiently independent of the regime in power to survive its fall.

All three forms of reaction featured in the Roman reform. Compromise might have been unavoidable in order to avoid failure, but this is hard to either prove or disprove. Tiberius compromised in two ways: he allowed the big holders of *ager publicus* a larger land allowance for their children, giving each family the right to hold up to 1,000 *iugera* (customarily equated with 622 acres); he also exempted them from rent on public land. He thus limited the impact of reform on the distribution of both income and land. Obstruction occurred when the land commission, under pressure from the Italian allies, was suspended and its powers of jursidiction vested in the consuls who were expected to evade implementation of the law. Consequently, the reform was indirectly brought to a halt before consummation.

Finally, reaction by reversal set in once the political forces exchanged places and the Gracchi brothers were overthrown. Though there has been disagreement over the extent of reversal, there is full agreement that it occurred. In the same year that Gaius Gracchus was killed, land alienation was made permissible and the preventive measure against future land accumulation was destroyed. Two years later the land commission was dissolved. Then the law on colonization was repealed and the colonies established by Gaius were disestablished. Finally, the stage was set for reconcentration by declaring all *ager publicus* held by individuals as private property subject to alienation. Probably one of the main reasons for reversal was that the opponents of reform had not been weakened sufficiently to prevent their counteraction. The fact that even among the reformers there was hesitation and willingness to compromise might also have contributed to the impermanence of the reform effects.

Reaction in the French reform was apparent mainly in the execution of supplementary measures, namely, in those areas dealing with land and land concession. The reform, primarily for the liberation of the peasants, was complete and quick, but once implementation was under way, obstruction started. Obstruction was possible owing to the ambiguity of the law, to the difficulty of separating personal from real rights, and to the fact that proof of title was put initially on the peasant. These regulations slowed down implementation until peasant pressure and rioting forced repeal of these obstructive policies.

Finally, reaction by reversal was reflected in the policy on sale of public land which was more favorable to the richer than to the poorer people. Reversal was, of course, more conspicuous after the Restoration when many former landlords recovered their land or received compensation. These reactionary policies were economic in character, directed toward rehabilitating the former landlords or strengthening the new big landowners. In no case did reaction affect the personal freedom that the revolution conferred on the *censier* or the serf.

Reaction was more conspicuous in the Russian emancipation, both as compromise and as reversal. Since the compromise was quite favorable to the landlords, they made no attempt to obstruct the reform. Compromise was effected mainly by manipulating the redemption settlement and the land value, and by permitting the landlords to choose the land they retained. As a result, the landlords were better off economically than they were before. Another form of compromise was the exclusion from redemption of complementary resources such as water and meadow land, giving the landlord economic weapons to bargain with and to safeguard some of his traditional advantages.

Reaction by reversal prevailed mostly after the death of Alexander II, the reformer Tsar. Almost immediately afterward repression and oppression mounted, and the peasants were personally bound and subjected once more to the authority of the nobility. In their assemblies and in their economic affairs the peasants were put under guardianship of the local nobility in a manner described by Robinson as being similar to serfdom of the old days. The reversal extended to the tenure rights of the peasant, and in 1893 his right of separation from the commune was further restricted in an attempt to perpetuate the communal form of tenure.

One might go farther and tie the Stolypin reform to the Emancipation rather than treat it as a separate reform measure. The Stolypin reform itself would then appear as reaction by reversal, since it advocated a retreat from the Emancipation communal tenure policy, replacing it with private tenure. Yet, even in implementing this policy there was reaction by compromise in favor of the nobility. The land committees entrusted with implementing the law were biased in composition and under the influence of the nobility. The land banks, which were the intermediaries in transferring the land to the peasantry, also favored the nobility by overvaluing the land and charging the peasants higher interest rates than those required of the landlords.

Evaluation of the Soviet reform is a little more difficult, since the conclusion will depend on one's point of departure. If, for instance, one looks at the reform from the standpoint of ownership, the reform was complete, rapid, and free of reaction. Land was nationalized and private ownership abolished in one act. But if one considers the agrarian policy concerning holding and operation of the land as part of the reform, reaction becomes evident. Also, if we were to evaluate each specific policy measure separately, reaction appears to have prevailed. If we look at the reform in its totality, however, reaction appears to have been a tactic necessary to bring about consummation rather than a way to obstruct change or to perpetuate the old situation.

Taking each Soviet measure separately indicates several instances of compromise, obstruction, or reversal. Compromise appeared first in 1917–18 when the peasants were permitted to seize land and property according to their abilities. The richer peasants got more this way than the poorer, and differentiation favoring the former continued. A second compromise was during War Communism when the Soviet government formed an alliance with the middle peasantry against the rich. Though a tactic, this policy compromised the objectives of the Land Decree and the basic goals of the reform. When the War Communism policy was successfully blocked by the peasantry, the Soviet reformers reversed it and reinstated free trade. They permitted tenancy and hired employment, and substituted a tax in kind for the requisitioning of farm products. This reversal probably was an unavoidable political tactic, but the fact remains that the reform was temporarily halted and the original policy modified.

When the economic and political goals of the NEP were considered fulfilled, reform was resumed in the direction of collectivization. When

196

the kulaks and richer peasants destroyed livestock and refrained from sowing the land in protest, Stalin suspended the drive for forced collectivization. The drive, however, was resumed and by 1938 collectivization was complete. The effects of Soviet reaction, however, were temporary in contrast to the permanent effects in other instances.

Reaction in Mexico was mainly by compromise and obstruction, though reversal at one point may be said to have prevailed. This was between 1925 and 1933, the period dominated by President Calles, who changed his views on the tenure status of the *ejido*. Under his influence, it became mandatory that land title be vested jointly in the ejido and the individual member and that land be parceled out to the members. But this period was short and its effects negligible, and therefore it need not be discussed.

Compromise and obstruction were more common and more effective. Compromise was due partly to the absence of a clear idea of reform and the vagueness that surrounded the status of the ejido. Thus, in the land decree of 1915 and the Constitution of 1917, eligibility to petition for land was so restricted that many landless rural groups were excluded, particularly the peones on haciendas who were most in need of land. The choice of land for redistribution was also based on compromise. Generally speaking, only the lower quality land was redistributed. Furthermore, concessions to the landlords were made in 1927 giving them representation on the census boards which determined the area of land to be distributed.

Obstruction was equally common. For example, execution of the law was made dependent on the initiative of the peasants who were illiterate and ignorant of their rights and of the letter of the law. This was particularly obstructive because it was difficult to prove title to the land or to prevent a court injunction in favor of the landlord.

The reaction in Japan started even before the reform bill was passed, as shown by the discrepancy between the proposed bill and the order of SCAP. It was an attempt to compromise with the landlords by raising the upper retention limit to 5 *cho* (12.25 acres). Compromise prevailed during implementation by excluding the forest and meadow land from the reform, leaving it in the hands of the landlord. But obstruction was more significant; it came in different forms, including intimidation, eviction, appeal to court, and pressure on the local land commissions. In fact, it became so evident that SCAP found it necessary to interfere and put an end to it.

Finally, reaction by reversal was contained in the legislative amendment of 1950 which allowed land transaction. While this action might be considered a contribution to freedom of the peasant, it was a factor in reversing the reform effects; it increased the number of larger holdings and encouraged a black market rent structure. These results suggest that when freed of control and preventive measures, the system of ownership in Japan tends toward land concentration. The latest attempt at reversal has been the bill introduced in the Diet session of 1963 to recompensate the landlords for their losses.

Finally, reaction in Egypt was by both compromise and obstruction. Toleration of landholdings larger than any size limit that had been suggested by earlier writers on reform and allowing the landlords to retain and dispose freely of their choice land were certainly compromises. The majority of the big owners continued to live on rent income as absentee landlords. Those who were expropriated were "generously" compensated, and the redistribution of wealth and income was quite limited while the majority of the peasants continued to live at or near subsistence.

Obstruction was attempted by the former landlords, using both legal and illegal methods. First they tried to prevent passage of the law, and when they failed, they tried to obstruct its effective application by removing livestock and grain from the estates, as happened in Soviet Russia on the eve of collectivization. They also tried to evade the law by failing to register the land in excess of the legal limit as required in preparation for reform. Now they are evading the rent regulation law, by reverting to black market rents, and thus partly reversing the distributive effects of the reform.

In contrast to these instances of reaction, there was none in the changes of the English tenure system. The tendency has been continuously in the direction of private tenure and land concentration. One may consider the spread of tenancy after the eighteenth-century enclosures as reversal, being reminiscent of the preyeomanry period, but not if one looks at the rise of yeomanry as a step toward concentrated ownership at the expense of very small landlords. Finally, it may be objected that the tendency in England has recently been not toward private property but away from it, as suggested by tenant protection, at least in the twentieth century. Protection of tenancy, however, regulates the right of contract only; it does not diminish the right of disposal.

The above observations suggest that land tenure reform has usually fallen short of expectations because of reaction in one form or another. In general, the form and degree of reaction have depended on who the initiator of reform was. Not only have the reforms failed to realize the expectations fully, but usually the reform process has undergone modification or reversal before reform has come to an end. The exception has been when the government followed an extreme policy of either abstaining from intervention as in England, or controlling the land system completely as in Soviet Russia. In the former case, the result was the entrenchment of private ownership; in the latter, its total destruction.

The significance of reaction, whichever form it takes, is that reform laws should not be interpreted at face value. Between legislation and execution there are many hurdles to be overcome. The reformers in most cases have objectives somewhat dissimilar to those of the peasants. They use reform for their own purposes, and as soon as they have obtained their own goals the movement for reform loses its tempo. This applies especially when the reformers in any way aspire to those positions occupied by the former elite or landlord class. The course of events or the fate of the reform is usually determined by the social position of the reformers vis-à-vis the former ruling class and by their objectives. The greater the conflict between the new and old ruling groups, the more radical and permanent the reform tends to be. Conversely, the more closely the new group identifies with the old, the less radical, more compromising, and less permanent the reform effects would be.

Permanence, however, is relative and reversal may come at a later date. In the above studies it has come usually within a generation of the beginning of reform and, except in the Soviet reform, always after the original reformers had disappeared from the scene of political activity. The shortest interval between initiation of the reform and its reversal was between War Communism and the NEP in Soviet Russia; the longest was in the Greek reform of Pisistratus, extending to more than two decades. Therefore, evaluation of the reform must allow enough time for belated developments to unfold, as well as for determination of the actual objectives of the reformers and their relationship with the landlords and the ruling elite.

XIII

COMPARISON AND CONTRAST III:
EFFECTS AND EVALUATION

In the last two chapters we have surveyed the background, objectives, and processes of reform and found that the objectives of reformers were often dissimilar to those of the peasants. The proclaimed objectives also differed from the real ones, which tended to be primarily political. We have also seen that implementation of the reform was almost always complicated by reaction of one form or another, which tended to limit the effects. In this chapter we will survey these effects, evaluate the impact of reform as a problem-solving mechanism, and estimate the degree to which the objectives were realized.

We may approach the effects of the reforms in two ways, by evaluating each reform either against its own background as seen in restrospect, or in terms of the problems and objectives delineated by the reformers themselves. The two approaches differ in that the former may be more comprehensive and precise in recognizing the needs of the rural people. We shall utilize both approaches.

(A) ECONOMIC AND TENURE EFFECTS

If, as in the previous chapter, one considers as economic problems only those relating to production and allocation of resources, then the discussion will be limited to only the English tenure changes, the Soviet, Japanese, and Egyptian reforms.[1] All the other reforms were motivated by social and political objectives, and the economic problem did not appear in the program. This does not mean that economic problems did not exist. On the contrary, production was relatively low, techniques primitive, and underemployment widespread. Yet in none of these cases was much attention paid to these questions. Even in the Roman case, where some attention was paid to unemployment in the city, underemployment on the land was ignored. The same may be said of the French reform, while the Russian emancipation aggravated underemployment by reducing the allotment land area. The Stolypin reform could only indirectly have stimulated labor mobility or reduced population pressure on the land. In Mexico, efficiency of production was considered only passively by exempting efficient estates from partition. Otherwise, there was no

200

attempt to increase production or productivity by changing methods or reducing population pressure on the cultivable land except for a small amount of colonization. Thus, in all these reforms productivity and allocation of resources were virtually ignored, and the impact on them was almost nil or, as was claimed by the critics of the Mexican reform, even negative.

In contrast, the Soviet and Egyptian reforms, and to a limited extent the Japanese reform, took direct steps to deal with these problems. Although accurate data are hard to obtain, certain results of the Soviet reform have generally been accepted, including mechanization and investment in agriculture, reduction of underemployment and transfer of surplus labor to the industrial sector, modernization of agricultural techniques, change of the composition of agricultural products to comply with the needs of industrialization, increase of total output, and opening new land for cultivation. Regardless of the degree to which these advantages have been attained or of the level of efficiency of applying these changes to production, it is debatable whether the same could have been achieved in the same time-span without the Soviet type of reform,[2] especially if population pressure on the land prevailed.

The Soviet reformers achieved a great number of the objectives they included in the 1918 Land Decree. However, there is no indication that these were the objectives of a majority of the peasants. We know that the richer peasants were opposed to the institutional aspects of these reforms, though they might have shared the same economic objectives. Generally speaking, the Soviet reform was successful and attained the economic objectives it set for itself at the start, though these were not necessarily those of the peasants.

The economic effects of the Japanese reform were quite limited. The scale of operation was hardly affected and mechanization was not advanced nor was agriculture integrated into a national plan for development, probably because Japan was already an industrialized country. There was an increase in land productivity, but there has been no evidence that labor productivity has risen. Underemployment persisted even though total output increased. The rise in per-acre productivity has been attributed to better use of fertilizer and expansion of credit and marketing coöperatives, which probably could have been achieved without land tenure reform.[3] Nevertheless, it is clear that the economic results common to the Soviet and Japanese reforms were associated with the development of large-scale operation as represented by the collective and the coöperative in Russia and Japan respectively. The Egyptian reform shares this common feature. Improvement of agriculture in all three cases was due to the large-scale operations associated with producer, credit, and marketing coöperatives.

This similarity of effects may be explained by the fact that in both

Egypt and Japan agriculture was labor-intensive prior to reform, and further improvement depended on capital investment and organized marketing, which were encouraged by coöperatives and by consolidation of farms or operation on a larger scale. However, mechanization, integration of effort in line with industrialization plans, and reduction of underemployment were peculiar to the Soviet reform, in which coöperation was carried many steps farther and was implemented on a national scale.[4]

The above results are comparable to the English experience, where individualism rather than collectivism evolved and yet agriculture developed and was mechanized and underemployment eliminated. Again the common features were large-scale operation and emphasis on operation of the land rather than on its ownership. But England was also able to overcome underemployment by simultaneously developing industry which absorbed the surplus labor, as occurred also in the Soviet Union.

In all four cases in which agriculture developed and productivity rose, the larger-scale advantages were obtained through fuller utilization of labor, by pooling of efforts, and by increased investment of indivisible capital. These changes were made possible by consolidating the farms either by concentrating ownership and tenancy, as in England, or by evolving collectivism, as in the Soviet Union, Japan, and Egypt. In the two cases where underemployment was reduced, industrialization was taking place rapidly enough to absorb surplus rural population; in those where underemployment persisted, solutions to this problem were sought in agriculture alone, and there was little integration with industrial development for absorption of rural labor by industry. This suggests that underemployment is easier to reduce if treated within the context of the total economy rather than of agriculture alone. It also suggests an interdependence between the rural and urban sectors of the economy and that unless industrial and commercial opportunities are created, surplus labor in the rural areas cannot be utilized.

Industry, however, was not the sole absorber of surplus labor. In England and in Soviet Russia colonization of new land was an important source of employment. Opening new land raised the effective land/labor ratio and compensated for loss of employment because of tenure change. Though attempted in Mexico and Egypt, among other modern reforms, the results were limited for lack of potentially arable land and the high cost of reclaiming it.

We should also notice that where economic effects were positive, emphasis has been shifted, in different degrees, from land ownership to land operation, resulting in larger-scale farming and in greater tiller security. Besides deriving the advantages of the larger scale and being able to invest more capital in the land, the tiller has become more secure to the extent to which operation of the land has become the focus of attention. A tentative classification would place the Soviet reform at one extreme of emphasis on land operation, with the French reform at the other end of the continuum; the former emphasizes operation, and the latter ownership. The Egyptian and English examples follow down the line, and then the Mexican and the Japanese, in which the least attention has been paid to the scale of operation. Put in terms of land tenure, nationalization is the highest degree of shift of emphasis to operation; it is followed by limited expansion of producer coöperatives; then comes protection of the tenant during the contract period; and finally the credit and marketing coöperatives. These signs of the shift may exist in combination, as, for example, where both greater security of the tenant and marketing and credit coöperatives have been established simultaneously. But when operation has not become the point of emphasis and the scale of operation has remained small, development has been retarded even when large-scale ownership prevailed, as in the ejido of Mexico where methods of cultivation have remained primitive and productivity low.[5]

The other extreme on the scale-of-operation continuum is the ownership and cultivation of uneconomically small and fragmented farm units. Although small-scale operation prevailed in most of the societies under study, none of them except the English and Soviet tenure changes, and the Egyptian to a limited degree, gave attention to this problem. The Stolypin reform provided for consolidation in the Law of 1911, but since its implementation period was short, the effects are hard to evaluate. In no other reform was anything done or proposed to deal with fragmentation or the small-scale farm units. Where land distribution took place, the plots were consolidated, albeit in small units. When the problem of size and fragmentation was recognized, the measures dealing with it applied only to the land subject to reform. The farmers benefiting from the reform were required to join producer coöperatives to enable them to pool their resources as well as to facilitate indivisible capital investments. Since the reformed land was a small portion of the total farming area, fragmentation and small-scale ownership and operation have remained significant features of the land systems in the post-reform era. After the French reform 66 per cent of the farmers held less than 4.9 acres each. The Russian Emancipation reduced the average size of 23.8 per cent of the peasant holdings to about 8.18 acres each; this was hardly changed by the Stolypin reform. As late as 1950, 84.2 per cent of the holdings in Mexico were of less than 12.355 acres (5 hectares) of crop land each, and 73.6 per cent of the holdings of all land fell within this classification. More than 40 per cent of the *ejidatarios* held less than 9.884 acres each. Of the Japanese holdings in 1954, 39.8 per cent were less than 1.25 acres each, and another 32.5 per cent were between 1.25 and 2.45 acres each. After the 1952 reform Egypt was still a country of tiny landholdings; 95 per cent of the owners held less than 5.19 acres and half of these had less than 1.038 acres each.

It is significant that the enclosures of England and the reform of Soviet Russia got rid of small units [6] and fragmented holdings by different methods, the one by allowing the economic forces to determine the pattern of holdings, and the other by regulating tenure in accordance with a plan based on socialist economic and social philosophy.

From this survey and comparison of economic effects it appears that the form of tenure is irrelevant to production and allocation, but land tenure reform may have a positive impact to the extent to which it promotes the following three conditions:

1. Large-scale operation allowing indivisible capital investment, and a shift of emphasis from ownership of the land to its operation. Such a shift permits fuller utilization of labor, mechanization, and improvement of methods of cultivation as well as increasing farmer security. Large scale-operation may, however, be accomplished under different forms of tenure — under private individual tenure as in England, coöperative tenure as in Egypt, or collective tenure as in Soviet Russia.

2. Integration of agriculture and industry in a national plan so that agriculture will contribute to industrial development, and industry will enhance agriculture by absorbing surplus labor. Thus, integration solves the problem of underemployment and aids industrialization. Of course, integration may be carried out either through the forces of the market over a long time-span, as in England, or through national economic planning over a shorter period, as occurred in Japan and Soviet Russia. The method chosen depends upon the objectives of reform and the pressures to obtain them, and on the social and political philosophy of the reformers.

3. Colonization to raise the effective land/labor ratio where potentially cultivable land is available. This may be the most important outlet for surplus labor in the absence of expanding industry or where expansion is at a relatively slow rate.

It should be emphasized that large-scale operation is a necessary but not a sufficient condition of development in agriculture. It is possible to operate the land on a larger scale and yet fail to derive any advantages of scale or to improve the methods of cultivation, as in the Mexican hacienda. The deviation from the above generalization may be explained by the fact that other factors are necessary for development. There may be debilitating institutional factors, such as the attitude of the hacendado as an entrepreneur, or the lack of adequate market pressure on agriculture to stimulate improvement. If, however, the institutional factors are favorable and large-scale operation is promoted, development may follow through the market mechanism as in England. But if these factors have a neutral or negative influence, then integration of the agricultural and industrial sectors and economic planning would be necessary to sub-

204

stitute for the entrepreneur or the market, and complement the large-scale operation and promote development, as in Soviet Russia.

(B) Social Effects

The social effects of land tenure reform must be evaluated against the general pre-reform social background for lack of a more objective criterion. When poverty and wealth were concentrated on opposite ends of the scale, reform was designed to reduce rather than eliminate the gap between them, but we do not know to what extent the gap was supposed to be reduced. It is therefore hard to determine whether or not the results were satisfactory. It may be possible, however, to determine if there was a change and to what degree the original problems were controlled with respect to both social conditions and social differentiation, and personal status of the peasant.

1. SOCIAL CONDITIONS AND SOCIAL DIFFERENTIATION

Polemic or bimodal class differentiation among economic lines was common to all the societies under study. Taking land ownership as a criterion, class differentiation was represented by inequality of land and product or income distribution,[7] and the existence of a large number of poverty-stricken landless people. The question then is to what extent inequality and poverty have been reduced as a result of land tenure reform.

Two of the ancient reforms were important in this regard — the reform of Pisistratus and that of the Gracchi. Solon's reform did not redistribute the land, but it did reduce inequality of income or product of the land. By abolishing the *Horoi* and freeing the *Hektemors*, that share of the product which had been acquired by the creditor now reverted to the freed peasant. The peasants, through the reform, presumably recovered their mortgaged land and secured its product. It is not known, however, how extensive the liberated land was or how effective the redistribution, remembering that the creditors who lost because of debt cancellation were compensated by the monetary reform. Yet, since no land was redistributed, and since the landless people did not directly benefit and production was not increased, the average real income remained low and the concentration of wealth high. The same conclusion may be inferred also from the continued attempts of the peasants to bring about land redistribution and raise their income, as seen from the promises they extracted from Pisistratus.

Pisistratus' reform had more effect on wealth distribution, since it redistributed some land. However, as only land of dead or exiled enemies of the regime and some public land were distributed, and as only his supporters benefited, it is difficult to imagine that redistribution was extensive or that per capita real income was greatly increased. That this was so is indicated by Pisistratus' construction and public work projects to reduce unemployment and raise average income. There is no evidence either that concentration of wealth was greatly diminished.

The Gracchan reforms distributed to about half a million people most of the restored *ager publicus* that had been illegally held, increasing the number of owners by about 25 per cent. Land restoration had a double effect by redistributing the *ager publicus* and by correspondingly redistributing income or product of the land. But this does not mean that land concentration was eliminated or that poverty was overcome. On one hand, only holders of *ager publicus* were affected by the distribution while holders of private property retained their holdings intact with the same degree of concentration. On the other, the gap between the upper and lower size limits on individual holdings of the former and new holders of *ager publicus* after reform was in the ratio of 33:1, the upper limit being 1,000 *iugera* (622 acres) and the lower 30 *iugera*. Inasmuch as land-holding was a criterion of class differentiation, social stratification remained polemic and the gap between the wealthy and the poor remained wide, despite the impressive vigor with which the reforms were carried out. Furthermore, the social effects of the reform were limited by what we have called discrimination by exclusion. By restricting the reform to a small land area and to a small proportion of the population, the overall effect was generally reduced.

The same may be said of the French reform regarding the distribution of wealth and income, especially if the *censiers* were considered owners. Even if not so considered, their benefit from the reform in this context was limited to the abolition of the small fixed rent they formerly paid. The *metayers* and landless people did not benefit at all. Finally, the sale of public land contributed to new concentration of landownership, which at least in part offset the positive effect of the reform. In the absence of any claims that the reform dealt with distribution and low income, we need not dwell more on this point. It is sufficient to point out that the effect was negligible as far as social differentiation based on wealth and income was concerned.

In contrast to the earlier reforms, the Russian emancipation had a negative impact on distribution and welfare. The peasants not only had to pay for the redistributed land, but they even lost some of the land they had held before, especially in the regions of good quality land. By enacting redemption payment the emancipation simply changed the composition of wealth but did not affect its distribution, and the *pomeschiki* remained the class of concentrated wealth. The impact on income distribution and peasant income was no different. Sometimes the peasant had to pay in redemption more than he earned from his land, or 25–30 per cent more than the market value of his allotment. His income was further depressed by the underemployment caused by the loss of land.

Actually, the emancipation had no effect on land concentration as a source of extreme wealth, or on the peasants' living standard.

As a result of the emancipation and the crisis in which the nobility found itself, social class differentiation was nevertheless undergoing change. A group of middle-class owners was emerging from among the peasantry and capitalists. This trend was encouraged later by the Stolypin reform; its effects on the distribution of ownership and wealth were also negative. A rich peasantry was evolving at the expense of the poorer peasants or by substituting land for other forms of wealth.[8] Thus both the emancipation and the Stolypin reforms aided proletarization of the peasantry and distortion of wealth and income distribution. Inequality and low peasant income outlived both these reforms.

The effects of the Soviet reform on the distribution of wealth and income are difficult to evaluate in view of the social philosophy adopted by the reformers and the new concept of social differentiation. In one act the Soviet reformers abolished ownership and eliminated inequality of land distribution.[9] Land concentration and social differentiation on the basis of ownership became impossible. Only tillers could hold land in quantities that, considering the techniques of cultivation, would allow full employment of the peasant. In this sense it may be argued that the Soviet reform promoted equality of land distribution and abolished social differentiation deriving from it.

The income distribution was not so easily or so equally modified. The actual results are not clear because of lack of data. It is certain, however, that differentiation has remained because certain collectives acquired better quality land than others, and probably a larger quantity per member. Distribution of the product among the members has also remained unequal, being determined by arbitrary norms adopted locally, and by the extensive differentiation between skills and position. Yet, since the higher paying positions are open to all according to ability, the impact of such income differentiation cannot lead to social class differentiation. Social mobility has actually been very high in the Soviet Union.[10]

The question of Soviet peasant income is further complicated by the fact that a large portion of the product is delivered to the government at low prices. This reduces remuneration of the peasant, which is already low because productivity is low. But as productivity began to rise in the 1950's, income of the farmers began to rise, although its level is still low in comparison with other groups in the society.

Therefore, while the Soviet reform abolished inequality of land distribution by abolishing private ownership, the distribution of holdings of farm land has remained unequal. The ultimate control over land, however, has been taken out of the hands of the farmers and placed in state hands. Though income differentiation has persisted, partly because of the principle of "to each according to his contribution," such differentiation does not prevent social mobility nor does it permit the formation of social classes.[11]

The Mexican reform had one major effect on class differentiation: it increased the proportion of landowners from the 3 per cent prior to reform (1910) to over 50 per cent of the rural population by 1950, including those who held the land under restricted tenure, but it was less impressive in terms of distribution of wealth and income from the land. The spread of ownership simply increased the number of small holders whose income was no more than enough for subsistence living. About 84.2 per cent of all owners have remained in dire need and at very low incomes, especially when compared with the wealth and income of the big landowners. The latter, as late as 1940, constituted less than one per cent of all owners and yet owned 79.5 per cent of all private holdings, and this trend has not changed substantially since. In contrast, almost 50 per cent of the rural population have remained landless, working on haciendas at poor wage conditions. The Mexican land tenure reform has solved neither the problem of concentration nor that of rural poverty, particularly because no substantial improvement has been made in production methods or in per capita output.

The Japanese land tenure reform changed the pattern of ownership even more than the Mexican, and four years after its initiation 91.2 per cent of the land had become owner-cultivated. Considering the high rents that were charged before the reform, this change should be expected to have raised the income of the farmer radically. And since the reform redistributed privately owned cultivable land, one should expect land concentration to have been effectively reduced. The latter expectation has come true to a large extent, but the first has not, because the effects of redistribution were offset by a diminution of the size of holding. The smallness of the holdings kept the farm family income low, and encouraged underemployment on the land by creating a stronger tie between the peasant and his tiny patch of farm land. Furthermore, since the farmers had to pay for the land they received, the distribution of wealth was not changed, but only its composition.[12] However, the farm income increased owing to higher land productivity resulting from extension services and extensive use of fertilizer, and from greater dependence on supplementary employment.

Though land concentration in Japan has been reduced, the relative impact of the pattern of ownership on social differentiation has remained high. The ratio between the averages of the upper and the lower size holdings is 10:1. The ratio would be higher if the forest and meadow land were included. Finally, the results of the reform have been slightly offset by the recurring concentration in the last few years which, though limited, suggests that the reform has not permanently overcome the land concentration problem. It is too early, however, to generalize on this last point.

The Egyptian reform has generally been considered conservative in its distribution effects. Land concentration has continued and the gap between the peasants and the large owners has remained relatively high. Since the landlords were compensated, only the form of their wealth rather than its level has been changed. The impact on class differentiation has been negligible. However, the peasants' income has risen by up to 50 per cent, but the gap between high and low incomes of the rural groups has remained in the same ratio as between large and small size holdings, or about 40:1.[13] In other words, the distribution of both wealth and income has remained a strong basis for class differentiation, especially in that only a small number of people and a small percentage of the land were affected.

In contrast, the English enclosure neither aimed at nor achieved any reduction of land concentration or of poverty of the peasants. It has led to greater inequality, but it has eliminated underemployment and raised the per capita income of the remaining rural population. The surplus rural population, either because it was displaced or induced by incentives of city employment, migrated from the land and only those fully engaged in agriculture found it worthwhile to stay. The higher effective land/labor ratio, coupled with rationalization of agriculture, raised the level of income of the farmer even as a tenant, since he was operating a larger farming enterprise.

Generalizing from this comparative analysis, we propose the following hypotheses:

1. Land tenure reform tends to reduce concentration of ownership and wealth to the extent that it restricts land transaction and limits the size of the individual holding. The extreme case of this was the Soviet reform, which absolutely prohibited land transaction; the other extreme was the perfectly unregulated land transaction which has led to a high degree of concentration in England.

2. In the absence of restriction, land tenure reform reduces inequality of income distribution from the land to the extent that it makes tilling the basis of landholding and contribution to the product the basis of remuneration. And to the extent that the functional principle of remuneration is made the basis of income from the land, such income is of little importance in creating social differentiation which perpetuates income groups or consolidates them as classes.

3. Land tenure reform raises rural per capita income to the extent that it raises productivity and/or increases the land/labor ratio, either by opening new land or by transferring the surplus labor to industry, or both.

This has been demonstrated in Soviet Russia, England, and to some extent Japan. Land redistribution in the manner applied in all the other reforms has had limited or no effects on the distribution of wealth and on the level of peasant income, even when land redistribution was extensive, as in Mexico.

2. PERSONAL STATUS OF THE PEASANT

The personal status of the peasant, in this context, may be distinguished from his tenure status or his relation to the land. Personal status refers to the peasant's position vis-à-vis a landlord; it identifies him as free or unfree, as these were differentiated in the state of feudalism. Three of the reform cases have been directly concerned with this question and have been primarily designed to solve it. These were Solon's reform, the French reform, and the Russian emancipation. We may also mention the Commutation as it related to this problem. Generally speaking, emancipation of the peasant has been swift and complete. Whenever complications arose, they were related to the economic consequences of conferring freedom on the peasant. The landlords were willing to free their peasants as long as they were compensated economically; only in one instance was there reaction or attempts to revive peasant servitude, namely, in the Russian emancipation.

When Solon abolished the debts and demolished the *Horoi*, the *Hektemors* were automatically freed from enserfment. No serious resistance seems to have been met with, especially since Solon tried to compensate the creditors for their economic loss. In fact, lack of resistance by the creditors might indicate that enserfment was itself an economic rather than a political phenomenon. When the economic causes for enserfment were eliminated, the state of bondage itself crumbled and there were no grounds for protest or resistance.

A similar situation prevailed in France. When the revolution abolished feudalism, conflict arose only when it became necessary to differentiate personal from real obligations to settle the issue of redemption. Resistance was against giving up what might have been the result of land concession and not of feudal subjugation.

Even in Russia, the main issue was not whether or not to emancipate the serf, but whether to emancipate him with or without land, and what amount he should pay in redemption. Actually, it was forbidden in Russia to discuss redemption of the person of the peasant. The nobility were not ready to give up their privileges, but once the economic advantages were isolated and redeemed, it became relatively easy to obtain personal freedom from them. In England, for example, the peasant continued to be bonded, even after his labor services were commuted, until he was explicitly freed of his villein status by his lord. However, when labor services were commuted, the landlords found it difficult to enforce their feudal rights and were more apt to free their villeins.

It seems, then, that: (1) Emancipation of the person of the peasant became easier to the extent to which the economic advantages of feudalism were isolated and redeemed separately. (2) Emancipation was easier and more complete than reform which conferred economic benefits on the peasant. And (3), although land tenure change might lead to personal emancipation, as long as personal subjugation was the result of a feudal right rather than of land concession, land tenure reform was neither necessary nor sufficient for emancipation. This was evident in pre-reform France and in medieval and early modern England.

(C) Political Effects

There is no doubt that the political objectives were the most important. It is logical, then, to expect the political impact of reform to be substantial in comparison with the economic and social results. The political effects may be evaluated in terms of three objectives: democracy, legitimacy, and stability. These objectives are, of course, interdependent. A stable democracy is by definition legitimate, as also legitimacy of any political system implies its stability.[14] On the other hand, an unstable democracy is only partially legitimate and within it lie the seeds of dissent to a degree that undermines the stability of that democracy. This interdependence is only one complicating factor in the analysis. A more significant one is agreement on the meaning of these terms. For example, what is the meaning of democracy? It is political democracy for which circulation of the elite and change of government by peaceful means are requisite? Is it a system in which a large middle class exists with an organized structure of checks and balances to guarantee the people a voice in the affairs of the state? And, if so, what is the minimum size of middle class that makes an effective democracy? What is a middle-class status? — does an owner of a few acres of land in a system of concentrated property belong to the middle class? Or, is democracy a classless society in which political stability is obtained by harmony rather than conflict, as in the ideal socialist system?

Then, what do we mean by legitimacy? Is it the legitimacy of the political structure or only of the ruling regime? Does it require a majority acceptance or would a plurality suffice? Also, what degree of legitimacy implies stability? And, is it justified to consider a system stable because the power elite circulates and the government changes hands by peaceful means, even if the circulating governments are all oligarchies ruling from above rather than from below? Furthermore, before we can consider the system stable, what lapse of time without violent attempts to change the structure or overthrow the regime is necessary?

These questions are relative and no absolute measure can be used in answering them. In our evaluation, we shall rely on two criteria: the conception of democracy held by the reformers and the degree to which that form of democracy was realized, and the stability of the political structure and its apparent legitimacy, as these are reflected in the events of the period following the reform.

In six of the reforms it was believed that a large middle class was a prerequisite for democracy, and the reformers sought to enhance democracy by creating such a class. The exceptions were the English case in which the political question was irrelevant, the Russian emancipation which had no intention of creating a democracy, and the Soviet case in which a different conception of democracy prevailed. The last of these will be treated separately, while the English case and the Russian emancipation will come up in the discussion only occasionally.

The ancient reforms were designed to rehabilitate the middle class, rejuvenate the army, and reestablish democracy by increasing the number of small landowners. Solon accepted this theory of democracy and therefore freed the *Hektemors*, and presumably conferred on them citizenship and the right to vote in the assembly. This he did successfully, but the impact was not extensive enough to avert revolution or create stability. Since there was no redistribution of land and since concentration of ownership persisted, the poorer people were disappointed and continued to request land distribution. Solon's constitutional reform was inadequate to satisfy their desires, as was the liberation of the *Hektemors*; they wanted land. In other words, the legitimacy and stability sought after could not be obtained and it was not long before a revolution erupted.

From the promises that Pisistratus had made to his followers we observe that his supporters were advocates of land distribution, and that they were discontented people whose faith in the political structure had been shaken. Pisistratus tried to satisfy them, and it has been claimed that he built the foundations of democracy and that for many centuries afterward no cries for land distribution were heard. Unfortunately, we do not know how much land Pisistratus distributed, what number of people benefited, or the amount of land each received. But we have inferred that the results could not have been sufficient to establish a strong middle class as a foundation of democracy. This inference is reinforced by the fact that during his lifetime Pisistratus ruled as a tyrant. After him his sons inherited his position as dictators and no signs of democracy were apparent. That he and his sons failed to earn legitimacy is indicated by their dependence on force and a mercenary army, both of which would have been unnecessary had their rule been willingly accepted by a majority. Even their oligarchic enemies would have been unable to overthrow them had they been able to win the support of a majority of the common people. In other words, whatever degree of stability they attained, it was by suppression, and as soon as opportunities prevailed, their opponents overthrew them violently.

It may be objected that the counterrevolution was organized by an oligarchy seeking power and not by a dissatisfied populace, but without popular backing even an oligarchy might have found it extremely difficult to carry out a counterrevolution successfully.

Creating a democracy is a long-term objective. It was not attained by the Greek reformers, but they realized short-term stability and legitimacy. The reform won temporary support for the revolution, and Pisistratus could maintain his power throughout his life. In other words, though the reform was not sufficient to achieve the long-term objective of a stable democracy, it was adequate to sustain the political regime, as distinct from the political structure.

Were the Gracchan reforms successful in achieving their political objectives? First, it is clear that a revolution from below was averted, assuming that otherwise it was imminent. The number of owners and citizens was increased by about 25 per cent, but there were no more signs of democracy after the reform than before it. Power, though formally transferred according to the constitution, circulated between two opposed oligarchies. When the opposition found it possible, they overthrew the Gracchi and undid their reforms by violent means. The fact that a counterrevolution took place contradicts any claim that democracy, legitimacy, or stability resulted from the reform. Therefore, there is no reason to believe that the pre-reform undemocratic structure was transformed into a more democratic stable one. Even the short-term goals were not realized. The Gracchi did not need to earn legitimacy for their own regime, but the policies they pursued were new and needed support to be effective and permanent. This support they failed to earn.

It is more difficult to evaluate the political effects of the French reforms. These had no long-term political objectives other than to free the peasant and overthrow the old regime. The land tenure reform was only a means to these ends and was not meant to create a middle class, since one had already evolved in the cities and urban areas and had carried out the revolution. The reformers wanted the support of the peasants to weaken the power of the old regime and stabilize their new position rather than to make the small owners the foundation of the new political structure. If we evaluate the effects of the reform in terms of legitimacy and stability, we can only conclude that it failed, since neither of these existed in France for a long time afterward. Whatever positive effects might have been obtained in this respect, they were probably due more to the creation of a new rich peasantry through sale of public land than to the land tenure reform proper.

Thus, if freedom of the peasant and abolition of feudalism were the only long-term objectives, the reform was definitely successful. But if democracy, legitimacy, or stability were the goals, the reform was a failure in all three. However, there is no doubt that the short-term support of the peasantry was obtained.

Before discussing the Stolypin reform, one question seems pertinent: what is the size of property requisite for middle-class status, and is the owner of a few acres a member of this class? Even if we answer the latter part in the affirmative, the Stolypin reform seems unimpressive. In either case most of the *mir* members would be middle-class people whether they owned the land individually or collectively, and their separation from the *mir* would be irrelevant. Even if middle class means rich peasantry, the Stolypin reform would still seem unimpressive because the number of rich peasants arising from among the peasantry was small, and because much of the land sold was acquired by people who were already of middle-class status. This conclusion may seem unjustified, since the reform did not have a sufficiently long time-span on which to base our evaluation. Looking at the reform in this perspective, we must conclude that the reform was not a success, since it failed to earn legitimacy and stability — we exclude democracy as there was no pretense that it was aimed at.

A class of small owners was certainly enhanced by the reform in Mexico. A large number of people became owners, but not all of them were of the middle class, unless the *ejidatorios* — the owners of a few acres of land — were regarded as such. The increase in the size of the middle class was mostly in urban areas, independent of reform. Though the rural middle class increased by 125 per cent between 1895 and 1940, it still constituted only 3.75 per cent of the population. If we subtract from this percentage the *rancheros* (family farms) who had that status before the reform, the impact of land distribution on the growth of this class would seem modest. This raises an important question about democracy and the size of the middle class requisite for its operation. Is the 15.87 per cent of the population classified as middle class a sufficient and dependable foundation of democracy, even when they are not a homogeneous group, as in Mexico? There is no objective criterion by which to answer this question. If concentration of poverty and wealth conflicts with democracy, undoubtedly democracy has not existed in Mexico, where 83.08 per cent of the population are in the lower class and 1.05 per cent are in the upper class and own more than half of all the wealth in the country.

The political objectives of the reformers have been short-term goals related to immediate stability and legitimacy. They were able to achieve these objectives now and again, but no permanent stability or legitimacy of the political structure can be claimed, as recent events have shown. Whenever pressure from the agrarians mounted, the incumbent officers of the government expanded distribution just enough to lessen tension and maintain the security of the regime. Therefore, to say that the agrarian problem of Mexico has been solved and no longer constitutes a threat to political stability would be misjudging the situation in which rural poverty and unequal distribution of land have persisted.

The reforms of Japan and Egypt are fairly recent, and it may be too early to know what the political effects are likely to be. Therefore, any conclusions reached at this point must necessarily be tentative and incomplete.

Evaluation of the Japanese land tenure reform is complicated further by the fact that channels other than reform were utilized in pursuing the same political goals, such as local autonomy laws which tended to break up the old system and decentralize the power structure. As far as land distribution was concerned, the effects were extensive. However, from the standpoint of the hierarchy, the effects were not so impressive, since the relative position of most rural people remained fairly constant, and those who have become owners have not automatically become middle-class people. Some may have gone up the social class ladder by deriving extra income from nonagricultural employment. This fact raises a significant question about the adequacy of any land tenure reform, short of nationalization — even one as extensive as the Japanese — to create a middle class large enough to be the foundation of a democracy. The question may be viewed from a different angle: in a country where the land/labor ratio is relatively low, is it possible to create democracy without depending primarily on the urban middle class? We shall deal with this question later in this chapter. At this point it is sufficient to suggest that the long-term objectives of democracy and stability have not been achieved by the land tenure reform. The reform has only satisfied the immediate objectives of the tenants and small owners by making them independent from absentee landlordism and thus reducing their potential threat to stability.

The same may be said of legitimacy. Formerly, the seeds of instability lay in the army and the urban middle-class people who were frustrated for different reasons. These have been satisfied only in the sense that the old ruling group has lost part of its power and has become relatively weaker, and that a balance of power between classes has been promoted. Otherwise the reform had no direct impact on legitimacy, nor do we as yet know that the new situation has become willingly accepted.

The political effects of the Egyptian reform are even more difficult to evaluate because the reform has not been concluded and the political order has not been finally defined — both are still in the process of change. The immediate results of the reform, however, have been positive: the new regime has been able to replace the old one, and also to win the support of the peasants. But to conclude that democracy, legitimacy, or stability have been created would be too hasty and unprovable. The people have not yet had a chance to express their views freely and therefore we do not know how legitimate the new political structure has become in a long-term perspective. Nor has the reform created a large enough middle class among the peasants to justify the assumption that democracy has been enhanced by the reform. If it has, it would be on the basis of the urban middle-class, which has been strengthened by the revolution, rather than of a rural one resulting from reform. The recent wave of confiscation, nationalization, and land distribution shows that the situation may not have reached a climax. On the other hand, the new concept of democracy — socialistic, coöperative democracy — may not have the same requisites as a western type of democracy. Since we do not know the requisites, it is not possible to pass judgment on the degree to which this democracy has been established.[15] In other words, the short-term goals of strengthening the revolution have been obtained, but the long-term objectives may or may not have been achieved.

Finally, let us examine the Soviet reforms and evaluate their political effects. These reforms had both long- and short-term political objectives. They aimed at a classless society in which the means of production would no longer be a source of power, and democracy would be based on harmony rather than on a balance between social classes, as in western democracy. As far as land is concerned, this aim has been achieved through land nationalization and prohibition of land transaction. Now there can be no class conflict on the basis of ownership. However, class differentiation based on the product of the land has survived and this may prevent realization of the hoped-for harmony. We have dealt with this question already, but it may be useful to reiterate our position. Insofar as distribution of the product is based on one's contribution to production, and in so far as opportunity is open to all, differential income distribution need not be a cause of conflict or instability as long as it does not lead to accumulation of wealth and power or to perpetuation of class differences on economic grounds. These ends are theoretically impossible in a society in which private ownership and inheritance of the means of production are prohibited. In this sense, we may conclude that the long-term objectives have been achieved formally.

This question cannot be evaluated adequately without considering the actual results and the degree of legitimacy and stability created. In theory, collectivization was carried out voluntarily and as such the new structure must be considered legitimized. But it is a known fact that compulsion was the rule rather than the exception, especially in the case of the richer peasants as a class. Even though this class has been liquidated, its impact on individuals has not been obliterated.[16] Even if the impact of the members of this class were not significant, we cannot conclude that the new structure has been legitimized as long as it is maintained by force or the threat of force. There has been no attempt to allow the

216

members to leave the collective or to express political dissension on principles should they desire to do so. This does not mean necessarily that the structure is unstable; it simply means that a definitive conclusion one way or the other is unwarranted. On the other hand, if one considers the difficulty of forcing a structure on the majority of the people, it would seem unreasonable to expect that, had the people been seriously opposed to the program, it could hold for long. Even though no overt attempts have been made to overthrow the political structure, and even though peasant revolts which had plagued the old regime are no more, the Soviet Union is still in a state of revolution. Until the new structure has been completely institutionalized, it is hard to conclude that the new system has become stable. But the fact that a whole new generation has evolved in the urral areas may be a source of loyalty to the system as a result of the process of socialization.[17]

Here one may ask: how long a time-span should elapse before one considers a situation stable? If sufficient time has passed since collectivization, then the Soviet reform has obtained the long-term objectives of a stable, legitimized, and harmonious democracy. But time may not be a sufficient criterion; force and the threat of force may be determining factors.

The Soviet reform had short-term political objectives as well. First, the aim was to win the support of all the peasantry against the nobility to sustain the new order and create at least temporary stability. Later the objective was to win the support of the poor peasantry against the rich. However, when the richer peasants proved too strong for the regime and a grave economic crisis developed, the Soviet authorities compromised and reversed their policy to regain the confidence of the peasants. In all three instances the authorities were able to attain their goals. In 1917 they allowed the peasantry to seize what they could and retain what they had. But when the Soviet authorities wanted to gain the temporary confidence of the rich peasantry, they allowed them to trade and employ workers and lease their land until the need for compromise no longer existed. At the beginning of the drive for collectivization, they engaged the poor peasants to set the example and exempted them from many burdens to which the richer peasants were subjected. Thus, in each case, land policy was adjusted to obtain temporary political objectives. The regime not only got the temporary support it sought from the rural areas, but it also found a leeway until it could strengthen the economy and its own political standing.

The above analysis shows that long-term political objectives were obtained in two reforms, the French and the Soviet reforms. Although their objectives were different, they had in common the facts that a substantial change in the class structure was effected and the reform was initiated from below — by a class lower than the one in power and a challenge to the latter.[18] Both reforms obtained their objectives with the aid of the urban classes, but in the French case the urban class was socially differentiated from the peasantry, even after the reform. This was not true in the Soviet case, since theoretically classes no longer exist. Another important difference was that in France the objectives were only partly achieved, namely, those which were social in character and not closely dependent upon land tenure reform. In Russia, the achievements included objectives that depended on land tenure reform.

Short-term goals that related to temporary acceptance of the reforming regime and to temporary stability of the system were obtained in all reforms except the Roman.

These relationships may be generalized as follows:

1. Land tenure reform may be effective in obtaining short-term political objectives. These objectives usually are relevant to the regime in power rather than to the general political structure.

2. Land tenure reform may be effective in obtaining long-term objectives only if applied equally to all the land and all the tenure groups. However, unless the change has been imposed from below by changing the political structure, the results tend to be limited and the reform ineffective.

3. Land tenure reform does not suffice to create a sufficiently large middle class to ensure democracy, as conceived in western political theory, unless aided by a strong urban middle class.

4. By nationalizing the land and prohibiting its transaction, the reform may lead to a classless, harmonious democracy as advocated by socialist political doctrine, at least in the rural sector.

PART IV

SUMMARY AND CONCLUSIONS

XIV

TOWARD A GENERAL THEORY
OF AGRARIAN REFORM

In this concluding chapter we shall pull together the strings and formulate possible bases for a general theory of reform. The proposal consists of two main parts: an analytic scheme and a set of propositions concerning reform policies. Finally, we shall summarize briefly the implications of the study for present-day developing countries that are contemplating reform.

In the form of a summary, it is enough to point out briefly what has so far been accomplished. The actual findings will be embodied in the general theory as illustrations and therefore need not be presented separately. In Part I we treated the concept of reform and proposed a functional definition according to which *agrarian reform* consists of *land tenure reform* — or any improvement of the land tenure system or title to the land — and *land operation reform*, which deals with the pattern of cultivation, the terms of holding, and the scale of operation. We suggested further that it is more meaningful and less confusing to discard the term land reform and replace it as applicable with one or the other of the components of agrarian reform.

Part II was a uniform summary presentation of the data or case studies which formed the basis of the analysis in Part III. Although the case studies varied widely in their contexts, there was enough uniformity among them to warrant the formulation of some general propositions. It seems, for example, that reform occurs only when certain conditions [1] have been fulfilled, such as land concentration, and extreme inequality of wealth, income, and power distribution. But most significant among the preconditions tend to be certain dynamic features that make reform or change seem inevitable. These dynamic features vary widely, ranging from a change in economic organization and international trade to a serious political instability that threatens the whole political structure with revolution.

Despite the contrasting historical and cultural differences between the societies studied, there seems also to be a similarity in the objectives of the reformers, in the processes of reform, and, consequently, in the results. Usually the objectives of the reformers, or their basic premises — in contradistinction to the objectives of the peasants or their actual eco-

221

nomic and social needs — determined the processes and hence anticipated or predetermined the results. In other words, there seems to be a pattern in the relationship between the objectives and processes of reform and the effects that may be attained. These relationships form the basis of the analytic scheme.

AN ANALYTIC SCHEME OF REFORM

The differences between the various reforms are either of substance or of emphasis and extent of implementation. The former relates to the philosophy and basic premises on which the reforms are based and arises from the close connection between the reforms and the economic and political systems to which they are intended or applied. The latter difference relates to policy matters and the extent to which the policy may be executed within the framework of the prevailing philosophy of tenure and property relations. These differences suggest a partial theoretical dichotomy between two extreme or ideal types or classes of reform: the one more consistent with, or leading to, capitalistic or a western type of democracy, and the other usually intended to bypass or evolve that democracy into a system of social and economic organization that is more consistent with socialism or communism. The first represents the approaches common in western and most contemporary underdeveloped countries;[2] the second has been approximated in contemporary socialist countries. Each of the two classes, as already implied, includes a wide variety of reforms which, though reconciled philosophically, differ in emphasis and extent. A third class, or a hybrid or a mixture of the basic features of the two main classes, may exist, such as the English, Mexican, and Egyptian reforms. Chart III depicts these two classes in an extreme form which may not be perfectly attained, although it may be approximated.

The chart is based on the assumption that reforms of both classes tend to have similar background environments or preconditions. As shown in the chart, criteria 1–5 are mutually exclusive in the sense that in the extreme case the reformers in each class adopt one rule or the other regarding the form of tenure. Whether or not this is true will be discussed below. It is significant, however, that once these basic premises or rules have been adopted, the processes become fairly determinate and the results predictable, regardless of the proclaimed aims of reform. Criteria 6–11 are variable in degree and therefore measurable on a continuum — Class I tending to one extreme and Class II to the other. In contrast, criteria 1–5 fall on two segments of a continuum — one segment of the continuum for each class of reform.

We shall not deal with criteria 6–11 since they have been dealt with in detail in Part III. The basic premises or the mutually exclusive criteria

1–5 require elaboration, as they distinguish the two classes of reform from each other.

CLASS I APPROACH

Advocates of the first type of reform, as in 1a–5a, propose reform within the framework of private property, individual holding, small family farm operation, and a certain degree of inequality of wealth and income which makes class differentiation and conflict possible. With these objectives in mind, they propose that political democracy can be attained or maintained and stabilized by containing the class conflict. Obviously each of these proposals has a rationale behind it. These reforms, for example, attach great importance to the institution of private property as it relates to the social, economic, and political organization of the community. Private property is considered essential for safeguarding the rights of the individual and is defended by several theories they have formulated on the subject.[3] Accordingly, they have adopted a meaning of equality which separates them from the Class II reformers. One's acquisitions are one's own as long as they have been acquired by legitimate means, and therefore should be respected. Equality is concerned with opportunity, and land tenure reform should not infringe upon the rights of the individual to his property, which is nothing but the accumulation of legitimate acquisitions. Therefore, when expropriation is necessary, compensation should be paid for the property surrendered, since otherwise the individual would be deprived of his rights and of future security toward his property.

In the same sense of private individualism, these reformers regard the small family farm as the basis of individual freedom and democracy. Without actually setting a limit to the size of the family farm — that obviously being relative — this approach has led to an argument for small-scale farm operations, which, of course, preclude mechanization, indivisible investment, and economic efficiency on the farm; all this in the name of the family farm. On the contrary, the advocates of this approach hold that nationalization of the land, which may permit large-scale operation, actually is inefficient. They maintain that it deprives farming of the incentive that private ownership creates and reduces the individual to a sort of nonentity and thus proves socially and politically inefficient, since it means loss of freedom for the individual.[4]

The argument about incentives and freedom under private tenure leads to the question of the state versus the individual and the significance of class differences. This problem has been recognized since the days of the Greeks, having been revived in the writings of Locke and Rousseau and later in those of Marx and Weber.[5] The Class I reformers hold that an increase or a decrease in the power of the state would decrease or increase the freedom of the individual. To avoid any encroachment upon his rights, state power should not interfere with private own-

223

CHART III

TYPES OF AGRARIAN REFORM

Class I   *OBJECTIVES*   Class II

Mutually Exclusive Features

	Class I	Class II
1a	Maintain and promote private tenure	Eliminate private tenure and promote public tenure
2a	Advocate individual holding and operation of the land	Advocate collective holding and operation
3a	Advocate and promote small family farms*	Advocate large-scale business farms*
4a	Advocate reduction of rural wealth and income inequality	Advocate elimination of rural wealth and income inequality
5a	Promote a democracy based on conflict with checks and balances	Promote a classless democracy based on harmony

Common Features

6a   Both advocate social and political mobility, but Class I tends to gradualism while Class II advocates overthrowing existing institutions and changing the criteria of status and power.

7   Both seek legitimacy of a political structure and put great emphasis on this political objective; however, Class I may do so to stabilize old or new political systems, while Class II does it to stabilize a new system.

PROCESSES

Mutually Exclusive Features

	Class I	Class II
1b	Involves no or only limited land distribution, and discriminates among tenure groups	Nationalizes the land and distributes to the tillers, and applies equally to all tenure groups
2b	Maintains individual operations	Creates collective operations
3b	Maintains small farms and pays little attention to productivity	Creates large farms and pays primary attention to productivity
4b	Maintains inequality of rural wealth and income, and advocates compensation	Eliminates inequality of rural wealth, but applies a new conception to income, and rejects compensation
5b	Maintains class differences	Eliminates class differences

Common Features

6b   Both use reform as a means to same end as in 6a, but Class I implements limited measures, while Class II introduces comprehensive ones.

8   Both follow a crisis.

9   Both involve reaction, though the impact in Class II is temporary.

EFFECTS

	Class I	Class II
1c–2c	Private individual tenure and tenancy	Public collective tenure and no tenancy
3c	Small-scale operation, little improvement of labor produc-	Large-scale operation, higher labor productivity, and reduc-

CHART III—Continued

Class I	Class II
tivity and toleration of under-employment	tion of underemployment
4c Continued inequality and concentration of wealth and income. Potentially incapable of creating equality	Elimination of ownership and hence of wealth concentration; differential income consistent with new meaning of equality
5c Continued class conflict and apparent instability of political system	Potentially capable of creating equality. Absence of class conflict and apparent stability of political system
6c Both cause social change, but in Class II the change amounts to an upheaval.†	
10 Both advance state control, but in Class I it is limited while in Class II it is complete.	
11 Dual tenure	Uniform tenure

---

* "Family" farm and "business" farm are used only partly in the sense of R. Schickele; the business farm has in common with his concept the form of organization, the farm being an enterprise like any other business enterprise. It differs from his concept because of the difference in the tenure relations accepted in the system. *Op. cit.*, pp. 736–739.

† Social change is considered mild when only a small percentage of the rural population and/or the land is affected by the reform, so that class differentiation in rural areas is retained to a large extent.

ership of the means of production, nor undertake actions that would eliminate class differences based on ownership. However, to ensure political stability, class conflict should be contained by a system of checks and balances which would regulate but not eliminate conflict. Conflict rather than harmony and integration of classes is the source of political stability.[6] Therefore, reform should be within the framework of private property and western democracy. And when political stability is sought after, the political structure need only be modified without changing the ranking order of the economic classes. Ownership may become more widely spread, but the institutional basis of the power structure would remain the same. A redistribution of power to contain conflict is acceptable, but no radical change is justifiable or necessary.

Given these basic premises, when these reformers introduce reform they tend, as in 1b–5b, to undertake only limited redistribution of land, to maintain private individual ownership and operation, and to keep farms on a small, uneconomical scale. They also tolerate concentration of ownership and inequality as well as class differences and conflict. Accordingly, the results are usually only a reduction of the original problems rather than their solution. In fact, the potential danger of new con-

225

flict remains, since the institutions from which conflict arose in the first place remain.[7] Criteria 1c–5c depict the limited impact of reform when based on these premises and when the analogous processes are applied.

CLASS II APPROACH

In contrast to the former, advocates of this approach hold that land is a means of production, that means of production are used for class exploitation if owned privately, and therefore that private ownership of the means of production, including land, should be abolished to prevent exploitation. Inheritance of productive wealth should also be abolished to prevent a revival of this source of exploitation. Another reason for abolishing private ownership, according to them, is that it hinders the flow of capital into agriculture and consequently the development of capitalistic farming, whatever the scale of operation.[8]

This approach is easier to reconcile with the former regarding equality, although they differ greatly on the meaning of that concept. Advocates of Class II reforms agree that equality should be one of opportunity, but they stipulate that people should start at the same level of opportunity; no means of wealth or production favoring one over another should be privately owned. Needless to say, this does not apply to the communist stage in which remuneration follows the theory "from each according to his abilities, to each according to his needs." Therefore, they argue, no compensation should be paid for expropriated property, since otherwise the distribution of income and wealth would hardly be affected and equality would remain a dream. Another justification for expropriation without compensation is the contention that accumulated property is the result of past exploitation by those who have property that should not have belonged to them in the first place.

The two approaches are even closer on the equality of income distribution. Actually, they are not in conflict on the principles, since both advocate rewarding each according to his contribution to the product, except in the extreme case of communism. However, the conflict arises in measuring the contribution of the producer and in identifying the means of production.[9]

Looking at the problem from an economic standpoint, in contrast to the metaphysical or ideological approach of Class I reformers, Class II reformers contend that efficient production requires large-scale farming in order to reap the fruits of economies of scale and to permit indivisible capital investment, and that this is possible only through consolidation of the small farms. To do this and still prevent exploitation of the small farmer, it is necessary to nationalize the land and collectivize its operation (or establish some equivalent, such as coöperatives). Furthermore, they hold that it is politically expedient to have large farms, since, in the words of Lenin, "it is easier to create the proletarian state in a country given to large scale production than in a country where the

226

small dominate." [10] It is also inevitable that large-scale should replace small-scale farming if commercial and efficient cultivation were to develop, since the larger scale is the "fundamental and main trend of capitalism . . . both in industry and in agriculture." [11]

These reformers also contend that private property, besides its exploitative role, sustains a society in which the state serves the purposes of the owners of the means of production against other classes. Therefore, to eliminate class conflict, the source of exploitation or private property should be abolished. The state would no longer be a tool of one class against another and that is what reform should accomplish,[12] and thus liberate the individual rather than oppress him, since the state would then serve the society as a whole. This achievement itself would be significant in another sense. It would promote a democracy based on harmony in contrast to that based on conflict as advocated by Class I reformers. Advocates of Class II reforms seek political stability by integrating the conflicting groups, reducing them to an identical status with respect to land holding, and preventing new conflict by abolishing the institutions from which conflict originally derived. Although new sources of power are substituted for landownership, these are independent of ownership of the means of production, and depend rather on status in the political organization.

On the basis of these contentions, advocates of reform Class II would apply the processes suggested in 1b–5b in the chart. They would nationalize the land, give its operation rights to the tillers, collectivize the farms, and create large-scale cultivation with an emphasis on improvement of production; they would also eliminate class differences based on land. Consequently, they obtain results, 1c–5c of Class II, that differ broadly from those of Class I. It is also clear that in conformity with these principles and the processes applied, change in Class I reforms is usually relatively mild in contrast to the upheaval that results from Class II, and state control is complete in the latter while it is partial in the former.

This idealized approach, however, should not blind us to the common features of the two classes as they are approximated in the real world. It is in fact quite clear that no reform has perfectly fitted in either of them, as can be seen in Chart IV, in which we have classified each of the case studies as I or II on each criterion of Chart III. Chart IV points out two distinct observations: that a reform may combine features of the two classes including the basic ones 1–5, as in the English, Mexican, and Egyptian cases, and that the more recent reforms have acquired more of the features of Class II than the earlier ones. This indicates that while the two classes may be mutually exclusive on specific criteria, they need not be so in reality on all the basic criteria. It also indicates

CHART IV

REFORM MOVEMENTS DESIGNATED BY CLASS FOR EACH FEATURE OF CHART III*

Features from Chart III	Greek Solon	Greek Pisis.	Roman	English Comm.	English Enclos.	French	Russian Emanc.	Russian Stolypin	Soviet	Mexican	Japanese	Egyptian
1a	I	I	I	I	I	I	II	I	II	I	I	I
2a	I	I	I	I	I	I	I−?	I	II	II	I	II
3a	I	I	I	I	II	I	N	I[1]	II?	I	I	I
4a	I	I	I	−	N	I	N	N		I	I	I
5a	I	II	I	−	−	II	−	−	II	II	II	II
6a	I	II	II	−	−	II	II	I	II	I	II	II
7	II	II	II	−	−	?	−	II	II	?	I	I
1b	I	I	II	I	I	II	II	I	II	II	I	II?
2b	I	I	I	I	I	I	I	I?[2]	II	I	I	II?
3b	I	I	I	I	II	I	I	I	II	I?	I?	II
4b	I	I[3]	I[3]	II	I	I[3]	I	I	II?	I[3]	I	I
5b	I	I	I	I	I	I	I	I	II	I	I	I
6b	I	−	I	−	I	I	I	I	II	I	I	I
8†	I	I	I	I	−	−	I	I	II	I	I	I
9	I	I	I	I	−	I	I	I	II	I	I	I?
1c–2c	I	I	I	I	I	−	I	I	II	I	I	I?
3c	I	I	I	I	II	I	I	I, II[1]	II	I	I	I, II[4]
4c	I	I	I	I	I	I	I	I	II	I	I	I
5c	I	I	I	I	I	I	I	I	II	I	I	I
6c	I	I	I	−	−	−	I		II	I	I	I
10	−	−	−	−	−	−	−	−	II	I	I	I
11	II	II	I	II	II	II	I	II	II	I	I	I

* Arabic numerals indicate the feature variable from Chart III bearing the same number; Roman numerals indicate the reform class.
† Common to both classes; no differentiation possible on this variable. ? = partial or questionable. − = the reform was neutral on this variable. N = the change was in the opposite direction from both reform classes.
[1] The Stolypin reform aimed at creating rich peasantry, which I have taken to mean large scale by implication.
[2] Efficiency was considered in the 1911 Act which aimed at consolidation, but the time was too short for effects to occur.
[3] Theory and fact did not coincide; in the Roman and French cases compensation was theoretically advocated but not applied; in the Mexican case it was allowed but not made automatic upon expropriation.
[4] Scale kept large on distributed land through coöperatives; otherwise fragmentation and small scale persisted.

that a certain closing of the gap between them has been taking place recently, both on basic questions as well as on the others.

In the last few decades national policies have tended to protect tenants against landlords, restrict inheritance to prevent fragmentation of the land, and aid the small farmers to overcome the defects of the tenure system. All these restrictions of and interferences with ownership have become acceptable, even though, formally at least, private ownership has remained the ideal of Class I reformers. The effect of this development has been a change in the meaning of ownership in the direction of increased social control in the interest of the community as a whole. This development has been common in most countries of the world.[13]

The immediate impact of this conceptual and policy evolution and of the increased regulation of the rights of the individual owner has been a shift of emphasis from ownership to operation of the land and to security of the actual cultivator. This change has resulted from and accompanied the increasing interest in production and agricultural policy, as mentioned in Part I. In turn, the change has brought closer together the two classes of reform with respect to formal ownership of the land and the functions of agrarian reform.

Thus, while continuing to idealize the small private family farm, Class I reformers have transferred their emphasis from ownership to operation and have rendered the actual size of the *property* of the farmer irrelevant. Now importance attaches to the operator of the land and to the scale on which he operates it. For example, a United States spokesman, though insisting that "production is greatest . . . when the individual can own the land he works . . . ," admits that security of tenure may be a sufficient condition. He also suggests that "land reform should be considered in terms of its objectives, rather than in terms of its legal framework."[14] Similar disregard for the legal framework and increased emphasis on objectives in relation to tenure have previously been voiced by Marx and by Lenin.[15]

The change in America has come simultaneously with a similar shift in Europe. It has been suggested that

the shift from interest in property distribution to distribution of operational holdings of farms is symptomatic of modern developments. The holder has gradually become more important than the owner. Inversely, it can be stated that the degree to which the stress lies upon one and the other aspect is significant of the degree to which this modern development has been realized.[16]

Hand in hand with this shift has come an indirect change of attitude toward the scale of operation. While promoting small farms, advocates of reform Class I have tried to overcome the inefficiencies of small scale by encouraging producer coöperatives among the farmers and landholders so as to reap the advantages of large scale and yet maintain the doctrinal attitude toward small farms. This certainly is a concession to the advocates of reform Class II, regarding both the scale of operation and tenure, since coöperatives are a form of collectives — the tenure advocated in socialist countries.

One may wonder why this shift has taken place. In popular policy declarations idealization of private property and the family farm has not receded and yet actual reform programs have been changing. It is highly probable that the shift has been due to a clear recognition of the limitations of traditional Class I reforms in handling social, economic, and political problems and the need to adopt new techniques without being ready to compromise the philosophy on which reform is based. This hypothesis brings us to the second part of the general theory of reform proposed in this study.

POLICY IMPLICATIONS

The above analytic scheme has ignored the pre-reform conditions and the relationship between these conditions and the objectives, processes, and effects of reform. This was possible because of the similarity of pre-reform conditions in most of the reforms. However, it is no longer possible to omit this important aspect. Evaluation of the effects of planning a policy must necessarily be closely tied to the problems to be dealt with, irrespective of the basic premises of reform. For example, if land concentration is recognized as a problem, regardless of the philosophy behind the reform, the effects of reform can be measured only by the degree to which concentration has been reduced. Similarly, if economic development is aimed at, it should be considered a reform objective and the results should be evaluated accordingly. Seen in this light, the findings of the study and the hypotheses emerging therefrom may be related to actual reform policies quite closely. The relationships implied are presented below in the form of tentative generalizations or propositions in recognition of the limited number of cases on which these generalizations are based. These generalizations are as follows:

(1) To the extent that private ownership of land is permitted and land sale is practiced, it is highly probable that there will be land concentration and, consequently, wealth, income, and power concentration unless specific restrictions are imposed on the accumulation of these values. And inasmuch as such concentration constitutes a social and political problem, land tenure reform usually tends to be used as a problem-solving mechanism, particularly if the problem is considered to be primarily political.

From Chart II it appears that private individual ownership and land concentration were common to all the economies under study during the period preceding reform. Though concentration was the result of

230

different factors in each case, it seems that in the absence of any regulation of land tenure change, the tendency has been in the direction of concentration. The English land tenure development serves as a perfect example of this tendency and of what one may expect in the absence of regulation of land sale and size of individual holding. In general, either as a survival of feudal organization, or through debt necessitated by the low income of the peasant, or through competition in which those who are wealthier buy out the poorer, land as an economic tool and as a source of power tends to be concentrated in the hands of a few to the disadvantage of the majority of the rural population. The latter end up as tenants or wage workers. Only in the English case did tenancy develop into a contractual business enterprise permitting the farmer a higher-than-subsistence income. These observations suggest that land concentration tends to be accompanied not only by a high degree of tenancy or landlessness, which is true by definition, but also by a highly skewed distribution of the product of the land. This arises because widespread tenancy implies widespread absenteeism, which in all but the English case tended to hinder agricultural development, as the landlords were not interested in investing in the land or supervising its cultivation.

These features were also accompanied by small-scale operation of the land. Except where the *latifundia* system prevailed, land tended to be fragmented into small plots either because of inheritance and population pressure, or as a survival of the old manorial organization of agriculture. This was true in all the tenure systems under study except the Roman and Mexican, which operated the land mostly as plantations. Even the English tenure system developed into fairly small-scale farms until the enclosures consolidated these and evicted many of the smaller peasants. Small-scale operation is significant in two respects: it distributes farm income among a larger population and thus keeps the income of the peasant family low; and it hinders efficient production and prevents capital investment in the land.

Because of land concentration, the reformers had to deal with related problems, such as low income, underemployment, inefficient use of the land, and waste of resources. Land concentration reflected also on the political relationships among the rural population in these different societies. Land was not only a source of economic but also of political power. Its concentration meant concentration of power and class division on tenure lines as these prevailed in each situation. In all cases, except preceding the Stolypin and Soviet reforms, the rural community was divided into two major conflicting classes — the class of landlords and the class of peasants. There was no tendency for the conditions of the peasantry to improve or for the landlords to compromise without direct intervention by the respective governments. The conflict between landlords and peasantry was due not only to land distribution but also to personal subjugation of the peasant to the rule of a feudal lord, which was equally disturbing to him. The reformers, therefore, had to deal not only with the economic and social problems of land distribution but also with the political status problems which kept the peasant in an inferior position.

(2) There is a certain relationship between land tenure and the system of economic organization and political structure. A change or tension in either or both puts pressure on the land tenure system. As the tension mounts, reform seems imperative. By the same token, a change in the form of tenure may cause change in economic organization and in the political structure. Whenever a change of economic organization takes place or is contemplated, land tenure reform becomes necessary to promote or sustain the new organization, and the more radical the change in one, the more extensive and fundamental it tends to be in the other. Furthermore, a modest land tenure reform at a time when a radical change in economic organization has taken place means that friction and instability in the community are highly probable.

As a corollary of this hypothesis, reform comes during or after a crisis because the ruling classes, who are usually one and the same as the big landlords, do not entertain ideas of reforming the land tenure system and improving conditions of the peasantry until such action becomes absolutely necessary. When, for example, it becomes apparent that in the absence of reform a greater disaster with higher losses of economic and political privileges might befall them, the landlords would compromise. Otherwise, only a revolution could bring about change in the form of land redistribution.

This proposition is supported by the evidence presented in Part III. The reforms were preceded by grave problems of which both the landlords and the peasants were aware. Yet in no case were serious attempts made to solve them until political and organizational circumstances necessitated immediate action. Even peasant violence was not a sufficient reason for reform. Reform took place and the landlords compromised only when dynamic factors caused a disequilibrium in the system and seriously threatened the position of the landlords and the ruling government. Threat to stability of the system came from different sources. First, the peasants demanded a change in the relations and backed their demands with violence. Second, certain "organizational" and class structure changes altered the functional relationships among social groups. The organizational changes ranged from a transition from barter to money economy, as in Ancient Greece, to a substantial growth of industrial and commercial activities ahead of agriculture, as in pre-Soviet Russia, Japan, and Egypt. Other changes included the opening of international markets, growth of international trade, and urbanization which added pressures on agriculture and the rural population. Finally, the

232

middle class was undergoing changes — either a decline as in Athens and Rome, or crystallization as in pre-Soviet Russia and Egypt. Hence, the stability that the system had apparently enjoyed for a long time was jeopardized.

Disequilibrium was reflected in the economic and political crises prior to reform. Economically, the crises were due to the increasing needs of the landlords and the corresponding pressures on the peasants, whose incomes had already been greatly depressed. Discontent and uprisings were related also to the prevalent political crises. The danger of revolution, pointed out by most of the nonrevolution reforms and later realized in the revolution reforms, suggests that prior to reform the legitimacy and stability of the political system were undermined. The ruling classes were in a critical position; hence their willingness to compromise and allow a reform.

(3) Though the objectives of reform are varied, the primary ones are usually political regardless of who initiates reform. The reformers use reform to win the support of specific groups, to create or restore political stability, to legitimize their own political positions, or to create what they consider to be democracy. The timing and extent of the reform are determined more by political pressure than by the genuine economic and social needs of the rural population. Furthermore, land distribution is closely associated with revolution and change of the regime in power. A new elite tends to distribute the land both to win support of the peasantry and to weaken its opponents, in contrast to the continuing elite or ruling class who try to prevent reform as long as possible, and when it comes, to preserve as much of the old structure as possible.

In every single case, legitimization of the regime or of the total political structure was a primary objective of the reformers. Equally evident is the fact that land was redistributed only during or after a revolution and a change of elite. Also, in all but the English case, one of the main objectives was to stabilize the political system in its old or new structure, respectively, according to whether it was a nonrevolution or a revolution reform. The nonrevolution reforms usually were designed to maintain the old structure, and the revolution reforms to replace it with a stable new one. From the days of Solon up to the present day of Nasser, we hear of reform as a means to create stability, democracy, equality, and so on, but in each case the peasants end up with little more in return for their full support of the political regime. Even in Soviet Russia where the agrarian policy was based more on doctrine than any other reform, the details of that policy and its timing were determined by the political objectives of the reformers and their need for support by one or the other of the peasant groups. The exception, of course, was the Japanese case, where peasant support was not sought, but here the reform was imposed from outside for political reasons.

233

(4) When there are political reasons for reform, it tends to have positive effects on the peasants. In general, land tenure reform improves the social conditions of the peasants in proportion to their significance to the stability of the reforming group — usually just enough to attain the political objectives of the reformers. If the reformers are of the previous regime they promote the social objectives just enough to quiet down the threats of the peasantry. If they are of a new middle class, they pursue the social objectives to the extent that attainment of these objectives weakens the old political order and strengthens the new one. Finally, the greater the antagonism between the revolting class and the old regime, the higher is the premium on destroying the former ruling class and changing the political order, and the more thoroughgoing would be the change in the sociopolitical structure when it comes.

Limitation of the effects of reform results from what may be considered reaction in the form of compromise, obstruction, or reversal. The form and degree of reaction depend on who initiates the reform and the extent to which they identify themselves with the former ruling class and the degree to which they aspire to their political status.

The social effects of reform seem to be limited also by the hesitation and compromise common in the process of reform. Reaction, by one form or another, tends to limit or offset the effects of reform and to maintain the gap between the beneficiaries of reform and the losers. The two groups seem to remain in the same economic and social ranking order in which they were before.

Compromise has usually consisted of allowing relatively high upper limits on the size of the individual holding, with special allowance for the children, and authorizing the landlord to choose the land he wished to retain. This often ended in concentrating the best land in the former landlord's hands. Or sometimes the compromise consisted of excluding the complementary resources, such as forest land, water sources, meadows and pastures, from the reform. As a result, the peasants were not much better off after the reform than before it and in most cases they continued to live at subsistence levels. The implications of such compromises are too obvious to be discussed. It is enough to point out that the reforms usually have received disproportionate credit as problem-solving methods and as means of improving the conditions of the peasantry.

Hesitation was reflected in the tendency to discriminate between tenure groups. In their attempt to minimize the negative impact of the reform on certain tenure groups and to introduce changes expedient for political purposes, the reformers have usually applied double standards. They have conferred benefits on certain groups and not on others, more on some than on others, or have placed restrictions on some owners and not on others. They have frequently used the reform to appease some, neutralize others, and weaken those whose land was the object of reform — all three actions being means of attaining the political objectives.

Such discrimination raises doubts regarding the usefulness of these reforms in solving the economic, social, and political problems that they usually are planned to deal with.

The exceptions to this observation have been the Soviet reform and the English tenure changes. Both applied uniformly to all tenure groups and to all the land — the former abolishing the whole situation of ownership and the latter precluding any control of tenure.

This comparison and contrast suggests that there is a common tendency to apply double standards of reform which usually results in dual tenure except where the government goes to the extreme either of abstaining completely from intervention, or of nationalizing the land. All in-between reform policies are discriminatory in character and loaded with potentialities of dissent and instability.

(5) Land tenure reform (or change) improves agricultural labor productivity to the extent that it promotes large-scale operation of the land and allows capital investment, regardless of ownership. Land tenure reform (or change) is accompanied or followed by a reduction of surplus labor on the land according to whether or not alternative sources of employment are available, such as putting new land to cultivation or expanding industry, trade, and commerce.

Economic effects have been evaluated in terms of the impact of reform on production and allocation which in this case relate mainly to labor resources. As shown in Chart II, only three reforms had any economic impact, other than the English tenure changes. These were the Soviet, Egyptian, and to an extent the Japanese, while in Mexico the reform seems to have had negative effects. Since the Mexican results have not been conclusively substantiated, we will not discuss them further.

In all cases in which tenure change had positive economic effects, the change has been in the direction of large-scale operation. In the English and Soviet cases this has been the general pattern; in the former by concentrating private ownership and operation, and by collectivizing the farms and operating them on large scale in the latter. The Egyptian reform retained small ownership but emphasized large-scale operation by creating producer coöperatives in cognizance of the relation between scale and efficiency of production. The impact in Japan has been due mainly to marketing and credit coöperatives, which also imply large-scale benefits. The impact of marketing and credit coöperatives has been more on the value of the product than on the volume, or on nominal returns than on physical productivity. When physical productivity was improved, it was due to larger investment in fertilizers and to extension of credit and supervision, both of which were made possible by encouraging large-scale organization embodied in the coöperatives.

235

Productivity was not improved in any of the other reforms, either because this was not one of the goals of the reformers or because the reforms tended to create farms of an economically inefficient size, as in Mexico. The only possible conclusion of this analysis is that improvement of production was closely associated with large-scale operation, regardless of the scale of ownership or tenure arrangement. Whether the land was publicly or privately owned, in large or in small sizes, and whether operated by the owner as in Egypt or by the tenant as in England, productivity improved according to whether or not the land was *operated* on an economically efficient scale.

On the other hand, only in two of the reforms has utilization of labor improved by reducing wasted capacity, surplus labor, and underemployment. These were the English enclosures and the Soviet reforms, both of which were operated on large scale. The Egyptian reformed land also was operated on large scale and yet there is no indication that surplus labor was removed or underemployment eliminated. This suggests that the scale of operation cannot be *the* determining factor. The only other possible explanation is that prior to or concurrently with tenure change there was an alternative source of employment to which surplus population was transferred. This was the development of industry, trade, and commerce. It is interesting to note similar results in England and Soviet Russia although the government remained virtually neutral in the former but took complete control of the land in the latter. Both these reforms involved an aggressive policy of consolidating and enlarging the farms. There is no evidence that in either case underemployment would have been overcome had there been no constructive outlet for surplus labor.

The outlet, of course, need not be industry and commerce. Where uncultivated land is available, colonization may be the easier alternative to absorb labor, but since the effective land/labor ratio has been relatively low in all the cases under study, industry and commerce seem to be the only possible outlets.[17]

It may be suggested, accordingly, that in the absence of new cultivable land for colonization, underemployment may be overcome by expanding nonagricultural employment at the same time as or prior to reform or change in the rural sector. This suggests a sort of unbalanced growth between the agricultural and nonagricultural sectors, with the latter taking the lead over the former. The extent to which nonagricultural expansion or development should precede that in agriculture depends on the amount of unemployment predicted and the rate at which it should be overcome.[18]

(6) Land tenure reform equalizes wealth and reduces concentration of land ownership to the extent to which it restricts land alienation and makes private ownership less absolute. Extending this hypothesis to income, it appears that land tenure reform equalizes income distribution

236

to the extent to which it emphasizes operation of the land and makes rural income proportional to the contribution to production. Expressed differently, income is equalized by reducing rent payment and distributing the product to the tillers. However, the average real income of the peasants depends upon improving productivity, raising the effective land /labor ratio, and eliminating underemployment. In contrast, land tenure reform may be quite effective in improving the personal status of the peasant and in freeing him from feudal obligations.

Personal freedom was relevant in four cases and in all of them it was obtained without much trouble and in complete form. These were the Greek, English commutations, the French, and Russian emancipation cases. Once they were compensated, the landlords who had obtained authority over the peasants through debt obligation or feudal grants were not adamant against conferring freedom on their serfs or subjected peasants. In the Greek case, the landlord creditors were indirectly compensated by depreciating the value of the debts. The commutations, on the other hand, did not confer personal freedom unless it was explicitly conferred upon redemption. The Russian *pomeschik* received compensation indirectly by manipulating the value of the redeemed allotment land. Only the French *seigneur* was formally and actually denied compensation. Nevertheless, it is safe to say that once the economic advantages derived from peasant subjugation were isolated, the landlord was willing to confer personal freedom on the peasant. The relationship between landlord and peasant was more significantly economic than social or political.

The effect on redistribution of wealth and income was less impressive, especially when evaluated against the general background of extreme inequality in distribution of wealth and income. But this may not be the proper test of achievement, since the objectives of the reformers were not to eliminate inequality of wealth distribution but to improve the conditions of the peasants and raise their income. This can be interpreted as any degree of improvement, and in fact in the majority of cases some improvement took place; the exceptions were the English and the Russian tenure changes which turned out to be to the material disadvantage of the peasant, although the income of the Soviet peasant began to rise by the 1950's. In all other cases at least some land was redistributed and/or the income of the peasant improved. Many farmers were raised from the status of tenant to that of owner, and many who had been paying exorbitant rates of rent now paid lower rents and held the land under contractual arrangements supervised by the government. Thus, when these results were the goals of the reformers, they have attained them in most cases.

The problem may be looked at from a different angle, namely, that of the impact of reform on land concentration, on the equality of income distribution, and on the level of income itself. In absolute terms the peasants gained some land and/or received somewhat higher incomes than they did before the reform in eight of the reforms under study. But in terms of level or per capita real income, the peasants remained at or near subsistence in all cases. Even though the income of the peasant farmer was raised, it was originally at so low a level that the impact on his living standard could not be great. On the other hand, despite the distribution of both income and of wealth in the form of land, though made more nearly equal, the relative position of the peasants vis-à-vis the former owners was practically unchanged. The gap remained wide and concentration of both income and wealth persisted with a ratio of more than 10:1 between the averages of high and low brackets of ownership and also of income from the land. The ratio in Egypt, where a new upper limit has been set at half the original post-reform upper limit, is still more than 30:1. The Soviet reform was an exception, since land concentration and inequality of distribution have been eliminated and steps taken to prevent their revival. Income distribution in Soviet Russia has remained unequal in absolute terms, but if viewed from the standpoint of functional remuneration, equality of income distribution seems to have been achieved, except for possible abuses.

(7) Land tenure reform may be useful in obtaining short-term political goals, such as stability and legitimacy of the regime in power, but it cannot satisfy the long-term objective of creating a middle class as a basis of democracy. The latter objective may be possible only if the reform substantially equalizes wealth. However, substantial equalization in most cases has come only after a revolution, and too late to avert one.

There are problems inherent in the evaluation of the reforms' political effects because of the ambiguity of the concepts and the difficulty of defining precisely the conditions necessary or sufficient for a stable or legitimate democracy. One problem is the difficulty of specifying the time-span necessary to elapse before one can judge the stability of the regime or the political system. Keeping these reservations in mind, one may assess the extent to which the political objectives were attained. As shown on Chart II, all the reforms except the Stolypin reform, and to a limited extent the reform of Solon, succeeded in obtaining the short-term objectives. They pacified the peasants, at least temporarily, and won their support. Where the reformers were of a middle class revolting against the old regime, they were able to sustain peasant loyalties and to strengthen their own position.

The results were different with respect to the long-term objective of creating a middle class and establishing democracy or eliminating classes. Of all the reforms only two may be considered to have succeeded in this respect — the French and the Soviet; the Japanese and the Egyptian reforms are too recent to evaluate on this point. It is doubtful whether we can justifiably accredit the French tenure change with creating a middle class or a democracy, since the middle class had already evolved and had carried out the revolution. The same skepticism applies to the small middle-class that had existed in Mexico and Egypt prior to the reform. The Soviet reform has succeeded in reconstructing the class structure along the lines predetermined by the reformers, namely, the abolition of economic classes.

In contrast, all the reforms that aimed at preventing revolution have failed, even though they may have delayed it. In other words, the problems were postponed by the reform, but not solved. Because of their limited effects on the distribution of wealth and income, the reforms had little impact on the class structure and failed to create a substantial middle class in the rural sector. By abolishing classes the Soviet reform was an exception.

It may be possible, of course, that long-term objectives can be enhanced by the reform indirectly if unattainable directly. The fact that the reform may augment the possibility of changing the political structure means that reform can be of great political value as a first step in the right direction. We do not deny this, but such a result is too unpredictable and reforms cannot be depended on to attain such objectives within a reasonably short period of time. Therefore, to solve these political problems other measures may be more important than reform of the traditional land tenure system.

IMPLICATIONS FOR CONTEMPORARY AND FUTURE REFORMS

What conclusions can we draw regarding current policies of reform? Movements for land tenure and land operation reform are still widespread. In fact, they are on the increase. The problems of the reforming countries are not different from those we have encountered. In most of them the basic problem is that the effective land/labor ratio is below optimum, causing underemployment, low per capita peasant income, and economic and political dependence as a result of the great maldistribution of wealth and income. These are all fundamental problems that require long-term solutions. Yet a cursory look at the reforms of the last two decades shows that they have dealt with the problems only superficially. They have actually been treating symptoms rather than causes, and have affected only a small percentage of the population and of the cultivable area, and hence are inadequate and cannot solve the basic problems. To do so it is necessary to raise the effective land/labor ratio and provide alternative employment for the surplus population, reduce dependence of the peasantry on the land and landowners, and raise their standard of living above subsistence. Until reform concentrates on these basic issues, it is doubtful that it can solve the problems that have for a long time plagued the rural population in most agrarian societies.

More specifically, to reduce land concentration the reforming countries will have to change the power structure either by internal or external forces, since otherwise the landowners will not permit any serious modification of the agrarian structure. But to do so it is necessary to either break up land concentration or change the criteria of power by taking land out of the system as a source of power, or both. They can get out of this vicious circle through internal forces either by means of reorganizing the economic structure, as happened in England, or by a political revolution, as in most other countries. Of course, it is safer in the absence of the first alternative to depend on external forces, such as influence and persuasion by outside agencies or countries, to bend the arm of the groups with vested interests.

But even if land concentration were broken up, unless preventive measures are taken, concentration is very likely to recur, as has been the tendency in Japan. Furthermore, the members of the old regime do not only put up a fight but also try to obstruct the reform or even reverse it. Unless they are overpowered, formal approval of reform by the landlords who stand to lose is no assurance that they will not try their best to subvert the whole program. This may, of course, be avoided if the whole political structure has been changed and the land tenure system greatly modified, or if preventive measures have been taken.

By these means, the reforming countries may effect the distribution of land, income, and political power. However, the general standard of living or the net per capita income will not rise unless agricultural methods improve and the effective land/labor ratio is raised to relieve underemployment by reducing population pressure on the land. Redistribution of land may be an acceptable short-term solution to relieve the poverty of the peasant, but in the long run it alone is inadequate, since the rural per capita income will decline unless agriculture has improved and aggregate income has increased at a higher rate than population. Thus, only if higher productivity and a higher land/labor ratio are brought about concurrently can both inequality of distribution and low living standards be dealt with simultaneously. To improve productivity and overcome underemployment and thus raise peasant income, it is necessary to eliminate the defects of the scale of operation and create alternative employment opportunities. However, since potentially arable land is limited, industry and commerce are the only domestic avenues for surplus population. Finally, to deal effectively with underemployment, emphasis should be transferred to the operation of the land so that the land will be in the hands of those who till it and who can be fully employed on it. Land consolidation, mechanization, and emphasis on accepted economic efficiency criteria are helpful means to that end when planning reform.

Putting it more formally, if the reform objective is to improve productivity and promote better use of resources, large-scale operation must be promoted; if the objective is to improve the social conditions of the peasantry, wealth and income from the land must be redistributed, private ownership restricted, and land transaction regulated. The more extensively these conditions are met the more positive the social effects will be. If the objective is only to raise the level of income of the peasantry without interfering with its distribution, productivity of the land must be improved and underemployment eliminated. This is possible either by opening new land for cultivation or by developing industry and commerce, or both. Finally, if more than one of these objectives are to be attained, the respective conditions must be satisfied simultaneously. The viability of prospective reforms depends on how well they satisfy these conditions and to what extent they contribute to the solution of the agrarian problems of the underdeveloped countries.

An equally important concern of agrarian reform has often been to change the political structure, to promote freedom of the peasant, to create democracy, or to avert revolution. First, it is essential to be clear about the nature of the objectives. If these are related to the basic political structure, a western type of reform (Class I) tends to be of limited impact, since it does not reach to the foundations of the system as do socialist reforms. This type of reform has not averted revolutions or created democracies, nor is it capable of doing so. It may, as in the past, create short-term stability, delay a violent eruption of hostilities between tenure groups, and recruit support for the reformer government. Therefore, if the reforming countries desire such short-term achievements, reform may be quite helpful. But if they genuinely desire a fundamental change, they should either institute fundamental changes in the tenure structure or utilize means other than land tenure reform.

Finally, it is important to recognize the role of the middle class in introducing and successfully implementing reform. The process and the effects of reform are closely related to the position of that class at the time of reform initiation, regardless of what the basic principles are. The stronger and more sympathetic toward the peasantry the middle class is, the easier and more extensive the reform tends to be. Conversely, the weaker the middle class and the more they aspire to the position of the landowners, the less-far-reaching and the less advantageous to the peasantry the reform is. As it happens, in most reforms nowadays the middle class tends to be conservative as seen from the standpoint of the peasants. They desire to replace the landowning class but not to elevate the peasantry to their own ranks. They use the reforms as a tool of propaganda, publicize greatly the limited reforms they undertake, and reduce

241

the tempo as soon as their own political and economic aspirations have been realized, to the disappointment of the peasants. Therefore, it is of great importance for groups genuinely interested in the masses of rural population to recognize these limitations of conventional reform movements. If they cannot improve the programs, at least they can advise the peasants not to expect more of the reform than is legitimately achievable. This warning is not offered as a service to the peasantry. It is, rather, a warning against staking political stability on measures that are inherently incapable of creating it, of easing tension, of averting revolutions, or of creating democracy.

This brings us back to where we started — by asking if reform attempts that are being promoted in underdeveloped countries suffice to solve the current problems. Even if carried out, do such reforms bring about results that are sufficient to eliminate the causes of tension and the seeds of rebellion? Remembering that the landlords are not easy to convince, that the peasants are too poor and numerous to be satisfied easily, that a restless middle class has been emerging at a high rate, and that impressive results have been obtained in socialist countries — remembering all that, can we depend on the limited effects of nonsocialist reforms to solve these problems and avert revolution? A most optimistic answer can be only conditionally in the affirmative.

CHRONOLOGY

Chapter III

594 B.C.   Solon elected archon or chief magistrate of Athens.
582–580 B.C.   A period of anarchy following Solon's reform, during which Damasias was archon unconstitutionally.
561–560 B.C.   Pisistratus begins his rule as tyrant and embarks on his reform.
528 B.C.   Pisistratus died.

Chapter IV

134 B.C.   Tiberius Gracchus elected Tribune in Rome, during which year he introduced his reform.
133 B.C.   Tiberius Gracchus killed.
129 B.C.   The Commission supervising the execution of the reform in Rome was suspended.
123 B.C.   Gaius Gracchus elected Tribune and the Commission revived.
121 B.C.   Gaius killed and the reform brought to an end.
121 B.C.   Reaction against the reform started by legalizing alienation of public land.
119 B.C.   The Commission formally dissolved.
111 B.C.   Rent payments on public domain abolished and holdings of public land declared private property in perpetual tenure.

Chapter V

A.D. 1236   Statute of Merton permitting enclosure of common and waste land.
1289   Statute of Westminster the Second reaffirming the right to enclose land.
1349   Statute of Labourers passed to stabilize wages and prices, regulate labor mobility, and assure land cultivation.
1381   Peasant revolt against the oppression and the Statute of Labourers.
1450, 1549, and 1607   Peasant riots against landlords and government.
16th-19th centuries   Period of enclosures.
1760–1845   Most active period of enclosure.

CHAPTER VI

1789   French Revolution precipitating changes leading to reform.

4–11 August, 1789   The National Assembly passed a series of acts instituting the reform and bringing the *ancien regime* to an end.

1789–1790   Peasant disturbances in France expressing discontent with letter and execution of the reform.

1792   National Assembly in France revised law and abolished all casual rights of landlords (rights not based on land concessions).

1792   National Assembly passed law allowing redemption of annual rights and casual rights separately, by groups or by individuals.

1792   National Assembly abolished all previous legislation on common land, and introduced new measures to speed up the destruction of feudalism.

1793   National Assembly suppressed land sale on cash terms and readmitted installment payments to help the peasants acquire land; it also provided for land distribution to the poor without reverting to auction.

1796   Terms of land purchase eased in favor of the peasants.

1803   Division of common land suspended.

1823   Indemnity paid to former landlords for expropriated lands.

CHAPTER VII

1856   Tsar Alexander II took a stand on abolishing serfdom to avoid revolution.

1861   Emancipation Act passed by Main Committee and signed by Tsar Alexander II.

1863   Reform regarding state serfs enacted by statute.

1866   Emancipation of state serfs.

1869   Emancipation of the Cossacks.

1881   Emancipation completed when "temporary obligation" was abolished.

1881, 1884, 1896   Government took action to ease the debt accumulation resulting from redemption payments.

1885   Peasants expressed discontent with reform by attacking property of landlords; disorder widespread; 192,000 complaints of damages filed in that year.

1889   Reaction by nobility and government through law providing for election of *zemskii* chiefs from among local nobility and giving them wide powers, extending in 1893 to land distribution.

1890   Peasant representation in *zemstvo* assemblies reduced and that of nobility increased.

1893   Rights of individual upon completion of redemption payments restricted to hereditary tenure in order to perpetuate the commune.

1905   Peasant revolt.

1905   All redemption payments canceled by edict.

1906   Land Organization Commissions established; some restrictions on personal rights abolished.

1906   Edict introducing the Stolypin reform.

1910   Edict of 1906 reaffirmed by legislation.

1911   Act permitting land consolidation by compulsion if necessary.

1917   Provisional Government made a proclamation recognizing peasant grievances.

1917   First Land Decree by the Soviets, abolishing private property in land, land alienation, and tenancy.

1919   Decree declaring individual farming as transitional, pending the establishment of collective farming.

1919   Decree reaffirming earlier provisions and generalizing further the relationship between farming and land holding.

1918–1921   Period of War Communism.

1922   New Economic Policy introduced and formally but conditionally permitting tenancy, hired labor, and private exchange of products.

1929   End of New Economic Policy and beginning of the Drive for Collectivization.

1938   Collectivization virtually completed.

CHAPTER VIII

1858–1861   The War of Reform.

1876   Diaz became president.

1906   Labor rebelled against conditions.

1910   Diaz announced his intention to seek reëlection.

1911   The Mexican Revolution which deposed Diaz and ushered in the era of reform.

1912   The Land Commission established by Madero, the new president, reported on the Indian village land.

1915   Land Decree introducing reform.

1917   The Constitution adopted, incorporating the Land Decree as Article 27.

1919   Zapata, the Indian leader who instigated reform, was killed.

1922   Law defining the land subject to requisition, the identity of the recipient, and the procedure for acquisition.

1923   Law dealing with colonization of public land.

1925   Regulatory Law concerning the Division of Ejido Lands and the Constitution of the Ejido Patrimony.

1927   Law dealing with the right to petition for land and with other procedures and details, including concessions to landlords.

1930 and 1931   Laws reversing the reform trend by augmenting private ownership in small holdings.

1933   Article 27 of the Constitution expanded, allowing division of ejido land and abolishing land distribution that was based on error or fraud.

1934   The Agrarian Code synthesizing previous legislation and redefining eligibility to acquire land, among other new provisions.

1937   President Cardenas abolished Article 45 of the Agrarian Code and made the *peones* automatically eligible to receive land.

1942   The Agrarian Code revised to protect efficient livestock farms.

Chapter IX

1868   Beginning of the Meiji period, basis of the tenure subject to reform.
1918   Rice Riots.
1924   The Tenancy Conciliation Law.
1926   The Regulations for the Establishment of Owner-Farmers.
1933   Conflict between landlords and tenants reached a peak.
1938   The Agricultural Land Adjustment Law.
1939   The Rent Control Order froze all rents.
1941   The Land Control Order regulated prices and land use.
1943   The Agricultural Land Adjustment Law amended by administrative order.
1945   The First Reform Bill passed the Diet, but on the same day was rejected by the Supreme Commander of the Allied Powers.
1946   The Second Reform Law on which the reform was based.
1947   The Local Autonomy Law.
1950   Cabinet Order No. 288 modified the Reform Law, permitting land transaction subject to size restriction.
1963   Bill introduced in the Diet to recompensate former landlords for losses inflicted by the reform.

Chapter X

1944–1952   Peasant revolts widespread.
1952   The Egyptian Revolution which led to reform. The Agrarian Reform Law passed.
1961   An amendment of the Agrarian Reform Law came into effect, restricting the size of individual ownership and tenancy.

NOTES

*Bibliographical details of works cited briefly
in the Notes are given in the Bibliography*

[1] W. A. Lewis, *The Theory of Economic Growth* (4th impression; London: Allen & Unwin, 1960), pp. 10–18, on inductive research and the current trend in economic studies.

[2] As far as I can ascertain, only two such studies have been made: R. Ciasca and D. Perini, *Riforme agrarie antiche e moderne* (Florence: G. C. Sansoni, 1946), which is basically a historical survey of specific reforms and does not undertake the comparative study we have suggested in order to derive laws or generalizations; and E. P. Cheyney, "Recent tendencies in the reform of land tenure," *Annals of the American Academy of Political and Social Sciences,* II (July, 1891-June, 1892), 309-23, which is an excellent study but is limited to the century following the French Revolution and to the European experience, both of which involve a limited experience of reform, especially in that the new tendencies had not yet started.

[3] In answering his critics for undertaking a comprehensive study, Toynbee quotes from M. R. Cohen's, *The Meaning of Human History* (p. 210): "History certainly justified a dictum of Einstein, that no great discovery was ever made in science except by one who lifted his nose above the grindstone of details and ventured on a more comprehensive vision." Toynbee adds that "a panoramic view will at any rate be a less misleading reflection of Reality than a partial view. And, while it is true that in the search for knowledge and understanding, as in all human activities, human achievements are never complete, it is one of Man's virtues that he has the intelligence to be aware of this and the spirit to go on striving, with undiminished zest, to come as near to his goal as his endowment of ability will carry him" (*A Study of History*, Vol. XII [London, New York, Toronto: Oxford University Press, 1961], p. 136).

[4] Marc Bloch, "Toward a Comparative History of European Societies," reproduced in Frederic C. Land and Jelle C. Riemersma, eds., *Enterprise and Secular Change* (Homewood, Illinois: Richard D. Irwin, 1953), p. 496; on comparative method, see also Arnold Toynbee, *op. cit.*, Vo. I, pp. 441–521.

[5] This method of data presentation has seemed preferable since it allows a uniform approach to the data and thus makes comparison possible. It will also relieve the analytic Part III from extensive footnoting and documentation which might render the reading tedious and confusing. Additionally, it permits evaluation of each experience individually. However, there is a risk of repetition of some of the material, which seems to be a justifiable price to pay for the hoped-for clarity. The reader who is well acquainted with a case study may choose to skip it without fear of a great loss to the analysis.

NOTES TO CHAPTER II

[1] Thomas Carroll, "The Concept of Land Reform," in *Documentation* (Prepared for the Center on Land Problems in Asia and the Far East, Bangkok, Thailand, 1954 [Rome, FAO, 1955]), p. 35.

[2] A definition of land reform will be developed later in this chapter. Land tenure here means the system of ownership or title to the land; more on this below.

[3] M. R. Ghonemy, "Resource Use and Income in Egyptian Agriculture Before and After the Land Reform with Particular Reference to Economic Development" (unpublished Ph.D. dissertation, North Carolina State College, Raleigh, 1953), pp. 8–9, and pp. 2–3 for his own definition.

[4] Doreen Warriner, *Land Reform and Development in the Middle East* (London and New York: Royal Institute of International Affairs, 1957), pp. 3–6.

[5] A. W. Griswold, *Farming and Democracy* (Yale University Press and Oxford University Press, 1952), p. 45.

[6] *Ibid.*, pp. 5, 29–31, 43–45.

[7] *Ibid.*, pp. 86–87.

[8] C. Hammer, "The Land Tenure Ideal," *J. Land and Public Utility Economics*, 19 (1943), 78. Although the trend toward tenancy was arrested after World War II, the decline of the small farms has continued; the number of farm units dropped from 6,800,000 in 1935 to 3,708,000 in the 1960's. From 1930 to 1960, farms of more than 1,000 acres have raised their holdings from 28 to 49 per cent of all agricultural land in the U.S.A. The indications tend actually toward intensification of the trend; Edward Higbee, *Farms and Farmers in an Urban Age* (New York: Twentieth Century Fund, 1963), pp. 9, 18, 31, 33. The trend is best shown in *U. S. Census of Agriculture*, Vol. II, General Report, chap. x, table 16, p. 1042. The official opinion that the trend has been reversed is based on misrepresentation of the statistics and also on manipulation of the concept of family farm to accommodate the new features in agriculture; actual examples and discussion are found in Higbee, pp. 80–81.

[9] Doreen Warriner, *op. cit.*, pp. 3–4. This conception is not so new as Miss Warriner implies; besides its usage in socialist countries, Rowntree used it as early as 1913. In fact, his conception of land reform went as far as dealing with farm labor, which is even broader than the "new" concept; B. S. Rowntree, "Rural Land Reform," *Contemporary Review*, 104 (1943), 609–623.

[10] Mao Tse-tung and Liu Shao-chi, *Significance of Agrarian Reforms in China* (Bombay, India: New Age Printing Press, 1950), p. 19.

[11] On the confusion of the concept of reform, see Doreen Warriner, *op. cit.*, pp. 2–6.

[12] United Nations, Department of Economic Affairs. *Land Reform: Defects in Agrarian Structure as Obstacles to Economic Development* (New York, 1951), pp. 4–5.

[13] Personal criteria will be more important, as with the *censiers* in France

and the villeins in England. See the chapters on France and England, respectively, in Part II.

[14] Strictly speaking, there is no justification for defining reform as an improvement because this implies the value-judgment of the parties concerned. One may suggest that reform simply means purposive change, which may or may not be an improvement except from the standpoint of the reformers. Because of the policy implications of reform, the wide acceptance of the improvement connotation, and primarily because there are certain objective criteria of improvement related to agrarian reform, I have retained the above definition. On the subjective aspects, my attitude is consistent with the conception of reform as a purposive change. For more details see my unpublished Ph. D. dissertation, "Economics, Politics, and Land Tenure Reform: A Comparative Study" (University of California, Berkeley, 1962), p. 25 (this reference will be indicated henceforth as MS).

NOTES TO CHAPTER III

[1] Reproduced with translation and annotation in Ivan M. Linforth, *Solon the Athenian* (University of California Publications in Classical Philosophy, Vol. VI; Berkeley: University of California Press, 1919), pp. 13–245. References to Solon's poems will be to this source.

[2] *Ibid.*, Appendix 4, p. 283; C. Gilliard, *Quelques réformes des Solon: Essai de critique historique.* (Lausanne: Georges Bridel, 1907), pp. 28–58.

[3] James Day and Mortimer Chambers, *Aristotle's History of Athenian Democracy* (University of California Publications in History, vol. 73; Berkeley and Los Angeles: University of California Press, 1962), pp. 1–24.

[4] M. Rostovtzeff, *A History of the Ancient World. I: The Orient and Greece,* tr. from the Russian by J. D. Duff (Oxford: Clarendon Press, 1926), pp. 218–219; this was also the opinion of Aristotle (Day and Chambers, *op. cit.,* p. 67).

[5] W. J. Woodhouse, *Solon the Liberator* (London: Oxford University Press [Humphrey Milford], 1938), pp. 86, 148–152; J. V. A. Fine, "Horoi: Studies in Mortgage, Real Security, and Land Tenure in Ancient Athens," *Hesperia,* Supplement IX (American School of Classical Studies at Athens, 1951), p. 206. Some suggest that inalienability of the land had been relaxed before Solon, but the bulk of evidence tends otherwise; Gilliard, *op. cit.,* pp. 184–185. If land were alienable, why was it not foreclosed and why should the debtor put his person up for security and be enslaved? On the other hand, Plutarch says that while Solon was designing his reform, friends of his knew of its contents and "purchased" land, knowing that he would not meddle with the land (*The Lives of Noble Grecians and Romans,* tr. by John Dryden and rev. by Arthur Hugh Clough [New York: Random House, 1932], p. 106); the same is mentioned in Aristotle, *Constitution of Athens and Related Texts* (tr. with an Introduction and Notes by Kurt von Fritz and Ernst Kapp [New York: Hafner, 1961]), p. 73. It is not explained how the land could be purchased if it were inalienable.

⁶ Gilliard, *op. cit.*, p. 222, for more detailed and different estimates; these figures are conjectural.

⁷ Plutarch, *op. cit.*, p. 104; one critic at least suggests that the Hill people, later the followers of Pisistratus, were not a part of a distinct social class at the time of Solon and became so only thirty years later; see P. N. Ure, *The Origin of Tyranny* (Cambridge: University Press, 1922), pp. 35–38.

⁸ Plutarch, *op. cit.*, p. 104; Aristotle says that the people were divided into those same social classes later defined according to property by Solon; *op. cit.*, pp. 74–75; Day and Chambers, *op. cit.*, p. 174.

⁹ Rostovtzeff, *op. cit.*, pp. 119–120, 219–219.

¹⁰ Woodhouse, *op. cit.*, p. 119; *The Cambridge Ancient History, IV*, ed. by J. Bury, S. A. Cook, and F. E. Adcock (Cambridge: University Press, 1926), pp. 32–33; Linforth, *op. cit.*, p. 50.

¹¹ Linforth, *op. cit.*, p. 50; Rostovtzeff, *A History of the Ancient World, I*, pp. 218–219; Gilliard, op. cit., pp. 11, 136–138; Woodhouse, *op. cit.*, p. 119; a different approach lays great stress on explaining the growing indebtedness of the small farmer on the role of population increase, soil exhaustion, and the need to shift to more intensive cultivation, but no mention is made of the role of the money economy as a factor; A. French, "The Economic Background to Solon's Reforms," *Classical Quarterly*, n. s., VI, nos. 1 and 2, (Jan.–April, 1956), 11–25.

¹² *Woodhouse*, op. cit., pp. 125–126; Rostovtzeff, . . . *Ancient World, I*, pp. 218–219; some authors have insisted that the *Hektemor* paid one-sixth only and kept the rest and that his grievance was primarily due to his social and political subjugation rather than to economic oppression; N. Lewis, "Solon's Agrarian Legislation," *American Journal of Philology* 62 (1941), 150–151. One should ask why the peasant was unable to repay the debt if his payments were so small, even by modern standards. Aristotle also has been interpreted to mean one-sixth and that enslavement resulted from default on the payments of "rents" or repayment of debts; *op. cit.*, p. 69. On the conflict of opinion regarding the peasant payment, see Day and Chambers, *op. cit.*, p. 168 and note 36.

¹³ Linforth, *op. cit.*, pp. 48–49, as also implied in Solon's poems, verses IX, XI, and XII; Plutarch, *op. cit.*, p. 104.

¹⁴ Linforth, *op. cit.*, pp. 50–52 and Solon's verse XII, p. 141; Woodhouse, *op. cit.*, p. 146.

¹⁵ A. Andrewes, *The Greek Tyrants* (London: Hutchinson's University Library [Anchor Press], 1956), p. 84.

¹⁶ Linforth, *op. cit.*, p. 62 and verse IX, p. 137.

¹⁷ This is implied in Solon's verse IX (*ibid.*, p. 137) in which he says of the black Earth: "and she who was a slave is now free. . . ." This interpretation is opposed by A. French, *op. cit.*, p. 21, who suggests that cancellation of debts could have been accepted by the landlords only if their claims to the debtor's mortgaged land were finally conceded and the land therefore could not have been restored. He also suggests that farm debts only were canceled rather than debts in general. I tend to accept the theory of restoration of mortgaged land on these bases: (1) on the assump-

tion of inalienability, restoration was within Solon's jurisdiction; (2) the landlords were anxious to avoid disaster and hence were willing to compromise; (3) their loss was not great because they must have been more than reimbursed while they held the land; and (4) those who were debtors among them were at least partially compensated by the monetary reform (note 21 below).

[18] *The Cambridge Ancient History, IV*, pp. 46–49; Woodhouse, *op. cit.*, pp. 201–202.

[19] *The Cambridge Ancient History, IV*, pp. 42–43.

[20] Gilliard, *op. cit.*, pp. 184–185.

[21] Aristotle, *op. cit.*, p. 77; here he says that the change was from 70 drachmae, in contrast to Plutarch, *op. cit.*, p. 106, who makes it from 73 drachmae. Such a reform could have benefited the farmers only if they had to repay debts, which is inconsistent with the above interpretation of the *seisachtheia*. A new interpretation suggests that there was no coinage in the Athens of Solon's days and therefore there could have been no such reform, but it is conceded that a reform of the exchange standard might have occurred; C. M. Kraay, "The Archaic Owls of Athens: Classification and Chronology," *Numismatic Chronicle*, 6th ser., XVI (1956), 46–47; also Day and Chambers, *op. cit.*, pp. 77–78.

[22] Plutarch, *op. cit.*, pp. 110–111.

[23] Aristotle, *op. cit.*, pp. 74–75; estimates of the land area thus owned by a member in each class vary; for details see Gilliard, *op. cit.*, p. 220. On the validity of attributing this classification to Solon, see Day and Chambers, *op. cit.*, pp. 79-83.

[24] Linforth, *op. cit.*, pp. 79, 85; however, Day and Chambers raise questions as to whether Solon did in fact introduce the *Thetes* to the assembly for the first time; *op. cit.*, p. 80.

[25] Some believe that "the greatest positive immediate achievements of Solon were a solution of the economic problem of Attica in his day" (*The Cambridge Ancient History, IV*, p. 57). This is not evident unless by inference we consider liberation of the *Hektemor* and encouragement of parents to train their children to trades as successful solutions to the problem.

[26] Linforth, *op. cit.*, p. 60; Solon himself makes that claim in verses VIII and IX, pp. 135–137; *The Cambridge Ancient History, IV*, p. 49.

[27] Aristotle, *op. cit.*, pp. 80–81; Andrewes, *op. cit.*, pp. 87–88.

[28] *The Cambridge Ancient History, IV*, p. 55; Gilliard, *op. cit.*, p. 220.

[29] Aristotle, *op. cit.*, p. 81; this description of the party of Pisistratus is challenged by Ure, *op. cit.*, pp. 37–38. Ure suggests that Pisistratus himself organized his faction from among the mineworkers to establish his tyranny; his interpretation is not consistent with the accepted fact that Pisistratus had to distribute land in fulfillment of early promises to his followers. Why would he have promised land to miners? On the distinction in terms of political philosophy, see the references in note 8 above.

[30] Although Solon openly criticized Pisistratus for seizure of power, he later approved many of his actions and gave him advice, Plutarch, *op. cit.*, p. 116; on the relationship between them, E. von Stern, "Solon and Pisistratus," *Hermes*, 48 (1913), 426–441.

[31] *The Cambridge Ancient History, IV*, pp. 65–66.

[32] *Op. cit.*, pp. 83–84.

[33] *The Cambridge Ancient History, IV*, pp. 65–66.

[34] Andrewes, *op. cit.*, p. 113; Ure, *op. cit.*, p. 291.

[35] Aristotle, *op. cit.*, pp. 84–85; Andrewes, *op. cit.*, p. 111. Ure describes all Greek tyrants as capitalists, including Pisistratus, but he uses the term capitalist quite loosely; *op. cit.*, pp. 290–291.

[36] The term legitimacy must be interpreted here with caution because acceptance of his rule or lack of it might have depended more on the traditional and tribal loyalties than on his own qualifications and achievements, as is usually true of charismatic leaders.

[37] For a critical evaluation, see Day and Chambers, *op. cit.*, p. 118.

NOTES TO CHAPTER IV

[1] *The Cambridge Ancient History, IX*, ed. by S. A. Cook, F. E. Adcock, and M. P. Charlesworth (New York: Macmillan; Cambridge: University Press, 1932), pp. 16–18; *Appian's Roman History, III*, tr. by Horace White (London: Heinemann; New York: Macmillan, 1913), pp. 15–17; this will be cited henceforth as Appian, *The Civil Wars*.

[2] In 367 B.C. the limit was set and might have been modified, but as late as 167 B.C. it was 500 *iugera* (yoke, the area that a pair of oxen can plough in one day) or about 300 acres (the customary equivalent is 1,000 *iugera* = 622 acres); *The Cambridge Ancient History, IX*, p. 19; in the *Civil Wars* Appian gives the equivalent of this to be one hundred cattle or five hundred sheep being kept on common pasture (p. 17).

[3] *The Cambridge Ancient History, IX*, p. 3.

[4] H. H. Scullard, *From the Gracchi to Nero* (New York: Praeger, 1959), pp. 19–20; M. Cary, *A History of Rome* (London: Macmillan; New York: St. Martin's Press, 1960), pp. 258–259.

[5] M. Rostovtzeff, *The Social and Economic History of the Roman Empire*, rev. by P. M. Fraser (Oxford: University Press, 1957), pp. 22–23.

[6] H. H. Scullard, *op. cit.*, p. 20.

[7] Th. Mommsen, *The History of Rome, III*, tr. by W. P. Dickson (New York: Scribner, 1895), p. 313.

[8] *Ibid.*, pp. 313–314. Distribution of public land was discontinued in 177 B.C., after which "a slow but steady decline" in the number of small holders resulted; M. Cary, *op. cit.*, p. 257.

[9] M. Cary, *op. cit.*, pp. 257, 263; *The Cambridge Ancient History, IX*, p. 7.

[10] *Ibid.*, pp. 5–6.

[11] V. Duruy, *History of Rome and the Roman People, II*, ed. by Rev. J. P. Mahaffy (London: Kegan Paul, Trench, 1884), pp. 302–304.

[12] M. Cary, *op. cit.*, p. 263.

[13] *Ibid.*, p. 263; H. H. Scullard, *op. cit.*, pp. 9–10.

[14] Mommsen, *op. cit.*, III, p. 303.

[15] H. H. Scullard, *op. cit.*, p. 10.

[16] Plutarch, *op. cit.*, p. 998; M. Cary, *op. cit.*, p. 282; H. H. Scullard, *op. cit.*, p. 25.

[17] M. Cary, *op. cit.*, p. 281.

[18] Plutarch, *op. cit.*, p. 998; M. Cary, *op. cit.*, p. 282; H. H. Scullard, *op. cit.*, p. 26.

[19] Plutarch, *op. cit.*, p. 998

[20] Mommsen, *op. cit.*, III, pp. 228, 319–320; H. H. Scullard, *op. cit.*, pp. 25–26.

[21] Duruy, *op. cit.*, p. 404.

[22] H. H. Scullard, *op. cit.*, p. 27; some have suggested that the size was left to the discretion of the executors of the law; *The Cambridge Ancient History, IX,* p. 23.

[23] For more details see Mommsen, *op. cit.*, III, pp. 320–327; Duruy, *op. cit.*, pp. 402–403; and *The Cambridge Ancient History, IX*, pp. 22–24.

[24] Appian, *The Civil Wars*, pp. 19–20.

[25] Mommsen, *op. cit.*, III, p. 337; some people have disagreed with this conclusion and suggest that the new decree restricted the power of the commission only with respect to the land of the Italians; E. G. Hardy, "Were the Lex Thoria of 118 B.C. and the Lex Agraria of 111 B.C. Reactionary Laws?", *Journal of Philology*, XXXI (1910), 272.

[26] For further details see *The Cambridge Ancient History, IX*, pp. 42–48.

[27] *Ibid.*, pp. 66–69.

[28] E. G. Hardy, *op. cit.*, p. 275.

[29] M. Cary, *o.p cit.*, pp. 289–90.

[30] *The Cambridge Ancient History, IX*, pp. 98–100; for more details on the failure of the agrarian reform see Appian, *The Civil Wars*, p. 55. Some hold that the post-Gracchan legislation was actually a completion rather than a reversal of the reform; it is held that these laws were to stabilize the confused situation generated by the Gracchi; E. G. Hardy, *op. cit.*, makes this the thesis of his article; I dealt with these views in Appendix I of Tuma, MS, pp. 501–502, and reached the following conclusion: "Since land alienation became permissible and holdings of *ager publicus* were made private property, and since the former landlords were politically rehabilitated, it seems plausible to conclude that the post-Gracchan land laws were reactionary and represented a reversal of the Gracchan reform."

[31] Mommsen, *op. cit.*, III, pp. 375–6.

[32] *The Cambridge Ancient History, IX*, p. 43.

[33] Rostovtzeff, *The Social and Economic History of the Roman Empire*, p. 43.

[34] *Ibid.*, pp. 23–24; similar views have been expressed by Hardy, *op. cit.*, p. 277; in *The Civil Wars* Appian says that "the condition of the poor became even worse than it was before" and shortly afterward "a still further decline in the numbers of both citizens and soldiers" resulted, and "about fifteen years after the enactment of the laws of Gracchus, by reason of a series of lawsuits, the people were reduced to unemployment" (p. 55).

[35] Rostovtzeff, *The Social and Ecomonic History of the Roman Empire*, p. 33.

[36] Plutarch, *op. cit.*, p. 1019.

[37] M. Cary, *op. cit.*, pp. 83, 85.

[38] *The Cambridge Ancient History, IX*, p. 25.

[39] *The Civil Wars*, p. 37, on the litigation under the reform law.

[40] Mommsen, *op. cit.*, I, pp. 387–389.

NOTES TO CHAPTER V

[1] There is no denying that the timing might be of importance in shedding light on the rate, process, and effects of change as these are related to other aspects of society.

[2] Hence the differences between the forms of tenure that evolved in England, France, and Scandinavia also. Where economic development has been limited, as in the countries of the Middle East, pressure for tenure change has not been forthcoming until recently, and therefore the same agrarian structure that the English people rid themselves of centuries ago has persisted.

[3] P. Vinogradoff, *Collected Papers*, Vol. I (Oxford: Clarendon Press, 1928), p. 129.

[4] E. P. Cheyney, "The Disappearance of English Serfdom," *The English History Review*, XV (1900), 20.

[5] E. A. Kosminsky, *Studies in the Agrarian History of England in the 13th Century*, ed. by R. H. Hilton, tr. from Russian by Ruth Kisch (Oxford: Basil Blackwell, 1956), p. 84.

[6] *Ibid.*, pp. 84–85.

[7] H. Nabholz, "Medieval Agrarian Society in Transition," *Cambridge Economic History*, Vol. I (Cambridge: University Press, 1941), p. 496.

[8] Kosminsky, *op. cit.*, p. 98. These calculations exclude five Cambridgeshire hundreds, since these show a comparatively higher percentage of small manors which would distort the picture.

[9] *Ibid.*, p. 168.

[10] *Ibid.*, pp. 168–169.

[11] H. Pirenne, *Economic and Social History of Medieval Europe* (New York: Harcourt, Brace, 1937), pp. 64–65. There is no need to deal with these conclusions in this context. It is sufficient to point out that Pirenne's conception of collectivism and equality is a peculiar one and only in that sense is it possible to describe the system as he does. Nor was equality a result of this system as shown by the amount of differentiation it involved.

[12] P. Vinogradoff, *The Growth of the Manor* (London: George Allen; New York: Macmillan, 1911), p. 307.

[13] *Ibid.*, pp. 307–308.

[14] *Ibid.*, p. 208.

[15] T. W. Page, *The End of Villeinage in England* (Publications of the American Economic Association, I, no. 2 [May, 1900]), pp. 10–11.

[16] *Ibid.*, p. 24.

[17] Vinogradoff, *The Growth of the Manor*, pp. 310–311.

[18] *Ibid.*, p. 309.

[19] For distinction between free and unfree in manorialism see Tuma, MS, Appendix II.

[20] This sketchy presentation is based on H. Pirenne, *op. cit.*, pp. 67–85; J. E. Th. Rogers, *Six Centuries of Work and Wages* (New York: Putnam, n.d.), pp. 226–230; Vinogradoff, *Collected Papers, I*, pp. 129–138; J. W. Thompson, *Economic and Social History of Europe in the Later Middle Ages* (New York, London: The Century Co., 1931), pp. 381–395; T. W. Page, *op. cit.*, pp. 64–72; and Cheyney, *op. cit.*, pp. 25–35.

[21] Kosminsky, *op. cit.*, pp. 319–352. Maurice Dobb applies a similar method of analysis, but he gives less weight to the role the growth of trade played in creating internal conflict. He stresses the importance of insufficiency of the production system, the growth of population of both the lords and the serfs, and the resulting pressure on the peasants. Hence the massive desertion which led to the breakdown of feudalism. *Studies in the Development of Capitalism* (London: Routledge, 1947), pp. 37 ff.

[22] Cheyney sees the courts to be inclined toward freedom of the serf, *op. cit.*, pp. 29–30.

[23] Harriett Bradley, *The Enclosures in England* (New York: Columbia University Press, 1918), pp. 64–72.

[24] J. E. Th. Rogers, *op. cit.*, pp. 228–229.

[25] Page, *op. cit.*, pp. 71–72; W. H. R. Curtler, *The Enclosure and Redistribution of Our Land* (Oxford: Oxford University Press, 1920), pp. 57–58.

[26] Curtler, *op. cit.*, p. 58.

[27] Kosminsky, *op. cit.*, pp. 354–355.

[28] Page, *op. cit.*, pp. 83–84.

[29] H. Heaton, "Enclosures," *Encyclopedia of the Social Sciences*, V–VI (New York: Macmillan, 1948), p. 523. See Curtler, *op. cit.*, pp. 77–80, for meaning of common rights.

[30] Heaton, *op. cit.*, pp. 523–524. A different classification is given by Curtler according to the impact on the common field system and on agriculture, and also with respect to the methods used in bringing about enclosure.

[31] R. Schickele, "Theories Concerning Land Tenure," *Journal of Farm Economics*, 34 (1952), 734–744.

[32] A. H. Johnson, *Disappearance of the Small Landowner* (Oxford: Clarendon Press, 1901), pp. 56–60; it is noted that the value of arable land increased by 23 per cent when converted into pasture (p. 56).

[33] R. H. Tawney, *The Agrarian Problem in the Sixteenth Century* (London, New York, Bombay, and Calcutta: Longmans, Green, 1912), pp. 191–192.

[34] Curtler, *op. cit.*, pp. 64, 70; Gonner, *op. cit.*, p. 43; Marx, *Capital*, Vol. I, p. 741.

[35] Tawney, *op. cit.*, p. 197; Curtler, *op. cit.*, pp. 65–67; there were enclosures motivated by still other causes, but these were minor.

[36] Some writers disagree that enclosure was necessary for improved agriculture. Slater suggests that improvement and substitution of the rotation

system "might take place independently of enclosure, and might not follow if enclosure did take place." G. Slater, *The English Peasantry and the Enclosure of Common Fields* (London: Constable, 1907), p. 95. Also Doreen Warriner challenges the theory that enclosure was necessary for agricultural progress and cites the examples of western and northern Europe where enclosure was not allowed and yet agricultural methods were improved. Miss Warriner holds that enclosures in England were a result of the political power of the landlords. *Economics of Peasant Farming* (London, New York: Oxford University Press, 1939), pp. 11–12.

[37] Bradley, *op. cit.*, pp. 105–107.

[38] This theory has also been advocated by Lord Ernle, who applies it to the eighteenth-century enclosures as well. Lord Ernle admits that "commercial motives, no doubt, operated to accelerate both changes . . . but from the economic point of view the movement was justified by the national interest in the maximum yield from the soil of the country" (*The Land and Its People* [London: Hutchinson, n.d.], p. 19).

[39] V. M. Lavrovsky, "Expropriation of the English Peasantry in the Eighteenth Century," *Economic History Review* (1956), pp. 271–272.

[40] Curtler, *op. cit.*, p. 82. The Statute of Merton allowed the lord of the manor to enclose the common as long as he left sufficient pastures for the tenants, and it was his responsibility to prove that he did so. The Statute of Westminster entitled manor lords to enclose against their neighboring manors or townships, unless a specific grant of common rights had been made to them. It is interesting to note that both statutes were reconfirmed as late as 1550, at a time when opposition to the enclosures was already running high. These two statutes continued to be of importance throughout the period of enclosures, particularly since the control of Parliament was indirect and application of the law was in the hands of the beneficiaries of the enclosures.

[41] T. E. Scrutton, *Commons and Common Fields* (Cambridge: University Press, 1887), p. 170.

[42] J. Collings, *Land Reform, Occupying Ownership, Peasant Proprietary and Rural Education* (London, New York, and Bombay: Longmans, Green, 1906), p. 140.

[43] *Ibid.*, pp. 150–158.

[44] Slater, *op. cit.*; most of these measures are mentioned in his Appendix D, pp. 322–330.

[45] R. H. Tawney, *op. cit.*, p. 25.

[46] Slater, *op. cit.*, pp. 130–131.

[47] Johnson, *op. cit.*, pp. 90–91. H. Heaton estimates the area enclosed between 1450 and 1650 to be only 500,000 acres, mostly in poor land. *Economic History of Europe* (rev. ed.; New York: Harper, 1948), p. 312.

[48] This question has been dealt with by many people, among whom are Slater, *op. cit.*, pp. 91–116; Curtler, *op. cit.*, pp. 233–250; opposite sides of the debate are represented by Paul Mantoux, *The Industrial Revolution of the Eighteenth Century*, English trans. (London, 1928), Part I, chap. 3, pp. 168–190, and J. D. Chambers, "Enclosures and Labour Supply in the Industrial

Revolution," *The Economic History Review*, 2d ser., V, no. 3 (1953), 319–343.

[49] Heaton, *op. cit.*, p. 554.

[50] Quoted in Slater, *op. cit.*, p. 128.

[51] Curtler, *op. cit.*, p. 244.

[52] Johnson, *op. cit.*, p. 66.

[53] A detailed discussion of this is found in Tawney, *op. cit.*, pp. 287–301.

[54] Slater, *op. cit.*, pp. 99–100.

[55] For supporting evidence see Abbas Gabriel, "Consolidation of Agricultural Holdings in Lebanon," in *Center on Land Problems in the Near East* (Salahudin, Iraq, 1955; Rome FAO, 1956) (mimeographed).

NOTES TO CHAPTER VI

[1] R. E. Cameron, "Economic Growth and Stagnation in France, 1815–1914," *Journal of Modern History*, XXX (March, 1958), 1–13.

[2] L. Gershoy, *The French Revolution and Napoleon* (New York: F. S. Crofts, 1933), p. 40.

[3] *Ibid.*, p. 44.

[4] J. H. Clapham, *The Economic Development of France and Germany: 1815-1914* (4th ed.; Cambridge: University Press, 1955), p. 14.

[5] Gershoy, *op. cit.*, p. 41.

[6] A. Marshall, *Principles of Economics* (8th ed.; London: Macmillan, 1922), p. 643, n. Sharecropper is the common translation of *metayer*, but it is not clear if *metayers* managed their farms as share-tenants or not.

[7] Clapham, *op. cit.*, p. 14.

[8] Gershoy, *op. cit.*, p. 42.

[9] *The Cambridge Modern History, Volume VIII: The French Revolution*, ed. by A. W. Ward, G. W. Prothero, and Stanley Leathes (London and New York: Macmillan, 1908), p. 62.

[10] Gershoy, *op. cit.*, pp. 43–44.

[11] Clapham, *op. cit.*, p. 14.

[12] Gershoy, *op. cit.*, p. 41.

[13] *The Cambridge Modern History, VIII*, pp. 62–63. One wonders why sharecroppers did not give up sharecropping to take advantage of the better opportunities available to landless workers, as this observation holds. Furthermore, what evidence is there to show that wages in English farming were "tolerable" in this period?

[14] Gershoy, *op. cit.*, pp. 40–41. For a discussion of whether the *censiers* should be considered owners or tenants, see Tuma, MS, Appendix III, in which I proposed considering them tenants.

[15] *The Cambridge Modern History, VIII*, p. 62.

[16] G. Lefebvre, "Les Recherches Relatives á la Repartition de la Propriete et de l'Exploitation Foncieres á la Fin de l'Ancien Regime," *Revue d'Histoire Moderne*, III (1928), 100.

[17] H. Sée, *Histoire Economique de la France*, Vol. I Paris: Libraire Armand Colin, 1939), pp. 173–175.

[18] *Ibid.*, p. 175.

[19] E. J. Lowell, *The Eve of the French Revolution* (Boston and New York: Houghton, Mifflin; Cambridge: Riverside Press, 1892), p. 25.

[20] *The Cambridge Modern History, VIII*, p. 53.

[21] *Ibid.*, p. 56.

[22] H. Sée, *Economic and Social Conditions in France During the Eighteenth Century*, tr. by E. H. Zeydel (New York: F. S. Crofts, 1931), pp. 77–78.

[23] *The Cambridge Modern History, VIII*, p. 54.

[24] Lowell, *op. cit.*, pp. 28–29.

[25] *Ibid.*, p. 25

[26] *Ibid.*, p. 70. The most conservative estimate describes them as being equally wealthy as the clergy.

[27] H. Sée, *Economic and Social Conditions*, p. 88.

[28] *Ibid.*, p. 208.

[29] Lefebvre, "Les Recherches . . . ," *op. cit.*, p. 112.

[30] Gershoy, *op. cit.*, p. 48. For more details on social classes see *The Cambridge Modern History, VIII*, pp. 48–63; Lefebvre, "Les Recherches . . . ," *op. cit.*, pp. 110–120, especially on distribution of land and size of farm; E. .J Lowell, *op. cit.*, pp. 25–37, 186–192, 228–229; and also H. Sée, *Economic and Social Conditions*, pp. 60–61, 76–79, 88–109, 208–210.

[31] H. Sée, *Economic and Social Conditions*, pp. 24–25.

[32] S. Herbert, *The Fall of Feudalism in France* (New York: F. A. Stokes, n.d.), p. 60.

[33] The *Cambridge Modern History, VIII*, pp. 66–71.

[34] Herbert, *op. cit.*, pp. 93, 94, for further details; also, H. Sée, *Economic and Social Conditions*, p. 45.

[35] T. S. Hamerow, *Restoration, Revolution, Reaction: Economics and Politics in Germany, 1815–1871* (Princeton, N.J.: Princeton University Press, 1958), p. 44.

[36] Herbert, *op. cit.*, pp. 111–112.

[37] Gershoy, *op. cit.*, p. 161.

[38] *Ibid.*, pp. 160–161.

[39] Herbert, *op. cit.*, pp. 191–192.

[40] *Ibid.*, pp. 193–194.

[41] *Ibid.*, pp. 195–196.

[42] Gershoy, *op. cit.*, p. 310.

[43] J. Loutchisky, *Quelques Remarques sur la Vente des Biens Nationaux* (Paris: Librairie Ancienne Honore Champion, 1913), pp. 25, 27.

[44] *Ibid.*, pp. 32–34.

[45] *Ibid.*, p. 40.

[46] *Ibid.*, pp. 41–42.

[47] *Ibid.*, pp. 64–72.

[48] G. Lefebvre, *Questions Agraires aux Temps de la Terreur* (Strasburg, 1932), pp. 30–31.

[49] Loutchisky, *op. cit.*, p. 48.

[50] F. Dovring, *Land and Labor in Europe 1900–1950: A Comparative Study of Recent Agrarian History* (The Hague: Martinus Nijhoff, 1956), p. 139.

[51] J. H. Clapham, *op. cit.*, p. 12. Common land in this context refers to the traditional concept of open commons used as pastures by the community as a whole.

[52] Loutchisky, *Quelques Remarques* . . . , pp. 8–9.

[53] *Ibid.*, pp. 106, 139–140, 148, 149, 150.

[54] Lefebvre, *Questions Agraires* . . . , p. 131.

[55] Clapham, *op. cit.*, p. 20. Also Gershoy, *op. cit.*, p. 311; also F. B. Artz, *France Under the Bourbon Restoration 1814–1830* (Cambridge, Mass.: Harvard University Press, 1931), pp. 176–178.

[56] Artz, *op. cit.*, pp. 176–177.

[57] *Ibid.*, pp. 176–177; Clapham, *op. cit.*, p. 20.

[58] G. Lefebvre, *The Coming of the French Revolution, 1789*, tr. by R. R. Palmer (Princeton, N.J.: Princeton University Press, 1947), p. 159.

[59] It may be observed in this context that competition between the bourgeoisie and the peasantry was replacing the alliance that characterized the earlier stages of the Revolution. Schism between the two classes arose regarding grain trade; the bourgeoisie wanted free trade while the peasants preferred a return to regulation. Thus class conflict was replacing alliance between the groups that had fought feudalism together. See *ibid.*, p. 519.

[60] Clapham, *op. cit.*, p. 10.

[61] Some peasants redeemed their feudal dues on church property after they had bought it, though payment to former lay seigneurs was not so common. Herbert, *op. cit.*, p. 170.

[62] The nobility recovered about half of their property and were indemnified for the rest, Artz, *op. cit.*, pp. 176–177.

[63] One may ask whether clerical property should not be classified as collective or corporate property, as was done in Mexico in the nineteenth and early twentieth centuries, but even so the tenure change after the reform would be in the direction of individual private ownership.

[64] Griswold, *op. cit.*, p. 97.

NOTES TO CHAPTER VII

[1] The method of approximation is the following: according to Litoshenko, the nobles had 87 million desiatines in 1862 and 77 million desiatines in 1877. If we generalize this change percentage-wise to the figures of Table 5, we obtain 82.5 million desiatines for the property of the nobility in 1862. This, however, is inaccurate, since part of what the nobility lost had been acquired after Emancipation upon settlement with the peasants, as we shall see below. A conservative estimate of this acquisition is 20 per cent, which should be deducted from the lords' holdings in 1862 and added to those of the peasants in that year — before the peasant had acquired land by purchase — which Litoshenko estimates at about 5,665,290 desiatines up to 1877.

[2] W. H. Mosse, *Alexander II and the Modernization of Russia* (London: English Universities Press, 1958), p. 12.

[3] J. Mavor, *An Economic History of Russia*, Vol. II (London and Toronto: Dent; New York: Dutton, 1925), pp. 273–275.

[4] L. E. Hubbard, *The Economics of Soviet Agriculture* (London: Macmillan, 1939), pp. 27–28.

[5] G. T. Robinson, *Rural Russia Under the Old Regime* (New York: Longmans, Green, 1949), p. 28.

[6] *Ibid.*; for a detailed discussion of this see Mosse, *op. cit.*, pp. 42–75.

[7] Robinson, *op. cit.*, pp. 28–29.

[8] The number of serfs is taken from Mosse, *op. cit.*, p. 14; Mavor, however, estimates the serf population to be 34.59 million in 1859.

[9] Robinson, *op. cit.*, pp. 36–37.

[10] Lenin, *Alliance . . .* , p. 34.

[11] *Ibid.*, pp. 36–38; Robinson, *op. cit.*, p. 40. Lenin presents this picture of differentiation with respect to the *mir*, but we have generalized it to the commune in the earlier period on the assumption that there was no reason for conditions to have been different.

[12] Robinson, *op. cit.*, pp. 56–57.

[13] *Ibid.*, p. 38.

[14] The loss of grain has been estimated at about 30 million rubles per year between 1830 and 1859; Mavor, Vol. I, *op. cit.*, p. 422.

[15] Robinson, *op. cit.*, p. 38; Mavor, however, rejects the idea that the serf population increased; on the contrary, he presents data indicating a decline from 44.93 per cent of total population in 1815 to 37.00 per cent in 1851, and to 34.39 per cent in 1859. However, he admits a small increase in the absolute number of serf population; Vol. I, *op. cit.*, pp. 418–419.

[16] Mavor, Vol. I, *op. cit.*, p. 419.

[17] Robinson, *op. cit.*, pp. 39–40.

[18] W. Kokovtzoff, "The Agrarian Question in Russia," *English Review*, XXXIX (London, 1924), 362.

[19] Mavor, Vol. I, *op. cit.*, p. 379.

[20] Quoted in Mosse, *op. cit.*, p. 48.

[21] *Ibid.*, p. 398.

[22] Robinson, *op. cit.*, p. 39. Robinson adds: "Such was the law, but history is more concerned with facts."

[23] Hubbard, *op. cit.*, pp. 29–30.

[24] For a detailed discussion of the maneuvers, see Mosse, *op. cit.*, pp. 47–48; Mavor, Vol. I, *op. cit.*, pp. 377–395.

[25] M. Dobb, *The Soviet Economic Development Since 1917* (New York: International Publishers, 1948), p. 50.

[26] Robinson, *op. cit.*, pp. 83–84.

[27] *Ibid.*, p. 82.

[28] Professor Gregory Grossman has suggested a different estimate of the value of the person of the serf in redemption as follows: the landlord used to receive half the product of the land as net income; by freeing the serf with a "beggarly lot" he is now to bear the cost of production; therefore,

he receives half the land as his share and another quarter in lieu of the cost of production or the value of the services of the freed serf.

Actually this analysis is relevant only to serfs bound to the land and can be contradicted by the facts concerning the other serfs, since those in household service were freed without having to redeem their person.

[29] A. Baykov, *The Development of the Soviet Economic System* (Cambridge: University Press, 1950), p. 10.

[30] Mavor, Vol. I, *op. cit.*, p. 383.

[31] Robinson, *op. cit.*, p. 82.

[32] Sir John Maynard, *Russia in Flux* (New York: Macmillan, 1949), p. 25, n.

[33] Robinson, *op. cit.*, pp. 82–84.

[34] Dobb, *Soviet Economic Development*, p. 51.

[35] Robinson, *op. cit.*, p. 89.

[36] *Ibid.*, pp. 89–91.

[37] Dobb, *Soviet Economic Development*, pp. 51–52.

[38] By two-thirds approval the commune could divide the land and establish hereditary ownership. This actually happened in the south, west, and southwest of Russia. The resulting system was called *podvorny* rather than *mir* as in the repartitional tenure. The peasants in the *podvorny* "made a final distribution of their holdings when they received them in 1861, and they distributed them in strips which they held as individual property, with certain limitations as to sale" (Sir Bernard Pares, "The New Land Settlement in Russia," *Russian Review*, I, no. 1 [1912], 60).

[39] For details, see Robinson, *op. cit.*, pp. 73–75.

[40] Lyashchenko, *op. cit.*, p. 384.

[41] L. Owen, *The Russian Peasant Movement*, 1906–1917 (London: P. S. King, 1937), p. 6.

[42] *Ibid.*, p. 6.

[43] Robinson, *op. cit.*, pp. 95–96.

[44] B. Pares, *A History of Russia* (5th ed.; New York: Knopf, 1949), p. 355.

[45] Robinson, *op. cit.*, p. 130.

[46] *Ibid.*, p. 131.

[47] Litoshenko, *op. cit.*, p. 196.

[48] *Ibid.*, p. 198.

[49] Lenin, *Collected Works, I*, pp. 348–349, quoted in Lyashchenko, *op. cit.*, p. 392.

[50] Litoshenko notes that in 1877 the average size of a bourgeoisie estate was 668 desiatines, and in 1905, 559 desiatines. On the other hand, in 1906, 83.5 per cent of the total area sold by the merchants was acquired by estates of more than 500 desiatines. Litoshenko, *op. cit.*, p. 197.

[51] Lenin, *Alliance* . . . , p. 34.

[52] V. I. Lenin, *The Development of Capitalism in Russia* (Moscow: Foreign Languages Publishing House, 1956), p. 172; for statistical results on the separate provinces, see his chap. ii, pp. 50–172; on differentiation and class conflict, see also Lenin, *Alliance* . . . , pp. 36–37.

[53] W. Kokovtzoff, *op. cit.*, p. 363.

[54] Robinson, *op. cit.*, p. 98. (1 *pud* = 16.38 kg. = 36.113 lb.)

[55] Lenin, *Development of Capitalism in Russia*, p. 266.

[56] L. Lawton, *An Economic History of Soviet Russia*, Vol. I (London: Macmillan, n.d.), pp. 7–8.

[57] M. T. Florinsky shows that change in techniques was very slow. Productivity per acre increased between 1860 and 1870 on privately owned estates because the nobility retained the best land. Florinsky, *op. cit.*, pp. 926–929.

[58] Lenin, *Alliance* . . . , p. 13.

[59] Mavor, Vol. II, *op. cit.*, p. 136; on penetration into the rural areas, see Sir John Maynard, *Russia in Flux*, p. 11.

[60] Mosse, *op. cit.*, pp. 158–173.

[61] Mavor, Vol. II, *op. cit.*, pp. 139–140.

[62] Robinson, *op. cit.*, p. 132.

[63] *Ibid.*, p. 132.

[64] S. Shidlovsky, "The Imperial Duma and Land Settlement," *Russian Review*, I (1912), 20.

[65] Mavor, Vol. II, *op. cit.*, p. 140.

[66] These figures have been approximated from figures given by Robinson, *op. cit.*, p. 114, and Kokovtzoff, *op. cit.*, pp. 365–366.

[67] Robinson, *op. cit.*, pp. 113–114.

[68] *Ibid.*, pp. 106–107.

[69] *Ibid.*, pp. 103 and 98.

[70] Owen, *op. cit.*, p. 8.

[71] This is best demonstrated by the impact of "advance payment" on the Mexican *peon*; see below, chap. viii.

[72] Robinson, *op. cit.*, p. 99.

[73] *Ibid.*, p. 131.

[74] *Ibid.*, p. 47.

[75] *Ibid.*, pp. 96–102.

[76] Owen, *op. cit.*, p. 20, and Mavor, Vol. II, *op. cit.*, p. 356.

[77] Owen, *op. cit.*, p. 20.

[78] Robinson, *op. cit.*, pp. 145–146.

[79] A. Manuilov, "Agrarian Reform in Russia," *Russian Review*, I, no. 4 (1912), 132.

[80] Mavor, Vol. II, *op. cit.*, p. 348.

[81] Maynard, *op. cit.*, p. 163.

[82] However, the separator was still required to give up his allotment land that had not been finally consolidated, and to belong to some peasant community. Robinson, *op. cit.*, pp. 209–210.

[83] Owen, *op. cit.*, pp. 43–44; Robinson, *op. cit.*, pp. 212–213.

[84] Owen, *op. cit.*, p. 60.

[85] *Ibid.*, pp. 61–62.

[86] Robinson, *op. cit.*, p. 222.

[87] Lyashchenko, *op. cit.*, pp. 749–751.

[88] *Ibid.*

[89] Manuilov, *op. cit.*, p. 133.

90 Lyashchenko, *op. cit.*, p. 748.

91 Manuilov, *op. cit.*, pp. 148–149. This criticism may in fact be applied to all the previous measures since, and including, Emancipation. This policy-making, reversal, and reformulation have not been based on study and sound judgment concerning the real needs of the peasant and efficient farming. Nor is this criticism limited to the Russian pre-Soviet land tenure reforms, but extends to most western reforms. Carroll suggests that only Communist tenure reforms have been part of a plan designed with great concern for economic efficiency and higher production. T. Carroll, "The Concept of Land Reform," *op. cit.*, p. 39.

92 Owen, *op. cit.*, pp. 68–69; Lyashchenko, *op. cit.*, pp. 749–751.

93 Maynard, *Russian in Flux*, p. 164.

94 On the impact of the reforms on the development of new revolutionary activities among the peasantry, see Lyashchenko, *op. cit.*, pp. 751–752.

95 Lenin, *Alliance* . . . , pp. 158–159.

96 Owen, *op. cit.*, p. 196.

97 *Ibid.*, p. 206.

98 V. I. Lenin, *The Land Revolution in Russia* (London: 1919), from the Appendix which includes the Land Decrees 17–19.

99 *Ibid.*, 21–23.

100 *Ibid.*, p. 23.

101 Baykov, *op. cit.*, p. 18.

102 *Ibid.*, pp. 17–18.

103 J. Stalin, *Problems of Leninism* (Moscow: Foreign Languages Publishing House, 1954), p. 213.

104 *Ibid.*, p. 214.

105 Dobb, *Soviet Economic Development*, pp. 104–106.

106 N. Jasny, *The Socialized Agriculture of the USSR: Plans and Performance* (Stanford, Calif.: Stanford University Press, 1949), p. 158.

107 M. Tcherkinsky, "Agrarian Policy in Soviet Russia," *International Review of Agricultural Economics* (Oct.–Dec., 1924), pp. 535–536.

108 Hubbard, *op. cit.*, pp. 80–81.

109 Dobb, *Soviet Economic Development*, p. 129.

110 Baykov, *op. cit.*, p. 132.

111 Lenin, *Alliance*, pp. 376–377.

112 Dobb, *Soviet Economic Development*, p. 138; quoted from *Selected Works*, Vol. IX, p. 178.

113 Hubbard, *op. cit.*, pp. 82–83.

114 The advantage accorded the middle and rich peasants led some people to describe the NEP as a concession to the kulaks, a reaction and return to capitalism, and a sign of weakness of socialism. Among these critics were Trotsky and Bukharin. Baykov, *op. cit.*, p. 133.

115 Dobb, *Soviet Economic Development*, p. 145.

116 Stalin, *op. cit.*, p. 413.

117 Dobb, *Soviet Economic Development*, pp. 215–216.

118 *Ibid.*, p. 222, quoted from the report to the Fifteenth Congress.

119 Stalin, *op. cit.*, p. 521; also A. Erlich, "Stalin's Views on Soviet Economic Development," *in* E. J. Simmons (ed.), *Change and Continuity in*

Russian and Soviet Thought (Cambridge, Mass.: Harvard University Press, 1955), pp. 91–97.

120 Baykov, *op. cit.*, p. 90.

121 Stalin, *op. cit.*, p. 609.

122 Hubbard, *op. cit.*, pp. 113–114.

123 *Ibid.*; Baykov, *op. cit.*, pp. 193–199. According to H. S. Dinerstein, "the peasant who had nothing to begin with was generally willing to enter a collective farm" (*Communism and the Russian Peasant* [Glencoe, Ill.: The Free Press, 1955], p. 19).

124 Stalin, *op. cit.*, p. 611.

125 Dobb, *Soviet Economic Development*, pp. 228–229; also *Baykov, op. cit.*, p. 200. Some writers disagree that resistance was by the richer peasants only, but no one has been able to deny that the peasants were treated differentially and that their responses were accordingly differentiated. Differential peasant attitudes toward the collectives in later years are observed by Dinerstein, *op. cit.*, p. 125.

126 Reproduced in Stalin, *op. cit.*, pp. 419–425.

127 Baykov, *op. cit.*, p. 327.

128 Dobb, *Soviet Economic Development*, p. 246.

129 G. Grossman, "Soviet Agriculture Since Stalin," *The Annals of the American Academy of Political and Social Sciences* (Jan., 1956), p. 62. M. I. Goldman estimates that it took up to 1952 "to recover not only from World War II but also from the trauma of the five year plans and collectivization," after which positive results started to show ("The Soviet Standard of Living, and Ours," *Foreign Affairs*, XXXVIII, no. 4, [July, 1960], 626).

130 The problem of evaluation is discussed in more detail in Tuma, MS, Appendix IV.

131 J. Maynard, "Collectivization of Agriculture: Russia and India; with Discussion," *Asiatic Review*, XXXIX (1943), 118.

132 D. Gale Johnson and Arcadius Kahan, "Soviet Agriculture: Structure and Growth," *Comparisons of the United States and Soviet Economics* (Washington, D.C.: Joint Economic Committee, Congress of the United States, 1959), p. 216. That mechanization was partly to replace the lost animal power means only that it was speeded up on that account, but it does not imply that mechanization would have followed anyway.

133 For more details see N. Jasny, "A Note on Rationality and Efficiency in the Soviet Economy: II," *Soviet Studies*, XII, no. 1 (July, 1961), 35–68, especially the section on agriculture. A specific example is given in F. Belov, *The History of a Soviet Collective Farm* (New York: Praeger, 1955), pp. 116–124.

134 A. G. Frank, "Labor Requirements in Soviet Agriculture," *The Review of Economics and Statistics*, XLI, no. 2, part 1 (May, 1959), 181, for this claim.

135 A. Kahan, "Changes in Labor Inputs in Soviet Agriculture," *Journal of Political Economy*, LXVII, no. 5 (Oct., 1959), 461.

136 *Ibid.*, pp. 457–458.

137 M. I. Goldman, *op. cit.*, p. 627.

[138] A. Nove, "The Incomes of Soviet Peasants," *The Slavonic and East European Review*, XXXVIII, no. 91 (June, 1960), 326. This article discusses in detail the question of differentiation among the peasants.

[139] N. Jasny, "Peasant Worker Income Relationships: A Neglected Subject," *Soviet Studies*, XII, no. 1 (July, 1960), 14–21. The peasant income has sometimes been depressed by bureaucratic and managerial ambition within the collection, as, for instance, when collective wage funds are used to build schools and hospitals; *New York Times*, Sept. 23, 1962.

[140] One may raise objections as to why one would associate these results with collectivization when many of these effects have come only after organizational reform in the collective had started. This objection is untenable for three reasons: (1) The collective was originally planned as a means toward these ends. On the other hand, it is not collectivization *per se* that counts, but the characteristics of the collective farm that count, such as large scale, mechanization, and intensive commercial farming. (2) The reforms introduced in the 1950's, with which positive results have been associated, were consistent with collective tenure. Actually the changes included larger scale and more highly mechanized collectives. And (3) the positive effects were delayed by the sudden social change inherent in a drive such as that for collectivization. Rapid industrialization and the war, rather than collective organization, were also responsible for the delay. This last point was recognized earlier by W. E. Moore in his *Economic Demography of Eastern and Southern Europe* (Geneva: League of Nations, 1954), p. 108.

[141] Looking at the problem differently, it is true that some groups were hit harder than others, which may be considered discrimination and favoritism. However, the end result involved no duality of tenure, as was the case in other reforms. The concept of duality will be discussed in detail in Part III.

[142] However, income differentiation may not perpetuate a group or create a class unless accumulation of wealth and inheritance are allowed. On the other hand, political power and status no longer derive from differential income. The land has been neutralized as a source of class differentiation, and social mobility has been extensive. See A. Nove, *op. cit.*, on income differentiation; on social mobility, see H. Dinerstein, *op. cit.*, pp. 26–27. More recent observations suggest that the rural communities tend to be in "class conflicts with the city-bred rural elite" or collective farm bosses; *New York Times*, Sept. 23, 1962.

[143] This is not to deny that the peasants have generally expressed antagonism to the methods of procuring the product from the collectives; whether in the form of tax or otherwise, the share of the product taken by the government has been so large that the peasants revert to cheating, black marketing, and other means of evading the regulation. This sort of opposition, however, is directed toward loss of the product rather than toward collectivism *per se*.

[144] Even before the October Revolution, to undermine the power of the Provisional Government, "the Bolsheviki had played for all it was worth the purely demagogic card of land reform, promising the peasant soldier the

267

division of the larger farms and estates . . . [and] for days and weeks, the army had been streaming away from the trenches and making its way home." to seize the land (G. F. Kennan, *Russia and the West Under Lenin and Stalin* [Boston, Toronto: Little, Brown, 1961], p. 29).

NOTES TO CHAPTER VIII

[1] Colonization is distinguished from colonialism, as was the case in Egypt; the former implies foreign settlement and permanence, while the latter involves sociopolitical and economic exploitation during the period of occupation without settlement.

[2] G. M. McBride, *The Land System of Mexico* (New York: American Geographical Society, 1937), pp. 134–135.

[3] *Ibid.*, pp. 103–104.

[4] *Ibid.*, pp. 24–28.

[5] Many of the *peones* had their claim to the land acknowledged even by the landlords, though there was no legal title; *ibid.*, p. 30. On how the *peon* was alienated from his rights and brought into the service of the landlord, and on the history of the *hacienda* see *ibid.*, pp. 43 ff., also E. N. Simpson, *The Ejido: Mexico's Way Out* (Chapel-Hill, N.C.: University of North Carolina Press, 1937), pp. 29–31, especially on the period immediately prior to the Revolution.

[6] McBride, *op. cit.*, p. 39.

[7] *Ibid.*, pp. 82–102.

[8] F. Tannenbaum, *Mexico: The Struggle for Peace and Bread* (New York: Knopf, 1950), p. 141.

[9] McBride, *op. cit.*, pp. 140, 143.

[10] Tannenbaum, *Mexico: The Struggle* . . . , p. 140.

[11] The best discussion of the fate of the Indian villages in Mexico that I have found in English is in Helen Phipps, *Some Aspects of the Agrarian Question in Mexico* (University of Texas Bull. no. 2515, April 15, 1925, Studies in History No. 2), chap. vii, pp. 112–130.

[12] *Ibid.*, pp. 122, 125.

[13] Clarence O. Senior, *Land Reform and Democracy* (Gainesville, Fla.: University of Florida Press, 1958), p. 15.

[14] C. C. Cumberland, *Mexican Revolution* (Austin, Texas: University of Texas Press, 1951), p. 4.

[15] *Ibid.*, pp. 4–5.

[16] McBride, *op. cit.*, p. 83.

[17] Cumberland, *op. cit.*, p. 4.

[18] McBride, *op. cit.*, pp. 99–102.

[19] Cumberland, *op. cit.*, p. 6.

[20] *Ibid.*, pp. 4–6.

[21] Senior, *op. cit.*, p. 39.

[22] *Ibid.*, p. 15. This is roughly the classification presented by McBride.

[23] Tannenbaum, *Mexico: The Struggle* . . . , p. 36.

[24] Senior, *op. cit.*, p. 14.

[25] *Ibid.*

[26] E. Simpson, *op. cit.*, p. 43.

[27] *Ibid.*, pp. 45–46.

[28] McBride, *op. cit.*, p. 158.

[29] As will be shown later, most of these signs of crisis were common to revolutions in the cases under study.

[30] Senior, *op. cit.*, p. 22.

[31] Cumberland, *op. cit.*, pp. 16–19.

[32] Quoted in Cumberland, *op. cit.*, p. 209. McBride suggests that agrarian reform was "the most fundamental part" of Madero's program, *op. cit.*, p. 157.

[33] Cumberland, *op. cit.*, pp. 210–213.

[34] Actually, the Mexican peasants were in this period doing what the French did after the French Revolution, and the Russians after the fall of tsardom in 1917.

[35] F. Tannenbaum, *Peace by Revolution: An Interpretation of Mexico* (New York: Columbia University Press, 1933), p. 198.

[36] *Ibid.*, p. 199; the behavior of the military commanders is quite significant in a country such as Mexico where the pattern of politics is personalistic and in which an important role is played by these military leaders and chieftains; see H. B. Parkes, "Political Leadership in Mexico," in *Annals of American Academy of Political and Social Sciences* (March, 1940), pp. 12–22.

[37] Cumberland, *op. cit.*, p. 212. A different version of the plan suggests that it requested restoration of illegally acquired land to which the legal owners still had title. Villages that had no land or title were to receive land expropriated from private properties "to the end that the pueblos and citizens of Mexico may obtain ejidos, colonies, *fundos legales*, and crop lands." The owners of these expropriated lands were to be indemnified for one third of the value of their land. E. Simpson, *The Ejido* . . . , *op. cit.*, p. 51.

[38] Tannenbaum, *Peace by Revolution*, p. 199.

[39] Simpson, *op. cit.*, pp. 56–58.

[40] These selections are taken from *ibid.*, Appendix C, pp. 751–755, which gives the full text of Article 27.

[41] F. Tannenbaum, *The Mexican Agrarian Revolution* (Washington: The Brookings Institution, 1930), Appendix D, pp. 518–527.

[42] *Ibid.*, p. 189.

[43] *Ibid.*, p. 197.

[44] *Ibid.*, p. 234.

[45] *Ibid.*, p. 239.

[46] Simpson, *op. cit.*, pp. 83–84.

[47] *Ibid.*, p. 84.

[48] *Ibid.*, p. 86.

[49] Tannenbaum, *Peace by Revolution*, p. 204.

[50] *Ibid.*, p. 207.

[51] Simpson, *op. cit.*, pp. 90–94.

[52] *Ibid.*, pp. 89–90. This law seems to repeat what the Stolypin reforms in Russia tried to achieve in the early years of the century. See chap. vii above.

[53] Simpson, *op. cit.*, pp. 114–116.

[54] *Ibid.*, p. 120; quote from Appendix B.

[55] *Ibid.*, p. 769, Article 45 of the Agrarian Code; text as Appendix D.

[56] N. L. Whetten, *Rural Mexico* (3d impression; Chicago: University of Chicago Press, 1958), pp. 132–133.

[57] United Nations, Bureau of Economic Affairs, *Progress in Land Reform* (New York, 1954), p. 282.

[58] J. H. Bradsher, "Agrarian Reform in Mexico Since 1934" (unpublished Ph.D. thesis, University of California, Berkeley, 1958), pp. 178, 185. Unfortunately it is not shown what percentage of ejidos were collective and what individual. However, as late as 1944, 86.5 per cent of the ejidos were individually operated, and 12.3 collectively, while 1.2 per cent were mixed. Whetten, *op. cit.*, p. 203. Between 1955 and 1959 another 548,700 hectares of cropland and 1,600,500 hectares of other land were distributed. U. S. Dept. of Agriculture, ERS–Foreign–39, *Land Redistribution in Mexico* (August, 1962), p. 7.

[59] Senior, *op. cit.*, p. 192. Figures on productivity of labor are not available.

[60] U.S. Dept. of Agriculture, *Land Redistribution in Mexico*, p. 10. An argument has been made that yield did not decline, but that there was substitution and reallocation of land owing to which the yield of certain products were down while that of others went up; the general attitude, however, supports the view that productivity suffered after partition of the land.

[61] Tannenbaum, *Mexico: The Struggle . . .* , *op. cit.*, pp. 102–103; for more details, see the whole chapter, "A Theory of Property," pp. 102–112.

[62] In England absolute ownership of land resided in the monarch throughout the history of that country, and private owners have formally been holders by grant only. According to some, the tradition of ownership in fee simply never existed in the Indian or Spanish heritage. "The Indian and Spanish heritage holds as queer and antisocial the doctrine that land can be bought and sold as can a sack of flour" (Senior, *op. cit.*, p. 184).

[63] Tannenbaum, *Mexican Agrarian Revolution*, pp. 202–203.

[64] In fact, the *ejidatario* has been described as "tenant" by Professor Lucio Mendieta Y Nunez, Professor of Agrarian Law, in his "The Balance of Agrarian Reform," *American Academy of Political and Social Sciences, Annals*, CCVIII (March, 1940), 130.

[65] Whetten, *op. cit.*, p. 45.

[66] *New York Times*, Dec. 3, 1961, p. 2; *San Francisco Chronicle*, June 12, 1962, p. 14; *New York Times*, Western ed., March 7, 1963, p. 3; *Wall Street Journal*, Jan. 29, 1963, p. 1; *Los Angeles Times,* Jan. 6, 9, and 10, 1963, and March 9 and 10, 1963.

[67] According to E. Flores, "land reform can be credited with being the

most important single factor responsible for the political stability and peaceful transference of power which Mexico — notorious for her former political truculence — has enjoyed during the last three decades" ("Land Use Changes in Economic Development in Mexico," *Land Economics*, XXXV, no. 2 [1959], 116).

[68] Whetten suggests that one of the defects of the reform was its rapid rate of land distribution, which did not allow enough time to make wise judgment concerning the land expropriated or the identity of the recipient; *op. cit.*, p. 148.

[69] See Table 23 in Senior, *op. cit.*, p. 239, for the annual amounts of land distribution to ejidos between 1916 and 1954.

[70] The period of intensive distribution was also the period in which the status of the *ejido* became more permanent; it coincided with the renewed drive for collectivization in Russia. Also, Trotsky was residing in Mexico at this time (mid-'thirties).

[71] Bradsher, *op. cit.*, p. 27.

[72] Simpson, *op. cit.*, pp. 98–108.

[73] *Ibid.*, p. 119. Actually some argue that the reforms were not intended to break up the *latifundia*, as implicit in the emphasis on restitution rather than on granting, especially in the early period of reform. See Tannenbaum, *Peace by Revolution*, p. 203.

[74] On Carranza's reactionary treatment of reform, see Tannenbaum, *Peace by Revolution*, p. 171. U.S. Dept. of Agriculture, *Land Redistribution in Mexico*, pp. 9–10.

[75] Tannenbaum, *Peace by Revolution*, p. 172.

[76] *Ibid.*, p. 26.

NOTES TO CHAPTER IX

[1] R. P. Dore, *Land Reform in Japan* (London, New York, Toronto: Oxford University Press, 1959), p. 14

[2] *Ibid.*, pp. 15–17. See footnote [6] to my Table 23 for tenure status definitions.

[3] L. I. Hewes, Jr., "On the Current Readjustment of Land Tenure in Japan," *Land Economics*, XXV, no. 3 (August, 1949), 251.

[4] *Ibid.*, pp. 18–22.

[5] Dore, *op. cit.*, pp. 19–20. The importance of this last factor seems doubtful, since low profits must have been unfavorable to the small owner and the tenant as well, keeping the relative economic position of each of these groups fairly constant and the comparative advantage of land ownership unchanged.

[6] L. I. Hewes, Jr., *Japan—Land and Men: An Account of the Japanese Land Reform Program—1945–51* (Ames, Iowa: Iowa State College Press, 1955), p. 31.

[7] Dore, *op. cit.*, p. 23.

[8] *Ibid.*, p. 24.

[9] *Ibid.*, p. 3; 1 *cho* = 10 *tan* = 0.99174 hectares = 2.45072 acres.

[10] *Ibid.*, p. 72.

[11] J. E. Embree, *The Japanese Nation: A Social Survey* (New York: Farrar and Rinehart, 1945), p. 117; for a fairly detailed discussion of social classes prior to the restoration of the Meijis, see *ibid.*, pp. 20–33.

[12] *Ibid.*, pp. 117–127, from which the rest of this section is taken.

[13] Dore, *op. cit.*, p. 78.

[14] On attempted reform see *ibid.*, pp. 80–85, 98–100, 106–112.

[15] *Ibid.*, p. 84.

[16] *Ibid.*, p. 89.

[17] *Ibid.*, pp. 95–96; according to Embree, the relationship between the army and the peasantry stemmed from the fact that many of the army personnel had come from the villages and had an affinity with the peasants, rather than from political expediency (*The Japanese Nation, op. cit.*, p. 121).

[18] *Ibid.*, p. 113.

[19] *Ibid.*, pp. 115–125.

[20] L. A. Salter, "Global War and Peace, and Land Economics," *Journal of Land and Public Utility Economics*, XIX (1943), 395.

[21] Hewes, *Japan: Land and Men*, pp. 41–42. Hewes suggests that some evictions were made in anticipation of reform which would affect absentee landlords; hence the landlords rushed back to their land in order to save what they could (p. 53).

[22] According to Dore, reform was bound to come, even had the Occupation Army not interfered, though maybe on a different level of effectiveness, for the following reasons: (1) weakening of the landlord's power of resistance against pressure for reform from official circles; and (2) release of political prisoners and freedom of political activity, including the resurgence of peasant unions. *Op. cit.*, p. 129.

[23] Hewes, *Japan: Land and Men*, pp. 52–53.

[24] Dore, *op. cit.*, pp. 132–133.

[25] Hewes, *Japanese Land Reform Program* (Tokyo: General Headquarters Supreme Commander for the Allied Powers, Natural Resources Section, Report No. 127, 1950), Appendix A, which gives the text of SCAP 411 (Dec., 1945).

[26] *Ibid.*, p. 97.

[27] Hewes, *Japan: Land and Men*, pp. 53–54.

[28] Dore, *op. cit.*, pp. 137–141.

[29] M. B. Williamson, "Land Reform in Japan," *Journal of Farm Economics*, XXXIII, no. 2 (1951), 174–175.

[30] Dore raises questions as to whether the land reform helped coöperatives or not; he suggests that at least indirectly it did, by raising the incomes of the farmers and thus enabling them to pay the dues and participate in these coöperatives (*op. cit.*, p. 293).

[31] *Ibid.*, pp. 174–175.

[32] One might argue that the reform increased fragmentation of owner holdings but not of operating units, since the owner holdings that were

broken up were not necessarily operated as units before the reform. Nevertheless, it cannot be denied that the reform increased the number of small operating units.

[33] "Orientation of Farming," *Oriental Economist*, XXV (1957), 461.

[34] Dore, *op. cit.*, p. 207.

[35] *Ibid.*, p. 212.

[36] *Oriental Economist*, XXIV (Oct., 1956), p. 486. F. Chia earlier raised questions regarding the impact of the Japanese land redistribution on the standard of living. He estimates that each family of "new tenant owners" might increase its annual income by 20 bushels of rice or an average of 3 bushels per capita. Considering the installment payments on land purchase, and the interest on the debt, the effects become very small. F. Chia, "On Land Tenure in Japan, A Reply," *Land Economics*, XXV, no. 4 (1949), p. 443.

[37] Dore, *op. cit.*, pp. 213–214. More recent data suggest rises in labor productivity from an index of 100 in 1950-1952 to 135.2 in 1958, measured in terms of population engaged in agriculture, and to 142.0 if in hours of labor; U.N., F.A.O., I.L.O., *Progress in Land Reform, 3rd Report* (New York, 1962), p. 43.

[38] J. P. Gittinger, II, *"Econimic Development Through Agrarian Reform"* (unpublished Ph.D. thesis, Iowa State College, 1955), p. 480.

[39] Dore, *op. cit.*, p. 329. This analysis may be elaborated by studying the distribution of power among social classes in relative terms. Those who owned more land still own more than the people who did not own any land but have not become owners. The economic gap between these two groups, though diminished by the reform, nevertheless persists.

[40] J. D. Eyre, "Elements of Instability in the Current Japanese Land Tenure System," *Land Economics*, XXVIII, no. 3 (Aug., 1952), 199.

[41] *Ibid.*, p. 199.

[42] Dore, *op. cit.*, p. 152.

[43] *Ibid.*, p. 163; some of these petitions, however, were by tenants wanting to restore land of which they had been dispossessed; these amounted to 11,000 cases.

[44] Hewes, *Japanese Land Reform Program*, Appendix F (4 Feb., 1948), p. 110.

[45] "Farmland Status," *Oriental Economist*, XXIII (1955), 400.

[46] "Farmland Tenure," *Oriental Economist*, XXV (1957), 236–238; U. N., *Progress in Land Reform, 3rd Report*, pp. 24–25.

[47] "Farmland Status," *op. cit.*, p. 400.

[48] For a more detailed treatment of this point, see C. D. Campbell, "Weak Points in the Japanese Land Reform Program," *Journal of Farm Economics*, XXXIV, no. 3 (Aug., 1952), 361–368.

[49] Dore, *op. cit.*, p. 263.

[50] *Los Angeles Times*, March 8, 1963, p. 11; the bill, however, has been shelved for this session but is expected to be a central issue in the 1964 session; see *ibid.*, March 15, 1963, p. 11.

¹ For a summary history of the modern land tenure system in Egypt, see A. Bonne, *State and Economics in the Middle East* (2d ed.; London: Routledge and Kegan Paul, 1955), pp. 192–193.

² C. Issawi, *Egypt at Mid-Century* (London, New York, and Toronto: Oxford University Press, 1954), pp. 131–132; the charitable *wakf* has been estimated at 93,000 *feddans* (one *feddan* = 1.038 acres.) or about 1.6 per cent of the cultivated area of Egypt; the *ahli* amounted to 600,000 or about 10 per cent of the total cultivated area.

³ *Ibid.*, p. 132.

⁴ Khalid M. Khalid, *Min huna nabda'* [From Here We Start] (Cairo: Dar al-Nil, 1950), p. 116.

⁵ In fact, fragmentation had been on the increase owing to the increase of population and the lag of the cultivated land behind population. In the half-century preceding the reform the population almost doubled while the land area under cultivation increased by only 15 per cent; Sayed Marei, *Agrarian Reform in Egypt* (Cairo: Iprimerie De L' Institut Français D'Archéologie Orientale, 1957), p. 19; see *ibid.*, p. 191 for more details on fragmentation.

⁶ Khalid M. Khalid, *op. cit.*, p. 118. (This excludes rent as cost of production.) Khalid says that the government set a bad example by charging exorbitant rates of rent; he reports that the Ministry of Wakf tried to operate the land but made a loss, after which they leased the land at rates that meant certain loss to the tenant and yet paid no attention to that expected result (p. 119). On tenancy rates see Issawi, *op. cit.*, p. 125, and also Marei, *Agrarian Reform*, p. 21.

⁷ According to Issawi, *op. cit.*, pp. 127–128: "For cotton, the landlord's share may be five-sixths, if he provides seeds, fertilizers, and draught animals and meets the taxes and half the expenses of picking; or it may be three-quarters, if he pays the taxes only, leaving all other expenses to the tenant; or it may be one-half, if the tenant meets all expenses, including taxes; or it may be some intermediary figure, based on a slightly different combination. In wheat, a common form is for a group of tenants to take over a piece of land ploughed by the landlord, to supply seeds, fertilizers, labor, and transport, and to receive one-third of the produce. In maize, the tenant's share varies from one-quarter to one-half, according to the proportion of expenses met by him."

⁸ M. Darling, "Land Reform in Italy and Egypt," *Yearbook of Agricultural Cooperation* (Washington, D.C.: Horace Plunkett Foundation, 1956) p. 14.

⁹ M. R. Ghonemy estimates the surplus labor in agriculture to be about 50 per cent of the labor force or 1.8 millions in 1947 ("Resource Use and Income in Egyptian Agriculture Before and After the Land Reform . . ." [unpublished Ph.D. dissertation, North Carolina State College, Raleigh, 1953], p. 82); on waste, see Issawi, *op. cit.*, p. 106.

¹⁰ M. R. Al-Ghanimi, "Land Tenure in Egypt — Its Economic and Social

Phrases" [Arabic], *Al-Abhath*, X (1957), 19–22; H. Abu al Su'ed, "A Study on Land Reform in Egypt," *Islamic Review*, XLV (1957), 14.

[11] Gabriel Baer, "Egyptian Attitude Towards Land Reform, 1922-1955," *in* W. Z. Laqueur, ed., *The Middle East in Transition* (New York: Praeger, 1958, p. 85.

[12] Mirrit Ghali, *Al-Islah Azzirai'* [Agrarian Reform], pp. 1-100, for a discussion of previous reform programs.

[13] Baer, *op. cit.*, p. 85; for further details on the attitudes of different political parties to reform, see *ibid.*, pp. 85–94.

[14] Al-Ghanimi, "Land Tenure in Egypt," *op. cit.*, p. 22. Of 182.623 feddans sold by the government between 1935 and 1950, the small owners bought 3,111 feddans or 1.7 per cent; 13,827 feddans or 7.6 per cent were sold to graduates of agricultural institutions; and 163,686 feddans or 90.7 per cent were sold to big landlords (p. 22).

[15] *Ibid.*, pp. 17–18. £E1 = $2.80 according to official exchange rates.

[16] *Ibid.*, p. 23; also Abu al-Su'ud, *op. cit.*, p. 14, and H. A. Dawood, "Agrarian Reform in Egypt: A Case Study," *Current History*, XXX (1956), 335.

[17] On the crystallization of the middle class and its role in the revolution, see Sadek H. Samaan, *Value Reconstruction and Egyptian Education* (New York: Columbia University Press, 1955), pp. 10–12.

[18] A. Morad, "The 1952 Agrarian Reform Law of Egypt, Its Limitations and Expectations" (unpublished Ph.D. thesis, University of Maryland, 1954), pp. 130–131; also Baer, *op. cit.*, p. 98, paraphrasing *Al-Ahram* (Arabic daily) of Sept. 4, 1954.

[19] *Ibid.*, p. 98.

[20] Al-Lajnah al-U'lia Lilislah azzirai', *Fajr Jadeed Ma' al-Islah azzirai'* [A New Dawn with Agrarian Reform]. Cairo, n.d.

[21] Baer, *op. cit.*, pp. 96–98.

[22] *Land Reform and Economic Development* (Cairo: National Bank of Egypt, 1955), p. 13.

[23] Baer, *op. cit.*, p. 98, from *Al-Ahram*, Sept. 4, 1954. This is similar to what the Tsar said about Russia almost a century earlier; see my chap. vii.

[24] Extracted and paraphrased from the text of the law presented in Sayed Marei, *Agrarian Reform, op. cit.*, pp. 361 ff.

[25] *Al-Ahram* (Arabic daily), July 26 and 27, 1961. More recently the estimate of land made available by the new size restriction has been 300,000 feddans (U.N. *Progress in Land Reform, 3rd Report*, p. 25).

[26] Doreen Warriner, *Land Reform and Development in the Middle East*, *op. cit.*, p. 12.

[27] Marei, *op. cit.*, pp. 22–27.

[28] Royal Institute of International Affairs, *The Middle East: A Political and Economic Survey* (2d ed.; London, New York: Royal Institute of International Affairs, 1954), p. 220.

[29] W. Thweatt, "The Egyptian Agrarian Reform," *Middle East Economic Papers* (1956), p. 159.

[30] Issawi, *op. cit.*, p. 137.

[31] Thweatt, *op. cit.*, p. 160 (1 *cantar* = 99.05 lb.)

[32] Public Relations Dept., Agrarian Reform General Organization, *Replies to United Nations Questionnaire* (Cairo: April, 1961), p. 31.

[33] *Land Reform and Development in the Middle East*, p. 41. A similar attitude is expressed by Egyptian officials; see *Replies to United Nations Questionnaire*, p. 38.

[34] A question may be raised about the validity of the assumption that speculation took capital away from productive investment. What is significant is real investment, not financial investment; therefore land speculation could not have diverted capital from productive investment and the reform would have no significance in this respect.

[35] Warriner, *Land Reform and Development in the Middle East*, p. 41. That little impact on investment has been observed can be seen from *Replies to United Nations Questionnaire*, pp. 55–56.

[36] Whether the rate of compensation was reasonable or not has been debated. If the market value prevailing in the inflationary period following the Second World War were considered the real value of the land, then the compensation rate would certainly be unreasonably low. The real value has been estimated at £E161 per feddan while the market value was £E700 per feddan, which has also been considered an abnormal price due to speculation and therefore should not be the basis of compensation. See Thweatt, *op. cit.*, p. 155. Ghanimi estimates the real value to be £E150 and the market value to be between £E800 and £E1,000; "Land Tenure in Egypt," *op. cit.*, pp. 17–18.

[37] *Replies to United Nations Questionnaire*, p. 21; other estimates are approximated by me on the basis of the figures on page 53 of these *Replies*.

[38] Warriner, *Land Reform and Development in the Middle East, op. cit.*, p. 34; K. H. Parsons, "Land Reform in the United Arab Republic," *Land Economics*, XXXV, no. 4 (Nov. 1959), 323.

[39] The average small holding is far below 5 feddans; in fact, it is a little more than one feddan and thus the ratio becomes almost 300:1.

[40] *Replies to United Nations Questionnaire*, p. 25.

[41] Thweatt, *op. cit.*, p. 152; official figures put the estimate at £E40 million (Marei, *op. cit.*, p. 251).

[42] Warriner, *Land Reform and Development in the Middle East, op. cit.*, p. 39.

[43] *Replies to United Nations Questionnaire*, p. 50.

[44] After the Agrarian Law amendment of July, 1961, the term "feudalism" has been applied to owners of more than 100 feddans, the new upper limit to the size of individual ownership.

[45] Thweatt, *op. cit.*, p. 150; this is similar to the policy of the Soviets in the first stage of their revolution.

[46] Beginning with 1956, and particularly in 1957, Nasser started talking about establishing a "Socialistic Democratic Cooperative" society. What this means has been unclear and it seems to imply what the actual policy has happened to be; see *Al Ahram*, Nov. 26, 1961, pp. 1–7.

[47] *Al Ahram*, July 25 and 26, 1961; also Jay Walz, "The Flash is Gone from Nasser's Grin," *N.Y. Times Magazine*, Nov. 19, 1961.

[48] Nasser has recently been frank on this. In his speech to the Preliminary Committee for the National Forum of the Peoples' Forces on November 25, 1961, he said that his recent social policies were part of the social revolution that had been delayed until the political revolution was consummated, and that happened only in 1957. However, he admitted that the "capitalists" had become entrenched in the new political structure and had been able to utilize top government officials in furthering their own purposes as they had used ministers under the old regime. Therefore, it became necessary to push forward the "social revolution" by leveling class differences. The text of his speech is reproduced in *Al Ahram*, Nov. 26, 1961.

[49] On these discussions a series of articles and news items has appeared in *Al Ahram* beginning November 25, 1961.

[50] Warriner expresses her apprehensions on these problems, except for the differential treatment of the graduates; *Land Reform and Development in the Middle East*, p. 49. For a detailed study of the reform impact on social development in Egypt, see Saad M. Gadalla, *Land Reform in Relation to Social Development*, University of Missouri Studies: Vol. XXIX (Columbia, Mo.: University of Missouri Press, 1962).

[51] Actually, Nasser has admitted that the agrarian reform was not *the* social revolution he had promised the country; it was only a test and expression of the need and readiness of the people for such a revolution. *Al Ahram*, Nov. 26, 1961, p. 7.

[52] This was similar to what the Kulaks did in Soviet Russia during the collectivization and product reacquisition periods. *Al Ahram*, Nov. 5, 1961, p. 3.

NOTES TO INTRODUCTION TO PART III

[1] This may not be true where land is extensively cultivated, as in Latin America, but even there the *effective* land/labor ratio is low in the sense that access to cultivable land is very difficult for most of the people living on the farms. This abstracts from nonagricultural sectors of the economy; the potentialities of industry will be referred to below.

NOTES TO CHAPTER XI

[1] Another category of private collective tenure may be the holdings of the Church in pre-reform France. However, since this tenure does not differ from private individual tenure as far as land mobility is concerned, we are treating it in the same way as the private individual tenure.

[2] It may be added that the form of tenure is relevant to the efficiency of agriculture, the scale of operation, and the pattern of cultivation. Such relevance is not discussed here on the assumption that efficient production does not depend on any form of tenure as long as an "economically efficient" scale of operation is possible.

[3] Absentee landlordism is used in the sense of being away from the

land and unconcerned with the decision-making that is inherent in owner operation.

[4] The French *censiers* and the Russian serfs are regarded as tenants; one may stretch this analysis a little to include the Greek *Hektemors* as tenants and their creditors as absentee landlords.

[5] In the Japanese and Egyptian cases, productivity per acre had increased, but this resulted from intensive cultivation based on underemployment rather than from improved methods or labor saving.

[6] We have ignored other classes, such as the clergy in prerevolutionary France and the *Hektemors*, the slaves, and serfs, because their interests were tied to either one or the other of the two major classes in each society.

[7] We differentiate between internal and external strength because sometimes the reformers or opponents of reform derived support from outside forces, as in Athens, Mexico, Japan, and Egypt.

NOTES TO CHAPTER XII

[1] Few reformers had plans for reform in advance and their preliminary objectives were not always known. This was true of the French, Mexican, and Egyptian reforms, as well as of the Stolypin reforms.

[2] These are the direct or proclaimed objectives of the reformers. There might be indirect ones, such as changing the social structure, promoting incentives, and increasing investment. These may be considered as effects rather than objectives and are treated in the next chapter.

[3] This difference has important implications regarding the distribution of the product and the efficiency of production, particularly when the interests of the individual and the community do not coincide.

[4] This is not, of course, to deny the advantages of freedom from serfdom, but to insist that these advantages were more social and political than economic.

[5] The Soviet reforms differ from the others regarding the meaning of equality, as will be discussed below.

[6] The peasants did not seem to think so, as implied by the small number who separated before the revolution.

[7] As we shall see below, most of the reforms were preceded by a revolution or other political upheaval.

[8] It is interesting that this association between democracy and the middle class and the class of small owners goes back to the days of Solon and the Gracchi; however, modern scholars have raised questions about the general validity of this association, as will be seen in chapter xiv.

[9] He conceived of land distribution and the creation of a class of small owners as the foundation of democracy, but no democracy was established during his or his sons' rule.

[10] Analysis of reform processes raises a significant question of dynamic behavior. It often happens that the process that starts as a means to an end undergoes transformation and becomes an end before consummation of

the reform. The transformation may also be in the opposite direction. The question becomes more complicated when means and ends are interwoven and difficult to separate. An example is the attitude of the Mexican governments toward the ejido tenure. Was the ejido a step toward private individual ownership, or was it an end in itself? It was one or the other at different times in the history of reform.

[11] It may be questioned whether the Japanese reform was part of a revolution. Since the reform was enforced by the Occupation Army in a similar manner to that of new forces carrying out a revolution in other countries, and since the Japanese political structure was modified greatly before the reform, it is reasonable to classify this reform among the revolution-reforms.

[12] The Soviet reforms have been excluded from this generalization, since they did not transfer land to other owners but applied nationalization equally to all the land.

[13] The bourgeois reformers were anxious not to allow reform without compensation for fear of setting a precedent that might be used in dealing with urban wealth and property, should such a contingency arise.

[14] In all three cases the value of the bonds depreciated gradually because of inflation in the years following reform.

[15] Although all social legislation may seem discriminatory by our definition, it is when such discrimination breeds social conflict that it becomes significant.

[16] Dual tenure is used differently from the way Tannenbaum applies it to Mexico in *Mexico: The Struggle for Bread and Peace*, pp. 102–112.

NOTES TO CHAPTER XIII

[1] I have some reservations in this respect about the Japanese reform.

[2] We shall discuss the example of England below. However, there is no other example that may be used to counteract the claim that the Soviet type of reform was necessary for this development. Only the Scandinavian countries may shed some light on this problem, but there the pressure of backwardness was relieved gradually at a time when sociopolitical tensions such as those of the Soviet Union did not exist. Also, the role of the government in the two areas has been different throughout.

[3] In fact, Egypt had expanded its coöperative movement and increased its consumption of fertilizer long before any land tenure reform was implemented.

[4] The experiences of Japan and Egypt were preceded by a similar experience in the Scandinavian countries where agriculture was developed with the aid of the coöperative or collective feature of operation within the framework of private family ownership.

[5] This actually is the problem that the English enclosures sought to overcome in order to facilitate development.

[6] An exception to this were the private garden lots in Soviet Russia.

[7] An attempt has been made to measure income distribution by measur-

ing land distribution in peasant economies; C. T. Stewart, Jr., "Land and Income Distribution in Peasant Economies," *Land Economics*, XXXVII, no. 4 (Nov., 1961), 337–346.

[8] The latter point refers to the fact that some of the newly acquired land came from sale by the nobility. In fact, the sale was a means of further skewing the distribution, since the buyers had to pay more than the market value for the land they bought. It is irrelevant that some of the nobility dissipated their wealth in the process, nor was such a result a function of the reform.

[9] We are here dealing with final results of the reform rather than with temporary effects experienced in the process. As such, we are evaluating the conditions after collectivization had been completed in the late 'thirties.

[10] H. Dinerstein, *Communism and the Russian Peasant*, pp. 26–27; a class here denotes relative consolidation and permanence, neither of which can evolve in the rural districts of Soviet Russia on the basis of income differentiation.

[11] Social class differentiation in terms of power distribution will be discussed below. Equality on a Lorenz curve cannot be achieved by the Soviet reform or any other reform we have studied. However, by adopting the functional theory of remuneration, the Soviet reform is potentially capable of creating functional equality.

[12] The real value of the compensation payment, however, has been greatly reduced by inflation to the advantage of the peasant.

[13] This would be the ratio after all the land subject to reform has been distributed.

[14] The latter relationship, however, is not reversible, since stability may be maintained by suppression rather than by acceptance; such a system would imply neither democracy nor legitimacy and it might represent short-term stability.

[15] After reading Arabic newspapers, one feels that even the proponents of the new democracy do not know what these requisites are; their approach is pragmatic and their theory reflects the flexible social and economic needs of the society — what works will be the goal!

[16] An admission has recently been made by Communist leaders that collectivization was not voluntary; see *New York Times*, Dec. 3, 1961, p. 11.

[17] This may not be a sound assumption; we notice from the attitude of the new generation that has grown up in the Israeli *kibbutz* that they seem to be restless and interested in urban life and individual ownership and effort, contrary to their communal upbringing.

[18] The same can be said of the Egyptian reform, but we are not in a position to evaluate that reform yet for the reasons mentioned above.

NOTES TO CHAPTER XIV

[1] Some highlights of a theory dealing with these preconditions may be discerned in Kenneth H. Parsons, "Agrarian Reform Policy as a Field of

Research," *Agrarian Reform and Economic Growth* (Farm Economics Division, Econ. Research Service, U.S. Dept. of Agriculture, March, 1962), pp. 17–29.

[2] Lenin classifies western reforms as the "American" revolutionary type which creates small peasant ownership and breaks feudal estates, and the "Prussian" type which results in large ownership, tenancy, and expropriation of the peasantry. Yet, both lead to capitalism. *Collected Works, op. cit.*, Vol. XI, pp. 348–349, as reported in Lyashchenko, *History of the National Economy of Russia . . .*, p. 392. Class I above is basically the "American" type; though it has historically prevailed, the "Prussian" type is not represented in Class I above because, as with most other reforms of its kind, it was not promoted by direct government action, which is a criterion in selecting our case studies; it is similar to the English case which we have included for contrast, and, as we have said of the latter, it is doubtful whether these tenure changes of the "Prussian" type may be called reforms. Other attempts have been made to classify reforms. The most serious attempt that has come to attention was made by R. Barlowe, "Land Reform and Economic Development," *Journal of Farm Economics*, XXXV (1955), 173–187. For an evaluation of his classification, see MS, pp. 471–473.

[3] Morris R. Cohen, "Property and Sovereignty," in his *Land and the Social Order* (New York: Harcourt, Brace, 1933), pp. 41–68.

[4] On the attitude of Class I reformers, see I. Lubin, "Land Reform Problem Challenges Free World," *U.S. Department of State Bulletin*, XXV (Washington, 1951), 467–475. Also G. Hakim, "Land Tenure Reform," *Middle East Economic Papers* (Economic Research Institute: American University of Beirut, 1954), pp. 76–90.

[5] For a discussion of this, see S. M. Lipset, "Political Sociology," *in* R. K. Merton, L. Broom, and L. S. Cottrell, Jr., eds., *Sociology Today* (New York: Basic Books, 1959), pp. 81–91.

[6] *Ibid.*, pp. 84–88.

[7] It may be argued that conflict has not always erupted in violence in the societies that have applied Class I reforms. A counter argument may be that stability has not been due to the "success" of reform, but to the progressive decline of the role of agriculture in the economy and the evolution of a stabilizing middle class in the industrial and commercial sectors. Conflict between the tenure groups has become a less dangerous source of instability, more as a result of industrial development than of land tenure reform. For more information on political stability, see the works of S. M. Lipset and I. Lubin, *op. cit.*; for a brief summary of attitudes toward land tenure, see "Land Policy" in F. Dovring, *Land and Labor in Europe, 1900–1950 . . .*, pp. 219–221.

[8] Marx, *Capital*, Vol. III, chap. 47; also Lenin, *Capitalism and Agriculture*, pp. 66–70.

[9] On equality under socialism, see V. I. Lenin, *State and Revolution* (New York: International Publishers, 1932), pp. 69–78.

[10] Quoted in D. Mitrany, *Marx Against the Peasant* (Chapel Hill, N.C., University of North Carolina Press, 1951), p. 63. Notice that Lenin actually

agrees implicitly that small farms tend to stabilize the nonsocialist political system as the proponents of Western democracy contend.

[11] Lenin, *Capitalism and Agriculture*, p. 27; Marx gives a detailed analysis of this problem in *Capital*, Vol. III, chap. 47.

[12] This debate certainly does not apply to the state of Communism, since the state would wither away and the conflict cannot exist; see Lenin, *State and Revolution*, pp. 7–20.

[13] Dovring, *op. cit.*, pp. 180–181.

[14] I. Lubin, *U. S. Department of State Bulletin*, 1951, pp. 467, 471. More recently even the meaning of the family farm has undergone modification in official U.S. circles, fitting the concept to the tendency in U.S. agriculture. Now the family farm is one in which the family provides at least half the labor and most of the management, but "it has no ownership or tenancy attribute because acquisition and management control is independent of ownership." Quoted in Higbee, *Farms and Farmers in an Urban Age, op. cit.*, p. 81.

[15] Marx, *Capital*, Vol. III, pp. 602–603; Lenin, *Development of Capitalism in Russia*, pp. 346–348.

[16] Dovring, *op. cit.*, pp. 146–147.

[17] The Second World War may be considered as an outlet for surplus rural population in Russia, where the total loss of human life was about 25 million people, many of whom came from the rural areas; on Soviet population see Warren W. Eason, "The Soviet Population Today," *Foreign Affairs*, 37 (July, 1959), 598–606.

[18] Population control might be suggested as an alternative solution. This is very complicated in illiterate societies and involves social and cultural values which require a long time to change. I therefore consider it an impractical solution for the contemporary underdeveloped and already overpopulated countries.

GLOSSARY OF NON-ENGLISH WORDS

Ager publicus: Public domain in ancient Rome.

Ahli, Wakf: Private or to the benefit of specific individuals.

Amparo: Court injunction.

Ancien regime: The regime overthrown by the French Revolution in 1789.

Archon: Chief magistrate of ancient Athens.

Calegoria politica: Political status.

Cantar (*see Quintal*): Weight used in the Middle East in various equivalents; here used as equal to 99.05 lb.

Capitation: War tax in pre-Revolution France.

Cens: Quit-rent or payments fixed by custom, made by the peasant to the landlord, prior to the French Revolution.

Censiers: Peasants who paid *cens* or quit-rent to the landlord, prior to the French Revolution.

Champart (*also called terrage*): a share payment by the peasant to the landlord in pre-revolution France, equal to one-eighth of the crop on the average.

Chevaliers: A social class, second highest, in ancient Athens, including those whose land produced 450 bushels or more but less than 750.

Cho: Japanese land measure equal to 2.45072 acres.

Creoles: Mexicans of the upper class; presumably of pure European stock.

Desiatine: Russian land measure equal to 2.7 acres.

Dominium eminens: Eminent domain, or the equivalent to the right of a sovereign state to dispose of real estate for the common welfare; ultimate right.

Ejidatario: Member of the ejido or communal farm in Mexico.

Ejido: Communal farm in Mexico.

Eta: The class of outcasts in pre-reform Japan.

Feddan: Egyptian land measure equal to 1.038 acres.

Fellahin (sing., *fellah*): Cultivators; used to designate the small farmers or peasants.

Fermier: Large-scale tenant farmer in pre-Revolution France.

Grossbauer: Wealthy peasant.

Guberniia: Russian for geographical region or province.

Hacendado: Plantation owner or lord of the hacienda.

Hacienda: Plantation in Mexico.

Hectare: A metric measure equal to 2.471 acres.

Heimin: The Japanese commoners after the 1868 restoration.

Hektemor: A peasant who had failed to repay his debt and has thus forfeited his usufruct rights to his land but continues to cultivate it for the creditor against a share of the crop; a form of serfdom in ancient Athens.

Horoi: Mortgage stones designating land that had been seized for failure of the peasant (hektemor) in ancient Athens to pay the mortgage.

Iugera (or jugera) (sing., *juger*): Land measure, equal to 28,800 sq. pedes (feet), or to 0.622 acres; more commonly equivalent to yoke or what a team of oxen can plough in one day.

Junker: A young German noble whose class was associated with large-scale commercial farming.

Kazoku: The class of nobility in the Meiji period (after 1868) in Japan.

Kibbutz: Collective settlement in Israel.

Kilogram: A metric weight equal to 2.2046 lb.

Koku: Japanese dry measure equal to 5.12 bushels.

Kolkhoz: A Soviet collective farm.

Kulak: A member of the rich peasants in Russia; also used to describe the peasants who opposed the Soviet agrarian policies up to the end of collectivization.

Laboureurs: Capitalist landowners who cultivated their land on a large scale prior to the French Revolution.

Latifundia: A system of large landed estates, characteristic of ancient Rome.

£E: Egyptian monetary unit, equal to $2.872 at the official rate on January 15, 1964.

Livre: A former French money unit of account; was replaced by the franc in 1795, at which time it was worth about 19.1 cents.

Lods et ventes: A sales tax on land equivalent to one-eighth of the sale price in pre-Revolution France.

Mainmortables: Serfs whose possessions and land fell to the landlord if they died childless.

Medimnes (sing., *medimnos*): A dry measure used in ancient Greece; equivalent to 1.50, 1.47, or 1.42 bushels according to source.

Mestizo: A Mexican of mixed blood or racial origin, often living on a small family farm.

Metayer: Shareholder (the size of the share varies).

Minifundia: A system of tiny farms in contrast to *latifundia*, a system of large plantations.

Mir: Pre-Soviet Russian communal village.

Pentacosiomedimnes: Upper class in ancient Athens, including those whose land-produce amounted to 750 bushels or more.

Peon: Plantation worker in Mexico.

Podvornee vladenie: Russian, hereditary tenure.

Pomestshik (Pometschik, Pomeshchik): Russian pre-Soviet landlord.

Pud (or Pood): A dry measure equal to approximately 16.38 kg. (36.113 lb.)

Pueblo: An Indian village in Mexico.

Quintal (*see Cantar*): Weight used in various countries as equivalent to different values; in the metric system it is equal to 100 kg. (220.46 lb.). Used in Egypt interchangeably with the Cantar, as equivalent to 99.05 lb.

Ranchero: Peasant owner in Mexico; owner of a *rancho*.

Rancho: Small family farm in Mexico.

Retrait: Right of the landlord to prevent the sale of land by his peasants by withholding approval, in pre-Revolution France.

Ruble (*or Rouble*): Russian monetary unit; prior to the First World War it equaled $0.5146.

Samurai: The warrior class prior to the Meiji restoration (1868) in Japan.

Seigneur: A feudal lord.

Seisachtheia: "Shaking off the burdens," relates to Solon's reform law which freed the lands of the enserfed peasants on account of debt from the creditors.

Taille: Head tax in pre-Revolution France.

Tan: Japanese land measure equal to one-tenth of a cho, or 0.245072 acres.

Thetes: Lowest social class in ancient Athens after Solon's reform, including those whose land produced less than 300 bushels.

Vingtième: Property tax in pre-Revolution France.

Wakf: Property held in trust for pious or charitable purposes, or to provide for support of specific persons.

Zemskii: A representative council in Russia.

Zemtsvo: In Russia, an elective local district and provincial administrative assembly.

Zeugites: The third social class, from the top, in ancient Athens, including those whose land produced 300 or more bushels but less than 450.

BIBLIOGRAPHY

Abu As-Su 'ud, Hassan. "A Study on Land Reform in Egypt," *Islamic Review,* XLV (April, 1957), 14–19.

Allen, G. C. *A Short Economic History of Modern Japan, 1867–1937.* London: Allen & Unwin, 1951.

———. "Japan Revisited," *The Oriental Economist,* XXIII, no. 531 (Jan., 1955), 27–29.

Anderson, Frank M. (ed.). *The Constitutions and Other Select Documents Illustrative of the History of France, 1789–1907.* Minneapolis, 1908.

Andrews, A. *The Greek Tyrants,* London: Hutchinson's University Library (Anchor Press), 1956.

Appian's Roman History: III, tr. by Horace White, London: Heinemann; New York: Macmillan, 1913.

Aristotle, *Constitution of Athens and Related Texts,* tr. with an Introduction and Notes by Kurt von Fritz and Ernst Kapp. New York: Hafner, 1961.

Artz, F. B. *France Under the Bourbon Restoration, 1814–1830.* Cambridge, Mass.: Harvard University Press, 1931.

Ashby, A. W. *Public Lands.* FAO Agricultural Studies, No. 31. Rome: U.N., FAO, 1956.

Auge-Laribe, M. "Structure agricole," *Revue d'economie politique,* no. 1 (Paris, 1939).

Badeau, John S. "A Role in Search of a Hero. A Brief Study of the Egyptian Revolution," *Middle East Journal,* IX, no. 4 (Autumn, 1955), 373–384.

Baer, Gabriel. "Egyptian Attitudes Towards Land Reform, 1922–1955," *in* Walter Z. Laquer, ed., *The Middle East in Transition: Studies in Contemporary History.* New York: Praeger, 1958. Pp. 80–99.

Barlowe, R. "Land Reform and Ecomonic Development," *Journal of Farm Economics,* XXXV (1953), 173–187.

Baykov, Alexander. *The Development of the Soviet Economic System: An Essay on the Experience of Planning in the U.S.S.R.* Cambridge: University Press, 1950.

Belov, Fedor. *The History of a Soviet Collective Farm.* New York: Praeger, 1955.

Belshaw, H. "Industry and Agrarian Reform," *Far East Survey,* XVI (1947), 153–156.

Black, A. G. "National Agricultural Plans and Programs," FAO Report No. 161 (Rome, 1953).

Blanco, Gonzalo. *Agriculture in Mexico.* Washington, D.C.: Pan American Union (American Agricultural Series), 1950.

Bloch, Marc. "Toward a Comparative History of European Societies," *in* Frederic C. Lane and Jelle C. Riemersma, eds., *Enterprise and Secular Change: Readings in Economic History.* Homewood, Illinois: Richard D. Irwin, 1953. Pp. 494–521.

Bonné, Alfred. *State and Economics in the Middle East: A Society in Transition.* 2d ed.; London, Routledge & Kegan Paul, 1955.

Borton, H. *Japan's Modern Century.* New York: Ronald Press, 1955.

Bourgin, Hubert. "L'histoire economique de la France de 1800 à 1830: etat des travaux," *Revue d'histoire moderne,* VI (1931).

Bourne, H. E. "A Decade of Studies in the French Revolution," *The Journal of Modern History* (June, 1929).

Bradley, H. *The Enclosures in England.* New York: Columbia University Press, 1918.

Bradsher, Julian Hill. "Agrarian Reform in Mexico Since 1934." Unpublished Ph. D. dissertation, University of California, 1958.

Branch, H. N. "The Mexican Constitution of 1917 Compared with the Constitution of 1857," *Mexican Commerce and Industry* (March, 1927), pp. 9–57. (Reprinted from the *Annals of the American Academy of Political and Social Science* [May, 1917].)

Breckenridge, J. C. "Landownership in its Relation to National Stability," *American Academy of Political and Social Science Annals,* CXXXIV, No. 223 (1927), 207–219.

Cahen, Georges, "L'economie sociale chretienne et la colonisation agricole sous la Restauration et la monarchie juillet," *Revue d'Economie* Politique (juin, 1903).

[*The*] *Cambridge Ancient History.* Volume IV: *The Persian Empire and the West.* J. Bury, S. A. Cook, F. E. Adcock (eds.). Cambridge: University Press, 1926. *Volume IX: The Roman Republic, 133–144* B.C. S. A. Cook, F. E. Adcock, and M. P. Charlesworth (eds). Cambridge: University Press, 1932.

[*The*] *Cambridge Modern History. Volume VIII: The French Revolution.* A. W. Ward, G. W. Prothero, Stanley Leathes (eds.). New York and London: Macmillan, 1908.

Cameron, R. E. *France and the Economic Development of Europe 1800–1904: Conquests of Peace and Seeds of War.* Princeton: Princeton University Press, 1961.

Campbell, C. D. "Weak Points in the Japanese Land Reform Program," *Journal of Farm Economics,* XXXIV, no. 3 (1952), 361–368.

Caroc, O. "Land Tenure and the Franchise. A Basis for Partnership in African Plural Societies," *Journal of African Administration,* VI, no. 4, (Oct., 1954), 152–160.

Carroll, Thomas. "The Concept of Land Reform," in *Documentation.* Prepared for the Center on Land Problems in Asia and the Far East Bangkok, Thailand, 1954, Rome, FAO, 1955. (Mimeo.)

Cary, M. *A History of Rome,* London: Macmillan; New York: St. Martin's Press, 1960.

288

Chambers, J. D. "Enclosures and Labour Supply in the Industrial Revolution," *The Economic History Review*, 2d ser., V, no. 3 (1953), 319–343.

Chénon, Emile. *Les Demembrements de la Propriete Fonciere en France: Avant et Après la Révolution*. Paris: Librairie de la Société du Recueil Sirey, 1923.

Cheshire, G. C. *The Modern Law of Real Property*. 8th ed.; London: Butterworth, 1958.

Cheyney, E. P. "Recent Tendencies in the Reform of Land Tenure," *Annals of the American Academy of Political and Social Science*, II (July, 1891–June, 1892), 309–323.

――――. "The Disappearance of English Serfdom," *The English Historical Review*, XV (1900), 20–37.

Chia, F. "On Land Tenure in Japan, A Reply," *Land Economics*, XXV, no. 4 (Nov., 1949), 433–434.

Ciasca, R., and D. Perini. *Riforme agrarie antiche e moderne*. Florence: G. C. Sansoni, 1946.

Clapham, J. H. *The Economic Development of France and Germany 1815–1914*, 4th ed.; Cambridge: University Press, 1955.

Cohen, Morris R. "Property and Sovereignty," in *Law and the Social Order: Essays in Legal Philosophy*. New York: Harcourt, Brace, 1933. Pp. 41–68.

Conacher, H. M. "The Relations of Land Tenure and Agriculture," Presidential Address in *Journal of Proceedings of the Agricultural Economic Society*, IV, no. 3 (Nov., 1936), 167–185.

Cook, Walter Wheeler. "Ownership and Possession," in *Encyclopedia of the Social Sciences, XI-XII*. New York: Macmillian [1948]. Pp. 521–525.

Cumberland, C. C. *Mexican Revolution*. Austin: University of Texas Press, 1952.

Cunningham, W. *The Growth of English Industry and Commerce*. Cambridge: University Press, Volume I, 1890; Volume II, 1892.

Curtler, W. H. R. *The Enclosure and Redistribution of Our Land*. Oxford: Oxford University Press, 1920.

Darling, M. "Land Reform in Italy and Egypt," *Yearbook of Agricultural Co-operation*. Washington, D.C.: Horace Plunkett Foundation, 1956. Pp. 1–26.

Dawud, Hassan A. "Agrarian Reform in Egypt: A Case Study," *Current History*, XXX (June, 1956), 331–338.

Day, James and Mortimer Chambers. *Aristotle's History of Athenian Democracy*, University of California Publications in History, vol. 73. Berkeley and Los Angeles: University of California Press, 1962.

Dinerstein, H. *Communism and the Russian Peasant*. Glencoe, Illinois: Free Press, 1955.

Dobb, Maurice H. *Studies in the Development of Capitalism*. London: Routledge, 1947.

――――. *The Soviet Economic Development Since 1917*. New York: International Publishers, 1948.

Dore, R. P. *Land Reform in Japan*. London, New York, Toronto: Oxford University Press, 1959.

Dovring, Folke. *Land and Labor in Europe, 1900–1950: A Comparative Study of Recent Agrarian History*. The Hague: Martinus Nijhoff, 1956.

Durant, Will. *The Life of Greece*. New York: Simon and Schuster, 1939.

Duruy, V. *History of Rome and the Roman People. Volume II*, ed. by Rev. J. P. Mahaffy. London: Kegan Paul, Trench, 1884.

Eason, Warren W. "The Soviet Population Today," *Foreign Affairs* 37 (July, 1959), 598–606.

Egypt. al-Lajnah al-Ulyali al-Islah al-Zira'i. *Fajr jadid ma' al-islah al zira'i* [A New Dawn with the Agricultural Reform]. Cairo: Maktab al-sahafah, 1954.

Embree, J. F. *Suye Mura, A Japanese Village*. Chicago: University of Chicago Press, 1944.

――――. *The Japanese Nation. A Social Survey*. New York: Rinehart, 1945.

Erlich, Alexander. "Stalin's Views on Soviet Economic Development," *in* Ernest J. Simmons (ed.). *Continuity and Change in Russian and Soviet Thought*. Cambridge, Mass.: Harvard University Press, 1955. Pp. 81–99.

Ernle, Lord. *The Land and Its People*. London: Hutchinson (n.d.).

Eyre, J. D. "Elements of Instability in the Current Japanese Land Tenure System," *Land Economics*, XXVIII, no. 3 (Aug., 1952), 193–202.

――――. "The Changing Role of the Former Japanese Landlord," *Land Economics,* XXXI, no. 1 (Feb., 1955), 35–64.

Fernandez y Fernandez, Ramon. "Land Tenure in Mexico," *Journal of Farm Economics*, XXV (Feb., 1943), 219–234.

Fine, John V. A. "Horoi: Studies in Mortgage, Real Security, and Land Tenure in Ancient Athens," *Hesperia*, Suppl. IX (American School of Classical Studies at Athens, 1951).

Flores, E. "Land Use Changes in Economic Development of Mexico," *Land Economics, XXXV*, no. 2 (May, 1959), 115–124.

Florinsky, Michael T. *Russia: A History and an Interpretation, Volume II*. New York: Macmillan, 1953.

French, A. "The Economic Background to Solon's Reforms," *Classical Quarterly,* n.s., VI, nos. 1 and 2 (Jan.–April, 1956).

Gadalla, S. M. *Land Reform in Relation to Social Development*, University of Missouri Studies, Vol. XXIX. Columbia, Mo.: University of Missouri Press, 1962.

Gamio, Manuel. "An Analysis of Social Processes and the Obstacles to Agricultural Progress in Mexico," *Rural Sociology* (June, 1937), pp. 143–147.

――――. "Geographic and Social Handicaps," *in* Special Issue: *Mexico Today, The Annals of the American Academy of Political and Social Science* (March, 1940), pp. 1–11.

Gershoy, Leo. *The French Revolution and Napoleon*. New York: F. S. Crofts, 1933.

Ghali, Mirrit B. *Al-islah azzira'i* [Agricultural Reform] Cairo, 1945.

Ghonemy, M. R. Resource Use and Income in Egyptian Agriculture Before and After the Land Reform with Particular Reference to Economic Development." Unpublished Ph.D. dissertation, North Carolina State College, Raleigh, 1953.

———. [Al-Ghanimi]. "Land Tenure in Egypt — Its Economic and Social Phases," *Al-Abhath,* X (April, 1957), 13–26 [in Arabic].

Gilliard, C. *Quelques reformes des Solon: Essai de critique historique.* Lausanne: Georges Bridel, 1907.

Gilmartin, W. M., and W. I. Ladejinsky. 'The Promise of Agrarian Reform in Japan," *Foreign Affairs,* XXVI, no. 2 (Jan., 1948), pp. 312–324.

Gittinger, James Price, II. "Economic Development Through Agrarian Reform." Unpublished Ph.D. dissertation, Iowa State College, 1955.

Goldman, M. I. "The Soviet Standard of Living, and Ours," *Foreign Affairs,* XXXVIII, no. 4 (July, 1960), 625–637.

Gonner, E. C. K. *Common Land and Inclosure.* London: Macmillan, 1912.

Gray, H. "Commutation of Villeinage in England Before the Black Death," *The English Historical Review,* CXVI (Oct. 1914), 625–656.

Griswold, A. Whitney. *Farming and Democracy.* New Haven: Yale University Press and Oxford University Press, 1952.

Grossman, Gregory. "Soviet Agriculture Since Stalin," *The Annals of the American Academy of Political and Social Science* (Jan., 1956), 62–74.

Grote, G. *History of Greece.* 3d ed.; London: John Murray, 1851.

Hakim, George. "Land Tenure Reform," in *Middle East Economic Papers.* American University of Beirut: Economic Research Institute, 1954. Pp. 76–90.

Hammer, Conrad. "The Land Tenure Ideal," *Journal of Land and Public Utility Economics,* XIX (1943), 69–84.

Hardy, E. G. "Were the Lex Thoria of 118 B.C. and the Lex Agraria of 111 B.C. Reactionary Laws?" *Journal of Philology,* XXXI, (1910), 268–286.

Harris, Marshall. "Legal Aspects of Land Tenure," *Journal of Farm Economics,* XXIII (1941), 173–184.

Heaton, H. "Enclosures," in *Encyclopedia of the Social Sciences, V-VI.* New York, Toronto, and London: Macmillan, 1948. Pp. 523–527.

Herbert, S. J. *The Fall of Feudalism in France.* New York: A. Stokes, n.d.

Hewes, L. I., Jr. "On the Current Readjustment of Land Tenure in Japan," *Land Economics,* XXV, no. 3 (Aug., 1949), 246–259.

———. *Japanese Land Reform Program.* Tokyo: General Headquarters Supreme Commander for the Allied Powers, Natural Resources Section, Report No. 127, 1950.

———. *Japan — Land and Men: An Account of the Japanese Land Reform Program — 1945–51.* Ames, Iowa: Iowa State College Press, 1955.

Higbee, Edward. *Farms and Farmers in an Urban Age.* New York: Twentieth Century Fund, 1963.

Hope, Clifford R. *The U. S. Concept of Agrarian Reform as a Foundation of World Peace.* Washington, D.C., U.S. Dept. of State Bulletin, XXV (1951), 998–1000.

Hubbard, L. E. *The Economics of Soviet Agriculture.* London: Macmillan, 1939.

291

Issawi, Charles. *Egypt at Mid-Century: An Economic Survey.* London, New York and Toronto: Oxford University Press, 1954.

Jasny, Naum. *The Socialized Agriculture of the U.S.S.R.: Plans and Performance.* Stanford, Calif.: Stanford University Press, 1949.

————. "Peasant-Worker Income Relationships: A Neglected Subject," *Soviet Studies,* XII, no. 1 (July, 1960), 14–21.

————. "A Note on Rationality and Efficiency in the Soviet Economy: II," *Soviet Studies,* XIII, no. 1 (July, 1961), 35–68.

Johnson, A. H. *Disappearance of the Small Land Owner.* Oxford: Clarendon Press, 1909.

Johnson, D. Gale, and Arcadius Kahan. "Soviet Agriculture: Structure and Growth," *Comparisons of the United States and Soviet Economics.* Washington, D.C.: Joint Economic Committee, Congress of the United States, 1959.

Kennan, G. F. *Russia and the West Under Lenin and Stalin.* Boston and Toronto: Little, Brown, 1961.

Kerensky, Alexander. "Russia on the Eve of World War I," *The Russian Review,* V, no. 1 (Autumn, 1945), 10–30.

Khalid, Khalid Muhammad. *Min huna' mabda'* [From Here We Start]. Cairo: Dar al-Nil, 1950.

Kokovtzoff, W. "The Agrarian Question in Russia," *English Review,* XXXIX (1924), 361–389.

Kosminsky, E. A. *Studies in the Agrarian History of England in the Thirteenth Century,* ed. by R. H. Hilton; from Russian by Ruth Kisch. Oxford: Basil Blackwell, 1956.

Kraay, C. M. "The Archaic Owls of Athens; Classification and Chronology," *Numismatic Chronicle,* 6th ser., Vol. XVI (1956).

Kramer, I. S. "Land Reform and Industrial Development in Meiji, Japan," *Land Economics,* XXIX, no. 4 (Nov., 1953), 314–332.

Lawton, Lancelot. *An Economic History of Soviet-Russia;* I, II. London: Macmillan, n.d.

Lavrovsky, V. M. "Title Commutation as a Factor in the Gradual Decrease of Landownership by the English Peasantry," *Economic History Review,* IV (1933), 273–289.

————. "Expropriation of the English Peasantry in the Eighteenth Century," *Economic History Review,* 2d. ser., IX (1956), 271–282.

Lefebvre, G. "Les Recherches Relatives à la Repartition de la Propriete et de l'Exploitation Foncieres à la Fin de l'Ancien Regime," *Revue d'Histoire Moderne,* III (1928), 103–130.

————. "La Place de la Revolution dans l'Histoire Agraire de la France," *Annales d'Histoire Economique et Sociale,* I (1929), 506–519.

————. *Questions Agraires aux Temps de la Terreur.* Strasbourg, 1932. [Collection de Documents Inédits sur l'Histoire Economique de la Revolution Française].

————. "La Revolution Française et les Paysans," *Cahiers de la Revolution Française,* I (1934), 7–49.

————. *The Coming of the French Revolution,* 1789 tr. by R. R. Palmer. Princeton: Princeton University Press, 1947.

Lenin, V. I. *The Land Revolution in Russia.* London: The Independent Labour Party, 1919.

———. *State and Revolution.* New York: International Publishers, 1932.

———. *Capitalism and Agriculture.* (Little Lenin Library, Volume XXX). New York: International Publishers, 1946.

———. *The Development of Capitalism in Russia.* Moscow: Foreign Languages Publishing House, 1956.

———. *Alliance of the Working Class and the Peasantry.* Moscow: Foreign Languages Publishing House, 1959.

Lewis, N. "Solon's Agrarian Legislation," *American Journal of Philology,* 62 (1941), 144–156.

Lewis, W. A. *The Theory of Economic Growth.* 4th impression; London: Allen & Unwin, 1960.

Linforth, Ivan M. *Solon the Athenian.* University of California Publications in Classical Philosophy, Volume VI. Berkeley, Calif.: University of California Press, 1919.

Lipset, Seymour M. "Political Sociology," *in* R. K. Merton *et al., Sociology Today: Problems and Prospects.* New York: Basic Books, 1959. Pp. 81–114.

Litoshenko, Leo. "Landed Property in Russia," *Russian Review,* II, no. 4 (1913), 207.

Loutchisky, J. *Quelques Remarques sur la Vente des Biens Nationaux.* Paris: Librairie Ancienne Honoré Champion, 1913.

Lowell, E. J. *The Eve of the French Revolution.* Boston and New York: Houghton Mifflin; Cambridge: Riverside Press, 1892.

Lyashchenko, Peter I. *History of the National Economy of Russia to the 1917 Revolution,* tr. by L. M. Herman; introduction by C. B. Hoover. New York: Macmillan, 1949.

MS: Elias H. Tuma, "Economics, Politics, and Land Tenure Reform: A Comparative Study." Unpublished Ph.D. dissertation, University of California, Berkeley, 1962.

McBride, George McCutchen. *The Land System in Mexico.* New York: American Geographical Society, 1923.

Maklakov, V. "The Agrarian Problem in Russia before the Revolution," *Russian Review,* IX, no. 1 (Jan., 1950), 3–15.

Manuilov, A. "Agrarian Reform in Russia," *Russian Review,* I, no. 4 (1912), 131–150.

Mao Tse-tung and Liu Shao-chi. *Significance of Agrarian Reforms in China.* Bombay, India: New Age Printing Press, 1950.

Marei, Sayed. *Agrarian Reform in Egypt.* Cairo: L'Institut Français d' Archéologie Orientale, 1957.

Marx, Karl. *Capital: A Critique of Political Economy, III.* Moscow: Foreign Languages Publishing House, 1959.

Mavor, James. *An Economic History of Russia, I, II.* 2d ed.; London and Toronto: Dent; New York: Dutton, 1925.

Maynard, Sir John. "Collectivization of Agriculture: Russia and India, with Discussion," *Asiatic Review,* XXXIX (1943), 113–127.

———. *Russia in Flux.* New York: Macmillan, 1949.

293

Mitrany, David. *Marx Against the Peasant: A Study in Social Pragmatism.* Chapel Hill, N.C.: University of North Carolina Press, 1951.

Mommsen, Theodor. *The History of Rome,* Vol. I (1908), Vol. III (1895). New York, Scribner.

Moore, Wilbert E. *Economic Demography of Eastern and Southern Europe.* Geneva: League of Nations, 1945.

Mosse, W. H. *Alexander II and the Modernization of Russia.* London: English Universities Press, 1958.

Nabholz, Hans. "Medieval Agrarian Society in Transition," *Cambridge Economic History of Europe, I.* Cambridge: University Press, 1941. Chap. viii, pp. 493–562.

Newth, J. A. "Soviet Agriculture: The Private Sector 1950–1959," *Soviet Studies,* XIII, no. 2 (Oct., 1961), 160–171.

Nobuo, Danno. "Japanese Agriculture After the Postwar Land Reform," *Japan Quarterly,* II, no. 1 (1955), 108–120.

Nunez, Lucio Mendieta y. "The Balance of Agrarian Reform," *Annals of the American Academy of Political and Social Sciences,* CCVIII (March, 1940), 111–131.

Owen, Launcelot. *The Russian Peasant Movement, 1906–1917.* London: P. S. King, 1937.

Page, Thomas Walker. "The End of Villeinage in England," *Publications of the American Economic Association,* 3d ser., I, no. 2 (May, 1900), 99.

Pares, Sir Bernard. "The New Land Settlement in Russia," *Russian Review,* I, no. 1 (1912).

———. *A History of Russia.* 5th ed. rev. and enlarged; New York: Knopf, 1949.

Parkes, H. B. "Political Leadership in Mexico," in *Annals of the American Academy of Political and Social Sciences* (March, 1940), 12-22.

Parsons, K. H. "The Concept of Land Reform." Paper delivered at the Center on Land Problems in the Near East, Salahudin, Iraq, 1955. Rome: FAO, 1956 (mimeo.).

———. "Land Reform in the Postwar Era," *Land Economics,* XXXIII, no. 3 (Aug., 1957), 213–227.

———. "Land Reform in the United Arab Republic," *Land Economics,* XXXV, no. 4 (Nov., 1959), 319–326.

Penn, R. J. "Public Interest in Private Property (Land)," *Land Economics,* XXXVII, no. 2 (May, 1961), 99–104.

Phipps, Helen. *Some Aspects of the Agrarian Question in Mexico.* University of Texas Bulletin No. 2515, Studies in History No. 2 (April 15, 1925).

Pirenne, H. *Economic and Social History of Medieval Europe.* New York: Harcourt, Brace, 1937.

Plutarch, *The Lives of Noble Grecians and Romans,* tr. by John Dryden and rev. by Arthur Hugh Clough. New York: Random House, 1932.

Public Relations Department (Egypt), Agrarian Reform General Organization, *Replies to United Nations Questionnaire.* Cairo, April, 1961.

Robinson, G. T. *Rural Russia under the Old Regime. A History of the*

Landlord–Peasant World, and a Prologue to the Peasant Revolution of 1917. New York: Longmans, Green, 1949.

Rogers, James E. Thorold. *Six Centuries of Work and Wages*. New York: Putnam, n.d.

Rostovtzeff, M. *A History of the Ancient World. I: The Orient and Greece*, from the Russian by J. D. Duff. Oxford: Clarendon Press, 1926.

———. *The Social and Economic History of the Roman Empire*, rev. by P. M. Fraser. Oxford: Clarendon Press, 1957. 2 vols.

Rowntree, B. Seebohm. "Rural Land Reform," *Contemporary Review*, CIV (1913), 609–623.

Royal Institute of International Affairs. *The Middle East: A Political and Economic Survey*. 2d ed.; London, New York: Royal Institute of International Affairs, 1954.

Salter, L. A. "Global War and Peace, and Land Economics," *Journal of Land and Public Utility Economics*, XIX (1943), 391–396.

———. *Tenure Policy Formulation in a Democracy*. Conference on Family Farm Policy: Proceedings, University of Chicago, 1946. Chicago: University of Chicago Press, 1947. Pp. 123–126.

Schickele, R. "Theories Concerning Land Tenure," *Journal of Farm Economics*, XXXIV (1952), 734–744.

Scrutton, T. E. *Commons and Common Fields*. Cambridge: University Press, 1887.

Scullard, H. H. *From the Gracchi to Nero*, New York: Praeger, 1959.

Sée, Henri. *La Vie Economique de la France Sous la Monarchie Censitaire (1815–1848)*. Paris: Librairie Felix Alcan, 1927.

———. *Economic and Social Conditions in France During the Eighteenth Century*, tr. by Edwin H. Zeydel. New York: F. S. Crofts, 1931.

———. *Histoire Economique de la France. I: Le Moyen âge et l'ancien régime*. Paris: Librairie Armand Colin, 1939.

———. *Histoire Economique de la France. II: Les temps modernes (1789–1914)*. Paris: Librairie Armand Colin, 1942.

Senior, Clarence O. *Land Reform and Democracy*. Gainesville, Fla.: University of Florida Press, 1958.

Shidlovsky, S. "The Imperial Duma and Land Settlement," *Russian Review*, I (1912), 18–26.

Simpson, Eyler N. *The Ejido: Mexico's Way Out*. Chapel Hill, N.C.: University of North Carolina Press, 1937.

Slater, G. *The English Peasantry and the Enclosure of Common Fields*. London: Constable, 1907.

Stalin, J. *Problems of Leninism*. Moscow: Foreign Language Publishing House, 1954.

Stern, E. von. "Solon and Pisistratus," *Hermes*, 48 (1913), 426–441.

Stewart, C. T., Jr. "Land and Income Distribution in Peasant Economies," *Land Economics*, XXXVII, no. 4 (Nov., 1961), 337–346.

Strauss, E. *Soviet Russia: Anatomy of a Social History*. London: Lane, 1941.

Supreme Commander for Allied Powers, Natural Resources Section, Report No. 148. *Agricultural Programs in Japan, 1945–51*. Tokyo: compiled under direction of M. B. Williamson, 1951.

Tannenbaum, Frank. *The Mexican Agrarian Revolution*. Washington: Brookings Institution, 1930.

———. *Peace by Revolution: An Interpretation of Mexico*. New York: Columbia University Press, 1933.

———. *Mexico: The Struggle for Peace and Bread*. New York: Knopf, 1950.

Tawney, R. H. *The Agrarian Problem in the Sixteenth Century*. London, New York, Bombay, and Calcutta: Longmans, Green, 1912.

Thayer, A. S. "Possession and Ownership," *Law Quarterly Review*, XXIII (1907), 175–194, 314–330.

Thompson, J. H. *Economic and Social History of Europe in the Later Middle Ages (1300–1530)* New York, London: Century Company, 1931.

Thweatt, W. "The Egyptian Agrarian Reform," *Middle East Economic Papers* (American University of Beirut: Economic Research Institute, 1956), pp. 143–175.

Timasheff, N.S. "Structural Changes in Rural Russia," *Rural Sociology*, II, no. 1 (March, 1937), 10–28.

Toynbee, Arnold J. *A Study of History, VIII*. London: Oxford University Press, 1954.

———. *A Study of History; XII: Reconsiderations*. London: Oxford University Press, 1961.

Trewartha, G. T. "Land Reform and Land Reclamation in Japan," *Geographical Review*, XL, no. 3 (July, 1950), 376–396.

Tuma, E. H. *See* MS

United Nations, Department of Economic Affairs. *Land Reform: Defects in Agrarian Structure as Obstacles to Economic Development*. New York, 1951.

United Nations. *Documentation Prepared for the Center on Land Problems in Asia and the Far East*. Bangkok, Thailand, 1954; Rome: FAO, 1955.

United Nations, FAO, ILO, *Progress in Land Reform*, Reports 1–3, 1954–1962.

United States Department of Agriculture. *Land Redistribution in Mexico*, ERS — Foreign — 39, August, 1962.

———. Farm Economics Division, Economic Research Service, *Agrarian Reform and Economic Growth*. March, 1962. Pp. 17–29.

United States Department of State. (Bulletin). "Land Reform Problem Challenges Free World." Washington, XXV (1951), 467–475.

———. *Land Reform — A World Challenge*. Washington: Department of State Publication 445 (Feb., 1952), p. 82.

———. (Bulletin). "Two Patterns for Land Reform: The Free World vs. the Soviet." Washington, XXVII, no. 704 (1952), 990–995.

Ure, P. N. *The Origin of Tyranny*, Cambridge: University Press, 1922.

Vinogradoff, Paul. *Villeinage in England: Essays in English Medieval History*. Oxford: Clarendon Press, 1892.

———. *The Growth of the Manor*. London: George Allen; New York: Macmillan, 1911.

———. *Collected Papers of Paul Vinogradoff. I: Historical*. Oxford Studies in Social and Legal History. Oxford: Clarendon Press, 1928.

296

Warde-Fowler, W. "Notes on Gaius Gracchus," *English Historical Review*, XX (1905), 209–227, 417–433.

Warriner, Doreen. *Land Reform and Economic Development*. Cairo: National Bank of Egypt, 1955.

———. *Land Reform and Development in the Middle East.* London and New York: Royal Institute of International Affairs, 1957.

Whetten, N. L. *Rural Mexico*. Chicago: University of Chicago Press, 1948.

Williamson, M.B. "Land Reform in Japan," *Journal of Farm Economics,* XXXIII, no. 2 (May, 1951), 169–176.

Woodhouse, W. J. *Solon the Liberator: A Study of the Agrarian Problems in Attica in the Seventh Century*. London: Oxford University Press, [Humphrey Milford], 1938.

INDEX

INDEX

Absenteeism, 170–171, 173, 231
Absolute ownership, 69
Ager publicus, 28, 34, 183, 194, 195, 206
Agrarian Mixed Commission, 120
Agrarian reform: approach to, 3–7; definition, 8–14; features, 165–179; objectives and processes, 180–199; effects, 200–218; general theory, 221, 222; analytic reform scheme, 222–230; policy implications, 230–239; other implications, 239–242. *See also* Egyptian reform movement; English reform movement; French reform movement; Greek reform movement; Japanese reform movement; Mexican reform movement; Roman reform movement; Russian reform movement
Aguascalientes, 110
Ahli, 148
Alexander II, Tsar of Russia, 73, 74, 82, 83, 185, 195
Alexander III, Tsar of Russia, 83
Alienation, land: land tenure types, 14; in Greece, 20, 21, 22; in Rome, 33, 34, 195; in England, 41, 53; in Russia, 93; in Mexico, 115, 125; in Japan, 129, 192; in Egypt, 148, 168, 192; general theory, 236
Allied Powers, 135
Allotment tenure, 69
Ancien régime, 57, 59, 60
Anglo-French treaty, 174
Appius Claudius, 33
Archon, 20, 25
Aristotle, 20, 26
Arment, 157
Asia, 129
Athens, 20, 21, 26, 175, 177, 233
Attica, 20, 21, 22, 175
Ayala, Plan de, 115

Baja California, 110
Bastille, 60
Beggarly allotments, 75, 76
Black Death, 41, 42, 45
Bolsheviks, 92
Bradley, Harriett, 42, 46

Cade, Jack, 47
Cadet Party, 87
Calegoria politica, 116
Calles, P. E., 118, 119, 186, 197
Campeche, 110
Cananera, 114
Capitation, 57, 59
Cárdenas, Lázaro, 120, 126, 127, 181, 186
Carranza, V., 115, 127, 186
Caucasus, 83
Cens, 55, 58, 59, 61, 64
Censiers, 55, 56, 57, 65, 66, 67, 195, 206
Cens-land, 57, 64, 67
Census Board, 120
Central Land Committee, 138
Champart, 55, 61
Chevaliers, 24
Cheyney, E. P., 5, 38–39, 42
Chiapas, 110
Chihuahua, 110, 115
Chinese reforms, 6, 11
Christian Copts, 149
Chuprov, M., 87
Coahuila, 110
Colima, 110
Collectivism, 8, 98, 99, 100–104, 105, 106. *See also* Soviet reform movement
Collegium, 33
Committees of the Village Poor, 95
Communes: French, 56, 62; hereditary, 76, 84; repartitional, 78; Russian, 68, 81, 84, 85, 87, 88, 89, 90, 91, 108, 167, 191; Mexican, 108,

301